Foreign Trade Regimes and Economic Development: TURKEY

Foreign Trade Regimes and Economic Development:

A Special Conference Series on Foreign Trade Regimes and Economic Development

VOLUME I

NATIONAL BUREAU OF ECONOMIC RESEARCH
New York   1974

TURKEY

by **Anne O. Krueger**
UNIVERSITY OF MINNESOTA

DISTRIBUTED BY Columbia University Press
New York and London

Nᴀᴛɪᴏɴᴀʟ Bᴜʀᴇᴀᴜ ᴏꜰ Eᴄᴏɴᴏᴍɪᴄ Rᴇsᴇᴀʀᴄʜ

*A Special Conference Series on Foreign Trade Regimes
and Economic Development*

Library of Congress Card Number: 74–77689
ISBN for the series: 0–87014–500–2
ISBN for this volume, Cloth Ed: 0–87014–501–0
                      Paper Ed: 0–87014–526–6

Printed in the United States of America

Relation of the Directors of the National Bureau to
Publication of the Country Studies in the Series on
Foreign Trade Regimes and Economic Development

The individual country studies have not passed through the National Bureau's normal procedures for review and approval of research reports by the Board of Directors. In view of the way in which these studies were planned and reviewed at successive working parties of authors and Co-Directors, the National Bureau's Executive Committee has approved their publication in a manner analogous to conference proceedings, which are exempted from the rules governing submission of manuscripts to, and critical review by, the Board of Directors. *It should therefore be understood that the views expressed herein are those of the authors only and do not necessarily reflect those of the National Bureau or its Board of Directors.*

The syntheses volumes in the series, prepared by the Co-Directors of the project, are subject to the normal procedures for review and approval by the Directors of the National Bureau.

Contents

Tables

Figures

Co-Directors' Foreword

This volume is one of a series resulting from the research project on Exchange Control, Liberalization, and Economic Development sponsored by the National Bureau of Economic Research, the name of the project having been subsequently broadened to Foreign Trade Regimes and Economic Development. Underlying the project was the belief by all participants that the phenomena of exchange control and liberalization in less developed countries require careful and detailed analysis within a sound theoretical framework, and that the effects of individual policies and restrictions cannot be analyzed without consideration of both the nature of their administration and the economic environment within which they are adopted as determined by the domestic economic policy and structure of the particular country.

The research has thus had three aspects: (1) development of an analytical framework for handling exchange control and liberalization; (2) within that framework, research on individual countries, undertaken independently by senior scholars; and (3) analysis of the results of these independent efforts with a view to identifying those empirical generalizations that appear to emerge from the experience of the countries studied.

The analytical framework developed in the first stage was extensively commented upon by those responsible for the research on individual countries, and was then revised to the satisfaction of all participants. That framework, serving as the common basis upon which the country studies were undertaken, is further reflected in the syntheses reporting on the third aspect of the research.

The analytical framework pinpointed these three principal areas of research which all participants undertook to analyze for their own countries.

Subject to a common focus on these three areas, each participant enjoyed maximum latitude to develop the analysis of his country's experience in the way he deemed appropriate. Comparison of the country volumes will indicate that this freedom was indeed utilized, and we believe that it has paid handsome dividends. The three areas singled out for in-depth analysis in the country studies are:

1. *The anatomy of exchange control:* The economic efficiency and distributional implications of alternative methods of exchange control in each country were to be examined and analyzed. Every method of exchange control differs analytically in its effects from every other. In each country study care has been taken to bring out the implications of the particular methods of control used. We consider it to be one of the major results of the project that these effects have been brought out systematically and clearly in analysis of the individual countries' experience.

2. *The liberalization episode:* Another major area for research was to be a detailed analysis of attempts to liberalize the payments regime. In the analytical framework, devaluation and liberalization were carefully distinguished, and concepts for quantifying the extent of devaluation and of liberalization were developed. It was hoped that careful analysis of individual devaluation and liberalization attempts, both successful and unsuccessful, would permit identification of the political and economic ingredients of an effective effort in that direction.

3. *Growth relationships:* Finally, the relationship of the exchange control regime to growth via static-efficiency and other factors was to be investigated. In this regard, the possible effects on savings, investment allocation, research and development, and entrepreneurship were to be highlighted.

In addition to identifying the three principal areas to be investigated, the analytical framework provided a common set of concepts to be used in the studies and distinguished various phases regarded as useful in tracing the experience of the individual countries and in assuring comparability of the analyses. The concepts are defined and the phases delineated in Appendix D.

The country studies undertaken within this project and their authors are as follows:

Brazil	Albert Fishlow, University of California, Berkeley
Chile	Jere R. Behrman, University of Pennsylvania
Colombia	Carlos F. Diaz-Alejandro, Yale University
Egypt	Bent Hansen, University of California, Berkeley, and Karim Nashashibi, International Monetary Fund
Ghana	J. Clark Leith, University of Western Ontario

India   Jagdish N. Bhagwati, Massachusetts Institute of Tech-
                   nology, and T. N. Srinivasan, Indian Statistical Institute

Israel   Michael Michaely, The Hebrew University of Jerusalem

Philippines   Robert E. Baldwin, University of Wisconsin

South Korea   Charles R. Frank, Jr., Princeton University and The
                   Brookings Institution; Kwang Suk Kim, Korea Develop-
                   ment Institute, Republic of Korea; and Larry E. West-
                   phal, Northwestern University

Turkey   Anne O. Krueger, University of Minnesota

The principal results of the different country studies are brought together in our overall syntheses. Each of the country studies, however, has
been made self-contained, so that readers interested in only certain of these
studies will not be handicapped.

In undertaking this project and bringing it to successful completion, the
authors of the individual country studies have contributed substantially to the
progress of the whole endeavor, over and above their individual research.
Each has commented upon the research findings of other participants, and
has made numerous suggestions which have improved the overall design and
execution of the project. The country authors who have collaborated with us
constitute an exceptionally able group of development economists, and we
wish to thank all of them for their cooperation and participation in the project.

We must also thank the National Bureau of Economic Research for its
sponsorship of the project and its assistance with many of the arrangements
necessary in an undertaking of this magnitude. Hal B. Lary, Vice President-
Research, has most energetically and efficiently provided both intellectual and
administrative input into the project over a three-year period. We would also
like to express our gratitude to the Agency for International Development for
having financed the National Bureau in undertaking this project. Michael
Roemer and Constantine Michalopoulos particularly deserve our sincere
thanks.

JAGDISH N. BHAGWATI
Massachusetts Institute of Technology

ANNE O. KRUEGER
University of Minnesota

Preface

The purpose of this study is to analyze Turkey's trade and payments regime and its effects upon Turkish economic growth. The book is not intended as a comprehensive study of the Turkish economy,[1] although a constant problem in writing it was to establish a dividing line between those factors affecting growth in general and those relevant for the analysis of interaction between foreign trade and growth. In limiting the discussion to the latter, I have been aware that the general reader may gain the impression that foreign trade is the central problem of Turkey's development. It is not. Agricultural productivity, education, population growth, organization of the State Economic Enterprises (SEEs*), political and social stability, as well as a host of other factors are also important: a comprehensive view of Turkish development is thus not to be expected from the present volume.

The justification for focusing exclusively upon foreign trade is twofold. Firstly, foreign trade is an activity over which government policy makers have had an unusual degree of influence. Unlike population growth, agricultural productivity and many other problems where government regulations and policies have been only one determinant of the outcome, government policies have been pervasive in their effects upon Turkish foreign trade. Insofar as those effects have been detrimental to Turkish development, a universally ac-

---

1 The reader looking for such a study can refer to Edwin J. Cohn, *Turkish Economic, Social, and Political Change*, Praeger (New York), 1970.

* See Appendix D for lists of the abbreviations, acronyms, and specialized terms used in this volume.

cepted goal of Turkish governments and major political parties, alteration of those policies may provide a relatively inexpensive way to increase the effectiveness of Turkish development policy. And secondly, because economic growth is such a complex process it would be more fruitful to attempt to understand in some depth the trade-growth relationship rather than to cover, at a more superficial level, general economic growth.

Part One is designed as a brief introduction to the Turkish economy and its development, and the remainder of the book focuses on trade and growth relationships.

A few words must be said about the use of English and Turkish citations, and the nature of Turkish statistics. In Turkey, some documents are translated by the government, some are published in both Turkish and English in a single volume, some have been translated by unofficial sources, and many are available only in Turkish. Thus the texts of the First and Second Five Year Plans were published in both English and Turkish, as were the first several Annual Programs; the *Monthly Bulletin of Statistics* (*Devlet İstatistik Enstitüsü*), published by the State Institute of Statistics (SIS*), has both an English and a Turkish title, and all column and row headings are in both languages; while the *Official Gazette* (*Resmi Gazete*) is published daily in Turkish, but is translated by private agencies into English.

How to cite various documents and, for that matter, how to quote them when more than one translation exists for the same word is a problem. The rule of thumb used here is the following: (1) standardized wording (as, for instance, "liberalized list") is used in the text, but the wording of official translations (as, perhaps, "liberation list," or "liberalization list") will be employed when it is so quoted in the translation; (2) when an English language translation or a document with an English title accompanying a Turkish title was employed as a source, the English title is cited; (3) when a Turkish language source was used (even if a translation existed but was not available to the author), the Turkish citation is used. Thus when the *Official Gazette* is cited, an unofficial English translation (usually from Turk Argus Ajansi) was used. Citation of the *Official Gazette* as the *Resmi Gazete,* however, indicates use of the Turkish source. English translations have been used in the text. Thus the Annual Programs of the State Planning Organization (SPO) in the late 1960's are not available in translation, and are cited as *Yılı Programı* in footnotes, but are referred to as Annual Programs in the text.

The nature of Turkish statistics presented more serious problems. Difficulties were threefold: (1) some series are simply not available; (2) many data are given by several sources, which are not always consistent and are sometimes scattered; and (3) many data are not available as a consistent series over time.

Little can be done when data are unavailable, although there are several "manufactured" sets of data in the text. The means by which they were constructed are indicated at the appropriate points. More serious were the problems of locating data from widely scattered sources and deciding upon which to use or how to reconcile them. For example, SPO and SIS each produced national income statistics in the 1960's.[2] SPO's estimates had the practical advantages of use of a single deflator for the period since 1950 and consistency with the Plans and Annual Programs which are the major source of data. SIS however estimates national income by sector of origin from 1950 to the present (at 1948 prices until 1961 and at 1961 prices thereafter). The decisions between the two series were essentially pragmatic: SPO data were used for computations of Gross National Product (GNP), and SIS data for national income when referred to by sector of origin.

In addition to consistency between estimates from alternative sources, another problem is that many data are unavailable in a consistent time series. The determination of a set of figures for national income by sector of origin at constant prices is a case in point; quarterly money supply estimates are unavailable before mid-1959 on the International Monetary Fund (IMF) definition; accounting techniques for foreign exchange reserves were altered early in 1970 so that data before and after that data are noncomparable; and the home goods price index was no longer constructed after 1968. There are many other such instances where a series does not cover the entire period.

I have attempted to use the data where internal consistency over time was greatest, at the cost of leaving some inconsistency between series, of failing to use better available data, and of using series other than those most frequently cited in Turkey. I have included in the notes to the tables any known inconsistencies within a series, and have attempted to point out major inconsistencies between data in the tables and data presented elsewhere.

The advice and assistance of a large number of people have made this book possible. None of them bears any responsibility, however, for the errors which remain, nor for the conclusions drawn from the facts presented. Mr. Tercan Baysan, a graduate student at the University of Minnesota, assisted me at every stage of the study, even at the cost of delay in his own graduate program. I am deeply indebted to him for his willing and patient help with Turkish data and sources. His comments upon the manuscript and about Turkey have been useful throughout the study. Ashok Kapoor of the University of Minne-

---

2 In the summer of 1972, SPO and SIS agreed upon a common series for national income starting in 1962, which compilations differ from either independent series. The data were received too late for incorporation in this volume and would in any event have had to be linked with the SPO or SIS series for earlier years. In general the revised estimates do not appear to imply any significant differences in growth rates from the estimates presented in the text.

sota and Nuri Doğan of Robert College also assisted at various stages of the research.

My foremost debt is to my friends and colleagues at SPO, who not only were invariably willing to answer questions and help find data, but who also provided moral support. Hikmet Çetin's willingness to withstand interruptions despite an incredibly busy schedule went far beyond the call of friendship. His help in guiding me to people who could answer specific questions, his discussion of Turkey's economy, and his advice are gratefully acknowledged. Tefvik Can was invaluable in his advice and in providing data. Şadi Cindoruk, Güler Canalp, and Sevil Korum were helpful at any number of points.

I benefitted greatly from discussions with Cahit Kayra of the Ministry of Finance, who also provided a great deal of useful data. I cannot begin to mention all the other Turkish businessmen and government officials who patiently answered questions and helped me locate data. My thanks go to them all, and especially to Izzet Aydin of the Central Bank, Erhan Işil of the Ministry of Industry and Technology, Zeki Avrioğlu of SIS, and Türgüt Özoktay of the Union of Chambers of Commerce and Industry.

İbrahim Öngüt of the Industrial Development Bank of Turkey has been a valued source of insight and of data throughout the study. Much of the information on DRCs contained in Chapter VIII was obtained through him. He also read and commented upon portions of the manuscript, and I benefitted from discussions with him on numerous allied topics.

Several people were especially generous in contributing their time and knowledge on individual topics. Betty Yaşer of the AID Ankara was extremely helpful with government budget accounts. She read large portions of the manuscript and made many useful suggestions. Tuncay Akşit, also of AID, was especially knowledgeable on the import regime. He provided a great deal of data, answered numerous queries, and commented in detail upon an earlier draft of Chapter VI. While he bears no responsibility for remaining errors, his commentary improved the chapter vastly. Maxwell Fry of the City University of London read and commented extensively upon the discussion of inflation and monetary policy in Chapter II. At an early stage of the study, Baydar Gürgen, now at the IBRD, helped introduce me to Turkish data.

Several economists were helpful in general discussion, including Emre Gönensay, Attila Sönmez, Selim İlkin, and Besim Üstünel. Baran Tuncer of Ankara University and Osman Okyar of Hacateppe University read an earlier draft of the entire manuscript, and made valuable comments and suggestions throughout. Their efforts are greatly appreciated, and the manuscript is vastly improved as a result of their comments.

Several AID officials were extremely accommodating. Kenneth Kauffman of AID Ankara was generous with both his time and resources. Bradshaw

Langmaid, Mary Wampler, and Constantine Michalopoulos, all of AID Washington, also deserve special thinks.

The study was undertaken as part of the National Bureau of Economic Research project on Foreign Trade Regimes and Economic Development. I am grateful to the National Bureau for its financial support, which in turn was made possible in major part under a research contract with the Agency for International Development. All of the participants in the project commented extensively on various findings from the study. Hal Lary of the National Bureau read the entire manuscript and commented extensively. To Jagdish Bhagwati, codirector of the project, I am grateful not only for his detailed and incisive comments on the entire manuscript, but also for stimulating discussions over many of the issues involved.

Betsy Frederick, assisted by Sandy Menssen, typed the entire manuscript. I am grateful to them both for their patience and forbearance throughout a trying time.

Anne O. Krueger
Minneapolis, Minnesota

Principal Dates

1919   Declaration of Independence of Turkish Republic.

1923   Treaty of Lausanne and settlement of the Ottoman debt.

1929   End of the Capitulations, under which foreign powers regulated Turkish tariffs.

1934   Inauguration of a Five Year Industrial Plan, and the start of developing State Economic Enterprises under a philosophy of Étatism.

1938   Formulation of a Second Industrial Development Plan; death of Atatürk.

1940   Abandonment of Second Plan due to disruptions associated with World War II.

1946   Devaluation of the Turkish lira: from TL 1.28 = $1 to TL 2.80 = $1.

1950   Elections give the Democratic Party, under the leadership of Prime Minister Adnan Menderes, a majority in Parliament. The Republican People's Party loses power for the first time since Atatürk founded it.

1953   Introduction of a *de facto* multiple exchange rate system.

1958   *De facto* devaluation from TL 2.80 = $1 to TL 9 = $1 (with exceptions) and inauguration of a Stabilization Program.

1960   Menderes is deposed in May 1960 by a group of military leaders. A new government is formed, called the National Unity Committee.

1961   Elections are held, and a new Constitution is adopted. The Republican People's Party forms a coalition government. Several different prime ministers follow.

1963   The beginning of the *First Five Year Plan,* 1963 to 1967.

1965 Elections give a majority in Parliament to the Justice Party, under the
      leadership of Prime Minister Demirel.
1968 The beginning of the *Second Five Year Plan,* 1968 to 1972.
1969 Elections return the Justice Party to power.
1970 Devaluation from TL 9 = $1 to TL 15 = $1 in August.
1971 Resignation of Prime Minister Demirel, at the insistence of the Turkish
      military. A government is formed under Prime Minister Erim in
      March. A second Erim government is formed in December. When the
      dollar devalues, Turkey maintains her parity with Western European
      countries, so the exchange rate becomes TL 14 = $1.
1972 Resignation of Prime Minister Erim and formation of a new govern-
      ment, under acting Prime Minister Ferit Melen and then under Prime
      Minister Suat Hayri Ürgüplü, with the backing of the Turkish military.

Foreign Trade Regimes
and Economic Development:
TURKEY

Part One

Introduction

CHAPTER I

The Turkish economy and its growth: an overview

I. Introduction

The Turkish economy underwent profound changes from the end of World War II to 1971. Real national income more than tripled, while the Turkish population increased from 20 to 36 million. The resultant increase in real per capita income and government efforts to accelerate development led to an increase in the share of GNP allocated to capital formation: from 9.7 per cent in 1948 to 21 per cent in 1970.[1] The share of agriculture in GNP fell from 51.3 per cent in 1948 to 29.1 per cent in 1970, while that of industry rose from 10.1 per cent to 17.5 per cent.

The purpose of this study is to examine the relationship of the Turkish foreign trade and balance-of-payments experience to Turkish economic growth. Obviously a country's growth is the outcome of a host of interacting factors, both positive and negative. No analysis of the role of any one factor can be undertaken without reference to these others. This chapter is therefore intended to provide an overview of the Turkish economy and its growth and to place the foreign trade sector in perspective. In the next four sections of the chapter the structure and growth of the Turkish economy and the major government policies influencing growth are discussed. A fifth section provides a summary of the chronological development of the Turkish foreign trade regime, which will be the subject of more intensive investigation in later chapters, and a final section of Chapter I indicates the plan of the work as a whole.

II. Turkish economic growth prior to 1950

The year 1950 will be used as a starting point in studying the relationship of the foreign trade sector and economic growth. Several reasons led to the

---

1. Throughout this book 1971 will be taken as the terminal year of the study, apart from a few references to developments in the early part of 1972 (see Appendix C). Use of an earlier final year will signify that later data are not available as of the summer of 1972.

choice of that year: by 1950, Turkey had recovered to a large extent from the extreme abnormalities of the early post World War II years; the availability and reliability of data decreases sharply as one goes further back in time; a new government was elected in 1950, one whose economic policies were important in shaping Turkey's economic growth throughout the subsequent decade; and since 1950 preceded the balance-of-payments difficulties which later emerged, use of 1950 as a starting point permits the analysis of factors which led to those difficulties.

Although the decade of the 1950's contrasts sharply with the earlier decades of the Turkish Republic, the earlier period was formative. The Turkish Independence movement started in 1919 as the Ottoman Empire dissolved, and led to the establishment of the Turkish Republic in 1923, the dominant figure in this evolution, from 1919 until his death in 1938, being Kemal Atatürk.

The 1920's constituted a period when Atatürk and his associates were concentrating primarily on forming the political and social structure of the new Turkish nation and on setting the outlines of the republic's foreign policy. With occasional exceptions, there was little conscious economic policy relating to development goals, although the transport system was nationalized and a State Monopolies Agency (alcohol and cigarettes) was established. The latter was intended primarily as a means of raising revenue. Insofar as there was conscious economic policy aimed at economic growth, it consisted primarily of relying upon private enterprise to provide it.[2]

The decade of the 1920's saw numerous reforms: Turkey switched from the Arabic to a modified Latin alphabet, purdah and the fez were abolished, and the state was declared secular rather than religious.[3] Partly because of the disruptions, especially the cross-migration of Greeks and Turks associated with the end of the war with Greece, partly because of debt-servicing obligations, and partly for other reasons, it appears that per capita disposable income in Turkey hardly changed during the 1920's.[4]

The new Turkish Republic had little control over the foreign trade regime before 1929. The Sultans under the Ottoman Empire had sold to foreign powers the rights to impose taxes and tariffs (the Capitulations) in exchange for various considerations. The Sultans had simultaneously accumulated huge debts, settlement of which was not made until 1923 with the Treaty of

2. For a fuller account of government economic policy during the period, see James W. Land, "The Role of Government in the Economic Development of Turkey, 1923 to 1963," *Rice University Program of Development Studies, Paper No. 8,* Fall 1970.
3. See Kemal H. Karpat, *Turkey's Politics — the Transition to a Multi-Party System,* Princeton University Press (Princeton) 1959, Chapters 2 and 3.
4. Z.Y. Hershlag, *Turkey: The Challenge of Economic Growth,* E.J. Brill (Leiden), 1968, p. 58.

Lausanne. Under this treaty, Turkey was obliged to permit the Capitulations to continue until 1929 and to repay a fraction of the Ottoman debt amounting to TL 129 million — which can be compared with total export earnings in 1923 of TL 85 million. Throughout the 1920's the new government found itself saddled with massive debt-servicing obligations but with little control over its ability to service them. The Ottoman debt was renegotiated sporadically throughout the 1920's and early 1930's, but not without embarrassment for the government on each round. As will be seen below, foreign indebtedness has continued to be a problem for the government of Turkey throughout its existence. Memories of the Capitulations and of the Ottoman debt settlement are undoubtedly an important influence on Turkish foreign trade policy.

The free enterprise orientation of the Turkish government ended with the Great Depression. The very slow rate of increase in per capita income throughout the 1920's contributed to general skepticism about free enterprise. The end of the Capitulations increased the government's range of policy alternatives, while the decline in export earnings attendant upon the Great Depression virtually forced a shift in economic policy.

The government shifted to the economic philosophy usually called "Étatism", a concept never clearly articulated.[5] The main thrust of this movement was that government-owned enterprises should be started in an effort to raise living standards, and that these enterprises should be the major stimuli to economic growth. It was during the 1930's that State Economic Enterprises (SEEs) were started in the industrial field. Two Five Year Plans were formulated.[6] These plans endorsed infant industry protection and placed emphasis on the development of domestic textile, chemical, sugar, building materials, coal, iron and steel, paper and cellulose, and other industries, primarily through government enterprises. SEEs have played an important part in Turkey's economic growth since the 1930's. The First Five Year Plan was implemented, but the Second was not implemented owing to the outbreak of World War II.

Hershlag estimates that Turkey's income per capita increased by 19 per cent in constant prices during the decade from 1929 to 1939, about 1.7 per

5. For a discussion of Étatism and its origins, see Osman Okyar, "The Concept of Étatism," *Economic Journal,* March 1965.
6. These five year plans generally focused upon industrial development, and were not comprehensive of all sectors of economic activity. They should not be confused with the Five Year Plans of 1963–1967 and 1968–1972, which are called the First Five Year Plan (FFYP) and Second Five Year Plan (SFYP), respectively. The first five year plan of the 1930's started in 1934. The second started in 1939, but was not really implemented, as World War II broke out. See Bernard Lewis, *The Emergence of Modern Turkey,* 2nd Edition, Oxford University Press (London), 1961, pp. 268–70, and p. 296.

cent annually.[7] Some progress had thus been made toward the goal of economic growth and higher living standards on the eve of World War II. However, growth had been slow and per capita income, by European standards,
was very low. Contrasted with nations which achieved independence after
World War II, Turkey's head start consisted primarily of the political and
social changes which had been accomplished rather than of solid progress on
the economic front.

The already high level of government intervention was increased with
World War II. And despite substantial tax increases, the disappearance of
foreign sources of supply and increased government expenditures simultaneously led to rapid inflation. Although some industries' output increased
markedly, supply bottlenecks prevented rapid expansion in most. James W.
Land estimates that the entire period of 1933—1948 saw an average annual
growth of income of three per cent annually, but only of two per cent per
annum from 1938 to 1948. This slower rate of growth during the latter
period is generally attributed to stagnation during the War years.[8]

There was some relaxation in controls over international trade after the
War, and to adjust for the rapid wartime inflation, the Turkish lira was
devalued in August 1946, from TL 1.28 per U.S. dollar to TL 2.80 per dollar.[9]
Work was begun on a five year plan in the summer of 1946. However, in the
rapidly changing economic environment of the late 1940's the plan was not
implemented. Simultaneously, political changes were occurring in Turkey.
Étatism, which implied widespread government intervention in economic activity, continued to be the underlying economic ideology. In 1950, the Republican Party — historically Atatürk's — was defeated, and the Democratic
Party under Menderes, elected.[10]

III. Development planning and economic policy, 1950 to 1970

Economic policy during the 1950's

Most writers have cited economic factors, and in particular the rejection of
detailed controls and/or Étatism, as a major factor in the Democratic Party's
victory.[11] However, all major political parties during the 1950 campaign

---

7. Hershlag, *op. cit.* (Note 4), p. 121.
8. See Land, *op. cit.* (Note 2), pp. 8 ff.
9. The cost of living index in Istanbul stood at 101.4 in 1939 (1938 = 100) and rose to
   354.4 by 1945. *Overseas Economic Surveys — Turkey,* His Majesty's Stationery
   Office (London), 1948.
10. See Karpat, *op. cit.* (Note 3), Chap. 8 for a fuller discussion.
11. See, for example, *ibid.,* and Lewis, *op. cit.* (Note 6), pp. 312 ff.

attacked the network of detailed controls and high taxes that had arisen under the banner of Étatism and campaigned for a greater scope for private enterprise. Menderes had campaigned on a platform that actually included selling many of the SEEs to private firms.

But such a sale did not transpire: there was political protest against selling the profitable ones, and no willing buyer for the unprofitable SEEs. Indeed, the SEEs expanded their share of industrial activity during the 1950's. In 1950 when Menderes gained power and hence Étatism theoretically ended, 63 per cent of value-added in Turkish industry originated from private firms and 37 per cent from SEEs. By 1960 when Menderes' government fell, 52 per cent of industrial value-added originated in the private sector and 48 per cent in the public.[12]

The main reason for this outcome appears to have had little or nothing to do with economic philosophy. Rather, initial attempts to sell the SEEs met with strong political objections. After the crop failure of 1954 the SEEs became a useful instrument for attaining government objectives when the approach of 1950–1953 appeared to have failed. The SEE investments increased rapidly, financed by Central Bank credits; the SEEs thus grew relatively faster than the private sector during the 1950's.

Economic policy during the years of the Menderes government can be divided into three periods. The first, from the election until 1954, was a period during which emphasis was placed upon increasing agricultural production. The second, from the massive crop failure of 1954 until August 1958, was characterized by domestic and foreign economic difficulties and economic policy consisted largely of *ad hoc* measures to counter them. The third period, starting with stabilization program and *de facto* devaluation in August 1958, came to an end with the Revolution of May 1960.

It should be pointed out before examining each of these periods that the common denominator of economic policy during the 1950's was lack of coordination. Prime Minister Menderes had a "seeming phobia about any aspect of economic planning"[13] which led to a lack of any clearly formulated overall economic policy, even for government expenditures.[14] Thus the pe-

12. See Land, *op. cit.* (Note 2), p. 29, Table 6 for the underlying data.
13. Walter F. Weiker, *The Turkish Revolution 1960–1961*, Brookings Institution (Washington) 1963, p. 12.
14. In 1953, a report by Hollis B. Chenery, George E. Brandow and Edwin J. Cohn, *Turkish Investment and Economic Development*, Foreign Operations Administration Special Mission to Turkey (Ankara), December 1953, was prepared under American auspices, calling attention to the inflationary danger and to the need for better coordination in virtually all aspects of government expenditure policy. "...The fact that it discussed at all the inflationary situation prevailing in Turkey was said to be representative of its negative approach. All Turks who had in any way helped in the preparation of the report were frowned upon and the few copies which had been

riods are characterized more by changes in economic conditions to which the government responded on a case-by-case basis rather than by consciously formulated and enunciated policy shifts.

1950 to 1954. The first three years of the Menderes regime were marked by a rapid expansion of agricultural output and a substantial increase in governmental infrastructure investments. The resulting boom also led to a buoyant economy generally, as demand grew rapidly in response to increases in agricultural income. Increases in agricultural production, especially of wheat and other grains, resulted primarily from extending the area under cultivation. Rapid output increases were accompanied by a decline in wheat yields, since much of the additional land was submarginal.

The government seems to have adopted the view that emphasis upon agricultural expansion was the best policy for economic growth. Several factors evidently contributed to this emphasis. (1) The political support for the Menderes regime originated largely from the peasantry; thus Menderes and his government gave priority to road-building and other investment projects within the rural sector. (2) Menderes' commitments to free enterprise and the pricing system were more consistent with agricultural price supports and other pricing incentives (liberal credit policies, etc.) than with direct intervention.[15] (3) In post-war Europe, where food shortage was perceived to be a major problem, Turkey was urged during Marshall Plan consultations to focus upon expansion of food output.[16]

The foreign exchange regime was very liberal during the years 1950 to 1953. With rapid increases in agricultural production, exports expanded sharply — as did also imports (see Table I-6 below) — since demand for both investment and consumption goods imports increased. By the end of 1953 the government was forced to impose controls over imports and exchange control was introduced in response to mounting short-term indebtedness and a large current account deficit. Domestic economic policy, however, did not basically shift until 1954, when a massive crop failure occurred.

1954 to 1958. Agricultural production dropped 20 per cent between 1953 and 1954, largely as a result of bad weather. By that time opportunities for rapid increases in agricultural output through extensive investment had largely ceased; but the massive crop failure sharply focused attention on the

circulated were confiscated by the Government...": *Public International Development Financing Research Project of the Columbia School of Law. Report No. 3* (New York), 1962, p. 18.

15. Columbia School of Law, *op. cit.* (Note 14), p. 11.
16. Reşat Aktan, *Analysis and Assessment of the Economic Effects Public Law 480 Title 1 Program Turkey*, no publisher indicated (Ankara), 1964, p. 36.

inherent difficulties of reliance upon agriculture. Meanwhile, the inflationary pressures resulting from financing agricultural price-support operations were intensified with the decline in agricultural output.

Government policy became increasingly interventionist, with continued resort to additional direct controls. Emphasis upon agricultural development was reduced. The balance-of-payments pressures which had emerged in 1952 and 1953 intensified. Thus on both the domestic and foreign fronts detailed government regulation and intervention in economic activity replaced the rather more liberal economic policies of earlier years. The years 1954 to 1958 were ones of increasing inflation, continued balance-of-payments difficulties and other economic problems.[17]

1958 to 1960. In August 1958 the government embarked upon a Stabilization Program with a *de facto* devaluation of the Turkish lira and an attempted halt to inflation. Tight credit ceilings and other measures taken in consultation with creditor countries resulted in a sharp drop in the rate of inflation, but by late 1959 the government began relaxing its credit and expenditure policies. In May 1960 the Menderes government was overthrown by a group of military leaders.[18]

Economic policy during the 1960's

A major motive for the takeover that ended the Menderes era appears to have been the fear that the government was reverting to the inflationary policies that dominated the pre-1958 period. The military intervened and appointed a civilian government which ruled for eighteen months, until elections were again held under a new Constitution.

The Republican Peoples' Party gained power in a coalition government after the elections of 1961. The Justice Party won the election in 1965 and was in power until April 1971. The Republican Party has advocated economic planning, a large role for government economic activity, and has been somewhat more suspicious of private enterprise, whereas the Justice Party assigned a greater role to the private sector. Nonetheless, economic policy had a considerable continuity throughout the 1960's that was in marked contrast to the 1950's. One of the major commitments of the revolutionary government was to greater coordination of economic policy. A State Planning Organization (SPO) was established, and its role was defined in the new Turkish Constitution.[19] Work began almost immediately on a comprehensive Five

17. The characteristics of this period are discussed more fully in Chapter II, below.
18. See Chapter IV, below, for a fuller discussion of the period.
19. See Chapter V, below, for a fuller discussion of the State Planning Organization and the role of planning in the 1960's.

Year Plan which officially began in 1963.[20] The Plan was implemented and its successor, the Second Five Year Plan of 1968 to 1972, marked a continuation of planning although with greater emphasis upon incentives to the private sector.[21]

Both Plans have adopted a target growth rate of 7 per cent annually. Each laid down sectoral targets which assumed importance in government investment policies and in setting incentives for the private sector. The development of Turkish industry has been stressed in each Plan, with particular emphasis upon the development of new industries. As such, import-substitution goals became a conscious element of development policy.

The important point for present purposes is that during the 1960's the foreign trade regime was viewed as one of the instruments to be used to attain development goals. Although balance-of-payments difficulties often forced adjustments in the payments regime, those difficulties themselves were largely the result of the development effort and its implied import demands. "Foreign exchange shortage" was perceived as a bottleneck to growth, and the SPO has encouraged export promotion and emphasized import-substitution in response to that perception. Of course had foreign exchange earnings been greater it is likely that import-substitution would have been encouraged at a slower rate. Many of the side effects of the payments regime were undoubtedly the unintended result of greater-than-anticipated foreign exchange stringency, and detailed administration of the payments regime on occasion departed from the intent of the plans. Nonetheless, the Turkish foreign trade and payments policy of the 1960's can generally be regarded as consciously coordinated with development goals, in sharp contrast to the 1950's when policy was formulated on an *ad hoc* basis in response to individual events.

IV. Economic growth since 1950

Growth of GNP

Table I-1 provides basic data on the gross national product and its composition over the 1950 to 1970 period, and the behavior of real GNP, investment, and consumption is plotted in Fig. 1. Real GNP tripled between 1950 and 1970, for an average annual rate of growth of 5.7 per cent and an annual growth in per capita income of 3.0 per cent. Per capita income in 1970 was

20. *First Five Year Development Plan 1963–1967*, Government of Turkey, Prime Ministry, State Planning Organization (Ankara), 1963.
21. *Second Five Year Development Plan 1968–1972*, Government of Turkey, Prime Ministry, State Planning Organization (Ankara), 1968. At the time of writing, the *Third Five Year Plan 1973–1977* is in the final stage of formulation.

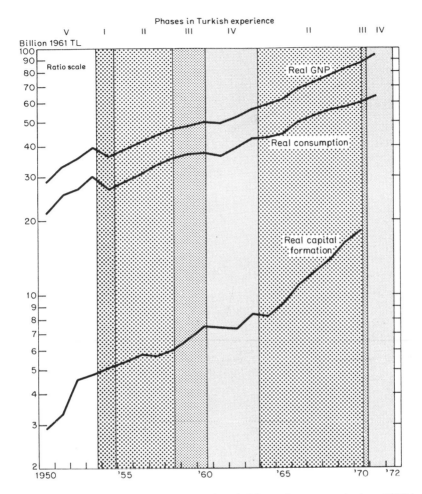

Fig. 1. Growth of real GNP, consumption and capital formation, constant prices, 1950 to 1971.

TL 3,764 or at the official exchange rate, $251. The Turkish population was estimated to be 35.7 million in 1970, having grown at an average annual rate of 2.7 per cent over the 1950–1970 period.

As can be seen, the growth of the Turkish economy has not been uniformly sustained over the entire period. Growth was extremely rapid from 1950 to 1953. Fluctuations in the growth rate have been associated with bad crop years (especially 1954) and growth was slowed down by the balance-of-payments crisis and readjustment that followed in the years 1958 to 1961. Thus net national product grew at an average annual rate of 7.5 per cent

Table I-1
Turkish GNP and its composition, 1948, and 1950 to 1971

	Current GNP (billions of TL)	GNP at 1961 Prices (billions of TL)	Per Cent Change from Pre-vious year	Percentage Distribution			
				Private Consump-tion	Fixed Capital Formation	General Govern-ment Con-sumption	Net Ex-ports
	(1)	(2)	(3)	(4)	(5)	(6)	(7)
1948	10.1	27.5	–	–	–	–	–
1950	10.4	28.5	–	75	10	16	−1
1951	12.3	32.8	15.1	78	10	14	−2
1952	14.3	35.6	8.5	75	13	17	−3
1953	16.8	39.6	11.2	76	12	15	−2
1954	17.1	36.1	−8.8	74	14	15	−3
1955	21.1	38.7	7.2	74	14	15	−2
1956	24.3	41.4	7.0	74	14	13	−1
1957	30.5	44.0	6.3	76	13	12	–
1958	36.1	46.3	5.2	77	13	12	–
1959	44.7	48.1	3.9	77	14	13	−3
1960	49.0	49.9	3.7	75	15	13	−2
1961	49.1	49.1	−1.6	74	15	14	−3
1962	55.2	52.1	6.1	75	14	15	−4
1963	63.3	56.1	7.7	76	15	14	−4
1964	68.0	58.9	5.0	73	14	14	−2
1965	73.2	61.6	4.6	72	15	14	−1
1966	85.7	67.9	10.2	73	16	13	−2
1967	95.2	72.1	6.2	73	17	12	−1
1968	105.0	76.9	6.7	72	18	12	−2
1969	117.1	81.7	6.2	70	20	12	−2
1970	135.6	86.4	5.8	69	21	12	−2
1971	173.5	94.3	9.1	67	18	15	0

Notes: a) SPO and SIS each have published GNP estimates since 1959. SIS's estimates are based on 1948 prices until 1961 and on 1961 prices thereafter. SPO esti-mates were used to provide opportunity for making comparisons with the real GNP series. The SPO estimates are based on SIS data, the difference being the estimate of agricultural production in 1958, and hence the weights used for estimating the growth rate in later years.

b) No estimate was made of inventory investment until the late 1960's. Con-sumption was estimated as a residual, and hence inventory accumulation was implicitly included in it. To maintain comparability, investment in stock, amounting to about one per cent of GNP, was included in the consumption data for later years.

c) 1971 data are provisional estimates.

Sources: Columns (1) and (2): SPO data, as given in *Economic and Social Indicators – Turkey,* U.S. Agency for International Development (Ankara), 1971.
Column (3): derived from column (2).
Columns (4) to (7): 1950 to 1968 from *Yearbook of National Accounts Sta-tistics;* 1969 and 1970 from SPO 1971: *Yılı Programı* (Ankara), March 1971.

between 1948 and 1953 and only 2.7 per cent per annum between 1953 and 1961. Growth since 1961 has averaged 6.5 per cent.

Gross capital formation over the entire period has risen from 10 per cent of GNP to 20–21 per cent, while private consumption has fallen, in percentage terms, from an average of 75 per cent in the period 1950 to 1954 to 69–72 per cent in the last half of the 1960's.[22] Government consumption, of which a sizeable fraction is defense expenditures,[23] has also declined relatively over the period. As indicated in Table I-1, there has been an import surplus over virtually the entire period, reaching its peak in the first half of the 1960's. It is evident that part of the increase in the rate of gross capital formation originated from an inflow of foreign credits, especially in the years from 1959 to 1965. The bulk of these credits came from foreign aid, as will be seen below.

Gross capital formation

Table I-2 indicates the composition of gross capital formation, the most rapidly growing component of GNP. Several notable features of the Turkish

Table I-2
Composition of gross domestic capital formation (percentage distribution)

	1951	1955	1960	1965	1969
A. *Private sector*					
1) Dwellings	22.8	30.1	20.6	21.9	22.6
2) Other buildings	9.1	9.2	6.5	6.4	6.6
3) Other construction	1.1	0.7	0.6	0.8	0.5
4) Machinery and equipment	28.9	17.6	22.3	15.2	14.5
Total Private	61.9	57.6	50.0	44.3	44.2
B. *Public sector*					
1) Dwellings	1.2	0.5	0.3	0.9	0.7
2) Other buildings	10.4	10.7	11.4	13.7	14.0
3) Other construction	19.1	22.1	24.8	28.1	26.8
4) Machinery and equipment	7.3	9.1	13.6	12.9	14.3
Total Public	38.1	42.4	50.0	55.7	55.8

Note: Due to rounding-off of uneven fractions, totals may not add up exactly to those given in the table.
Source: *National Income, 1938, 1948–1970. Pub. No. 625,* State Institute of Statistics (Ankara), 1972.

22. But see Note b to Table I-1.
23. According to Frederick Shorter, military expenditures averaged 7.3 per cent of GNP over the fifteen-year period 1948–1962. See Frederick C. Shorter, "Military Expenditures and the Allocation of Resources," in Frederick C. Shorter (ed.), *Four Studies on the Economic Development of Turkey,* Frank Cass & Co. Ltd. (London), 1967, p. 43.

economy are evident from the data. First, the government's share of total investment is high, and has increased throughout the period, rising from 38 per cent in 1951 (1950 data are not available) to about 56 per cent in the late 1960's. Government investment has taken place not only in infrastructure but also through the SEEs in manufacturing, mining, and so on. A second notable feature of the Turkish economy is the very high fraction of total capital formation which originates in construction activities.[24] Only 28.8 per cent of gross capital formation, both public and private, was allocated to machinery and equipment in 1969. This figure contrasts sharply with percentages in other countries in 1968: Argentina, 45; Chile, 45; Greece, 40; Israel, 41; Italy, 36; Spain, 49; and Taiwan, 53.2.[25]

Composition of output by sectors

Table I-3 presents estimates of the sectoral origin of national income. The estimates are in 1948 prices for the years 1951 to 1961 and in 1961 prices for later years. Because of data unavailability, no attempt was made to convert to a comparable price basis for the two decades. The trends nevertheless stand out clearly. Agriculture's share in national income has gradually declined from 51 to 30 per cent over the two decades. Manufacturing has meanwhile grown more rapidly than GNP, rising from 9 per cent of national income in the early 1950's to 17 per cent in 1967. The share of other non-agricultural sectors has risen somewhat over the period.

Hence Turkey's comparatively rapid growth has been accompanied by a structural change as the relative importance of agricultural production has declined, although this factor still remains large.[26] The growth of manufacturing production has been relatively rapid, stimulated primarily by·import-substitution.

24. It is generally believed that the unusually large fraction of investment in construction is attributable to Turkish tax law, which encourages new building. New residential buildings are exempted from tax for five to ten years, and even commercial buildings are exempt for three years. The tax rate for buildings thereafter is 0.3 per cent of assessed value, with rental income above TL 5,000 not subject to tax. Capital gains on buildings sold four or more years after construction, moreover, are tax-exempt. See R.A. Newberry, *Taxation in Turkey* (Istanbul), September 1964, and Hüsnü Kızıyallı, *Türk Vergi Sisteminin Ekonomik Etkileri,* State Planning Office (Ankara), 1965.

25. Data from *Yearbook of National Income Accounts,* United Nations, 1969, country-pages.

26. Turkey appears to have a strong comparative advantage in a number of agricultural commodities, including fresh fruits and vegetables and livestock, for which Western Europe is a natural market and the income elasticity of demand is high. Thus one would not expect the share of agriculture to decline with GNP growth as much as in some other countries.

Table I-3
Industrial origin of national income, 1951 to 1970 (billions of TL)

A. 1948 Factor Prices

	1951	1952	1953	1954	1955	1956	1957	1958	1959	1960	1961
griculture	5.5	5.8	6.4	5.1	5.6	6.1	6.2	7.3	7.3	7.4	7.2
ining	0.1	0.1	0.2	0.1	0.1	0.2	0.2	0.2	0.2	0.2	0.2
anufacturing	1.0	1.0	1.1	1.2	1.2	1.3	1.4	1.4	1.5	1.5	1.5
lectricity, gas, water	0.0	0.0	0.0	0.0	0.1	0.1	0.1	0.1	0.1	0.1	0.1
onstruction	0.5	0.6	0.8	0.7	0.7	0.7	0.9	0.9	1.0	1.0	0.9
holesale & retail trade	1.1	1.2	1.3	1.1	1.2	1.3	1.4	1.5	1.7	1.7	1.7
ransport & communication	0.5	0.7	0.7	0.8	0.9	1.0	1.0	1.0	1.2	1.3	1.3
inancial institutions	0.2	0.2	0.2	0.3	0.3	0.3	0.3	0.4	0.4	0.4	0.4
rivate services	0.4	0.5	0.5	0.5	0.6	0.6	0.7	0.7	0.8	0.8	0.9
welling ownership	0.3	0.3	0.3	0.3	0.4	0.4	0.5	0.6	0.6	0.7	0.8
overnment services	0.9	1.0	1.2	1.2	1.2	1.2	1.4	1.5	1.6	1.6	1.8
come from rest of world	−0.0	−0.0	−0.0	−0.0	−0.0	−0.0	−0.0	−0.0	−0.0	−0.0	−0.0
ational income	10.5	11.4	12.7	11.5	12.3	13.2	14.0	15.7	16.3	16.7	16.7

B. 1961 Factor Prices

	1961	1962	1963	1964	1965	1966	1967	1968	1969	1970
griculture	19.0	20.2	21.7	21.7	21.0	23.4	23.6	24.0	24.0	24.3
ining	0.8	0.8	0.8	0.9	1.0	1.1	1.1	14.1	15.5	15.9
anufacturing	6.5	7.0	7.7	8.2	9.0	10.0	11.4			
lectricity, gas, water	0.3	0.3	0.3	0.4	0.3	0.4	0.4			
onstruction	2.9	3.0	3.2	3.5	3.7	4.1	4.5	5.0	5.4	5.7
holesale & retail trade	3.6	3.9	4.2	4.5	4.8	5.2	5.7	6.1	6.6	7.0
ransport & communication	3.4	3.7	4.0	4.2	4.5	4.9	5.2	5.6	6.1	6.5
inancial institutions	1.3	1.4	1.5	1.6	1.7	1.9	2.1	2.3	2.5	2.7
rivate services	2.4	2.6	2.8	3.0	3.2	3.4	3.7	4.0	4.3	4.6
welling ownership	2.3	2.4	2.5	2.7	3.0	3.2	3.5	3.8	4.2	4.6
overnment services	4.4	4.6	5.0	5.3	5.7	6.2	6.7	7.3	8.0	8.7
come from rest of world	−0.3	−0.3	−0.2	−0.2	+0.2	+0.5	+0.2	+0.2	+0.4	+1.2
ational income	46.5	49.5	53.4	55.8	58.2	64.3	68.0	72.6	77.0	81.1

otes: a) Provisional estimates for 1967 and 1968.
       b) Preliminary estimates for 1969 and 1970.
ource: *National Income, 1938, 1948–1970, Pub. No. 625*, State Institute of Statistics (Ankara), 1971.

Table I-4
Exports, imports, and GNP, various dates

	1950	1952	1955	1958	1961	1963	1965	1968	1970
(billions of TL)									
Exports	0.7	1.0	0.9	0.7	3.1	3.3	4.2	4.5	6.4
Imports	0.8	1.6	1.4	0.9	4.6	6.2	5.2	6.9	10.3
GNP	10.4	16.8	21.1	36.1	49.1	63.3	73.2	105.0	134.2
(percent of GNP)									
Exports	6.7	6.0	4.3	1.9	6.3	5.2	5.7	4.3	4.8
Imports	7.7	9.5	6.6	2.5	9.4	9.8	7.1	6.6	7.7

Sources: GNP from Table I-1. Exports and imports from *Statistical Yearbook of Turkey
1968, Pub. No. 580,* State Institute of Statistics (Ankara), 1969; and *Aylık
Bülten,* Central Bank, October–December 1971.

The importance of exports and imports in GNP is indicated in Table I-4.
Imports have averaged about 8 per cent of GNP, while exports have declined
somewhat in relative importance. The constancy of the import share reflects
the fact that capital formation has a much higher import content than consumption and has grown much more rapidly than GNP. Thus despite the
stability of the overall share there has been considerable import-substitution.

The relatively low share of foreign trade in Turkish GNP understates the
importance of the trade sector in the Turkish economy. Because of the import-substitution which has taken place, Turkish industry is dependent upon
intermediate goods imports, while there is a wide range of capital goods
which are not produced in Turkey.

Moreover, Turkey is committed to joining the Common Market. Under a
1963 Protocol, the 1960's were a preliminary period during which Turkey
received tariff-quota preferences on some of her major exports, but had no
reciprocal obligations.[27] In July 1970 Turkey and the European Economic
Community (EEC) formally concluded the preliminary period, and the first
twelve-year stage of a twenty-two year transition period was embarked upon.
After the completion of the two stages, Turkey will become a full member of
the EEC under the terms of the agreement.[28] Thus Turkey will eventually
harmonize her trade policies with those of other EEC countries. She is committed as such to a pattern of open economic development, at least in the

27. Vural Savaș, "Foreign Trade of Turkey and the European Common Market," in
Foreign Trade and Economic Development, Economic and Social Studies Conference
Board (Istanbul), 1968.
28. *Turkish Economic Review,* August 1970, p. 14.

long run. As will be seen below, there can be little doubt that that pattern will result in a higher share of foreign trade in GNP than has been the case over the past two decades.

Fiscal and monetary developments

As was seen in Table I-2, the government has been extremely important in Turkey's growth, not only in setting the environment for the private sector, but in its own investment activities. Moreover, there are key government enterprises affecting virtually every phase of economic activity: TMO (Toprak Mahsulleri Ofisi: Soil Products Office, a SEE) is a major purchaser of agricultural commodities and has established minimum prices for most major agricultural commodities throughout the period under review. Etibank, one of the first SEEs, controls and operates all mining output of copper, chrome, mercury, lead and sulphur.

Government policy therefore affects economic growth in all the usual ways and in addition contributes directly to it through the SEEs. It will be seen below, in analyzing various aspects of the Turkish experience, that the role of the SEEs has been important, not only in their own performance and growth but also in their financing. Because their operations are integrally intertwined with the government accounts and cannot readily be disentangled, meaningful data on government accounts are difficult to obtain, and such data as are available are difficult to interpret. At this stage, therefore, aggregate data which may be of some use in providing an overview of the Turkish economy are presented, although the reader is warned to interpret them with extreme care.

Table I-5 presents the basic data. The first column gives the money supply as of the end of each year. The money supply more than doubled during the period 1954 to 1958, reflecting primarily the Central Bank financing of SEE deficits.[29] The rate of increase in the money supply fell off markedly in the 1960-to-1965 period and rose again thereafter.

Central government expenditures over the 1950-to-1968 period rose from 13 per cent of GNP to about 20 per cent of GNP. Tax revenues have risen with expenditures, although a portion of government expenditures has been financed by aid flows, the sale of savings bonds and deficit financing. The increase in government expenditures has been partly responsible for the rise in the rate of capital formation, while the increase in tax revenues has been a significant factor in raising the savings rate.

The last columns of Table I-5 give the price indices for home goods and wholesale prices on a 1958 base. These indices are subject to several down-

---

29. This phenomenon will be explored more fully in Chapter II. Suffice it to say here that SEE accounts are separate from those of the central government budget.

Table I-5

Money supply, government accounts, and price level, 1950 to 1970

	Money Supply	Central Government		Price Indices	
		Expenditures	Tax Revenues	Home Goods	Wholesale
		(billions of TL)		(1958 = 100)	
1950	1.59	1.300	1.312	42	48
1951	2.02	n.a.[a]	n.a.[a]	44	51
1952	2.42	n.a.[a]	n.a.[a]	47	52
1953	2.95	2.148	1.971	48	53
1954	3.37	2.507	2.222	54	59
1955	4.21	3.172	2.627	60	63
1956	5.36	3.455	2.999	74	73
1957	6.87	3.965	3.821	90	87
1958	7.42	4.887	4.430	100	100
1959	8.70	6.568	5.928	119	120
1960	9.26	7.204	6.096	117	126
1961	10.03	8.447	7.187	119	130
1962	10.96	8.940	7.625	125	137
1963	12.17	10.924	9.291	132	143
1964	14.00	12.483	10.060	128	145
1965	16.43	13.462	11.206	135	156
1966	19.78	16.008	13.389	146	164
1967	22.68	18.179	16.787	158	176
1968	25.97	20.893	17.567	163	185
1969	30.13	n.a.[b]	n.a.[b]	n.a[c]	195
1970	35.27	n.a.[b]	n.a.[b]	n.a[c]	207

Notes: a) The Land-SIS data are not available for 1951 and 1952. On a different definition, government expenditures and receipts were reported in *Statistical Yearbook of Turkey,* SIS 1968, p. 330, as:

	Expenditures	Receipts
1950	1.467	1.419
1951	1.590	1.645
1952	2.248	2.235
1953	2.294	2.272

b) SIS economic accounts are not yet available after 1968. Budget appropria-
tions and tax revenues were:

	Expenditures	Tax Revenues
1968	21.612	16.240
1969	25.697	19.114
1970	28.860	24.060

From *Bütçe Kanunları,* Ministry of Finance.

c) Not published after 1968.

Table I-5 (continued)

Sources: Money Supply: *Aylık Bülten,* Central Bank, October–December 1971. End-of-
year figures.
Government Accounts: 1950 and 1953 to 1962, James W. Land, *Economic
Accounts of Government in Turkey, Pub. No. 566-17,* SIS (Ankara), 1969.
1963 to 1968: data kindly provided to the author by SIS.
Price Indices: Home goods index – Istanbul Chamber of Commerce index as
reported in *International Financial Statistics.*
Wholesale price index: Ministry of Commerce index reported in *International
Financial Statistics.*

ward biases: (1) the weights are those of 1938, and thus the rise in the price
of manufactured commodities relative to agricultural commodities is under-
weighted,[30] and (2) prices used in compiling the index are official prices in
the many instances – especially in the 1955-to-1958 period – when commodities were subject to price controls. Hence there is every reason to believe
that the index understates the actual degree of inflation, especially in the
mid-1950's. But even by these figures the rapid inflation Turkey experienced
in the mid-1950's is evident. The price level doubled between 1955 and 1959,
according to the official index. The rate of inflation since 1960 has been
considerably more moderate, averaging less than 3 per cent annually between
1960 and 1965 and about 6 per cent annually since 1965.

V. Payments regimes: delineation of phases

It is the purpose of the remainder of this study to focus upon Turkey's
trade and payments regime and its effects upon and interaction with resource
allocation and economic growth in the 1950-to-1971 period. Various aspects
of the Turkish experience will be separately analyzed in later chapters.

To place each of these aspects in perspective it will be useful to start with
an overview of the evolution of the payments regime in accordance with the
phases outlined in the Foreign Trade Regimes and Economic Development
research project. Although any demarcation contains some arbitrary elements, the best delineation appears to be:[31]

1950 to September 1953	Phase V
September 1953 to December 1954	Phase I
January 1955 to August 1958	Phase II

30. Sevil Korum, *Türkiyede Toptan Eşya Fiyatlari Endeksi,* Sevinç Matbaasi (Ankara)
1968.
31. See Appendix D-2 for definitions of "Phases" as used in the project.

August 1958 to August 1960	Phase III
August 1960 to December 1963	Phase IV
January 1964 to August 1970	Phase II
August 1970 to December 1970	Phase III
January 1971 to Summer 1972	Phase IV

1950 to September 1953: Phase V

A payments deficit was emerging during this period, but the conjunction of massive aid inflows (which covered 80 per cent of the net current account deficit between 1950 and 1955[32]), favorable world prices for Turkey's exports and the emergence of wheat exports obscured the underlying situation. Moreover a massive increase in imports, permitted under a fairly liberal trade regime, offset inflationary pressure that would otherwise have resulted in price increases. Table I-6 gives summary balance-of-payments data. As can be seen, imports virtually doubled between 1950 and 1952; the current account deficit in 1952 amounted to 3 per cent of GNP despite the fact that export earnings had risen by $100 million, or 40 per cent in the two-year interval.

The payments regime remained fairly liberal until September 1953. Exports were generally free from licensing requirements, although exporters were supposed to surrender all proceeds to the Central Bank within three months of the date of export, with the exception of proceeds from a few designated "minor exports" (about 3 per cent of exports by value) which could be retained for purposes of importing a specified list of goods not otherwise legally importable. Imports were all subject to license. Most goods, however, were on a "liberalized" list for which licenses were automatically granted. Some commodities were subject to global quotas, but these were the exception rather than the rule. Guarantee deposits were required against import license applications, but only in an amount equal to 4 per cent of the value of the license, and were subject to refund if the license was not granted within a month.[33] Foreign investment was encouraged, required little paperwork, and guarantees were given for repatriation of profits and capital.[34]

September 1953 to August 1958: Phases I and II

September 1953 saw the first moves toward restricting international transactions. It was decreed that all imports would be subject to "strict licensing."

---

32. *Economic Situation in Turkey, 1959,* OEEC (Paris), 1960, p. 30. Henceforth, this will be cited as OEEC, *Turkey, 1959.*
33. Imports on government account were excluded from these regulations.
34. For a summary of the regime during 1952 see *Fourth Annual Report, Exchange Restrictions,* International Monetary Fund (Washington), 1953, pp. 278–81.

Also, the provision that exporters could use their foreign exchange under certain conditions was abolished and in its place a *de facto* multiple exchange rate system was introduced. Subsidies of 25, 40, and 50 per cent were payable on certain exports, while taxes of 25, 50, and 75 per cent were levied on "nonessential" imports. This decree was quickly followed with another on November 1, which removed all items from the Liberalized List (for which licenses were then fairly automatically granted) except machinery, industrial raw materials and spare parts. Other commodities could be imported only if they were "needed for economic development" and import surcharges of 25 to 75 per cent were imposed upon them.

Thereafter the control system was subject to frequent modification. Both quantitative controls and multiple rates were generally used and subject to rapid changes. Buying rates by the end of 1957 ranged from TL 2.82 to TL 5.75 per dollar. Most imports, when licenses could be obtained, came at TL 3.995 per dollar (2.82 plus a 40 per cent exchange tax).

Despite the increasing surcharges and tighter controls, the Turkish balance-of-payments situation deteriorated almost continuously and Turkish short-term international indebtedness mounted. Export earnings fell steadily from a peak of $396 million in 1953 to $247 million in 1958. A sizeable black market developed and, as indicated in Table I-6, net errors and omissions became large and negative. Even so, the situation was so bizarre that the International Monetary Fund was warning readers of an estimated $100 million or more of unrecorded imports and other significant inaccuracies in the Turkish balance-of-payments records.[35] Finally, in the summer of 1958 import licensing was virtually suspended, and the Central Bank was unable to cover its immediate debt-servicing obligations. These circumstances left the government no choices other than declaring international bankruptcy or accepting foreign credits and the conditions attached to them. At that point the government chose to borrow and accepted a Stabilization Program as a condition for debt restructuring.

August 1958 to August 1960: Phase III

Turkey's international indebtedness was staggering when the Stabilization Program was agreed upon. It was estimated that as of December 1957 Turkey's foreign debt was $1,011 million,[36] contrasted with 1957 exports of $345 million.

The Stabilization Program had several parts: (1) alterations in the ex-

35. *Balance of Payments Yearbook, Volume 13,* International Monetary Fund (Washington), *Turkey,* p. 2.
36. OEEC, *Turkey, 1959, op. cit.* (Note 32), p. 30.

Table I-6
Turkey's balance of payments, 1950 to 1970 (millions of U.S. dollars)

	1950	1951	1952	1953	1954	1955	1956
Exports f.o.b.	262	314	363	396	335	313	305
Imports f.o.b.	252	354	489	468	421	438	358
Trade balance	11	−40	−126	−72	−86	−125	−53
Net goods and services	−42	−84	−182	−141	−159	−130	−25
Net donations	56	40	52	49	45	51	89
Net private capital	9	−30	43	141	76	12	−29
Net official capital	8	28	90	−49	28	113	7
Errors and omissions	−32	46	−3	0	10	−45	−42

	1957	1958	1959	1960	1961	1962	1963
Exports f.o.b.	331	247	363	336	365	399	395
Imports f.o.b.	346	284	433	422	448	567	588
Trade balance	−15	−37	−70	−86	−83	−168	−193
Net goods and services	−34	−84	−127	−117	−123	−235	−256
Net donations	67	91	91	91	99	105	78
Net private capital	−61	73	14	25	−34	50	−7
Net official capital	126	−47	86	−30	25	111	187
Errors and omissions	−97	−33	−64	31	33	−31	−2

	1964	1965	1966	1967	1968	1969	1970
Exports f.o.b.	433	479	494	530	498	537	588
Imports f.o.b.	475	505	639	608	688	726	850
Trade balance	−42	−26	−145	−78	−190	−189	−262
Net goods and services	−89	−30	−109	−87	−228	−179	−132
Net donations	23	21	27	29	70	46	62
Net private capital	58	−1	−8	−2	11	−10	78
Net official capital	20	39	109	127	193	192	129
Errors and omissions	−12	−29	−19	−67	−46	−49	−137

Source: International Monetary Fund, *Balance of Payments Yearbook* (Washington), various issues.

change-rate system, which (2) enabled an immediate inflow of imports; (3) removal of the source of inflationary pressure; and (4) restructuring and consolidation of Turkish foreign indebtedness. Substantial changes were also made in domestic monetary and fiscal policy. Multiple exchange rates were maintained, but primarily on the export side. A uniform TL 6.20 per dollar "exchange surtax" was imposed on all purchases of foreign exchange for imports, invisibles and capital transactions, thus giving an actual TL 9 per dollar exchange rate for payments abroad. Export rates were simplified, as all exports were divided into three classes with rates of TL 4.90, 5.60 and 9.00

per dollar. To allow some imports into the country, credits totalling $203 million were granted by the IMF, the U.S., and the OEEC. Simultaneously, the European Payments Union (EPU) advanced a credit of 25 million units of account. In addition there was considerable debt rescheduling, so that the total credit was in effect much larger. This enabled import licensing to resume. To remove the sources of inflationary pressure, the Turks were asked to balance the central government budget and to raise SEE prices (to eliminate SEE deficits; see below, Chapter II). SEE prices and civil servants' salaries were raised by about 20 per cent in May 1959, an action which was immediately reflected in the price level. But Turkish prices remained virtually constant through the end of 1961. Since that time Turkey has been a moderate-inflation country, never again experiencing inflationary pressures nearly as severe as those of the mid-1950's.

There was a sizeable short-term response to the Stabilization Program, resulting in a net shift in Turkey's balance of payments over and above the credits received, of over $200 million by the end of 1959. In this atmosphere the Menderes government introduced a clearly inflationary budget early in 1960. After the Revolution in May, however, the budget was substantially altered; one of the first acts of the new government was to devalue the Turkish lira officially to a new rate of TL 9 to the dollar and virtually all vestiges of a multiple exchange rate system were eliminated.

August 1960 to December 1963: Phase IV

This was the period during which the State Planning Organization developed and began implementing the First Five Year Plan. An indication of the degree of success of devaluation is that over the life of the FFYP export earnings exceeded their plan levels (and planned rate of increase) in each year. From $249 million in 1958, exports rose to $336 million in 1960 and $395 million in 1963 (just below the 1953 level).

With the rapid growth of export earnings and relatively slack import demand in the years 1960 and 1961 following the Revolution, the import control system was further liberalized. Bilateral payments agreements were terminated as they came up for renewal. Goods were transferred from the import Quota List to the Liberalized List (for which licensing was automatic), and goods previously not listed were added to the group of commodities which could be legally imported. While some deletions from the list of eligible imports were made, the motive appears to have been protection on newly-started domestic production rather than balance-of-payments strain. Although a 50 per cent tax was imposed on foreign exchange purchases for purposes of foreign travel, the motive again appears not to have been balance-of-payments considerations, but rather that of taxing luxury consumption.

Thus the early 1960's passed in an atmosphere of relatively little strain in the balance of payments. However, while the FFYP underestimated export (and other foreign exchange) earnings, it also underestimated import requirements and overestimated the likely magnitude of foreign aid. By the end of 1963 a payments deficit was re-emerging, with imports mushrooming to $588 million in that year from $284 million in 1958 and $422 million in 1960.

January 1964 to August 1970: Phase II

A period of foreign exchange shortage followed. In 1963 and 1964 the government reduced the number of items on the Liberalized List, tightened quotas, raised guarantee deposit requirements, and imposed an import surcharge of 5 per cent on landed cost (equivalent to about 10 per cent of c.i.f. price) in an effort to control the flood of imports. Further steps toward tightening the import regime were taken in subsequent years.

Although imports fell sharply to $542 million in 1964, the structural shifts the planners were attempting to effect − a higher rate of capital formation, more import-substitution, etc. − led to sharp increases in import demand, with the balance-of-payments situation remaining difficult throughout the rest of the decade. Premia (see definition in Explanation of Terms, Appendix D) on import licenses rose from virtually nothing in 1963 to 40−50 per cent of the value of the license by early 1965 and continued rising in later years.

Thus Phase II in the mid-1960's was entirely different from that in the mid-1950's. First, the lessons of the 1950's led to an extreme reluctance to resort to deficit financing: inflationary pressures were much smaller than in the 1950's. Whereas Phase II in the 1950's resulted from the generalized pressures of excess demand, the consequent shift in relative prices, and decline in export earnings, Phase II in the 1960's had its origins in a structural shift in the demand for imports resulting from an altered development strategy and the increased rate of capital formation.

The Turkish economy lurched through a series of increasingly severe payments difficulties and consequent mountingly restrictive regimes, with small breathing spaces in which things relaxed somewhat, from 1964 until devaluation in 1970. These difficulties very quickly led the Turks to develop export premia, a special tourist exchange rate and other measures to buffer the foreign-exchange-earning sector from the disincentive effects of the import premia that were emerging. In fact, an export rebate scheme had become law in 1963 but did not begin to become a significant element in export incentives until 1966.

Export earnings consequently rose in every year until 1968. Workers' remittances, encouraged by special premia, became a large and significant factor

ings. But the growth of demand for imports increased
the inflow of foreign aid did not. The licensing mecha-
into Liberalized List goods for which licenses were
nd quota goods for which licenses were issued up to a
remained unaltered on paper. In practice, however,
nly as foreign exchange was available and a backlog of
Other devices were also used to restrict imports: the
ed to 15 per cent in 1967 and 25 per cent in 1969 and
irements rose to over 100 per cent of the value of
gories of imports. This latter, given delays and other
bably the equivalent of a 25 per cent duty on some

969 that speculation against the lira developed on a
ticipation of elections in 1969, the government intro-
budget which resulted in a 10 per cent increase in the
9. Export earnings which had fallen off in 1968 barely
level in 1969, and imports were simultaneously cut
reduce the $228 million current account deficit which
968.

nber 1970: Phase III

e lira was devalued *de jure* to the new rate of TL 15 =
f 9:1, and many of the devices introduced in the middle
either relaxed or eliminated. Thus the special tourist and
rates were abolished, the stamp tax was reduced from 25
cent and guarantee deposit requirements were sharply
ebates continued for non-traditional exports, and ex-
to 3 per dollar were imposed on traditional exports.
ion in 1958, however, the response to devaluation was
ed. There was, moreover, little interruption of domestic
although domestic prices rose sharply.

January 1971 to Summer 1972: Phase IV

With the rapid increase in foreign exchange earnings immediately after
devaluation, Liberalized List import licenses were granted quickly and virtually automatically. Although exchange control continued, it was much less
pronounced in its effects than in the late 1960's, and premia on import
licenses virtually disappeared. Turkey's exchange reserves by the spring of
1972 exceeded $900 million, contrasted with $218 million in July 1970,
while foreign exchange earnings were continuing to increase over their 1971
level.

VI. Plan of the book

In the following chapters various aspects of the Turkish experience will be examined. In keeping with the focus of the project on Foreign Trade Regimes and Economic Development, primary attention is given to three phenomena: Phase III from August 1958 to August 1960; the nature and effects of Phase II in the middle and late 1960's; and the resource-allocational and growth effects of the Turkish trade and payments regimes in the 1960's.

Part Two, consisting of Chapters II to IV, is concerned with the Phase III episode of 1958 to 1960. Chapter II contains an analysis of the factors leading up to 1958. In Chapter III an evaluation of the Stabilization Program is given. Chapter IV is devoted to tracing the results of the devaluation package.

Part Three, consisting of Chapters V to VII, evaluates Phase II of the mid-1960's. Chapter V concerns the role of planning in the 1960's and its interaction with the trade and payments regime. Chapter VI contains an analysis of the import regime and its administration. Chapter VII analyzes the determinants of foreign exchange earnings, with primary attention to export behavior.

Part Four focuses upon the resource-allocational and growth effects of Turkey's trade and payments experience. Chapter VIII is concerned with the microeconomic effects of Turkish foreign trade policies and with such evidence as is available about the income-distributional effects of those policies. Chapter IX evaluates the interaction between Turkish foreign trade and economic growth at a more macroeconomic level, and Chapter X summarizes the main conclusions of the study.

There are four appendices. Appendix A contains the details of the computations of effective exchange rates for exports and imports used throughout the book and Appendix B provides data underlying results reported in Chapter III. Appendix C reports briefly upon the devaluation of 1970 and its aftermath. Although insufficient time has elapsed for detailed analysis of the 1970 episode, the preliminary data are sufficiently interesting and suggestive to warrant at least brief mention. Appendix D is divided into three sections: (1) defines the general concepts used in the entire series; (2) delineates the "Phases" used in tracing the exchange control regimes; (3) lists important Turkish names, abbreviations, and acronyms used in the study.

Part Two

The Devaluation-Cum-Liberalization Episode

CHAPTER II

Phase II: 1953 to 1958

The focus of this part is upon the devaluation of 1958 and its effects. Understanding and analysis of that episode requires consideration of the factors leading to payments imbalance in the 1950's. Knowledge of that period is also valuable in understanding many aspects of the exchange control regime in the 1960's.

Consideration is given in the present chapter to the nature of the imbalance in the 1950's and to other aspects of the experience that are relevant for subsequent analysis — subject, of course, to severe limitations of data availability. It is simply not possible to obtain meaningful data on a variety of aspects of the Turkish experience prior to 1958. The lack of data is in part attributable to inadequate data collection in the 1950's. In fact, many of the data used below were developed in the early 1960's by the staff of the State Planning Organization, who found them necessary for planning purposes. Another factor contributing to the lack of information is that the Menderes regime was discredited after the May 1960 Revolution, and as a result many of those who could have provided insights into events of the 1950's have not done so. In addition, the nature of the payments regime and the partially suppressed inflation which resulted precluded reliable information. The economic environment was one in which data *a priori* were subject to wide margins of error. As indicated in Chapter I, even Turkish balance-of-payments statistics are believed to be subject to sizeable error for the latter half of the 1950's. Meaningful price data are impossible to obtain, since price controls were legally in force. Although black markets were prevalent, there are no records of those transactions. Many statistics simply were not collected at all, owing partly to the government's lack of interest in coordination of economic policy.

Subject to data limitations, then, three questions about Phase II of the mid-1950's must be considered: (1) the nature of the trade and payments regime; (2) the factors contributing to the payments imbalance; and (3) the effects of those factors and of the balance of payments on the Turkish economy. Each of these questions is considered, in turn, in this chapter.

I. The trade and payments regime of Phase II in the 1950's

Once exchange controls and multiple exchange rates were imposed in 1953, they were constantly changed in response to continued balance-of-payments difficulties. Thus the exchange rates applicable to various transaction categories, licensing regulations, guarantee deposits and other aspects of the trade and payments regime were in a constant state of flux. The proliferation of detailed, generally *ad hoc*, measures sometimes resulted in a system of internally inconsistent regulations.[1]

In addition to the factors creating continuing payments imbalance discussed in Section II below, another source of difficulty confronted the Turkish government. That factor, already existing in late 1952, was an accumulated short-term indebtedness. Because of its effects on other aspects of the regime and even upon the interpretation of those statistics that are available, we start by considering Turkey's foreign debt and its effects upon the trade and payments regime.

Foreign indebtedness

Nothing better illustrates the lack of coordination in economic policy during the Menderes years mentioned in Chapter I than the management, or more accurately its absence, of Turkey's international indebtedness. From 1952 until 1958 the debt hung over the entire exchange regime and affected everything: even export data and export prices are incomprehensible, except in that light.

Difficulties were already immense by late 1952. Despite the rapid increase in export earnings in the early 1950's, imports rose much more sharply. With a fairly liberal regime many of these imports were financed by suppliers' credits: Turkish importers were able to buy goods on short-term credit. The volume of those obligations was far in excess of the Central Bank's foreign exchange resources. Turkey was the first country to overdraw her IMF quota, and the first to request an extension of time when payment came due.[2]

By 1952 a large volume of overdue debt had already accumulated. The Central Bank always had a negative free-foreign-exchange position, from late 1952 until 1958, and Turkish importers were often unable to buy foreign exchange from the Central Bank to pay their commercial debts, despite their having been issued import licenses at earlier dates.

1. *Three Monthly Economic Reports, Turkey,* Economist Intelligence Unit, *No.21,* March 1957, pp. 3–4. Hereafter, various issues of this publication will be cited as EIU.
2. Keith Horsefield, *The International Monetary Fund 1945–1965,* International Monetary Fund (Washington), 1969, p. 347.

The precise amount of arrears and total debt during the 1952–1958 period has never been known. When debt consolidation was agreed upon by Turkey and the European Payments Union (EPU) governments in 1958, the EPU governments were forced to advertise within their countries in an effort to learn the extent of Turkish indebtedness.

Various estimates have been made about the volume of outstanding overdue and total debt at different dates. Table II-1 provides these estimates. However, the only official figure in Table II-1 is the Central Bank's estimate in early 1958 – at that time long- and short-term debt amounted to TL 3,550 million not counting arrears, which were estimated at TL 644 million.[3] As of early 1958 total indebtedness thus exceeded 10 per cent of GNP. Arrears alone were over 2 per cent of GNP and almost equal to 1958 exports.

Despite its large and growing size during the 1950's there was considerable turnover of the debt. Starting in 1954, Turkey made a series of bilateral agreements with various Western European countries for exporting and debt repayment: first Germany, then Switzerland, Italy, England and others.[4] All of these agreements had a similar format, although they varied in detail. For Turkish exports of specified commodities, a certain fraction of the export earnings was retainable by Turkish creditors. For example, an export-import firm in Germany could, if it imported DM 500,000 of hazelnuts, pay the Turkish exporter DM 250,000 and retain DM 250,000 against overdue Turkish debt. The Turkish debtor then paid the Turkish exporter the TL equivalent of DM 250,000.

These bilateral agreements have certain important consequences for the interpretation of Turkish trade and balance-of-payments statistics in the mid-1950's. First, not all of Turkey's foreign exchange earnings from exports – even those officially recorded – were available as free foreign exchange for the Central Bank. The picture of declining export earnings therefore understates the decline in free foreign exchange. Second, the fact that EPU creditors could receive repayment of their loans only if they imported from Turkey resulted in their willingness to buy Turkish commodities at prices above those in the world market. Failure to do so cost, at a minimum, foregone interest (or profits) for an unknown period and, at a maximum, implied an increased probability that the debt might not be repaid at all.[5] Hence the bilateral-agreement device enabled Turkey to export at a time when, as will be seen below, Turkey's export prices were non-competitive.

---

3. EIU, *op. cit.* (Note 1), *No. 25,* February 1958, p. 2.
4. Unfortunately there are no official records of the value of exports to Western Europe that moved under these bilateral agreements. In export data for the 1950's, exports to EPU countries include exports under bilateral debt payment agreements.
5. EIU, *op. cit.* (Note 1), *No. 21,* March 1957, p. 6.

Table II-1
Turkey's foreign debt, various dates (millions of TL)

Date	Central Bank Assets and Liabilities		Arrears	Balance	Total Debt
	Assets				
	Gold	Foreign Exchange			
2/54			420		
12/54	402	172	584		
12/55	402	188	799	−209	
12/56	402	242	732	−88	2,800
12/57				−160	4,200
8/58			1120		

Source: EIU, *op. cit.* (Note 1), various issues.

The eventual consolidation of arrears in 1958 amounted to $436 million. It is likely that this figure was below the actually overdue debt at that date. Moreover, by that time many creditors had accepted repayment of part or all of their loans at a discount under the bilateral-agreement arrangements.

Exchange rates[6]

Turkey had in effect a multiple exchange rate system from 1953 to 1960. The official rate, however, remained at TL 2.80 per dollar throughout the period. Multiple rates were achieved by imposing taxes on imports and other foreign exchange purchases, and by paying premia of differing heights for various categories of foreign exchange sales.

Import EERs.[7] When exchange control was instituted in September 1953, a system of surcharges on various categories of import transactions was inaugurated, along with import licensing. Once surcharges were established, commodities were frequently transferred from one category to another and the rates payable were changed frequently. The details of these surcharges and their EER equivalents are given in Appendix A.

Although import licensing was the dominant means of import control in

6. Data in this section, except as otherwise indicated, are drawn from: EIU, *op. cit.* (Note 1), various issues; and *Annual Report Exchange Restrictions,* IMF, 1952 to 1958.

7. For the definition of Effective Exchange Rates (EERs) and Price-Level-Deflated EER: (PLD-EER) mentioned below, see the Definitions and Concepts used in the Project on Foreign Trade Regimes and Economic Development included in this volume (Appendix D-1).

the 1950's, exchange surcharges of 25, 50, and 75 per cent were decreed for various categories of "luxury" imports in September 1953. Within two months, however, import licensing was restricted to permit only imports "essential to development," while the surcharges were extended to cover many of those goods.

The three-tier surcharge system remained in effect until 1958. Turkey switched from specific to *ad valorem* tariffs in 1954, with a general rise in the average rate of duty paid and thus an increase in EERs in that year. In 1957 a 40 per cent "exchange tax" was imposed on all purchases of foreign exchange, this tax lasting until December 1958.

Table II-2 summarizes the resulting import EERs for the 1953-to-1958 period. As can be seen, the EERs for all categories of transactions rose substantially over the period. However, as will be seen below, the price level rose sufficiently rapidly so that the PLD-EERs (see list of Definitions and Concepts used in the Research Project on Foreign Trade Regimes and Economic Development, Appendix D-1) for imports actually decreased (see Table II-3 below). It is noteworthy that as the nominal EERs rose the disparity in rates between import categories fell. Thus despite the initial intention of the government to favor capital goods, the increased use of multiple exchange rates reduced the differential between capital goods and other import categories.

Export EERs. At the same time that exchange control and import surcharges were imposed in 1953, premia were started for a few export categories. These were all marginal exports and had accounted for only about 3 per cent of Turkey's export earnings in 1952. The premia were: 50 per cent for exports earning "free" dollars, 40 per cent for proceeds from EPU coun-

Table II-2
Import EERs, 1953 to 1957 (TL per U.S. dollar of c.i.f. value)

	1953	1954	1955	1956	1957
Construction materials	3.58	3.76	4.25	4.55	6.16
Machinery and equipment	3.22	3.48	4.02	4.72	5.97
Intermediate goods and raw materials	3.78	4.14	4.38	4.54	5.35
Consumer goods	5.60	6.09	6.37	6.54	7.47

Sources: Construction Materials and Investment Goods EERs: Table A-10. Intermediate Goods and Raw Materials, and Consumer goods: 1954 and 1957 from Tables A-11 and A-14. 1955 and 1956: the percentage change from 1954 to 1957 was prorated over the intervening years in proportion to the change in construction materials.

Table II-3
Nominal and PLD-EERs, 1953 to 1957

	1953	1954	1955	1956	1957
A. Nominal EERs (TL per dollar)					
Sales of foreign exchange					
Traditional exports	2.80	2.85	2.89	2.91	2.94
Nontraditional exports	3.92	4.48	4.50	5.00	5.00
Tourists and invisibles	2.80	2.80	2.80	5.75	5.75
Capital account	2.80	2.80	2.80	2.80	2.80
Purchases of foreign exchange					
Capital goods imports	3.22	3.48	4.02	4.72	5.97
Consumer goods imports	5.60	6.09	6.37	6.54	7.47
Tourists and invisibles	2.80	2.80	2.80	5.25	5.25
Capital account	2.80	2.80	2.80	2.80	2.80
B. PLD-EERs (1958 TL per dollar)					
Sales of foreign exchange					
Traditional exports	5.83	5.28	4.82	3.93	3.26
Nontraditional exports	8.16	8.30	7.50	6.76	5.55
Tourists and invisibles	5.83	5.18	4.66	7.77	6.39
Capital account	5.83	5.18	4.66	3.78	3.11
Purchases of foreign exchange					
Capital goods imports	6.71	6.44	6.70	6.38	6.63
Consumer goods imports	11.67	11.28	10.62	8.84	8.30
Tourists and invisibles	5.83	5.18	4.66	7.09	5.83
Capital account	5.83	5.18	4.66	3.78	3.11

Notes: a) Capital goods import rate taken as the machinery and equipment rate.
b) PLD-EERs were computed by dividing the nominal EER by the home goods wholesale price index (1958 = 100) given in Table I-5.
c) Capital account sales of foreign exchange does not include capital repatriated by Turks after 1956, which was subject to the TL 5.25 = $1 exchange rate.
Source: Appendix A.

tries, and 25 per cent for earnings from bilateral-agreement (generally Eastern European) countries.

Premium rates were introduced in subsequent years for additional categories of exports, the number of commodities eligible for the basic premia was increased, and the premium rates themselves were altered periodically. Some premia, such as those for raisins and figs, were specific and were altered frequently. One effect of the premia was to encourage exports to Eastern European countries at relatively high prices, thereby enabling Turkish exporters to earn the premia. The importers in turn resold Turkish commodities in Western European markets at lower prices, recovering their losses through high prices on the goods exported to Turkey. These transactions, known as "switch deals," were reported to be widespread in the mid-1950's. The government even stopped premia on cotton exports in 1957 (thereby virtually halting the exportation of cotton) to investigate the extent of switch-dealing.[8]

In addition to export premia, exporters of certain commodities were accorded foreign-exchange retention privileges. Chrome and manganese exporters, for example, were allowed to retain and use 100 per cent of export earnings from 1956 to March 1957. Another system, with 1 to 15 per cent retention, was introduced in August 1957 and later rescinded. It was not possible to calculate the value of retention rights in computing export EERs. However, their sporadic and limited use suggests that little bias in estimating export EERs results from their omission. Export EERs are given in Appendix Table A-1 and are summarized in Table II-3.

As can be seen, Turkey's major exports — tobacco, cotton, raisins, figs, hazelnuts, chrome and copper — received virtually the official exchange rate until 1956. Even after that date the premia for most traditional exports were relatively low. Even the marginal export commodities were subject to EERs below those applicable to imports.

Invisible and capital account transactions. Until October 1956 virtually all invisible and capital account transactions were subject to the official rate of exchange. An 87.5 per cent surcharge was imposed in October 1956 on payments for services and purchases of foreign exchange by Turks for foreign travel. The effective rate, TL 5.25 per dollar, thus applied to purchases of foreign exchange on current account except for dividend and interest payments. A premium of 105 per cent was simultaneously extended to foreigners' purchases of Turkish lira for tourist purposes, to repatriation of capital held abroad by Turks, and to some minor exports. The intent of introducing these new rates was apparently the hope of diverting foreign exchange transactions from black-market to official channels (see below, Section III). These rates remained in effect until August 1958.

Spread of EERs. Table II-3 presents the nominal and (price-level-deflated) PLD-EERs on various classes of transactions during the 1953-to-1957 period. As can be seen, the disparity between sales and purchase rates increased over the period. The amount in real terms received by traditional exporters per dollar of sales decreased by 45 per cent, and even that for non-traditional exports fell 32 per cent. The real exchange rates for capital goods imports, by contrast, remained virtually constant over the period, and the consumer

8. EIU, *op. cit.* (Note 1), *No. 22*, May 1957, p. 7.

goods import rate, initially 75 per cent above the capital goods import rate, fell to 25 per cent above it. Thus while the export rate depreciated markedly, that for imports fell by a considerably smaller magnitude and the spread between import rates decreased. As inspection of the detailed tables in Appendix A indicates, the spread within categories of both export and import rates was even greater than that shown in Table II-3.

Quantitative restrictions

Although there were frequent changes in EERs during the 1950's, the basic instrument used to control the balance of payments was quantitative restriction. Both imports and exports were subject to licensing, and the rules governing each were frequently changed. Initially, the intent of import licensing was to limit expenditures upon imported goods, while export licensing was primarily aimed at insuring that foreign exchange earnings would enter official channels. But regulations were rapidly modified in attempts to prevent the evasions of the system which had developed. Moreover, the restrictiveness of the system increased as foreign exchange earnings declined. We consider quantitative restrictions on imports and exports in turn.

Import licensing and price checks. It was decreed in the initial decision to employ exchange control that all imports would be subject to licensing and that machinery, equipment and raw materials would be licensed fairly freely, while other items could be imported only "if needed for development."[9] The regulations governing import licensing increased in complexity and detail thereafter. In 1954 all importers were required to possess "importer's certificates," and their annual imports were limited to their highest annual imports of the years 1948 to 1953.[10] Not more than one-sixth of this amount could be imported in any two-month period. The system was further tightened and modified in mid-1955, but by the end of that year it was decided that the Ministry of Finance and the Minister of Economy and Commerce should determine the import needs of the private and public sectors and decide on their foreign exchange allocations.[11] The government gradually became the sole importer of a variety of raw materials and other goods.

Guarantee deposits against applications for import licenses from the private sector were a part of the control system throughout the 1953-to-1958 period. These requirements were increased at intervals, rising from 4 per cent in 1953 to 20 per cent in 1958.

9. *Sixth Annual Report on Currency Restriction,* IMF, 1954, p. 301.
10. *Seventh Annual Report on Currency Restriction,* IMF, 1955, p. 294.
11. *Eighth Annual Report on Currency Restriction,* IMF, 1956, p. 290.

There were frequent "holidays" on the issuance of import licenses as the government's foreign exchange holdings became smaller. It often happened that applications for licenses, even for those commodities whose importation was supposed to be liberal, were delayed two to eight months before action was taken on them. In the last few weeks prior to August 1958, indeed, no import licenses were issued. Licensing in earlier years had on occasion been suspended for periods of several weeks, and delays were frequent.

As evidence of large premia on imports developed in the mid-1950's, the government placed a number of goods on a "restricted import" list. These goods were to be eligible for importation only if the importer could arrange foreign credit of more than a year's duration to finance the import.[12] The intent of the "restricted import" list was to increase the flow of imports of high-premium goods without worsening Turkey's indebtedness situation in the short run. One result of the regulation was a major increase in imports in this category, apparently financed by foreign credits, but often actually paid for by black-market foreign exchange.[13]

In an effort to stem the growing black market, the government developed a system of import price controls. Price committees were established to verify that import prices were in line with those in world markets. No licenses were issued after 1956 and no goods cleared customs without an official price certificate.[14]

There was also increasing resort to bilateral agreements with Eastern European countries throughout the 1953-to-1958 period in order to step up the flow of imports and to find export markets. As those agreements affected both imports and exports, they are dealt with separately below.

It should be recalled that the many changes in the licensing system and its administration interacted with changes in import EERs discussed above. The brief description of the control mechanism given here fails to convey more than the barest outline of the import controls applied during the 1950's. It will be seen below that the curtailment of imports flowing through official channels was pronounced and had considerable impact on the economy.

Export licensing. Whereas the purposes of import controls were to restrict the flow of imports and to plug loopholes in the system, export licensing was apparently intended primarily as a means of preventing extra-legal flows of exports. In addition to bilateral agreements, to be discussed below, the major instrument used in connection with exports was the system of price controls, or price registrations.

12. EIU, *op. cit.* (Note 1), *No. 10,* July 1954, p. 5.
13. *Ibid., No. 15,* September 1955, p. 3.
14. *Ibid., No. 19,* August 1956, p. 4.

It should be noted first that the pricing policies of the SEEs and other government agencies were and are a major factor influencing exports.[15] During the 1950's the export prices set by government agencies, especially for traditional agricultural exports, were significantly above international prices. Thus even in the absence of export price controls there would have been severe problems associated with exporting those commodities.

Price controls on exports were intended to prevent under-invoicing of exports and the diversion of export proceeds to the black market, but the manner of their administration led to additional difficulties. In general an export price was "registered" applicable to a particular commodity category. Once that price was established, no export licenses were issued for prices lower than the registered price.

A priori, one would expect price registration of this form to have several drawbacks. Firms attempting to develop export markets or penetrate new ones would be hampered in so doing; quantity discounts would be difficult to make; and firms with below-average quality would encounter difficulty in obtaining export orders, since they could not cut price to reflect lower quality. Attempts to get approval of exports at less than the registered price would entail delays, and hence shifts in world market prices would be difficult to adjust to. An exporter with an unusually high-priced order would be reluctant to accept it for fear that the price would become the registered price and hence prejudice future sales (unless of course he resorted to under-invoicing). Bilateral agreement countries would also become increasingly attractive export markets relative to convertible currency markets, since prices paid under those agreements were generally higher.

There can be little doubt that throughout most of the 1950's there was an incentive to under-invoice exports. Despite the legal export premia indicated above, the black-market rate (see below) was considerably in excess of the legal premium rate, generally by a factor of two or more. While this consideration might have warranted some sort of minimum prices for exports, the actual administration of registered prices was done in a way that made their effects even more pronounced than *a priori* arguments would suggest.

Price registration for hazelnuts will illustrate. The minimum export prices for the 1955 crop were $140, $110 and $104 per 100 kilos in 1955, 1956 and 1957, respectively; the 1956 crop had a minimum export price of $130 in 1956 and $110 in 1957, contrasted with world prices in those years of $55–$60.[16] Stocks consequently built up to 40,000 tons by the beginning of 1957, and thereafter declined to 23,000 tons after the government granted special import rights to the exporters. As of November 1, 1957, however, no

---

15. See Chapter VII for a fuller discussion.
16. EIU, *op. cit.* (Note 1), *No. 23*, November 1957, p. 4.

sales of that year's crop had yet been made, as the minimum export price had not yet been established. When the price was finally set at $100 per 100 kilo, it was well above the international price, but also below the internal price, and the Exporter's Union was expected to take the loss on export sales.[17]

Other export commodities suffered similar fates. Neither tobacco nor figs could be exported at the start of the 1957 export season owing to delays in establishing registered export prices.[18] In general, registered prices for exports appear to have been set well above international prices. Turkey often lost export markets as a consequence, ending up with large stocks of exportable goods. In many instances the government finally exported at a later date, incurring sizeable losses. In other cases excessive stocks were sold at above-world prices under bilateral debt-repayment agreements, in which cases free foreign exchange earned was much smaller than export proceeds.

In examining the decline in export earnings, the price control policies of the government should be borne in mind. Given the decline in the real exchange rate for exports, there would in any event have been a downward shift in export supply. That decline was accentuated by price registration.

Bilateral agreements. As the Turkish foreign exchange position became increasingly stringent, Turkey resorted more and more to bilateral clearing agreements as a means of obtaining some imports, and of finding some export markets at the relatively high prices of her export goods. These agreements were different from the bilateral arrangements referred to above, which focused upon debt repayment. By 1957 there were fifteen such bilateral agreements in effect.[19] Whereas only 7 per cent of Turkey's imports originated from bilateral trading partners in 1952, 29 per cent of all imports originated from those countries by 1955. Similarly, 14 per cent of Turkish exports were destined for clearing-agreement partners in 1952, and 32 per cent in 1955.[20]

With a general shortage of imports, Turkish importers were willing to pay higher prices than those prevailing in Western Europe for imports from bilateral agreement countries, thus offsetting the above-world prices charged for Turkey's exports. The switch-deal phenomenon was one outcome. In effect, some Eastern European countries were involved in an entrepôt trade, buying

17. *Ibid.,* p. 6.
18. *Ibid.,* p. 4.
19. They were with Brazil, Bulgaria, Czechoslovakia, Egypt, Finland, East Germany, Hungary, Iran, Israel, Japan, Poland, Romania, Spain, U.S.S.R., and Yugoslavia.
20. By 1955 Turkey's imports from her bilateral trading partners were 33 per cent greater than her exports to them. The absolute value of imports from clearing agreements countries then fell from TL 404 million in that year to TL 259 million in 1957, contrasted with exports to those countries of TL 285 million in 1955 and TL 238 million in 1957.

Western European goods to sell to Turkey and buying Turkish exports for resale on the Western European market.

There is no hard evidence as to the extent of switch-dealing, although most people interviewed on the question indicated they thought it to be widespread. The large increase in Turkey's traditional exports to Eastern Europe is sometimes cited as presumptive evidence of the argument that Turkey's Eastern European trading partners could not have absorbed so much tobacco, cotton, hazelnuts and dried fruit. A further indication is the fact that the government adopted several measures to attempt to stop switch-dealing. As indicated above, cotton exports were halted at one time while switch-dealing was investigated. On other occasions, the government imposed quantitative regulations on the fraction of exports that could go to Eastern Europe. For example, the government decreed in 1955 that 75 per cent of every cotton exporter's shipments should go to EPU countries,[21] and in 1956 hazelnut exports to non-EPU destinations were limited to 1,000 tons.[22]

II. Sources of inflationary pressure and imbalance

Five interrelated factors must be examined in evaluating the causes of Turkey's inflation and payments difficulties of the mid-1950's. These are: (1) the government's budget policies, (2) agricultural price support policy, (3) the losses of the SEEs, (4) the expansion of the money supply, and (5) exogenous shifts in Turkish agricultural production. Each of these factors is considered in turn in this section, and the combined consequences of all five phenomena are evaluated thereafter.

Government budgets

In Turkey the general government budget is separate from that of public enterprises, except insofar as there are transfers from the general government to the public enterprises. Hence the government revenue and expenditure figures presented here do not include the activities of the SEEs, which will be considered separately below.

Table II-4 provides the basic data on the public finance of the Government of Turkey during the 1950's. As can be seen, real government expenditures rose rapidly, especially in the early 1950's. With an average annual 11 per cent growth rate of real GNP, government expenditures rose from 15.6 per cent of national income in 1950 to 17.4 per cent of national income in 1955. Although tax revenues were less than expenditures, transfers, primarily from

21. EIU, *op. cit.* (Note 1), *No. 16,* December 1955, p. 7.
22. *Ibid., No. 17,* March 1956, p. 7.

Table II-4
Central government expenditures and receipts, 1950 to 1957

	1950	1953	1954	1955	1956	1957
A. (millions of TL)						
Current outlays	1,236	1,809	2,140	2,635	2,693	3,025
Capital formation	134	339	367	537	762	940
Total expenditures	1,370	2,148	2,507	3,172	3,455	3,965
Tax receipts	1,312	1,971	2,222	2,627	2,999	3,821
Transfers	120	241	230	522	295	264
Net domestic borrowing	−62	−64	55	23	161	−120
B. (per cent of national income)						
Current outlays	13.9	12.3	14.5	14.5	12.7	11.4
Capital formation	1.7	2.3	2.9	2.9	3.6	3.5
Total expenditures	15.6	14.6	17.0	17.4	16.3	14.9
Tax receipts	14.9	13.4	15.0	14.4	14.1	14.3
Transfers	1.2	1.6	1.6	2.9	1.4	1.0
Net borrowing	−0.5	−0.4	0.4	0.1	0.8	−0.4

Notes: a) Transfers consist predominantly of use of TL counterpart funds.
b) These accounts are on an economic basis, and do not coincide with the Turkish classification of current and capital accounts.
c) Central government budget includes the general and annexed budgets. See Land, *op. cit.*, for details.

Source: Land, *op. cit.* (Table I-5).

abroad, covered most of the disparity until 1954. Thus inflationary pressure from the government budget originated more from the rapid increase in real expenditure than from the financing of that expenditure in the early 1950's.

The big surge in government expenditures came just at the time when agricultural production fell sharply in 1954. Hence whatever inflationary pressures would otherwise have been generated by the rapid increase in expenditures were intensified by exogenous events. After 1955 government expenditures continued to increase, but not as rapidly as GNP. As a means of finance, domestic borrowing assumed some importance in the years 1954 to 1956, but was not large by any absolute standard.

Thus if the government budget was inflationary, it was the very rapid increase in real government expenditures that provided the stimulus. Even so, there is no way in which government fiscal policy (aside from the effects of SEE financing) could have resulted in the amount of inflation actually experienced. While government fiscal policy may have contributed moderately to Turkish inflation, it did not do more than that.

Agricultural price supports

During the early 1950's the government attempted to encourage rapid growth in agriculture through high price supports on major agricultural products, especially cereals, and other measures. The result was rapid output expansion for a few years, which was the major factor in the very rapid GNP growth. The costs of that expansion however were strong inflationary pressures and an uneconomic land utilization pattern.[23]

Government policy toward agriculture had several parts: (1) maintenance of high prices for agricultural commodities through price support programs and purchases by state agencies, (2) the subsidization of inputs and especially of tractors, and (3) the development of roads and infrastructure in agriculture. Of these policies, the first was most important and is of particular concern here. Support prices were announced for a number of agricultural commodities early in the year. Various government agencies then stood ready to buy at those support prices. Those agencies were either SEEs or Agricultural Cooperatives under government control (although membership by farmers is voluntary). Focus for present purposes is upon TMO (Toprak Mahsulleri Ofisi — Soil Products Office) which was organized as a state enterprise in 1938. TMO is responsible for price intervention in wheat and other cereals,[24] and in addition is the sole importer and exporter of cereals for Turkey. Grains account for about 70 per cent of the value of Turkish agricultural output.

Table II-5 gives estimates of acreage, production, yield, and net trade in wheat over the 1950-to-1957 period. As can be seen, the response to high support prices was a rapid increase in acreage devoted to wheat. The area

23. Expansion of cereals output was accomplished primarily through the conversion of pastureland and forests to cropland. The evidence is that almost all the converted land had a higher marginal product in livestock or forests than in cereals production. Not only did yields decline in cereals production, but livestock yields must also have fallen. It is estimated that, by 1956, total livestock output was declining. The decrease in livestock production is not taken into account in the national income statistics. See Eva Hirsch and Abraham Hirsch, "Changes in Agricultural Output Per Capita of Rural Population in Turkey, 1927–60," *Economic Development and Cultural Change,* July 1963.

24. There are also SEEs for livestock and fish (Et ve Balık Kurumu — EBK — Meat and Fish Company), sugar (Şeker Fabrikasi Kurumu — Sugar Factories Company), and tobacco (State Monopoly). Other products are handled by sales cooperatives. The EBK has set ceilings on livestock prices, which have been below the prices prevailing in Turkey's southeastern neighbors. This is a major factor accounting for a large smuggling trade in livestock over Turkey's southeastern border as well as very very low rates of capacity utilization in EBK, averaging 7 per cent for sheep and 21 per cent for cattle in 1960. See Olan Forker, *Agricultural Price Intervention by the Government of Turkey,* mimeograph (Ankara), August 1967.

Table II-5
Wheat acreage, yield, production, and net trade, 1950 to 1957

	Acreage (thousands of hectares) (1)	Production (thousands of tons) (2)	Yield (kg. per hectare) (3)	Exports Minus Imports	
				(thousands of tons) (4)	(millions of dollars) (5)
1950	4,477	3,872	864	−189	−122.0
1951	4,789	5,660	1,169	−69	−7.1
1952	5,400	6,447	1,194	462	59.4
1953	6,410	8,000	1,248	601	58.7
1954	6,405	4,900	765	950	67.3
1955	7,060	6,900	977	−63	−4.9
1956	7,335	6,400	872	−9	+1.0
1957	7,157	8,300	1,159	−444	−37.7

Notes: Palmer's data are reworked SIS estimates and do not accord with SIS figures.
They are not consistent with balance of payments data.

Sources: Columns (1) to (3). Edgar Z. Palmer *et al., Agriculture in Turkey,* Robert
College (Istanbul), 1966, Chapter 8.
Columns (4) and (5). *Yearbook of International Trade Statistics, U.N.,* various
issues.

sown increased from 4.5 million hectares in 1950 to 7.0 million hectares in
1955. Production also increased markedly; Turkish wheat production in 1950
was 3.9 million tons, and 189,000 tons were imported. By 1953, a bumper-
crop year, production of wheat had more than doubled, resulting in an export
surplus of 601,000 tons (adding $58.7 million to Turkey's export earnings in
that year) and a sizeable increase in TMO's stocks.

The price at which TMO exported wheat was well below the price at which
TMO purchased wheat. Although the government had earlier declared its
intention of compensating TMO for its resulting losses, no such compensation
was made. Rather, TMO financed its deficits by borrowing from the Central
Bank,[25] and did not repay its loans. The outstanding amounts of TMO's
credits from the Central Bank were: TL 196 million, 1950; TL 519 million,
1952; TL 708 million, 1954; and TL 1,371 million in 1958. By 1958, 31 per
cent of all Central Bank credit was extended to TMO. Of the increase of TL
5,516 million in high-powered money between 1950 and 1958, TL 1,175
million, or 21 per cent, resulted from TMO losses alone. Moreover, for the
years 1950 to 1954 the net increase of TL 512 million in TMO's Central Bank

25. TMO had inadequate storage facilities. Some of its losses were caused by the resulting depletion of grain stocks.

credits accounted for over 31 per cent of the increase in high-powered money.

Other agricultural commodities also benefited from high price supports, with consequent losses on export sales (by other agencies not included in the central government budget), although TMO's losses were the largest. That TMO's operations were clearly an important inflationary factor was observed at the time. According to the Chenery report, written in 1953:

> Normally, it is not possible to identify any one factor as inflationary; it is the aggregate excess of investment over intended savings which is significant. In the present situation, however, there is one element of investment which clearly stands out as the marginal factor. This is the accumulation of cereals stocks by Toprak [TMO] and its borrowing from the Central Bank to cover not only the stock accumulation but the difference between the prices which it pays for cereals and their sale price....Toprak's investment in stocks in the past two years has been equal to half of the inflationary gap between investment and total savings.[26]

There can be little doubt that the government's cereals policy was responsible for much of the initial inflationary pressure experienced within the Turkish economy. The large import surpluses in the years 1951 to 1953 and the rapid increases in agricultural output offset much of the inflationary pressure and there were relatively small rates of price increase. With the first crop failure in 1954, however, the effects of TMO policies and their financing were immediately felt.

State economic enterprises

Once inflation was underway, the government attempted to stop it through a variety of direct interventions. One such measure was instructions to the non-agricultural SEEs to keep their sales prices constant. With rising costs, the SEEs were soon unable to cover their expenditures from current revenues and they too borrowed heavily from the Central Bank.[27]

In 1956 a law was passed regulating legal profit margins on private transactions, as well as imposing legal ceilings on SEE prices.[28] Although enforcement was fairly strict over the private sector for a short time, the inevitable black market soon developed. For SEEs, caught with rising input costs and fixed output prices, the magnitude of borrowing simply increased.[29]

As indicated above, SEE budgets are not included in the Turkish govern-

26. Chenery *et al., op. cit.* (Note 14, Chap. I), pp. 40–41. Acquisition of stocks was of course the result of export-pricing policies.
27. Aktan, *op. cit.* (Note 16, Chap. I), p. 336.
28. Law No. 6731 passed June 6, 1956 and published in the *Official Gazette No. 9329,* June 11, 1956.
29. Okyar, *op. cit.* (Note 5, Chap. I), pp. 104–5.

ment accounts. Credits from the Central Bank to the SEEs were of major importance in the latter half of the 1950's. They had much the same inflationary impact that a central government deficit financed by Central Bank borrowing would have had. Credits to SEEs from the Central Bank stood at TL 745 million in 1950. By 1956 they were TL 1,844 million. In 1958 they were TL 3,247 million. Thus, whereas TMO operations had their biggest impact on Central Bank credits in the early 1950's, deficits of other SEEs were huge in the 1956-to-1958 period.

Little or nothing can be inferred from the SEE losses about their efficiency during the 1950's, since it was government policy which forced them to sell below the cost of production. However, insofar as increases in the money supply led to excess demand, which in turn was met by the SEEs with heavier losses and additional borrowing and consequent money creation, the anti-inflation price controls of the government became in fact the chief source of continuing inflationary pressures. Elimination of the SEE deficits and alterations in SEE pricing policies in 1958-1959 were among the important components of Turkey's devaluation package.

Money supply and money income

It is clear that TMO and other SEE borrowings from the Central Bank largely explain the rapid increase in Central Bank credits from 1953 to 1958. It remains only to link up the behavior of money income and the price level with that of the money supply and Central Bank credits.

Table II-6 presents data on the amount of high-powered money (currency plus Central Bank credits) for the years 1950 to 1958. The top part of the table gives the amount of high-powered money at the end of each year. As can be seen, the amount of high-powered money almost quadrupled in the eight-year period 1950 to 1958, with the biggest increase in the years 1956 and 1957. The role of SEE credits from the Central Bank in the total increase in high-powered money stands out clearly. Part B of Table II-6 gives the year-to-year changes in high-powered money.

Fry has extensively investigated the relationship between high-powered money, money stocks and money income in Turkey.[30] In evaluating the relationship of high-powered money to the money supply, his results were that:

> It is clear that long-run movements in all definitions of money have been primarily determined by changes in high-powered money. Over the period 1950–1968, the contribution of high-powered money to the change in all definitions of the money supply exceeded 90 per cent.[31]

30. Maxwell J. Fry, *Finance and Development Planning in Turkey*, E.J. Brill (Leiden), 1972.

31. *Ibid.*, p. 85.

Table II-6
High-powered money expansion and its origins, 1950 to 1958 (millions of TL)

| | Cur-rency | Central Bank Credits | | | | Total High-Powered Money | Per cent SEE Credits of High-Powered Money |
		SEEs	Govern-ment	Other	Total		
		A. Absolute Amount					
1950	900	745	263	63	1071	1971	37.8
1951	1048	933	298	88	1319	2367	39.4
1952	1146	1145	263	131	1539	2685	42.6
1953	1333	1444	242	126	1812	3145	45.9
1954	1397	1562	439	227	2228	3625	43.1
1955	1805	1643	616	193	2452	4257	38.5
1956	2322	1844	892	119	2855	5177	35.6
1957	2936	2566	1021	153	3740	6676	38.4
1958	3052	3247	1000	188	4435	7487	43.3
		B. Change from Previous Year					
1951	148	188	35	25	248	396	–
1952	98	212	−35	43	220	618	–
1953	187	299	−21	−5	273	160	–
1954	64	118	197	101	416	480	–
1955	408	81	177	−34	224	632	–
1956	517	201	276	−74	403	920	–
1957	614	722	129	34	885	1499	–
1958	116	681	−21	35	695	811	–

Note: Much of TMO's borrowing was reflected in expansion of currency in circulation, as TMO bought up crops. Thus, the column of "SEE credits" fails to reflect the combined effect of TMO and other economic enterprises.

Source: *Aylık Bülten,* Central Bank, June–September 1971.

Fry concluded that for the period 1950 to 1961, with the annual average increase in money stocks of 14.5 per cent, 14.1 per cent was accounted for by changes in high-powered money.[32]

Thus the mechanism of credit creation to finance the government agricultural policies and SEE deficits contributed directly to increases in the money supply during the 1950's.

Fry found a strong link between the money supply and money income in Turkey. In view of the fact that government price policy and weather conditions are the chief determinants of agricultural money income, it is not surprising that Fry found the best fits for money supply and money income

32. *Ibid.,* p. 84.

excluding agricultural income. Fry attempted to estimate the lag between money stock and non-agricultural money income for all definitions of the money supply. With only annual data at hand, he found that the lag between money supply and non-agricultural money income was about two years. The constant term in his estimating equation was insignificant, and for the period 1950 to 1969 Fry's estimates are:

$$\Delta \log Y_t = 0.91 \, \Delta \log M_{t-2} + 0.03 \, \Delta \log i_t \qquad (1)$$

where Y_t is non-agricultural income in year t, and M_{t-2} is the money supply (defined as currency in circulation, commercial sight deposits, sight deposits at the Central Bank, savings time deposits,[33] and commercial time deposits) lagged two years. The symbol i_t stands for the rate of inflation in year t — a proxy for the cost of holding money — and was insignificant. Of the variance in the rate of change of money income, 62 per cent is explained by eq. (1).[34] These results imply that a one per cent increase in high-powered money in year t–2 gives rise to a 0.91 per cent increase in money income with a two-year lag.

Fry also attempted to test the link between money supply and real income. All tests were insignificant, lending strong support to the view that the Turkish inflation of the 1950's was induced, proximately, by the behavior of the money supply. That behavior in turn was largely the result of Central Bank creation of high-powered money, much of which was forced upon the Central Bank by the agricultural and SEE pricing policies of the government.

Exogenous shifts in agriculture

Given Fry's results, the increases in high-powered money in the early 1950's would have led to inflationary pressures within Turkey even if supply conditions had been stable. However, at the same time that monetary policy was resulting in strong inflationary pressures, after increases in the money supply of 21, 12, and 19 per cent in the years 1951 to 1953, respectively (see Table I-5 above), agricultural production dropped sharply.

The year 1954 was an extremely poor one for Turkish agriculture and 1955 was little better. Judged by the national income accounts, agricultural production fell by 20 per cent between 1953 and 1954; wheat production fell 38 per cent; output of other cereals declined by 25 per cent; and tobacco output fell 13 per cent.[35] Agricultural production in 1955 was still 12 per

---

33. *Ibid.*, p. 87. Savings time deposits can normally be withdrawn on demand in Turkey.
34. *Ibid.*, p. 101.
35. Data are from Palmer, *op. cit.* (Table II-5), p. 52.

cent below the 1953 level. Cereals production did not reattain the 1953 level
until 1957.

Available data indicate that food prices did not rise more than the general
price level in 1954 and 1955. The Istanbul Chamber of Commerce and Industry price index gives the following estimates, by components, on a 1948
base:[36]

	Food Prices	Overall Prices	Ratio
1953	113	109	104
1954	120	119	101
1955	129	134	96

The International Labor Organization, which derived its estimates independently by direct sampling, indicates the same movements in the domestic terms
of trade.[37] Hence stock sales of TMO and other agricultural organizations
prevented an increase in the relative price of food. The fact that agricultural
production declined so sharply must nonetheless have accentuated the inflationary pressure generated by money supply increases.

The net inflationary impact

We are now in a position to estimate the contribution of each of the
above-mentioned factors to excess demand and inflationary pressures in
Turkey during the 1950's. Any such estimates must necessarily be somewhat
heroic, but they nonetheless serve to give an idea of the separate contribution
of various factors to excess demand.

The model chosen is exceedingly simple: changes in the money supply are
assumed to have been determined, in accordance with Fry's results, by
changes in high-powered money. Changes in the money supply are in turn
assumed to determine later changes in money income, which is assumed equal
to aggregate demand. Supply shifts are taken to be exogenously determined.
Thus the increase in real agricultural output, in constant prices, is taken as a
fraction of the previous year's real income. The non-agricultural sector's capacity is assumed to have grown at a constant rate, equal to 3 per cent of the
previous year's national income over the period (this implies a 10 per cent
annual increase in manufacturing capacity and a 5 per cent average increase in
capacity in all other nonagricultural sectors). Given inflationary pressures, it
is reasonable to assume that capacity was generally fully utilized. The change
in imports was determined by the foreign trade regime, and is also linked to
the previous year's national income.

36. *Monthly Bulletin,* Central Bank, July–December 1960.
37. *International Labour Review, Statistical Supplement,* International Labour Organization, various issues.

Formally,

$$\frac{Y_t - Y_{t-1}}{Y_{t-1}} = \frac{M_{t-1} - M_{t-2}}{M_{t-2}} \tag{2}$$

$$\frac{Y_t - Y_{t-1}}{Y_{t-1}} = \frac{Q_t - Q_{t-1}}{Q_{t-1}} + \frac{P_t - P_{t-1}}{P_{t-1}} \tag{3}$$

$$\frac{Q_t - Q_{t-1}}{Q_{t-1}} = \frac{A_t - A_{t-1}}{Q_{t-1}} + \frac{N_t - N_{t-1}}{Q_{t-1}} + \frac{I_t - I_{t-1}}{Q_{t-1}} \tag{4}$$

where Y is money income, M is the money supply, Q is the physical quantity of output evaluated at the previous year's prices, P is the price level, A is agricultural output in previous-year prices, N is non-agricultural output (equal to capacity) at previous-year prices, and I is imports. Changes in the money supply and in the three right-hand variables of eq. (4) are taken as exogenous.

Table II-7 presents the results of the computation. As can be seen, fluctuations in agricultural output would have been very important in the early 1950's had their influence not been damped by TMO operations. In 1954 the reduction in agricultural output was equal to over 10 per cent of 1953 national income. Sales from TMO stocks in 1954 undoubtedly led to the smaller-than-predicted (26.9 per cent) increase in prices and the relatively small (8.9 per cent) increase in the money supply, which served to damp inflationary pressures in 1955. It is interesting to note, however, that the combined 1954 and 1955 predicted price increases were very close to the actuals: TMO operations evidently delayed inflation but did not suppress it for long. By and large, inflation was less than predicted in the period 1952–1954, and about equal to the predicted amount after 1955. Given the crude nature of the estimates, however, inferences must be drawn with care.[38]

The role of SEE credits in the period 1955 to 1958 stands out clearly via its influence on the money supply, and therefore on aggregate demand. Even if agricultural output had increased steadily at 5 per cent of national income — a very high rate of increase — there would have been considerable inflationary pressure: only in 1954 and 1957 would the situation have significantly improved on the assumptions underlying the model.

It may be objected that one should use the change in the export surplus as an indicator of the foreign trade sector's contribution to excess demand. The reason for not doing so was that there is considerable evidence that the volume of exports was a result of demand pressures rather than a cause. That

---

38. The same estimates were made with alternate lags in the money supply, but the results were essentially unaffected.

Table II-7
Predicted and actual inflation, 1952 to 1958
(percentage of previous year's real national income)

	Supply Changes				Demand Changes	Inflation	
	Agri-culture (1)	Non-Agri-culture (2)	Imports (3)	Total (4)	$\dfrac{\Delta M_{t-1}}{M_{t-2}}$ (5)	Esti-mated (6)	Actual (7)
1952	2.8	3.0	3.4	9.2	21.2	12.0	6.8
1953	5.3	3.0	−4.6	3.7	11.7	8.0	2.2
1954	−10.2	3.0	−0.9	−8.1	18.8	26.9	12.5
1955	4.3	3.0	0.3	7.6	8.9	1.3	11.1
1956	4.9	3.0	−1.2	6.7	28.0	21.3	23.3
1957	0.8	3.0	−0.1	3.7	25.2	21.5	21.6
1958	7.8	3.0	−0.7	10.1	22.6	12.5	11.1

Sources: Agricultural output: from national income accounts, at constant prices, as given in Table I-3.

Non-agricultural output: estimated capacity growth as a per cent of national income.

Imports: Lira value of imports (as recorded at a constant exchange rate) as a per cent of previous year's national income.

Money income: the change in the money supply as given in Table I-5 between $t-1$ and $t-2$ as a per cent of the money supply in $t-2$.

Estimated $\Delta P/P$: column (5) minus column (4).

Actual price increase: percentage increase in Istanbul Chamber of Commerce home goods price index, given in Table I-5.

is, exports appear to have been determined largely as a residual: given the level of domestic production, exports were the part of that production remaining after domestic demand was satisfied.[39]

We therefore conclude that fluctuations in agricultural production were themselves a fairly minor factor in leading to inflation. However, agricultural price supports and the ensuing credit creation were the major factors leading to increases in the money supply and initiating inflation. Inflation was thereafter fed through SEE deficits, which led to further money supply increases. Hence the proximate cause of the Turkish inflation in the 1950's was the behavior of the money supply.

39. See Chapter VII, below.

III. Effects on trade and growth

Interaction of foreign trade and the domestic economy

If the Turkish economy had been autarkic during the 1950's the Turkish inflation would still have resulted in some domestic economic dislocations. Conversely, if Turkey had not experienced inflationary pressures in the 1950's she might nonetheless have had some balance-of-payments difficulties at the existing exchange rates even in the absence of foreign indebtedness.

In fact, Turkey was dependent upon foreign trade for a wide variety of goods, and the misallocative effects of inflation were proximately felt through balance-of-payments difficulties and the consequent shrinkage of imports. While other factors might have led to some payments imbalance, their effects were completely swamped by the pressures of excess demand and inflation on the payments situation.

Thus the domestic inflation had its most distortive effects via the associated decline in foreign trade. In this section, consideration is first given to the behavior of foreign exchange earnings and receipts, and the reasons for it. The effects on the domestic economy will be examined thereafter.

Export earnings

As seen in Table I-6, Turkey's export earnings rose from $262 million in 1950 to a peak of $396 million in 1953. Thereafter they declined until 1958, with a minor interruption in 1957, when they were $249 million. Virtually every export category except tobacco shared in the decline, although there were sizeable year-to-year fluctuations in agricultural exports. As indicated above, the recorded decline in export earnings understates the decline in official foreign exchange receipts, since many exports were made under bilateral debt repayment agreements, where part of the receipts were retained in the importing country for debt-repayment purposes.

The first task is to separate the decline in export earnings into that part attributable to changes in international prices and the part attributable to volume changes. With peak export earnings coming in 1953, many have naturally blamed the fall in export earnings on terms-of-trade changes.[40] To quantify the relative importance of terms-of-trade and volume changes, detailed commodity trade statistics for the period 1953-to-1958 were examined and three alternative computations were made. (1) If unit prices had remained at their 1953 levels, what would the value of exports have been given actual export volumes? (2) Given unit prices prevailing in each year, what

40. Hershlag, *op. cit.* (Note 4, Chap. I), p. 180.

value would exports have had if Turkey's commodity-specific export volumes had remained at their 1953 levels? (3) If Turkey had retained her share of each commodity-export market, what would the value of exports have been? The first computation enables one to infer the degree to which changes in export earnings were attributable to volume changes. The second computation permits an inference about the degree to which export prices declined.[41] Those two computations, contrasted with the actual level of exports, indicate the relative importance of price and quantum changes over the 1953-to-1958 period. The share calculations make it possible to estimate the way in which export earnings might have increased had Turkish trade and exchange rate policy allowed Turkey to maintain her share of each of her export markets.[42]

Details of the computations are given in Appendix B. Table II-8 summarizes the results. The decline in export earnings for recorded exports is more than accounted for by a reduction in export volumes. Some have claimed that the reduction in wheat exports accounts for this. However, inspection of the detailed commodity figures in Table B-3 indicates that reduced volumes of exports were the rule rather than the exception. Between 1953 and 1958 cotton exports fell 66 per cent in quantity terms, chrome 24 per cent, copper 29 per cent, wool 29 per cent, and so on. When it is recalled that the dollar prices of minor exports − not included in the computations − were more probably rising than falling, there was undoubtedly a significant decline in the volume of minor exports whose quanta were not individually reported.[43] Had Turkey maintained her share of export markets her export earnings would have increased 26 per cent, contrasted with an actual decline of 45 per cent.

Thus there can be little doubt that the sharp reduction in export earnings

Table II-8
Decomposition of export earnings decline, 1953 to 1958 (millions of TL)

	1953	1954	1955	1956	1957	1958
Actual exports	945	827	738	642	721	519
Exports at 1953 prices	945	854	629	605	658	517
Exports at 1953 volumes	945	1013	1112	979	972	945
Exports at constant share	945	939	907	1070	1197	1192

Source: Appendix B.

41. The fact that export prices were high due to bilateral debt-repayment agreements does not alter the validity of the tests, since focus is upon the reasons for the decline in recorded export earnings.
42. Turkey's share of the world market is relatively low for most of her exported commodities. See Chapter VII, below.
43. See Chapter VII for estimates of the determinants of minor exports.

was attributable to reduced export volumes, and we must now consider the reasons for this. Several factors must be considered. First, the deteriorating real EER for exports was undoubtedly an important factor, since the profitability of exporting was declining. Even beyond that, however, domestic prices were well above international prices, a phenomenon which had two effects: (1) there was little incentive to export out of given volumes of production, since the domestic market was attractive, and (2) foreign purchasers were often unwilling to pay Turkish prices, especially when the registered export prices were set above those prevailing in other countries, even when Turks would have been willing to export at those prices. In addition, however, it is likely that there was a considerable volume of unrecorded or underrecorded exports, since foreign exchange earnings could then profitably be sold on the black market at a higher EER.

It has already been shown (Table II-3) that the PLD-EERs declined sharply for exports during the 1953–1958 period. By 1958, the most favorable import-exchange rate was virtually double that of traditional exports. Evidence on the responsiveness of exports to changes in the real exchange rate is given in Chapter VII.

The sharp declines in export PLD-EERs would by themselves have resulted in some diminution in export volumes. However, the domestic prices of exportable goods were generally well above the prices received for exports, even taking export premia into account. Price quotations for selected commodities in 1957 are revealing. Prices received in the domestic wholesale and export markets in Kuruş/kilogram were as follows:[44]

	Domestic Wholesale	Export	Ratio
Wheat	44.0	23.8	1.85
Beans	205.2	47.2	4.34
Hazelnuts	445.8	263.0	1.69
Figs	98.7	92.8	1.06
Raisins	172.9	105.5	1.64
Cotton	433.3	182.0	2.38

Although the commodities may not be entirely homogeneous between domestic sales and exports, the price discrepancies are much larger than can be accounted for by nonhomogeneity or quality variation.

Thus there was little incentive for private traders to export at the premium-inclusive exchange rates. Most exports that did occur were undertaken by government agencies, usually with sizeable losses. In addition, the higher prices received under both kinds of bilateral agreements may have made some exports privately profitable. In general, however, legal exportation was not

44. *Monthly Bulletin of Statistics,* Ministry of Finance, January 1967.

profitable, and that factor undoubtedly explains the decline in recorded export earnings.

Smuggling and faked invoicing

   Virtually all commentators on Turkish economic conditions during the 1950's cite the prevalence of a black market (in both internal and external transactions) as a characteristic of the period.[45] Many government actions were undertaken in an effort to control or reduce evasions of the regime. Those actions themselves attest to the incidence of extra-legal activities. Efforts to halt "switch" deals and to verify import prices have already been discussed. The declared purpose of the special tourist rate, introduced in 1956, was to shift funds back into legal channels.[46] Some quotations of black-market rates are given by the Economist Intelligence Unit. These, and their respective dates, were:[47]

September 1955	TL 12	= $ 1
March 1956	TL 9.6	= $ 1
October 1956	TL 11	= $ 1
August 1957	TL 12.5	= $ 1
May 1958	TL 17	= $ 1

In interviews conducted in July 1971 businessmen were asked about conditions prior to the 1970 devaluation. Many cited 1969–1970 black-market exchange rates, but volunteered that they were far below the levels of the 1950's, when the rate reached TL 25 to TL 30. The fact that memories of the 1950's dwarfed those of a much more recent episode attests to the magnitude and extent of the black market in the mid-1950's. Whether a TL 25–30 rate was reached or not, a black-market rate of even TL 17 was six times the official rate and more than three times the highest EER.

   One measure of the extent of evasion, both for exports and for imports, is to compare Turkish trade statistics with those of her major trading partners. Such a procedure does not pick up those transactions unrecorded by both parties, such as the large livestock trade over Turkey's southeastern border. Moreover, it can at best provide only a partial insight into the possible order

45. Aktan, *op. cit.* (Note 16, Chap. I), p. 36; Columbia School of Law, *op. cit.* (Note 14, Chap. I), p. 22; Hershlag, *op. cit.* (Note 4, Chap. I), p. 147; FFYP, p. 19.
46. EIU, *op. cit.* (Note 1, Chap. II), *No. 20,* December 1956, p. 2.
47. *Ibid., No. 15,* Sept. 1955, p. 2; *ibid., No. 17,* March 1956, p. 1; *ibid., No. 20,* Dec. 1956, p. 2; *ibid., No. 23,* August 1957, p. 1; *ibid., No. 26,* May 1958, p. 4.

Table II-9

Comparison of Turkey's trade statistics with those of her largest trading partners
(millions of dollars)

	Exports Reported by:			Imports Reported by:		
	Turkey	Trading Partners	Ratio	Turkey	Trading Partners	Ratio
1954	244.2	312.0	0.783	338.2	355.4	0.952
1955	214.7	247.0	0.869	337.1	400.8	0.841
1956	220.7	246.3	0.896	268.8	347.5	0.773
1957	265.7	270.2	0.983	304.2	369.5	0.823
1958	182.0	201.3	0.904	238.7	330.1	0.723
1959	252.2	290.4	0.868	313.4	385.1	0.816
1960	208.7	247.3	0.843	346.9	399.8	0.867
1961	225.6	262.1	0.860	379.0	409.7	0.925
1962	259.6	308.4	0.841	444.7	431.5	1.032

Note: Turkey's eight largest trading partners, in decreasing order of trade size, were: United States, United Kingdom, France, West Germany, East Germany, Italy, Czechoslovakia and Israel.

Source: Data from *Direction of International Trade,* International Monetary Fund (Washington), various issues.

of the magnitude of evasions, so that the results must be interpreted with care.[48]

To estimate the extent of false recording of merchandise trade, Turkey's recorded transactions with her eight largest trading partners (as reported by Turkey over the 1954–1962 period) were cross-tabulated against the transactions recorded by those trading partners. These eight accounted for over 75 per cent of Turkish recorded merchandise trade, and it is probable that most invoice faking took place in transactions with those countries.[49]

Table II-9 presents the computations. Turkish records of Turkey's exports f.o.b. are compared with her trading partners' records of imports c.i.f. from Turkey. Since there is normally a 10 per cent discrepancy between the f.o.b. value of exports and the c.i.f. value of imports, it is to be expected that

48. See Jagdish Bhagwati, "Fiscal Policies, the Faking of Foreign Trade Declarations, and the Balance of Payments," reprinted in his *Trade, Tariffs and Growth,* Weidenfeld and Nicolson (London), 1969 for a full discussion of the merits and shortcomings of the procedure. Bhagwati used Turkish data for 1960 and 1961 to estimate under-recording of trade.
49. It is likely, however, that smuggling activities may have been sizeable with other countries.

Turkey's estimate of exports will be less than the partner countries' recorded imports. The same procedure was followed with regard to Turkish import records. In that case Turkey's import statistics were compared with those of her trading partners' exports. The *a priori* expectation is that Turkish imports would exceed recorded partner exports by about 10 per cent.

On the export side, exports reported by Turkey f.o.b. were less in every year than the c.i.f. imports from Turkey reported by her eight largest trading partners. But the ratio is too high, especially in 1957 and 1958. This result may reflect the influence of "switch deals" or the incentive to over-invoice exports which were legally undertaken in order to obtain export premia. However, in view of the fact that most exports were effected by government agencies, it is difficult to interpret the results.[50]

The picture is strikingly different on the import side. Whereas Turkish records of imports should exceed the trading partners' exports by 10 per cent or more, imports recorded by Turkey were less than 85 per cent of the trading partners' reports in each year from 1955 to 1958. The fact that the ratio falls off sharply in 1956–1958, the years of greatest foreign exchange shortage, increases the likelihood that the disparity in statistics reflects under-invoicing, since those were the years when black–market activities and premia were greatest, and licenses were issued in value terms.

An important question is how under-invoicing of the magnitude implied by the data in Table II-9 was financed. Some Turks indicated in interviews that proceeds from smuggled exports were used. Another possibility, somewhat less likely in view of Turkey's debt arrears, is that some under-invoiced imports were financed with suppliers' credits. Whatever financing was used, it seems clear that under-invoicing and/or illegal entry of imports assumed sizeable importance in the mid-1950's. Although no hard evidence is available, it is probable that a high fraction of non-recorded imports were consumer goods whose legal importation had virtually ceased and upon which premia were enormous. This factor should be borne in mind when evaluating the decline in recorded imports discussed below.

Effects upon the domestic economy

With declining export earnings and huge arrears in foreign indebtedness, the Turkish government sharply curtailed imports from 1953 onward. As seen in Table I-6, Turkey's recorded imports increased from $252 million in 1950 to $489 million in 1952 and then fell steadily to $284 million in 1958, representing a change from 9.5 to 2.5 per cent of current GNP in six years. Although import-substitution was taking place, partly as a matter of govern-

---

50. Separate data for government and private exports are not available.

ment policy and partly as a result of the rising domestic prices of imported goods, such a sharp drop in imports must, *prima facie*, have caused severe domestic economic dislocations.

In reviewing the events of the 1950's, the SPO declared that:

> ...because money declined in value while the exchange rate was nevertheless maintained artificially at a high level, exports fell, imports increased, and the resulting shortage of foreign exchange led to the imposition of physical controls on all foreign trade. This situation gave rise to capital flight in addition to the instability and arbitrariness it introduced.
>
> Perhaps the worst consequence of inflation and controls was the disruption of the price mechanism and the disappearance of normal markets. As a result, the economy was strangled by a very unproductive regulatory system on the one hand, while, on the other, there developed a misallocation of resources whose harmful effects are felt even today... Production was interrupted as a result of bottlenecks and, what was worse, investments were channelled to fields which were unproductive for the economy as a whole.[51]

Virtually all commentators describe the economic situation in the 1955-to-1958 period as one of "very severe economic and social disruptions,"[52] "permanent crisis,"[53] and "grave internal and external difficulties."[54] Little hard evidence is available with which to quantify the degree of dislocation in the domestic economy. Moreover, it is difficult if not impossible to disentangle the direct effects of inflation from the indirect effects associated with the declining flow of imports.

It is clear that GNP growth declined markedly from the rate of the early 1950's (see Table I-1). However, the high early-fifties growth rate was at least partially attributable to the once-and-for-all opportunity to increase agricultural output through extensive investment. Growth in agriculture based on conversion of additional land to crops could not have been sustained even under ideal economic policies and was undesirable in any event.[55]

The years of slowest growth were from 1959 to 1961. It is tempting to conclude that the slow growth of those years was part of the cost of inflation and balance-of-payments difficulties earlier in the 1950's, and there is undoubtedly an element of truth in that conclusion. But the recession of 1960–1962 was in large part attributable to other factors, as will be seen in Chapter IV.

51. FFYP, *op. cit.* (Note 20, Chap. I), p. 22.

52. Columbia School of Law, *op. cit.* (Note 14, Chap. I), p. 28.

53. *Ibid.,* p. 18.

54. OEEC, *Turkey, 1959, op. cit.* (Note 32, Chap. I), p. 5.

55. Hirsch and Hirsch, *op. cit.* (Note 23), believe that the conversion of pastureland to selected cropland was followed immediately by a sharp reduction in livestock output, a computation not included in the national income accounts. If that is so, official figures overstate the real rates of growth for the period 1950 to 1956.

Even if the poor performance of the Turkish economy in the 1958-to-1962 period could be blamed on earlier economic policies, there are many Turks who believe that the excess demand conditions of the mid-1950's, coupled with import shortages, provided an atmosphere in which domestic entrepreneurship could develop. They point to the establishment of many small firms in a variety of import-substitution lines, some of which survived the ensuing Stabilization Program. Evidence is not available to evaluate the overall costs and benefits of the economic policies of the mid-1950's. Several side effects of the payments regime and consequent import shortage can be mentioned, however.

Perhaps most important is the fact that real investment declined and that investment in plant and equipment suffered relative to construction investment. There is also some evidence that many firms were unable to operate near full capacity due to a shortage of imported intermediate goods. We consider each of these effects in turn.

Import behavior and real investment.   All categories of goods shared in the decline in imports from 1953 to 1958, although consumption goods and construction materials imports declined proportionately more than the other two categories.[56] In the case of consumer goods, it is probable that a large part if not all of the decline was offset by increased smuggling and perhaps some under-invoicing of imports. Smuggling of consumer goods is generally easier than that of other categories because (1) they can be brought in as personal property, (2) they are generally relatively small, high-value items, and (3) resale of small quantities is comparatively easy.

The decline in raw material imports undoubtedly affected capacity utilization, as will be seen below. But declining imports of investment goods had a pronounced impact on the level and composition of real investment. Table II-10 provides estimates of gross domestic capital formation and its composition for the 1953–1958 period. The first row gives the c.i.f. value of construction materials in each year and the second row gives the landed cost of those imports. The increase in EERs for imports can be seen by inspection of the ratio of c.i.f. costs to domestic value of imports.[57] Although imports

---

56. The dollar value of imports in each end-use category was (millions of dollars):

	1953	1958
Construction materials	85	27
Machinery and equipment	192	109
Consumption goods	105	38
Raw materials	150	140

Source: *Aylık Bülten,* Central Bank, various issues.

57. Landed cost includes the TL paid to the Central Bank to finance the import, duties and surcharges, and costs of unloading the goods. Domestic value is equal to landed cost plus wholesalers' mark-up on the goods.

Table II-10

Investment composition and import content of investment, 1953 to 1958

	1953	1954	1955	1956	1957	1958
A. (millions of TL — current prices)						
Construction investment						
Construction materials imports, c.i.f.	210	180	223	134	112	94
Domestic value of imports	336	310	456	268	324	261
Domestic materials	355	369	456	633	800	1289
Domestic value added	796	1019	1258	1412	1800	2074
Total construction investment	1487	1698	2170	2312	2923	3624
Machinery and equipment investment						
Imports, c.i.f.	425	390	420	376	249	369
Domestic value of imports	569	560	696	721	628	894
Domestic goods	86	100	115	193	276	441
Total machinery and equipment investment	655	660	811	914	903	1335
Total investment:	2142	2358	2982	3226	3827	4960
B. (percentages)						
Composition of total investment						
Construction	69	72	73	72	76	73
Machinery and equipment	31	28	27	28	24	27
Imports (domestic value) to investment in						
Construction	23	18	21	12	11	7
Machinery and equipment	87	85	86	79	70	67

Source: Kenan Gürtan, *Yatırım Hesaplarının Tevhit ve Tashihine Müteallik Proje Çalışmaları Hakkında Rapor,* State Planning Organization (mimeograph), 1962.

of construction materials declined sharply, the value of domestic materials used in construction tripled between 1953 and 1958. The data are in current prices, but imports represented 22.6 per cent of the value of construction investment in 1953 and fell to 7.2 per cent in 1958. The construction materials industry was already well established in Turkey in 1953, and large increases in output of cement, bricks and other building materials enabled the continued growth of construction in the 1953—1958 period.

Imports of machinery and equipment, by contrast, represented 86.8 per cent of the value of machinery and equipment investment in 1953. Turkey was virtually entirely dependent upon imported machinery, as the domestic goods could not have accounted for much more than transport and installation. Despite the sharp decline in imports, the imported component of machinery and equipment fell only to 67 per cent in 1958.

No official data are available providing a breakdown of investment in

Table II-11
Estimates of real investment, 1953 to 1958 (millions of TL)

	1953	1954	1955	1956	1957	1958
Construction investment	655	660	811	914	903	1335
Implicit deflator	0.698	0.595	0.538	0.433	0.360	0.297
Construction investment at constant prices	457	393	436	396	325	397
Machinery investment	1487	1698	2170	2312	2923	3624
Implicit deflator	0.853	0.768	0.648	0.564	0.516	0.454
Machinery investment at constant prices	1268	1304	1406	1304	1508	1645
Total investment (1948 prices)	1725	1697	1842	1700	1833	2042

Notes: a) For the construction investment deflator, the implicit deflator for the construction sector of the national income accounts was used.

b) For the machinery and investment deflator, the domestic component was deflated by the implicit deflator for manufacturing in the national income accounts. The imported component was deflated by the implicit EERs given in Gürtan's data for machinery and equipment, reported in Appendix A.

Sources: Current price investment data, Table II-10. Implicit deflators, *National Income Total Expenditure and Investment of Turkey, 1938, 1948–1969, Pub. No. 607,* SIS (Ankara), 1970, Table 1.

constant prices. To estimate the effects of the decline in imports, the machinery and construction investment data given in Table II-10 were deflated by components by the author, using methods indicated in the notes to Table II-11. According to those estimates, real investment in construction increased by 30 per cent between 1953 and 1958, while real investment in machinery and equipment fell by 13 per cent, and total real investment increased as the share of construction in total investment rose.

It may be argued that real investment fell from 1953 to 1958 and that declining imports were a result of that decline. The contrary conclusion is suggested by the following considerations: (1) real construction investment rose; (2) there was considerable excess demand and investment was extremely profitable; (3) the absolute level — not just the share — of real investment in machinery and equipment declined; (4) the domestic price of machinery and equipment rose 135 per cent while that of new construction rose 85 per cent; and (5) after the Stabilization Program the share of imports in machinery and equipment rose again to 78 per cent in 1960, whereas the share of imports in construction never again rose above 11 per cent. These facts are all consistent with the interpretation that import-substituting production was much more difficult to achieve in machinery and equipment than in construction materials, so that the lack of imports led to a decline in real investment in plant and equipment.

Excess capacity. Excess capacity due to a shortage of imports was reported to be widespread as early as 1954.[58] As the decline in imports continued, various types of dislocation of economic activity undoubtedly resulted. As described by the Economist Intelligence Unit,

> ...There has been no rise in the monthly import bill and shortages are now very serious. Stocks of many raw materials are non-existent and many concerns work short-time, with periodic complete shutdowns. Very few plants are working at full capacity – a fact which helps to set the factory expansion programme in its true perspective...[59]

It is impossible to estimate the degree to which productive capacity was underutilized. As indicated above, price-control laws were in effect, and the consequent black-market evasions led to failure to report actual production levels in the private sector. A few concrete examples of underutilization can be cited, but there is no indication as to how representative these examples are.

It seems fairly clear that the mining sector was particularly affected by a lack of spare parts and transport. As reported by the EIU,

> Chrome ore production, particularly by the private mines, which in recent years were responsible for about three-quarters of total output, is being checked by insufficient mining equipment and inadequate transport facilities...
>
> This is in line with the proposal put forward earlier this year by U.S. firms, which offered to buy 800,000 tons of chrome ore over a five-year period. It was reported that these firms were prepared to pay for part of the ore deliveries in advance and to provide lorries and tyres, which are in very short supply to move them to the ports. This proposal was rejected by the Turkish authorities because they feared that it might encourage black-market transactions...[60]

Earlier, deliveries under existing contracts had not been met "because shortages of spares and tyres for transport trucks meant that supplies of ore could not be moved to the ports."[61]

The number of trucks in use rose only 5 per cent between 1955 and 1958.[62] With a 28 per cent increase in the level of economic activity over the period, an increasing average age of the vehicles and some strains in the transport sector undoubtedly resulted. The volume of imported tires reported in the official trade statistics certainly declined drastically – from 10.14 thousand metric tons in 1954 to 7.79 thousand metric tons in 1957 and 5.37 thousand metric tons in 1958.[63] Since Turkey had no domestic production

58. EIU, *op. cit.* (Note 1, Chap. II), *No. 12,* January 1955, p. 10.
59. *Ibid., No. 24,* November 1957, p. 7.
60. *Ibid., No. 19,* August 1956, p. 8.
61. *Ibid., No. 18,* May 1958, pp. 11–12.
62. *Economic Developments in the Middle East 1958-1959,* United Nations, Department of Economic and Social Affairs (New York), 1960, p. 87.
63. *Yearbook of International Trade Statistics,* United Nations, various issues.

capacity at that time, the shrinkage in imports in the face of increasing demand undoubtedly did cause difficulties.

Beyond this scattered and impressionistic evidence, it is difficult to estimate the extent to which excess and underutilized capacity resulted from import shrinkage during the 1955-to-1958 period. Two things however seem certain: (1) by mid-1958 government authorities believed that import shortages were seriously impairing both the level of economic activity and their ability to continue their investment programs; and (2) further cuts in imports would have been necessary (given the government's inability to borrow further) had action not been taken. Additional reductions in imports, or even continuing imports at the 1958 level, would undoubtedly have had a pronounced negative effect on the level of economic activity. Thus we turn to consideration of the Stabilization Program introduced in August 1958.

CHAPTER III

The stabilization program

I. Introduction

On August 8, 1958 the Turkish government announced a series of sweeping changes in virtually every aspect of the foreign trade regime and in many aspects of domestic economic policy. Consideration is given in this chapter to the political and economic factors that led to the decision to change and the nature of the changes. In Chapter IV the effects of the program are analyzed.

Some preliminary background is required on political developments prior to 1958. The economic developments of the mid-1950's, reviewed in the last chapter, had political ramifications long before 1958, and earlier political developments were important in the evolution of the Stabilization Program.

It seems fairly clear that the Menderes government enjoyed strong political support for its policies in the early 1950's. The Democratic Party was returned to power in the election of 1954 with 57.6 per cent of the popular vote, compared to the 52.9 per cent it had received in the 1950 elections. The first signs of unrest came in the fall of 1955. Despite the fact that the Menderes government had earlier appeared fairly strongly entrenched, revolt broke out within Menderes' own party, with ten prominent members of Parliament resigning from the party and joining the opposition. Consequently, the entire cabinet resigned; but the Prime Minister formed a new government, the key change being the appointment of a new Finance Minister. Most contemporary observers cited the government's economic policies as the basic cause of the unrest.[1]

There apparently was considerable discussion within the administration in late 1955 and early 1956 as to the policy changes which should be made. Notwithstanding a speech by the Prime Minister in December 1955 when he declared that "...we shall never consider any change in the value of our money despite all sorts of propaganda to the contrary..."[2] there was evident-

---

1. Eleanor Bisbee, "About-Face in Turkey," *Foreign Policy Bulletin,* April 15, 1956, pp. 113-4.
2. Cited by Hershlag, *op. cit.* (Note 4, Chap. I), p. 145, taken from *Prime Minister's Speech on Government Programme,* Anatolian Agency (Ankara), December 24, 1955, pp. 13-14.

ly a serious devaluation plan under consideration. Several government officials interviewed in the 1960's recalled that a devaluation plan was prepared
and ready for adoption, with a new exchange rate of TL 6 to the dollar, when
opposition to the program emerged from within the Cabinet.

A series of changes was finally made in 1956. These included: (1) the
special TL 5.25 and 5.75 rates for tourist and other current account transactions; (2) the price control law; (3) increased export premia; (4) ceilings on
commercial bank credits; and (5) an increase in the Central Bank discount
rate to 6 per cent, contrasted with a rate of inflation well in excess of 10 per
cent.

These measures appear to have had some effect during 1956. The black-
market rate for the lira declined slightly, the trade balance improved somewhat in the second and third quarters of 1956, and the Central Bank's net
foreign exchange deficit was somewhat reduced. The wholesale price index
actually declined 6 per cent (part of which was a normal seasonal pattern)
between the second and third quarters of 1956, and there is some evidence
that the level of economic activity was somewhat depressed during that period. Electricity production declined from a monthly average of 131 million
kilowatt hours in the first quarter of 1956 to 123 and 124 million in the
second and third quarters, respectively. Even the production of cement, one
of the most rapidly growing industries during the 1950's, declined by 10 per
cent between the second and third quarters, despite a normal seasonal trend
to the contrary.

The effects were short-lived, as evasion of the price-control law by the
private sector, increases in the money supply resulting from increased SEE
deficits, and abandonment of commercial credit ceilings soon transpired.

Political disaffection was evidently mounting by 1957 and elections were
scheduled. Despite increasingly restrictive curbs on opposition political activity[3] and large increases in expenditures designed to woo the electorate,[4] the
Democratic Party's share of the popular vote fell to 47.9 per cent. The Party
nevertheless won 424 out of 610 seats in Parliament, as changes favoring the
Democratic Party had been made in the electoral laws.[5] Once the elections
were over the regime continued its *ad hoc* efforts to meet the foreign exchange shortage and inflationary financing of the SEEs continued.

3. Weiker, *op. cit.* (Note 13, Chap. I), p. 11.
4. Columbia School of Law, *op. cit.* (Note 14, Chap. I), p. 22.
5. Nuri Eren, *Turkey Today and Tomorrow,* Praeger (New York), 1963, p. 37.

II. The devaluation decision

Given inflation, import shortages, retarded economic growth, a flourishing black market, multiple exchange rates and constant arrears in foreign indebtedness, there can be little doubt as to the economic rationale for the Turkish devaluation decision. However, all those phenomena were present from at least 1953 onward. Inflationary pressure grew after 1955, but it is difficult to argue that the underlying economic difficulties caused by inflation and overvaluation were more massive in 1958 than in 1956 except in the sense that those difficulties had continued longer. Then too, the import curtailment of 1957–1958 may have made those difficulties more visible than they were earlier.

It seems clear that Turkey delayed the devaluation decision long past the point where most other governments would have taken action. When devaluation did occur, *The Economist* commented

> ...Few countries have put off inevitable devaluation longer or with greater damage to their economies than Turkey. For at least ten years the Turkish lira has been artificially valued at its parity of TL 2.80 to the dollar. Since 1953 the effects of this overvaluation on the balance of payments have been partly but quite inadequately cushioned by a cumbersome system of differential surcharges on imports and subsidies on exports...[6]

Thus while it is straightforward to analyze the underlying economic reasons for devaluation, it is much less easy to determine the causes of the timing of devaluation or the factors that weighed in the decision. At least three separate factors undoubtedly contributed to it: (1) the apparent disruption of domestic economic activity, (2) domestic political dissatisfaction, and (3) pressure by foreign creditors and donors. We consider each of these in turn.

Disruption of economic activity

Enough was said in Chapter II to indicate that the payments situation and inflation had damaging effects upon the Turkish economy as early as 1954. Import stringency became so severe as time went on that capital goods, imported earlier, were left idle. Eren, for example, reported that:

> Within ten years, the Turks plunged from an unequalled affluence to an unexpected scarcity. Even coffee, rationed but available during the war, disappeared totally... The cement mixer and steel for ferroconcrete were everywhere....The horns of trucks and tractors broke the immemorial silence of the Anatolian plateau. But the sugar plant in Erzurum starved for beets, the cement factory in Sivas was without coal, and the

6. *The Economist*, August 9, 1958, p. 468.

thousands of tractor owners in Adana and in Izmir scrambled in the black market for spark plugs and batteries....[7]

Export earnings in the first two quarters of 1958 were 40 per cent below the corresponding level in 1957. By June 1958, with foreign exchange earnings declining, no available sources of credit and mounting arrears, import licensing ceased. It must have been evident that the situation could not continue without some sort of change.

An important question is the diagnosis of ills made by the Turkish leadership. There are two possibilities. These gentlemen may have concluded that import shortages were retarding growth and were the source of the problem. Alternatively they may have become convinced that past economic policies, including expenditure, finance and foreign trade issues, were ill-advised.

If the first interpretation is correct, additional imports were deemed the sole requirement for eliminating difficulties and the government would have adopted the Stabilization Program in order to obtain additional badly needed foreign credits. On the second view, the 1958 Program was adopted in the belief that the entire set of policy changes was necessary for Turkey's future sound development.

The question of which interpretation is correct is important in analyzing the course of events after August 1958. Unfortunately, no clear-cut evidence is available. Dr. Sturc, who was an active participant in the discussion prior to August 1958, clearly believes that the Turkish leaders were convinced of the desirability of both devaluation and stabilization.[8] If they did believe stabilization to be an essential part of the program, the second interpretation is valid. Others,[9] however, take the view that the Prime Minister and his cabinet reluctantly accepted the stabilization components of the program as a necessary cost of receiving foreign credits.

It seems clear that the regime at least recognized that failure to take action would entail further reductions in imports and regarded the probable economic and political costs of such reductions as prohibitive. As such, the economic dislocation and unavailability of additional foreign financing without government action were necessary conditions for the adoption of the Stabilization Program. Whether the government initially believed that the stabilization aspects of the Program were desirable will be considered in Chapter IV.

7. Eren, *op. cit.* (Note 5), p. 50.

8. Ernest Sturc, "Stabilization Policies: Experience of Some European Countries in the 1950's," *International Monetary Fund Staff Papers,* July 1968, p. 207.

9. Edwin J. Cohn, *Turkish Economic, Social, and Political Change,* Praeger (New York), 1970, p. 24.

Political disaffection

There appears to be little doubt that large segments of the Turkish population were adversely affected by inflation and import shortages by 1957–1958, and were unhappy with the Menderes government. Although all commentators agree that political discontent had its origins in the administration's economic policies,[10] they are not unanimous in their diagnosis as to the aspects of those policies upon which criticism focused. The diagnoses are not mutually inconsistent, however. According to Simpson,

> There is considerable political unrest in Turkey today, and most of it is directly traceable to the government's economic policies. Critics of the Democratic party argue that the major evil is "planlessness." This point is in many respects well taken. It is a fact that the government has never published a plan or even an outline giving the impression that an orderly, balanced development of the country and its resources was under way. As a result, there are cases of waste, duplication and the misuses of funds, resources and manpower. Moreover, a sizeable number of Turkish industrial projects have been undertaken, not for their own intrinsic soundness, but for the political advantages to be gained...[11]

Contemporary foreign observers agreed that economic conditions were at the heart of political difficulties, but placed the discontent as originating more from other aspects of the economic situation.

> The biggest practical stick with which the opposition can belabor the government is the serious economic condition in that country...The cost of living is rising and supply shortages are acute...Coffee is nonexistent...[12]

Sturc's analysis is somewhat more subtle, and perhaps more plausible. He argues that

> It was only late in 1957 that increasing resistance to government policy became noticeable. The Government had lost the support of some intellectuals as early as 1954, and it lost more after it had abandoned an abortive stabilization attempt in 1956. The Government believed, however, that the changed attitude of the intellectuals was caused mainly by their dislike of certain noneconomic aspects of its program...The Government overlooked the fact that the intelligentsia came to the conclusion that the sacrifices demanded of it were not yielding the expected benefits to the nation as a whole.... The Government later found that, when the external supply of capital goods on credit also diminished, it could still proceed albeit temporarily, with infrastructure development projects, such as village water wells, irrigation sys-

10. Another factor leading to discontent was the increasingly repressive political measures taken by the government. See Nuri Eren, "Turkey: Problems, Policies, Parties," *Foreign Affairs,* October 1961, p. 97.
11. Dwight Simpson, "Turkey: Problems and Prospects," *Foreign Policy Bulletin,* June 1, 1958, p. 142.
12. *The Economist,* April 19, 1958, p. 223.

tems, roads, power dams, with the existing machinery. (It used military trucks and bulldozers when civilian equipment wore out.) Construction thus progressed: there were new roads, new dams, and new harbors, but no new vehicles on the roads. Industrial consumer goods, based upon imported raw materials, also disappeared from the market, and prices began to rise sharply. It was only when this stage was reached that the Government came to accept the need for a stabilization policy...[13]

In many regards, Sturc's analysis seems more appropriate than that of those who argue that political disaffection caused the administration's changes in policy. On his interpretation, dissatisfaction with existing economic policies made devaluation appear a viable alternative since there would be little opposition to it. Civil servants' salaries were virtually unchanged between 1954 and 1959. The deterioration in their real income surely led many within the government to react against inflation. But that would not have been sufficient to bring about changes in the thinking of the political leadership. The Menderes government was, after all, reelected in 1957; under the Constitution, it had until 1961 before it would face the electorate again. Moreover, despite the smaller plurality received by the Democratic Party in 1957 than in earlier elections, the regime was firmly in power.

Role of foreign lenders

As evidenced by the amount of foreign assistance forthcoming in August 1958, the major foreign lenders and international organizations clearly supported the Stabilization Program enthusiastically. Devaluation had been urged upon the Turks from at least 1953 onwards, but the

> Government did not heed the advice from successive IMF missions and from OEEC and the International Bank for Reconstruction and Development that, in order to attain its objectives, it must reform internal policies and adjust its trade and payments system so that exports could move again and foreign suppliers would be forced by a more liberal import licensing policy to compete for the Turkish market.[14]

The fact that foreign governments urged devaluation as early as 1953 raises the question of why they should have been successful in 1958 and not in earlier years.

Foreign governments and international organizations had two related influences on Turkish economic policy in the mid-1950's: (1) some believe that had foreign credits not been forthcoming in the early and mid-1950's the devaluation decision would, of necessity, have been undertaken much earlier; (2) there is some support for the view that the regime finally decided to

13. Sturc, *op. cit.* (Note 8), p. 207.
14. *Ibid.*

adopt the Stabilization Program only when it was realized that no additional foreign credits would be received without such action.

Role of donors in perpetuating overvaluation. Perhaps the most forceful statement of the view that creditor countries were largely to blame for perpetuating the imbalance is that of the authors of the Columbia School of Law study:

> Although it is true that the international development financing has been a crucial factor in making possible the investments of the past decade and the increases in income to which they have given rise, it is also true that the Turkish inflationary crisis could not have been prolonged for a period of almost eight years without any corrective measures being taken, had it not been for the lack of coordination of the lending policies of the Western countries.[15]

While the availability of foreign credits certainly enabled the government to continue its policies at lower cost than would otherwise have been possible, it is difficult to see what action foreign creditors and donor countries could have taken that might have led to an earlier decision. The World Bank Mission to Turkey, for example, tried to discuss the inflation with the government in 1954 and refused to grant credits requested. The government's response was to request the termination of the Mission in Turkey on the grounds that the loan had not been granted and that the Mission had interfered in domestic affairs (by mentioning the inflationary threat).[16] Even if all Western countries and international organizations had withdrawn all support from Turkey it is questionable whether action would have been taken much sooner. First, the Turks could have resorted to bilateral payments agreements and other arrangements with Eastern European countries even more than they did. Second, the administration was certainly not reluctant to accumulate arrears in indebtedness, so it would have required not only cessation of official lending, but the Western governments' imposition of restrictions upon the private transactions of their own firms to prevent the use of suppliers' credits. Even then Turkey might have made fewer payments on arrears had new suppliers' credits been cut off. Third and perhaps most convincing, the regime's demonstrated lack of concern about the consequences of its economic policies is virtually proof that total cessation of foreign credits would not have resulted in a rapid change in outlook and behavior.

Of course the subject of what would have happened had there been no international development financing can only be conjectural. At most, however, continuing foreign credits were one additional factor at the margin en-

---

15. Columbia School of Law, *op. cit.* (Note 14, Chap. I), p. 164. The authors of the study were Osman Okyar and Cihat Iren.
16. *Ibid.*, p. 16.

abling Turkish economic policies to continue. The Turkish disregard for the views of creditor countries seems striking, and it is doubtful whether anything short of really extreme measures would have influenced Turkish policy.

Expectations of additional aid and donor pressures.   It appears that until some time in 1957 or early 1958 the governing body continued to believe that additional foreign credits would be received if the situation became sufficiently desperate. One factor leading to the adoption of the Stabilization Program in 1958 was probably a reversal of that belief.

From 1955 onward the United States, the source of virtually all aid to Turkey before 1955, became increasingly reluctant to extend additional credits. The Turks sent several delegations to Washington and sought generally to secure a large American loan of $300 million. The American government did not act on repeated requests.[17]

Actual American aid disbursements exclusive of PL 480 shipments were $68 million, $84 million and $39 million, respectively, in the years 1956, 1957 and 1958. Given the lag between authorization and disbursements (and the large American loan of August 1958), these figures suggest that American support was indeed withheld or diminished in 1956 and 1957.

There were undoubtedly political and military factors influencing aid to Turkey. Early in 1958 the Turkish administration sent a delegation to Moscow with the reported purpose of obtaining Soviet aid. Whether or not this was an attempt to obtain aid from the Western powers cannot be judged. It was subsequently announced that the Moscow negotiations had broken down. *The Economist* concluded:

> ...They (the Turks) may be beginning to realize that if they do not put their house in order, they may not get it (aid)...[18]

In July 1958 there was a revolution in Iraq. The pro-Western government was ousted and Iraq withdrew from the Central Treaty Organization. To what extent the resulting increased military and political importance attached to Turkey influenced the aid forthcoming in August 1958 is an open question.[19] Negotiations with respect to the Stabilization Program were undoubtedly proceeding prior to the Iraqi revolution. The fact remains that the Stabilization Program was announced within several weeks of the Baghdad coup.

As explained by the authors of the Columbia School of Law Study,

> ...the situation from the point of view of external financing became desperate after 1954...Short term measures of a stop gap nature were resorted to such as the effort to persuade the United States Government finally to agree to the demand for a large

17. Simpson, *op. cit.* (Note 11), p. 143.
18. Columbia School of Law, *op. cit.* (Note 14, Chap. I), pp. 23-4.
19. *The Economist,* April 19, 1958, p. 152.

loan; efforts to obtain more bilateral credits from European countries, especially from Germany; effecting imports on credit arrangements; making severe cuts in imports of consumer goods and raw materials; and the piling up of new commercial arrears by delaying payment on current imports. These were essentially stop gap measures intended to make it possible to go along a little bit further with the policies of expansion and inflation while hoping for something to turn up. The Government probably did not lose hope for a large United States loan without conditions until very late, only during 1957–58. Import cuts, severe inflation at home and the price control system introduced in June 1956 and later changed several times were causing severe disruption in the whole economy. Devaluation and an attempt at stabilization had finally to be carried out in August 1958 when the Government realized that it could not continue to meet its most essential commitments and that large scale aid would definitely not be forthcoming without conditions.[20]

The appropriate evaluation is probably that two preconditions had to be met before the regime would consider the adoption of the Stabilization Program: (1) the government could not obtain further credits without conditions; and (2) the high and rising economic costs of import shortages had to have become highly visible and increasingly politically unpopular. It is unlikely that the Stabilization Program would have been adopted even then had it not been for the willingness of foreigners and international agencies to extend credit contingent upon the acceptance of the Stabilization Program. Whether the government believed that the entire program was desirable or only half-heartedly accepted it remains an open question.

III. Components of the program

On August 3, 1958 a decree was issued declaring that: (1) the foreign trade regime would be changed; and (2) no international transactions would be permitted until new regulations were promulgated. Hence except for a few tourist transactions all international financial dealings between Turkey and the rest of the world ceased. Import licenses were not again issued until the announcement of the First Import Program at the end of September; and new export regulations were not issued until early October. The initial impact of the change, therefore, was virtually a complete suspension of foreign trade.

The components of the program emerged over the next several months. There were essentially seven parts: (1) the *de facto* exchange rates were altered and largely unified; (2) Turkish external debt was consolidated and rescheduled and Turkey agreed not to use suppliers'-credit financing; (3) Turkey received massive credits from international lenders; (4) a ceiling was imposed upon Central Bank and commercial bank credits and upon govern-

20. Columbia School of Law, *op. cit.* (Note 14, Chap. I), p. 20.

ment budgets; (5) the import regime was substantially liberalized; (6) the export regime was altered; and (7) SEE prices were raised and price controls were removed.

The first five parts of the package were announced in August 1958, although debt consolidation and rescheduling was not completed for some time. The export and import regimes were gradually liberalized over the succeeding two years; and SEE prices were finally raised in May 1959. We discuss each of these measures in turn.

(1) *The* de facto *exchange rate*

Turkey did not alter the official parity in August 1958. Records of international transactions were kept on the basis of the TL 2.80-per-dollar exchange rate until August 1960.[21] As of August 1958, however, an exchange tax of TL 6.22 per dollar was imposed on all imports, invisible expenditures, and capital transactions.[22] Tariffs were applied on the basis of the TL 9.02 rate, thus making the devaluation complete, *de facto,* on the purchase of foreign exchange. For foreign exchange earnings, a premium of TL 6.20 per dollar was set for all invisibles, capital transactions, and exports other than those indicated below.

Chrome, copper, tobacco and opium exports, which were subject to the TL 2.80 exchange rate until the moment of devaluation, were granted an exchange premium of TL 2.10 per dollar, thus making the EER for those exports – almost half the total value of exports in earlier years – TL 4.90. Dried fruits (figs, hazelnuts and raisins), which had received premia varying from TL 0.70 to TL 2.38 per dollar, were accorded a uniform premium of TL 2.80 per dollar. Thus while the exchange rate was unified completely for foreign exchange expenditures, the structure of premia on the foreign exchange earnings side was simplified considerably but was not immediately unified.

Over the next eighteen months the premia on exports initially receiving less than TL 9 per dollar were gradually raised: chrome was accorded the TL 9 rate in May 1959. The premia on exports of copper, raisins, figs and hazelnuts were subsequently increased, so that by November 1959 only tobacco and opium were subject to a lower rate. The EER for these commodities was increased to TL 5.60. Thus by the fall of 1959 only two export rates

---

21. Thus recorded imports, c.i.f., for 1959 were TL 1,315 million and $470 million, implying a TL 2.80 = $1 exchange rate even though no imports (except a few for SEEs, see below) entered at that rate.
22. The one exception involved the earnings of foreign oil companies. Under the Petroleum Law foreign oil companies were assured that they could repatriate their profits at the rate of TL 2.80 per dollar, regardless of the exchange rate, up to a certain percentage of their invested capital.

were in effect and all commodities except opium and tobacco were subject to the TL 9 = $1 rate. The tobacco rate was increased to TL 9 in February 1960. Finally, in August 1960 the exchange rate was altered *de jure*. At that time the diagnosis was:

> ...Altogether, the main effect of the formal devaluation will be to relieve the banks of a great deal of paper work which the premia system entailed...[23]

Paperwork had resulted, of course, from the payment and recording for the premia and for the foreign exchange transactions by different government agencies.

Thus one can regard the 1958 EER changes, covering as they did invisible and capital transactions, as a *de facto* devaluation accompanied, in effect, by the imposition of export taxes on several commodities. Although devaluation is generally thought to occur when the *de jure* parity is changed, the Turkish case represents an instance when the *de jure* alteration was simply recognition of a *fait accompli*. Thus we shall speak of the Turkish devaluation as having occurred in 1958; the 1960 parity devaluation will be referred to as the *de jure* change.

Three interesting questions arise with respect to the method by which devaluation was effected. (1) Was there any advantage in doing it *de facto* rather than announcing a *de jure* devaluation and imposing export taxes?[24] (2) What was the motive for imposition of export taxes, or, more accurately, failure to accord some exports the otherwise-uniform premium? (3) On economic grounds, what can be said about the imposition of export taxes?

De facto *versus* de jure *devaluation.* The answer to the first question appears to be that on balance there were disadvantages to the *de facto* approach, although as events actually transpired, it made little difference. Ignoring for the moment the taxation of exports, the effects on buyers and sellers of foreign exchange of imposing uniform premia and taxes were identical to the effects that would have been experienced under *de jure* devaluation. The only conceivable defense of the method actually used is that it reserved for the administration the option of increasing premia and surcharges at a later date. The difficulty with that defense is that if the government was uncertain as to what the new exchange rate should be it should have allowed the rate to float. For the very act of imposing premia and taxes without formal devaluation could have fueled (and probably to a small extent did fuel) speculation

---

23. EIU, *op. cit.* (Note 1, Chap. II), *No. 36*, November 1960, p. 6.
24. In 1970 the *de jure* devaluation was accompanied by declaring different exchange rates for some export commodities; again, this was equivalent to the imposition of export taxes. See Appendix C, below.

that there would be further *de facto* exchange-rate changes and thus slowed reaction to the altered exchange rate. Since exchange premia and taxes had been increased repeatedly since 1953, anticipation of further rate adjustments was a reasonable expectation, and could only end with *de jure* devaluation. By fixing the premia and surcharges the government gave one-sided certainty to private traders and thus increased the likelihood of speculation on further changes in the exchange rate.

The government's actual motive was probably not associated with uncertainty as to the proper exchange rate. Although no evidence is available on the point, the motive for the *de facto* approach probably lay simply in the government's unwillingness to use the word "devaluation," especially after past pronouncements on the subject.[25] It is doubtful whether in the actual course of events *de jure* devaluation would have altered the short-term response to the Stabilization Program very much. In the longer run of course the rate was altered *de jure*.

Export taxes.   Quite aside from the manner of devaluation, there is the question of the motive for imposing export taxes and of their economic effects. Sturc, the only participant in the negotiations to write on the subject, says that the main motive was to provide the country with "substantial noninflationary revenue" since a sizeable trade deficit financed by foreign credits was planned.[26] It will be seen below that there was indeed a fiscal impact from the premium system. Although the imposition of export taxes for revenue purposes *per se* is ideally no better than a second or third best policy, an economic and political rationale for some export taxes, imposed at the time of devaluation and gradually reduced and eliminated, can be provided.

We note that as seen above the domestic wholesale prices of most agricultural exports were generally well above their international levels before devaluation. Thus some exchange-rate adjustment for those commodities was called for to provide an incentive to private traders to export at all. The question is whether an exchange-rate adjustment of a magnitude sufficient to raise the export price only to the level of the domestic price was warranted, or whether all exports should have been accorded the new rate, thereby increasing the domestic prices of those commodities. Since the exchange-rate adjustments actually made were sufficient to raise the domestic receipts from

25. In the absence of evidence, it is difficult to reach any judgment on the subject, but there is the consideration that the imposition of exchange taxes and premia is a purely domestic matter. The government could have rescinded or increased the rates unilaterally, and thus it did retain its future options. Whether this consideration had any bearing on the manner of devaluation is unknown.

26. Sturc, *op. cit.* (Note 8), p. 208.

export to their level in the domestic market, focus in this discussion is upon failure to raise the rate fully to the new *de facto* exchange rate.

By August 1958 crops were already planted and harvest was approaching. It was impossible that the 1958 production of agricultural commodities could be significantly affected by changes in domestic prices. Thus in the short run there was likely to be little if any supply response to domestic price increases. There is also an institutional income-distributional argument. That is, for the taxed agricultural export commodities, opium, tobacco, figs, raisins and hazelnuts, small growers sell their crops to wholesalers against cash advances well before the harvest. An immediate move to the TL 9 = $1 rate would not have been reflected in prices received by those producers during 1958. It would have resulted in large windfall gains to wholesalers who had already purchased the crop at lower prices and to the larger, presumably wealthier, producers who had not yet entered into sales contracts. For the agricultural commodities which were effectively taxed, moreover, it can be plausibly argued that Turkey had some degree of short-run monopoly power, given her share of the world market in those commodities (see Chapter VII, below). Thus the export taxes on agricultural commodities could be defended on optimal tariff grounds.

Despite these arguments there was one adverse side effect of the lower premia accorded to traditional exports of agricultural commodities: given that all other exchange rates were adjusted, there was speculation that the premia for the traditional exports would be increased. Indeed, as will be seen below, it was precisely such speculation that forced fairly rapid adjustment of the premia.

As to chrome and copper, it is difficult to find a satisfactory rationale for maintaining the lower EER. Turkey's share of both the copper and chrome markets was relatively smaller than her share for the major crop commodities, and both minerals have close substitutes even in the short run. Exports of both commodities had eroded over the preceding decade as domestic costs had risen with a declining real EER. There could be no doubt that the erosion was largely supply-induced, and that the short-run supply response to an increase in the real EER for the minerals was likely to be considerably greater than that for agricultural commodities. In fact, the government recognized its mistake fairly early, as the EER for chrome was the first to be adjusted after August 1958.

Thus whereas the imposition of export taxes on agricultural commodities could at least in principle be defended as a sensible part of the devaluation package, those on minerals were almost certainly a mistake. The effects of the taxes on the short-run behavior of exports is examined in Chapter IV, below.

(2) *Consolidation and rescheduling of Turkish debt*

It was agreed as part of the devaluation package that Turkey would negotiate multilaterally for a consolidation of outstanding commercial debt. As of August 1958 Turkey had cleared debts with United Kingdom creditors only up to March 1953. Debts had been cleared up with other OEEC countries until 1956 and 1957.[27]

By the spring of 1959 a debt repayment schedule had been agreed upon in principle with the OEEC countries. The agreement covered all amounts due to OEEC creditors prior to August 5, 1958, and payments due before December 1963 against previous capital goods imports. The total consolidated debt was put at $422 million. Payments were scheduled to begin with $14 million in 1959, rising $5 million per year until 1963, with the balance paid in equal installments through 1970.[28] Interest was set at 3 per cent per year.

Table III-1 gives the scheduled repayments of consolidated debts and interest.[29] Since the prevailing market rate of interest on international borrowing was considerably in excess of 3 per cent, debt consolidation contained a large element of foreign aid. If one assumes that Turkey could otherwise have borrowed at 6 per cent (unlikely in view of her past performance) the present value of the debt consolidation to Turkey was about $65 million, according to the repayment schedule given in Table III-1.

Official debt at the end of 1961, including consolidated debt, was estimated by the Turks to be $690 million. This figure included indebtedness and arrears not covered by the consolidation, additional credits received during the 1959-to-1961 period and payments due the OEEC not covered by the consolidation agreement. Thus it would appear that about half of Turkey's 1958 foreign debt and arrears was covered by the agreement.[30]

In a sense, however, the chief value to Turkey of the consolidation agreement lay in its permissive aspect: without consolidation it is unlikely that Turkey would have been able to meet her international obligations and the chaotic debt management of previous years would likely have been resumed. A large part of the reform in the Stabilization Program was predicated upon the Turks' ability to manage their foreign exchange expenditures and receipts

27. EIU, *op. cit.* (Note 1, Chap. II), *No. 27*, August 1958, p. 3.
28. The figures do not accord with those given in Table II-1 because: (1) only arrears to OEEC countries are covered; (2) indebtedness to the OEEC not in arrears but payable before 1963 was included; and (3) Table II-1 is in TL and the OEEC agreement in U.S. dollars.
29. Debt rescheduling took place in the mid-1960's, so the data in Table III-1 do not reflect actual repayments. See Chapter V, below.
30. With $14 million paid in 1959, $19 million in 1960, and $24 million in 1961, the balance of consolidated debt in 1961 would have been $365 million.

Table III-1

Consolidated debt repayment schedule, December 1960 (millions of U.S. dollars)

	1961	1962	1963	1964	1965	1966	1967	1968	1969	1970	1971
Principal	24.5	29.3	34.4	32.5	32.9	32.9	32.9	32.9	32.9	32.9	8.7
Interest	8.5	8.3	7.6	6.6	5.7	4.7	3.7	2.8	1.8	0.3	
Total	32.9	37.6	32.1	39.2	38.5	37.6	36.6	35.6	34.7	33.2	8.7

Note: Principal and interest do not add to totals due to rounding.
Source: *Mali Yılı Bütçe Tasarısı Gerekçesi,* 1962, p. 61.

in a way which the chaotic arrears of the 1950's had made impossible. To the very considerable extent that the Turks succeeded, debt rescheduling was a necessary prerequisite and had a value in excess of the $65 million interest subsidy.

(3) *Foreign credits*

In addition to debt consolidation, Turkey received sizeable foreign credits at the time of devaluation. These totaled $359 million and included a $75 million credit from the OEEC countries and $25 million from the International Monetary Fund. The remainder came almost entirely from the United States.

An important question is the economic rationale for these foreign credits or, stated alternatively, whether large loans were a desirable part of the Stabilization Program. For loans received at the time of devaluation are typically used to finance increases in the current flow of imports, which was the case in Turkey. The question is whether increasing the current flow of imports over a one- or two-year period has a sufficiently high marginal product to justify the cost of the loan.

Although no answer can be given in general, it is the author's judgment that the foreign credits received by Turkey in 1958 did have a marginal product in excess of their cost. There are several considerations. (1) The increased flow of imports was an important factor in eliminating inflation.[31] Part of the productivity of the imports, therefore, was in the improved resource allocation resulting from generally stable prices. (2) Given the reports of bottlenecks and idle capital due to shortages of spare parts, the marginal product of some of the increased import flow must have been extremely high as idle and underutilized resources were available as complementary inputs. This consideration is all the more important when it is recognized that even

31. See Table IV-6, below.

after debt consolidation, Turkey had virtually no free foreign exchange and the import bill would have had to be reduced from its early-1958 level, at least until mid-1959 when additional export earnings were received. (3) After four or more years of import shortages there were inevitably once-and-for-all demands for imports for restocking and catching-up purposes. Unless this demand was satisfied liberalization of the import regime would have been virtually impossible, and in the absence of the foreign credits the initial spurt in demand could not have been met. (4) A large increase in imports was needed to eliminate the premia on import licenses, even at the new import EERs. Elimination of the premia probably had a large social product, as entrepreneurs shifted their energies from seeking premia to other economic activities.

None of these arguments is quantitative, and thus conclusive evidence on the cost-benefit ratio for foreign credits cannot be given. What is clear is that imports would have had to be much smaller in the eighteen months after devaluation had foreign credits not been available. As such, the actual course of events after devaluation would have been very different, and the large increase in imports actually recorded was an integral part of the Stabilization Program.

(4) *Limitations on monetary and fiscal policy*

A key component of the Stabilization Program was a series of limitations accepted by the Turks on monetary and fiscal policy and the financing of foreign transactions. One provision that requires little comment was that no external borrowing could be undertaken except by the administration and that all imports had to be financed by letters of credit. These provisions were designed essentially to preclude the resort to suppliers' credit financing and "thus gradually restore the country's shattered creditworthiness."[32] Suppliers' credits did not again become an issue in Turkey's management of her foreign exchange regime during the period under review in this study.

On the domestic monetary and fiscal side the Stabilization Program was far more complex. Ceilings, to be periodically negotiated with the IMF, were imposed on the issuance of Central Bank credit, the magnitude of commercial bank credit, the amount of government expenditure, the amount the government could borrow from the Central Bank and the financing of SEEs' current and investment expenditures.

For 1958 (1) commercial bank credit was not to exceed its June 1958 level; (2) the central government budget was to be balanced, with a ceiling (not publicly announced) on government expenditures; (3) agricultural sub-

32. Sturc, *op. cit.* (Note 8), pp. 208–9.

sidies were to be included in the government budget; (4) SEE prices were to be raised so that they covered current expenses out of current receipts, and SEEs were to finance their investments only from their own resources or other "non-inflationary sources"[33]; and (5) the interest rate payable to bank depositors was increased.[34]

These restrictions were wide-sweeping and were generally well observed during 1958, although the initial increase in SEE prices turned out in the event to be inadequate to meet the provisions of the agreement, and SEE prices were increased again in 1959.[35] The restrictions amounted to a complete reversal of government policy of earlier years. As will be seen in Chapter IV, the effects, particularly of tight money, were quickly felt within the economy. As evidence of the effects of the monetary restrictions mounted in 1959, the government weakened its adherence to various parts of the program. In analyzing the effects of the Stabilization Program in the year immediately following devaluation, however, the sweeping changes introduced in monetary and fiscal policy must be borne in mind.

(5) *Import liberalization*

The August 3 announcement that all import licensing was to cease pending the preparation of new import regulations caused all foreign exchange purchases, with only minor exceptions, to remain suspended for several months. For although the First Import Program was announced at the end of August and went into effect in September, no import licenses were issued under it until November. Since orders could not be placed until licenses were received, and given the lag between orders and delivery, it was not until late in the winter of 1959 that the flow of imports to Turkey began increasing. For that reason alone no effect, except possibly anticipatory, could be felt from import liberalization until the spring of 1959.[36]

33. In 1961 the government assumed the debt of certain SEEs, issuing 100-year Treasury bonds as obligations against the General Budget. SEE debt figures are therefore not comparable between the 1950's and 1960's.
34. *Annual Statement*, Türk Sınai Kalkınma Bankası, 1958, p. 28.
35. Columbia School of Law, *op. cit.* (Note 14, Chap. I), pp. 25 ff.
36. When deliveries did start in the winter of 1959, the Istanbul port very quickly became unusually congested, which further delayed the delivery of imports to final users. Two factors accounted for the delays: 1) the port's ability to handle cargo was basically limited, with the port ordinarily somewhat congested; 2) the severe financial stringency resulted in some importers' inability to raise funds for customs duties and other charges before they could land the goods. Those importers therefore left their goods in the ports until the time they could raise funds to clear customs. In some cases goods were left in warehouses until they were sold, whereupon the seller used part of the proceeds to pay customs clearing charges. This practice continued throughout the 1960's.

The Import Programs were the major regulatory tool for controlling imports after 1958. Their characteristics are discussed in Chapter VI, below. We concentrate at this juncture only on those aspects of the first few Import Programs relevant for understanding the adjustment to devaluation and its timing.

The total amount of the first three month program was $150 million which was over 40 per cent of 1957 total imports, thus implying a 60 per cent increase in imports. The quotas were heavily weighted toward producers' intermediate goods and raw materials. Of the $150 million total allocation, more than two-thirds were for major items required by producers, including allocations in excess of $10 million each, for vehicle spare parts, tires and tubes, chemicals, iron and steel intermediates and petroleum products.[37] It is clear that producers' demands for spare parts, intermediate goods and raw materials were deemed by the authors of the Import Program to be the most pressing needs.

The First Import Program decreed that all import-license applicants would be required to put up a 100 per cent deposit with the Central Bank against the value of the license within a week of its issuance. Despite tight credit ceilings, applications in the amount of $588 million were placed for $108 million of licenses to be allocated to the private sector. At that point it was announced that 20 per cent of the value of licenses applied for must be deposited at the time of application, subject to forfeit in the event the remaining 80 per cent were not deposited within a week of the receipt of license. Applications against the $108 million allocation thereupon fell to $116 million.[38] While the former figure, $588 million, gives some idea of the degree of speculative activity following devaluation, the fact that $116 million of applications were made within a very short time period, despite credit stringency, is indicative of the degree to which Turkey was import-starved by September 1958.[39]

Subsequent Import Programs continued to emphasize producers' goods and the increased flow of imports. Imports in the first and second halves of 1959 were $204 and $266 million, compared to $128 million in the last half of 1958.

Other features of the import regime also changed. Import price controls under the first few Import Programs were relaxed for some commodities and abandoned for others. Import price checks were virtually a dead letter by the time of *de jure* devaluation in 1960 (although some remained on the books), and little use of them was made during the 1960's.

37. EIU, *op. cit.* (Note 1, Chap. II), *No. 28*, November 1958, pp. 1–2.
38. *Ibid.*,
39. The figure is all the more noteworthy in that the 40 per cent surcharge on imports remained in effect until December 1958. See Table III-2, below.

In the 1956-to-1958 period state organizations had been given exclusive rights to import certain "essential" commodities, which they then resold to end-users. With the initiation of the Import Programs, private firms were allocated many import licenses directly, thus representing a shift toward "actual user" licensing. This shift undoubtedly offset the impact of increased import prices to many private firms, as the prices they had previously paid for imported commodities were probably at least equal to if not greater than the post-devaluation cost of direct importation.

(6) *Export liberalization*

It has already been seen that the exchange rates for major export commodities were gradually moved to the new exchange rate over the two-year period starting in August 1958. Exports during that same period were gradually liberalized in several important regards. Most significant, many minimum export prices were further adjusted to somewhat more realistic levels or abandoned during the 1958-to-1960 period. By mid-1959 the system of export price control was fundamentally altered, in that exporters registered the prices at which they were exporting, and the price checks for most commodities became *ex-post* rather than *ex-ante*. This change entailed considerable relaxation of the export regime as it reduced delays and uncertainties prior to exporting, and frequently gave Turkish exporters latitude to enter into firm export contracts without awaiting approval of the contract before signing it. [40]

Even for those commodities where minimum export prices remained in effect, most observers believed that the prices set after 1958 were considerably closer to realistic international prices than the prices decreed prior to devaluation. [41] Thus even where the formal machinery was not abandoned, the manner in which it was employed was considerably relaxed subsequent to devaluation.

(7) *SEE prices and price controls*

In Chapter II it was shown that one of the major contributing causes of the inflation of the mid-1950's was the failure to raise prices of SEE products in the face of rapid inflation with financing of the resulting deficits by Central Bank credits. Civil servants (including SEE white collar and managerial

---

40. The practice of prior price checks on exports was reinstituted in the spring of 1971. Delays at port became so great that the regime announced as one of its goals for 1972 a target of 3 weeks rather than 3 months as the average delay in the approval of an export price.
41. EIU, *op. cit.* (Note 1, Chap. II), *No. 30*, May 1959, pp. 5–6.

personnel) had received negligible increases in salaries since 1954, despite the rapidity of the inflation.

Among the measures taken as part of the Stabilization Program was an increase in the prices of SEE products, effected in the hope that the SEEs would be able to finance their investments from their own resources rather than with Central Bank credits. It was simultaneously judged desirable to increase civil servants' salaries substantially. Thus increases in SEE prices had to be sufficient to cover not only the existing costs of SEE products but also the increase in the wage-and-salary bill.

Some price increases were effected shortly after devaluation, in August 1958, but these were insufficient to accomplish the goal. The major adjustments in SEE prices and civil servants' salaries were effected in May 1959. SEE prices were raised an average of 20 per cent at that time, while civil servants' salary levels were raised an average of 41 per cent.[42]

Price controls over the private sector relaxed as SEE prices were increased. Although the basic legislation enabling government controls over prices and profits in the private sector was not repealed until 1960, price controls were in fact lifted in 1958 and 1959 for all commodities except wheat, coal and electric power.

It will be important to bear in mind these institutional changes and their timing when evaluating the degree of inflationary pressure set off by the devaluation and the short-term response to the Stabilization Program. Two things in particular will be noted. The SEEs were sufficiently dominant in enough commodity markets for the increase in their prices alone to be sufficient to give a major fillip to all price indices in the second quarter of 1959. Furthermore, the removal of price controls, even though they could not have been completely effective, undoubtedly resulted in increases in at least a few commodity prices. The official price indices, moreover, drew their observations heavily from controlled prices and ignored the existence of black markets in many commodities. Thus increases in controlled prices had a larger impact on price indices than they did on the actual increase in the price level. Secondly, the increase in the government budget in 1959 can be interpreted only in light of the huge salary increases negotiated as a part of the devaluation package. Ignoring the salary increases, the real expenditures of the Turkish government in 1959 probably did decline from their 1958 level, so that part of the increase in government expenditures can be interpreted primarily as a "catch-up" in wages and salaries from prior inflationary pressure, and was offset in large part by increased SEE prices and government tax revenues.

---

42. Civil servants' salaries were increased by 20 per cent again in 1961. See OEEC, *Turkey, 1961, op. cit.*, p. 13.

IV. Changes in effective exchange rates

The nominal devaluation of the Turkish lira, from TL 2.80 to TL 9 per dollar, was undoubtedly one of the largest nominal devaluations effected by any country since World War II. As already seen, however, many circumstances contrived to make the relevant magnitude of the change in the effective rate far less than the inspection of official rates would indicate. First, the change was accomplished over a two-year period. Second, the multiple exchange rates which had developed prior to 1958 meant that the *de jure* price of foreign exchange was considerably below the actual price, even on the export side.

Table III-2
EER changes, 1957 to 1959 (TL per dollar)

	December 1957	August 1958	December 1958	December 1959
Exports				
Minerals	2.80	4.90	4.90	9.00
Traditional crops	2.94	5.14	5.14	6.77
Cotton	3.78	9.00	9.00	9.00
Marginal exports	5.00	9.00	9.00	9.00
Weighted export rate	3.17	5.87	5.87	7.76
Imports				
Consumer goods	7.47	22.26	18.66	18.66
Intermediates and raw materials	5.35	16.35	12.75	12.75
Capital goods	5.38	16.15	12.55	12.55
Imports with domestic substitutes	8.29	24.82	21.22	21.22
Weighted import rate	5.94	17.90	14.31	14.31
Tourism	5.25–5.75	9.00	9.00	9.00
Other invisibles	2.80	9.00	9.00	9.00
Capital transactions	2.80	9.00	9.00	9.00

Notes: a) The weighted import rate was derived by using the percentages of total imports in each category. For imports competing with domestic production, however, judgment was used in deriving the weight. Weights used were: consumer goods, 0.106; raw materials, 0.291; capital goods, 0.482; and imports competing with domestic production, 0.121.

b) Data for capital goods imports are based on Table A-13 and do *not* agree with Gürtan's estimates used in Table II-10. Gürtan's data give an average figure for 1958 as a whole, and therefore could not be used to estimate the post-devaluation changes.

Source: Appendix A.

Table III-2 summarizes the estimates of the change in nominal EERs. One should recall that the nominal devaluation rate was 220 per cent. The weighted export EER rose from TL 3.17 at the end of 1957 to TL 5.87 in August 1958 and to TL 7.76 in 1959. Thus the export EER depreciated by only 85 per cent in August 1958. And the weighted import rate was TL 5.94 in 1957, jumping to TL 17.90 in August 1958, and falling to TL 14.31 by the end of 1958 when the 40 per cent tax on imports was lifted. Thus there was effective depreciation on the import side of only 140 per cent between the end of 1957 and the end of 1958. Neither of these percentage rates come close to the nominal devaluation rate of 220 per cent, although both are sizeable.

An important feature of the changes in EERs is that the weighted import EER was 1.87 times the export rate in 1957, three times the export EER in August 1958, and 1.84 times the export EER in December 1959. Thus devaluation did not result, at least prior to 1960, in any narrowing of the

Table III-3
Price-level-deflated EERs, 1957 to 1960 (Dec. 1958 TL per dollar)

	December 1957	August 1958	December 1958	December 1959
Exports				
Minerals	3.74	5.62	4.90	8.70
Traditional crops	3.93	5.89	5.14	6.54
Cotton	5.05	10.32	9.00	8.69
Marginal exports	6.67	10.32	9.00	8.69
Weighted export rate	4.23	6.73	5.87	7.50
Imports				
Consumer goods	9.97	25.53	18.66	18.03
Intermediates	7.14	18.75	12.75	12.32
Capital goods	7.18	18.52	12.55	12.13
Imports with domestic substitutes	11.07	28.46	21.22	20.50
Weighted import rate	7.93	20.53	14.31	13.83
Tourism	7.34	10.32	9.00	8.70
Other invisibles	3.74	10.32	9.00	8.70
Capital transactions	3.74	10.32	9.00	8.70

Note: The home goods price index for the first quarter of 1958 was set equal to 100, and the fourth quarter 1957, third quarter 1958 and fourth quarter 1959 indices were computed from that base.

Sources: EERs from Table III-2. Deflators from home goods price index, quarterly data given in *International Financial Statistics*.

differential between export and import EERs. It should be borne in mind that the import EERs are the prices paid if the import licenses could be obtained, and therefore do not take into account the premia. Even so, the fact that the Stabilization Program did not alter the differential against exports is remarkable. If data on the size of the premia were available, the premium-inclusive EER differential would undoubtedly have been reduced somewhat, although as will be seen below, it remained large in the 1960's.

Table III-3 presents estimates of the PLD-EERs over the devaluation period. December 1958 was used as a base period from which to make the estimates. As can be seen, when price-level changes are taken into account, the magnitude of the devaluation on both the import and the export side was far smaller than even computation of the nominal EER suggests. Thus the real export rate depreciated from TL 4.23 in December 1957 to TL 7.50 in December 1959, an overall depreciation of 77 per cent in a two-year period. On the import side there was a 74 per cent depreciation in the PLD-EER between the end of 1957 and the end of 1959.

We therefore conclude that the "true" order of magnitude of the real devaluation was probably about 80 per cent. While the basis of the estimates is necessarily somewhat rough, the 80 per cent figure much more closely approximates the magnitude of the devaluation than does the nominal exchange rate change.

Of course an 80 per cent devaluation in real terms is large by any standard and is indicative of the severe dislocation of the Turkish economy in 1958. Moreover the devaluation, large as it was, was only one component of the Stabilization Program. Other components also represented major shifts in the Turkish economy in 1958, and one would expect sizeable responses to them on *a priori* grounds. In the next chapter, analysis of the short-term response to the program is undertaken.

CHAPTER IV

Response to stabilization: Phases III and IV

As indicated in the last chapter, the Stabilization Program had many components, not all of which were effected in August 1958. The response of the Turkish economy to the Stabilization Program is traced in this chapter. An effort is made to analyze the separate effects of the various components of the program and to evaluate its optimality on the basis of that response.

Three factors cloud the analysis. First, there were so many changes undertaken simultaneously that it is difficult to sort out the effects of the separate parts of the Stabilization Program. Second, detailed data, especially on quarterly and monthly changes, are woefully lacking even for key variables. Third, the political events of 1959 to 1962 had strong economic repercussions and must be taken into account in the analysis. It will be useful at the outset to provide the reader with a brief chronology of the period. Thereafter the shifts in monetary policy, fiscal policy, the trade regime and other variables are examined, along with their effects. Next, consideration is given to the relationship of the Stabilization Program to the recession experienced by Turkey. Finally, an effort is made to assess the degree to which the Program was optimal from the viewpoint of Turkish economic growth.

I. Macroeconomic indicators

Figure 2 charts the course of the major macroeconomic variables over the 1959—1961 period, with indicators for the preceding and subsequent years given to enable comparisons. As can be seen, the years 1959 to 1961 were a time of extremely slow growth. The average annual growth of real GNP over the three years was 2 per cent, less than tha rate of population growth. Thereafter the growth rate rose sharply. The proximate cause of the slow growth rate was recession, although the fact that agricultural output grew at even less than its trend rate also contributed. The evidence suggests that there were really two recessions. One started in 1958 and was largely the result of tight money and thus of the Stabilization Program. It appears to have reached a trough in the spring of 1959, after which economic activity began expanding. By the spring of 1960 economic activity appears to have been fairly buoyant with few signs of recession left. The second recession started in the summer of 1960 after the May Revolution and reached a trough sometime during late 1961.

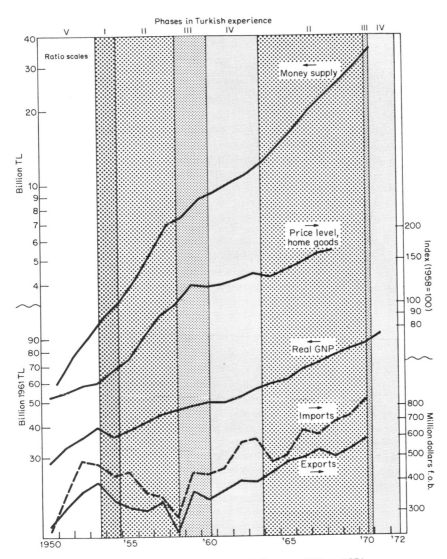

Fig. 2. Selected macroeconomic indicators, 1950 to 1971.

Perhaps the most remarkable fact about the period 1959–1961 is that after the spring of 1959 the Turkish price level remained stable through 1961. Price increases, in fact, were relatively modest throughout the 1960's. Thus the Stabilization Program was a complete success in breaking the inflationary spiral that had existed in Turkey prior to the inauguration of the Program.

This can be seen by the dramatic change in the course of the price level in Fig. 2. Analysis of the factors that led to the change will be undertaken in detail in Section II.

The government appears to have adhered fairly closely to most aspects of the Stabilization Program until the summer of 1959. Thereafter the money supply started to expand more rapidly than had been agreed to. By the winter of 1960 it appeared that the government intended to resume its expansionist policies, as a very expansionary budget was presented to Parliament.[1]

In May 1960 a bloodless revolution occurred when a group of military leaders calling themselves the National Unity Committee (NUC) took over the government. The causes of the revolution lay in discontent over both political repression and economic policy.[2] The NUC quickly reversed some of the expansionist policies of the Menderes government and announced complete adherence to the Stabilization Program. Thus in contrast to Cooper's conclusion that devaluations increase the probability that politicians will lose their jobs,[3] in Turkey it was the failure of the government to adhere to the Stabilization Program that contributed to its fall.

The flow of imports increased markedly after 1958. Premia on import licenses and the active black market of the mid-1950's virtually disappeared. Although exports and other foreign exchange receipts increased, the change was not enough to compensate for the large rise in foreign exchange expenditures. Among other charges made by the NUC against the Menderes government was the fact that almost the entire foreign credit received in 1958 had already been exhausted.[4] Imports nonetheless continued increasing rapidly in the first three years after the revolution and the foreign trade regime became increasingly liberal. Thus the period 1960-to-1963 can be regarded as Phase IV.

II. Components of the Stabilization Program and their effects

Monetary and fiscal changes

As indicated above, the use of official prices (which were controlled by law) in the construction of the price indices of the mid-1950's led to an understatement of the true rate of inflation during that period. The average

1. Columbia School of Law, *op. cit.* (Note 14, Chap. I), p. 20.
2. Weiker, *op. cit.* (Note 13, Chap. I), Chapters 1 and 2.
3. Richard N. Cooper, "Currency Devaluation in Developing Countries," *Essays in International Finance No. 86*, International Finance Section, Princeton University, June 1971, p. 30.
4. Weiker, *op. cit.* (Note 13, Chap. I), p. 13.

annual rate of increase in average wholesale prices from 1955 to 1958 was 19 per cent, even by official statistics, contrasting with an average annual rate of 1.5 per cent between final quarters from 1959 to 1962.

Four factors were primarily responsible for the change: (1) monetary policy, (2) the increased flow of imports, (3) the exchange-rate changes, and (4) abandonment of the price control law and changes in SEE pricing policy. Fiscal policy changes were of secondary importance. Brief consideration is given in this section to fiscal policy and especially the fiscal impact of the revenue generated by net receipts from the system of exchange taxes and premia. Monetary policy changes are discussed thereafter.

Fiscal policy. Table IV-1 presents data on central government expenditures and receipts as a per cent of national income over the period 1957 to 1963. As pointed out in Chapter II, the government accounts do not include the operations of the SEEs. Thus an incomplete picture of the impact of the government sector on economic activity is provided. However, since the effect of SEE finances was primarily felt through money creation, the impact of SEEs on governmental activity can be more appropriately considered when evaluating monetary policy.

Inspection of the data in Table IV-1 suggests that there was little change in central government fiscal impact after 1958. The central government budget was if anything somewhat expansionary. Expenditures rose from 14.5 per cent of national income in 1958 to 18.1 per cent in 1961. Tax revenues also rose, but their increase did not keep pace with that of expenditures, and net government borrowing increased substantially in 1960. Thus both the in-

Table IV-1

Central government expenditures and receipts, 1957 to 1963

(per cent of national income)

	1957	1958	1959	1960	1961	1962	1963
Current outlays	11.4	11.0	12.1	12.4	14.3	13.5	14.1
Capital formation	3.5	3.5	3.6	3.9	3.8	3.7	4.2
Total expenditures	14.9	14.5	15.7	16.3	18.1	17.2	18.3
Tax receipts	14.3	13.1	14.2	13.7	15.4	14.6	15.6
Transfers	1.0	1.6	1.7	1.6	2.2	2.1	1.6
Net borrowing	−0.4	−0.2	−0.2	1.0	0.5	0.5	1.2

Note: The government's assumption of the consolidated SEE debt is not included in 1961 central government borrowing.

Source: Same as Table II-4.

Table IV-2
Government net revenues from foreign trade taxes, 1956 to 1962

	1956	1957	1958	1959	1960	1961	1962
Tax revenue (millions of TL)							
Net foreign trade taxes	399	744	873	1565	1507	1553	1918
Total tax receipts	2999	3821	4430	5928	6096	7187	7625
Net foreign trade taxes as percentage of:							
Tax revenue	13.3	19.5	19.7	26.4	24.7	21.6	25.2
Imports c.i.f.	35.0	66.9	99.0	118.9	68.1	33.9	34.3

Sources: Tax data from Land, *op. cit.* (Table I-5).
Import data from *Statistical Yearbook, 1968, Pub. No. 580* (Ankara), 1969,
p. 309, State Institute of Statistics.

crease in government expenditures and its financing probably led to mild
expansionary pressures upon the Turkish economy.[5]

One interesting aspect of the Stabilization Program was the use of exchange taxes and premia. Their net effect was equivalent to that of imposing
export taxes. Since all purchases of foreign exchange were taxed TL 6.20 per
dollar while many sales of foreign exchange were accorded smaller premia,
the net receipts from the tax were sizeable, especially given the import surplus. Table IV-2 gives the net revenue from foreign trade taxes and premia in
relation to total tax revenue and to imports for the period 1956 to 1962. As
can be seen, net revenue from foreign trade taxes increased almost five-fold
between 1956 and 1959. The large increase between 1956 and 1957 originated in the 40 per cent "Treasury Tax" imposed then on most imports.

Until 1958, export premia accounted for a relatively small drain on import
tax receipts, so that net tax receipts were just slightly less than gross receipts.
Export premia were sizeable from 1958 until 1960 and the difference between import taxes collected and export premia paid out became significant.
After August 1958 gross tax receipts on imports were more than two and one
half times imports (recorded at TL 2.80 per dollar), as the tax per TL 2.80 of

5. As indicated above, part of the increase in government expenditures in 1959 was
attributable to the adjustment in salaries of government servants. For the government
as a whole (including social security institutions and local governments), wages and
salaries in relation to current expenditures on goods and services were as follows
(millions of TL):

	1958	1959	1960	1961	1962
Current expenditures	3226	4578	4762	5852	6231
Wages and salaries	1592	2424	2560	3276	3483
Per cent wage & salary	49.3	52.3	53.8	56.0	55.9

See Land, *op. cit.* (Table I-5).

imports c.i.f. was TL 6.20 and import duties were charged over and above that. With an average premium on exports of about TL 2.70 and exports much less than imports, net receipts from foreign trade taxes were greater than the recorded TL value of imports in 1959. The export premia were increased and the exchange rate was finally unified, so that by 1961 import taxes were about the same fraction of imports as in 1956. But since the exchange rate had increased so sharply foreign trade taxes generated about 25 per cent of total tax revenue in 1962, contrasting with only 13 per cent in 1956.

The net revenue from the tax-premium system in 1959 and 1960 was therefore a significant element in keeping the government budget from being even more expansionary than it was. Between 1958 and 1959, 46 per cent of the increase in total tax revenues originated from the changes in net foreign-trade tax receipts, and to some extent the 1958 figures already reflect the incidence of the tax-premium system. While there would have been some increase in foreign-trade tax receipts resulting from the increased flow of imports in 1959, the incremental revenues resulting from the tax-premium system, amounting to 1.6 per cent of 1959 national income, were undoubtedly an anti-inflationary factor of significance.

Monetary policy. Whereas fiscal policy was mildly expansionary in the years 1958 to 1960, monetary policy was extremely tight from August 1958 to mid-1959. It will be recalled that one component of the Stabilization Program was the ceilings imposed on Central Bank and commercial bank credit.

Table IV-3 gives data on the money supply at the end of each quarter as reported by the EIU. The money supply had increased by more than 10 per cent between March and September 1958, with virtually the entire increase coming in the period before August. The money supply then actually contracted about 5 per cent from September to December, with a further 1 per cent decline in the first quarter of 1959.[6] The shift from rapid monetary expansion to monetary contraction was therefore abrupt. After the second quarter of 1959 rapid expansion of the money supply resumed, with an increase of over 16 per cent in the last six months of 1959. After the NUC assumed power in May 1960 the money supply remained virtually stable until the middle of 1961. Thus two distinct tight-money periods can be distinguished: the first lasted from August 1958 until mid-1959; the second started in the second quarter of 1960 and continued well into 1961.

6. The data given in Table IV-3 are based on EIU reports. The OEEC reported a 2 per cent drop in the money supply between June and October 1958 but did not present data for later periods. OEEC, *Turkey, 1959, op. cit.* (Note 32, Chap. 1), p. 23.

Table IV-3
Money supply, quarterly, 1957 to 1962
(billions of TL — at the end of each period indicated)

Year	Quarter			
	I	II	III	IV
1957	4.6	4.9	5.1	5.5
1958	5.6	6.0	6.2	5.9/9.0
1959	8.9	9.0	9.4	10.5
1960	10.8	10.6	10.8	10.9
1961	10.8	10.7	10.9	11.7
1962	11.7	11.6	12.3	13.0

Notes: a) The EIU changed series at the end of 1958, so that figures are not comparable between periods. Until 1958, only currency and demand deposits were included. Thereafter, currency and all commercial bank deposits are included. The figure before the slash for the fourth quarter of 1958 is comparable with earlier data. The TL 9.0 figure is comparable with figures for later quarters.
b) The data are not comparable with those given by the Central Bank or with those given in *International Financial Statistics*. However, issues of the Central Bank's *Monthly Bulletin* for the period 1958 to 1962 were not available to the author, and *International Financial Statistics* does not report quarterly data on the Turkish money supply until the second quarter of 1959.

Source: EIU, *op. cit.* (Note 1, Chap. II), *Nos. 28, 32, 35, 39, 40, 43,* and *47.*

There is ample evidence that the sharp shift in mid-1958 from rapid monetary expansion to a stable money supply had immediate effects on the Turkish economy. As reported by the EIU,

> The authorities certainly appear to be determined ... to maintain the credit squeeze, but the latter, both by stifling demand and making it more difficult to finance essential imports, is undoubtedly hitting industry hard; many factories, particularly in the textile field, have closed down or are working part-time ... At present, the import market is finding credit stringency a less serious handicap than are manufacturers and exporters ... It is already clear that certain of the smaller manufacturing concerns set up speculatively during the import famine of recent years will have to close down permanently. In the end, ... some credit relaxation would appear inevitable; failing this, the continuing slump in demand would nullify the effects of any increase in output arising from a more liberal import policy.[7]

Detailed examination of the effects of tight monetary policy will be undertaken in Section III, below. The important points for present purposes are that: (1) the shift in monetary policy was large and abrupt; (2) the tight money policy was abandoned in the second half of 1959; and (3) tight money was resumed in the summer of 1960. One question of importance for under-

7. EIU, *op. cit.* (Note 1, Chap. II), *No. 31,* August 1959, p. 10.

standing the timing of the response to the Stabilization Program is what led to the abrupt resumption of monetary expansion and the inflationary budget of 1960.

Two interpretations are possible. One is that the Menderes government never seriously intended to carry through the Stabilization Program. The other is that the credit stringency and other effects of tight money and the Stabilization Program were sufficiently pronounced to lead the government to abandon the program as politically unpalatable and/or economically undesirable. Okyar and Iren[8] take the former view, while Aktan takes the latter.[9] Which interpretation is correct is closely related to the question raised in Chapter III: whether the government accepted the Stabilization Program because that was a necessary price for obtaining foreign credits or, alternatively, whether it believed that its past policies were in general need of reform. A definitive judgment is impossible in the absence of direct evidence. On either interpretation, however, it is likely that the visible effects of extremely tight money must have made the abandonment of the Program more appealing and perhaps speeded the time at which rapid monetary expansion resumed. We shall return to this question below when evaluating the optimality of the Stabilization Program.

SEE finances and their effects.   In August 1958 the prices of many SEE products were raised. However, the initial increase proved to be inadequate to enable the SEEs to cover their expenses, and a second large round of price increases took place in May 1959.[10]

In view of the important role of the SEE deficits in contributing to the money supply increases prior to August 1958, raising SEE prices was essential if rapid expansion of the money supply was to be halted. After 1959 SEE deficits never again became a major drain on Central Bank credits, although financing their investment programs remained something of an issue. As such, the Stabilization Program succeeded in eliminating one source of inflationary pressure.[11]

8. Columbia School of Law, *op. cit.* (Note 14, Chap. I), p. 20.

9. Aktan, *op. cit.* (Note 16, Chap. I), p. 36.

10. Columbia School of Law, *op. cit.* (Note 14, Chap. I), p. 25.

11. There is one interesting sidelight on the period which may be indicative of government intentions. After the Stabilization Program was in effect, the SEEs were still in financial difficulties. The government responded initially by failing to charge the TL 6.20 tax on their imports, and the SEEs did not pay the government tax liabilities they incurred. These practices stopped only after the IMF protested. See Columbia School of Law, *op. cit.* (Note 14, Chap. I), pp. 25 ff.

The inflow of imports

Table IV-4 gives quarterly export and import figures for the years 1957 to 1960. The export response to the Stabilization Program will be evaluated in more detail below. It is sufficient for present purposes to note that the increase in exports in the first half of 1959 was attributable to delays in exporting the 1958 crop and to some reductions in inventory following the Stabilization Program. It will be recalled that new export regulations were not promulgated immediately in August 1958 and that there was therefore a delay before exporting at the new exchange rates could begin. Until the final quarter of 1959 the increase in exports was thus achieved primarily through reductions in inventory rather than through increases in production.

In the absence of estimates of inventory investment, the increased flow of imports which really began in the first quarter of 1959 should therefore be regarded as a net deflationary factor.[12] Thus for the first three quarters of 1959 the increase in imports was $73.7 million. In the final quarter of 1959 the increase in the net inflow (imports minus exports) was $38.4 million. The deflationary effect of the import flow can be placed at $112 million for 1959 as a whole. Converted at the TL 9 per dollar exchange rate, that represented 2.4 per cent of 1959 national income and 3 per cent of 1958 national income. Thus the increased net inflow of imports, allowing for the part of

12. Of course part of the recorded increase in imports may reflect an increase in the fraction of imports entering legally or a reduction in under-invoicing. The data in Table II-9 suggest that that was not a significant factor until 1961, however.

Table IV-4
Imports and exports, quarterly, 1957 to 1960 (millions of U.S. dollars)

Year	Quarter				Total
	I	II	III	IV	
Exports f.o.b.					
1957	90.4	94.6	62.4	97.7	345.2
1958	81.5	50.5	38.6	76.6	247.2
1959	103.4	81.3	49.6	119.5	353.8
1960	98.6	59.0	54.4	108.7	320.7
Imports c.i.f.					
1957	90.5	98.2	101.4	107.0	397.1
1958	86.0	100.8	58.9	69.3	315.1
1959	98.4	105.9	115.1	150.6	469.9
1960	115.9	115.6	129.6	107.3	468.1

Source: *International Financial Statistics,* 1967/68 Supplement.

exports originating from inventory disinvestment, constituted a sizeable deflationary factor.

Net effect on prices

Table IV-5 presents quarterly wholesale and home-goods price indices for the period 1958 to 1962. Data for home-goods prices in 1958 are unfortunately not available on a quarterly basis. It seems clear, however, that both wholesale prices and home-goods prices rose at least until the first quarter of 1959. Some of that rise, of course, resulted from the first increase in SEE prices, and part of it may have been the result of recording procedures.[13] The home-goods price index shows prices falling somewhat after the first quarter of 1959, while the wholesale price index shows increases, albeit at a far slower rate than in earlier periods. On either index, however, it is evident that inflation had ceased by early 1959. The annual figures therefore obscure a great deal about the timing of price changes.

13. As indicated above, the government recorded official prices in the price indices during the inflation years. Thus when prices were decontrolled the prices actually recorded rose more than market prices. See OEEC, *Turkey, 1961, op. cit.* (Note 42, Chap. III), pp. 11–12.

Table IV-5
Quarterly price indices, 1958 to 1962 (1958 average = 100)

Year	Quarter				Annual
	I	II	III	IV	
Wholesale prices					
1958	90	95	104	111	100
1959	116	119	120	124	120
1960	129	128	123	125	126
1961	129	129	129	132	130
1962	140	139	133	137	137
Home-goods prices					
1958	n.a.	n.a.	n.a.	n.a.	100
1959	129	118	117	119	119
1960	122	121	114	116	117
1961	119	117	118	121	119
1962	125	124	122	127	125

Note: There is a discrepancy between the annual figures and the average of the quarterly figures for the 1959 home-goods price index. The reason for the difference is not known.

Source: Same as Table I-5.

Both indices indicate a return to moderate price increases in the final quarter of 1959 and the first quarter of 1960, after which prices declined for the remainder of the year and remained highly stable until the final quarter of 1961. Thus, contrasted with an annual average rate of inflation of over 15 per cent between 1956 and the first half of 1958, prices were either stable or rose only a few per cent annually between 1959 and 1961, even without allowing for bias in the statistics.

To estimate the factors contributing to the change, the same methodology is used as was employed in Chapter II with regard to the inflation of the mid-1950's. The results are reported in Table IV-6.

It is of interest that the predicted rate of price increase for 1959 to 1961 almost equals the actual price increase. But whereas the simple model developed in Chapter II predicts a very low rate of inflation in 1959 followed by rates of 10.6 and 8.4 per cent in 1960 and 1961, the actual rate of price increase was 19 per cent in 1959, negative in 1960, and only 1.7 per cent in 1961.

The difference between predicted and actual timing may have resulted from several factors. As already seen, part of the increase in prices in 1959 was attributable to the "catch-up" in SEE prices, which was a necessary condition for the cessation of additional inflation and which can to a large

Table IV-6
Predicted and actual inflation, 1959 to 1962
(percentage of previous year's real national income)

	Supply Changes				Demand Changes $\frac{\Delta M_{t-1}}{M_{t-2}}$	Inflation	
	Agri-culture	Non-Agriculture	Imports	Total		Estimated	Actual
	(1)	(2)	(3)	(4)	(5)	(6)	(7)
1959	0.0	3.0	3.0	6.0	6.9	0.9	19.0
1960	0.6	3.0	-0.2	3.4	14.0	10.6	-1.7
1961	-1.1	3.0	0.6	2.5	10.9	8.4	1.7
1962	2.6	3.0	2.6	8.2	7.6	-0.6	5.0

Sources: Given in Table II-7, except for imports, which had to be adjusted because of the exchange-rate change. The 1961 TL value of imports was linked to national income in 1961 prices. TL values for 1960 and 1962 were then computed by multiplying the 1961 figure by the ratio of the other year's dollar value of imports to the 1961 dollar value of imports. The same linkage procedure was followed for earlier years, except that the 1961 TL value of imports was multiplied by the ratio of 1961 national income at 1948 prices to 1961 national income at 1961 prices to obtain a base figure.

extent be attributed to the pent-up inflation of earlier years rather than to the degree of inflationary pressure in 1959.

Computed 1959 excess demand was virtually zero. Compared with computed excess demands of 21.3, 21.5, and 12.5 per cent in the preceding three years, the magnitude of the shift was truly remarkable and attests to the severity of the Stabilization Program. If time is required before altered underlying conditions are reflected in changed expectations, the virtual price stability of 1960–1961 may have resulted from a downward shift in expectations, which offset excess demand from other sources.

Another feature to be noted is that agricultural production, according to SIS national income estimates, contributed virtually nothing to whatever adjustments occurred following devaluation. Although the 1958 crop was perhaps good,[14] the disagreement over the size of the crop renders analysis difficult. After 1958 all sources appear to be in agreement that increases in agricultural production were relatively small. Thus it cannot be concluded that fortuitous weather conditions were a factor in bringing inflation to a halt. From 1959 to 1961, on the contrary, agricultural production contributed little to growth in aggregate supply.

It should also be noted that the estimates in Table IV-6 contain the implicit assumption that the growth of non-agricultural capacity was invariant with respect to the devaluation and stabilization. Not only is that a questionable assumption, but it will be seen below that there is evidence that it is wrong. On balance, however, it is doubtful if the short-term shifts in supply were sufficient to render the orders of magnitude given in Table IV-6 inappropriate.

The evidence then is mixed. Certainly in 1959 the influx of imports constituted a major anti-inflationary factor. The increased revenue from foreign trade taxes also undoubtedly absorbed a significant amount of purchasing power previously accruing to importers. These factors, as well as any improvement in resource allocation and increase in capacity utilization, led to stronger anti-inflationary pressures than would have taken place from monetary shifts alone. Without the shift in monetary policy, however, inflation would have been temporarily retarded but certainly could not have been stopped. Thus primary responsibility for stopping inflation must go to the shift in monetary policy; other components of the Stabilization Program enhanced the impact of the monetary shift.

14. There is dispute over the 1958 crop. This dispute lies at the basis of the divergence between SIS and SPO national income data. SIS estimates of national income at 1948 prices imply a 17.7 per cent increase in agricultural production between 1957 and 1958 with no increase between 1958 and 1959. SPO estimates imply no increase between 1957 and 1958 and a 6 per cent increase in agricultural output between 1958 and 1959. In recent years a consensus has begun emerging to the effect that the truth lies somewhere between the two estimates.

The role of exchange-rate changes

It has already been seen that the most remarkable result of the Stabilization Program was Turkey's transformation from a rapid-inflation country to one with virtual price stability. A natural question is the role of the EER changes in the Stabilization Program. While the increased flow of imports helped in the transformation, it was Turkey's receipt of foreign credits rather than exchange-rate policy which was the primary factor enabling additional imports. To the extent that imports entered at a higher EER not fully offset by increased government payments of export premia, some purchasing power was absorbed which contributed to the shift to price stability.

The questions therefore arise as to whether: the EER changes had any effects separate from those of the other components of the Stabilization Program and whether the EER changes can be viewed as separate from the Stabilization Program aside from their revenue-generating effects which, in any event, came at least as much from the import surplus as from the differential EERs between imports and exports.

The first question has three separate parts: (1) the behavior of exports after August 1958; (2) the behavior of other components of the balance of payments; and (3) the resource-allocational effects of EER changes. The resource-allocational effects of EER changes are considered in Section III, since they were closely interrelated with the overall determinants of the level of economic activity. It should be noted at this juncture that the primary resource-allocational effects of the EER changes were not immediately felt, and can be better considered as part of a longer-run response to devaluation.[15]

Export behavior.   Although exports increased between 1958 and 1959, their expansion was by no means dramatic. A number of factors obscure analysis of reasons for the increase that did occur. First, it has already been seen that export statistics prior to August 1958 were difficult to interpret, reflecting "switch" deals, bilateral debt repayment arrangements and associated artificially high prices for exports, and perhaps some faking of invoices as well as unrecorded export transactions. Second, many of the export transactions undertaken in 1957 and 1958 were carried out by government and quasi-government agencies, often at a loss. Since those transactions were somewhat less closely tied to profitability than were exports undertaken by private traders, one would not necessarily expect the same sort of response as if the profit motive had dominated all exports. Third, as was seen in Chapter III, the export EERs were not fully unified in August 1958, and export premia increased for different commodities at various dates from August 1958 to 1960.

15. See Chapter VII, below.

With these factors in mind, we can examine data on the quarterly behavior of exports given in Table IV-7. The first column gives quarterly exports seasonally adjusted at annual rates for the period 1957 to 1960. The second column gives the quarterly figures for exports of traditional commodities. With the exception of cotton, those commodities did not receive the TL 9 rate until various dates in 1959 and 1960. Many commodities were exported primarily by government agencies. The third column gives the behavior of other "minor" exports, all of which were accorded a TL 6.20 premium in August 1958 and were predominantly the domain of private traders.

Inspection of the second and third columns of Table IV-7 indicates that

Table IV-7
Short-term export response, 1957 to 1960 (millions of U.S. dollars)

Year and Quarter	Total Exports (seasonally adjusted annual rate)	Major Exports (actual quarterly figures)	Minor Exports (actual quarterly figures)
1957			
I	295.7	67.3	23.1
II	487.6	77.0	17.6
III	380.5	42.9	19.5
IV	272.9	78.1	19.6
1958			
I	287.0	74.9	6.6
II	260.3	42.6	7.9
III	235.3	15.7	22.9
IV	214.0	50.1	26.5
1959			
I	364.0	75.7	27.7
II	419.1	57.3	24.0
III	302.4	22.6	27.0
IV	333.8	79.1	40.4
1960			
I	347.2	66.7	31.9
II	346.5	31.9	27.1
III	331.7	19.4	35.0
IV	303.6	70.0	38.7

Notes: a) Seasonal adjustment factors were computed for the period 1948 to 1970. The year was taken from the second quarter of one calendar year to the first quarter of the next, since the crop export season overlaps the calendar year.
b) Major exports are: chrome, cotton, hazelnuts, raisins, tobacco and wheat. Minor exports are the difference between total and major exports.
c) Actual quarterly export totals are the sum of major and minor exports and are given in Table IV-4.

Source: Data from *International Financial Statistics*, various issues.

there were significant differences in the behavior of major and minor exports following August 1958. The exportation of major commodities appears to have been delayed somewhat until new export regulations were issued, so that the third quarter 1958 exports were less than they would otherwise have been and the subsequent three quarters' totals were perhaps slightly higher. Exports of major commodities were still 11 per cent below their 1957 level in 1959. Although they rose 28 per cent over 1958, that was primarily attributable to the spillover in exports from calendar year 1958 to calendar 1959, as exporters awaited higher premia on traditional exports.[16] In all, the response of traditional exports to the changed EERs was very moderate and generally disappointing. It will be seen in Chapter VII that a major reason for this is that price signals from the international market are generally not reflected to producers in Turkey, so that the quantity of exports depends much more upon government policy than upon EERs themselves.

In contrast to major exports, minor exports had declined much more sharply during the mid-1950's and were $77.8 million in 1957 compared to $116 million in 1953. The striking feature is the shrinkage in minor exports in the first half of 1958. Although the decline was steady from 1953 on, much of the drop in the first half of 1958 may have represented speculative inventory accumulation in anticipation of devaluation.[17] This is the more plausible because it seems unlikely that any production response to the altered EERs could have been felt by the end of the third quarter of 1958 and little could have occurred by the end of the year.

Even if the change in minor exports between the first and second halves of 1958 was entirely attributable to offsetting inventory changes, it is noteworthy that the flow of minor exports increased in each subsequent year. Minor exports in 1959 were $109 million, compared to $80 million in 1957. They had thus virtually reattained their 1953 level. By 1960, minor exports were $133 million. Thus minor exports seem to have responded to the altered EERs. Although the relative response appears impressive, the minor exports were too small a component of total exports to have a sizeable effect on total export earnings.

It will be seen in Chapter VII that there is ample evidence of the responsiveness of most minor and some traditional exports to changed real EERs. But in the short-run period from August 1958 to 1961 the export response was not pronounced.

16. Mustafa Renksizbulut, "Analysis of Turkey's Foreign Trade and Some Estimates about Future Developments," *Turkish Economic Review,* May 1962, p. 21.
17. There is little, if anything, in contemporary comments to suggest that devaluation appeared any more likely in 1958 than in earlier years until at least the second quarter. Thus although the data are strongly suggestive of speculative activity, there is no corroborating evidence.

Capital flows. When there are expectations of exchange-rate changes, people attempt to hold the currencies they expect may appreciate. One effect of changes in EERs is that funds previously held in other currencies may be repatriated. Although such repatriation represents a once-and-for-all increase in foreign exchange receipts, it can potentially be used to finance some liberalization of imports. It is of interest to attempt to estimate the magnitude of the speculative flow in Turkey.

As indicated in Chapter II, the reliability of the balance-of-payments statistics in the 1950's left much to be desired. Official data can therefore provide only a rough approximation as to the size of the speculative flow and must be interpreted with care.

Recorded net private capital outflows were $29 million in 1956 and $61 million in 1957. By contrast, inflows of $73 million were recorded in 1958 and an additional $39 million is reported for the next two years (see Table I-6, above). It is probable that most of the 1958-to-1960 private capital inflow reflected the return of speculative funds. Since there were probably net capital outflows in the first eight months of 1958, the capital inflow over the last four months was very likely larger than $73 million, but there are no quarterly data available. Even accepting the $73 million estimate would indicate a reversal of $131 million between 1957 and 1958 in private capital flows, all of which represented a net improvement in the balance of payments.

Errors and omissions in the official balance-of-payments statistics continued to be negative until the end of 1959, although the largest negative figure (minus $97 million) was recorded in 1957. Although negative errors and omissions in 1958 might have been the outcome of a negative balance on unrecorded capital flows for the first eight months and a positive balance for the last four months, the fact that errors and omissions were still negative in 1959 suggests that something more systematic was wrong. Given the unreliability of the data, it is difficult to reach any firm conclusions, but it seems inadvisable to count the change in errors and omissions as part of the speculative reversal following devaluation.

Expectations. With the frequent changes in exchange taxes and export premia in the mid-1950's, it would be surprising had the August 1958 changes removed all expectations of future increases in EERs. There is some evidence that supports the hypothesis that many persons indeed anticipated further exchange-rate adjustments. Uncertainty about future premia probably lasted until *de jure* devaluation in 1960. Thus the EIU reported in early 1959 that:

In recent weeks, there have been many rumours in Turkish business circles that with the second global import quota, the premium rate for imports, now TL 9.02 = $1, would be adjusted to an average TL 12 = $1, with separate rates for specific categories of goods..."[18]

This uncertainty may account in part for the fact noted in Chapter III that initial applications for import licenses under the First Import Program totaled almost four times the amount allocated for that period. On the export side, it was reported that exporters continued holding stocks of some commodities in anticipation of further changes in the export premia.[19]

One indicator of expectations about future exchange rates is the price of gold. The price of gold coin, fairly symptomatic of the gold market's behavior, reached a peak of TL 128 per gram in 1958, a level not reattained until the late 1960's. Although expectations of future changes may have persisted, the disparity between prevailing and expected future exchange rates fell after 1958.

Interaction between exchange-rate changes and stabilization.   Given the relatively limited short-term response of foreign-exchange receipts to changes in export EERs, it is apparent that the primary impact of the Stabilization Program, at least initially, was the cessation of inflation. An interesting question, therefore, is whether inflation could have been equally effectively stopped had the Stabilization Program not contained provisions for EER changes.

Two separate factors must be considered. First, the large inflow of imports was a sizeable deflationary factor and would have been considerably less so had the 1957 import EERs remained in effect. Second, there is the consideration that exports would almost certainly have stagnated, if not declined further, had export EERs not been altered.

It seems incontrovertible that a sizeable increase in imports was a necessary precondition for substantially halting Turkey's inflation. Those imports were financed primarily by foreign credits and therefore could have taken place at the old EERs (had the creditor countries not insisted upon EER changes as a precondition for receipt of the foreign credits). Had imports increased at 1957 nominal import EERs, a much smaller fraction of the premium on import licenses would have been absorbed by the government. It has already been seen that the net revenues (which were less than the increase in payments for imports by reason of the increased premium payments to exports) from foreign trade taxes in 1959 were 2.4 per cent of national income, and that the additional domestic purchasing power absorbed by the altered import EERs was at least twice that amount.

The effects of tight money would have been substantially reduced had

18. EIU, *op. cit.* (Note 1, Chap. II), *No. 29*, February 1959, p. 5.
19. *Ibid.*, *No. 28*, November 1958, p. 3.

import EERs not been increased. While a contraction of the money supply of sufficient magnitude to reduce demand for imports via deflation might have similarly reduced the premium, the adverse consequences of a contraction of that magnitude would almost certainly have been unacceptable. In the context of inflationary expectations which existed in mid-1958, it seems reasonable to conclude that given the shift in monetary policy which actually occurred, failure to increase import EERs would have impaired if not eliminated Turkey's chances of transition from a high-inflation to a moderate-inflation country. Thus increases in import EERs were in this author's judgment an integral and necessary part of the program to achieve price stability, in that the economic costs of increasing import EERs were far less than would have been the costs of reducing the money supply by enough to absorb the premium on imports at the old EERs.

On the export side, it is not as obvious that altered EERs contributed significantly to reduction in the rate of inflation in the first several years after August 1958. First, there is the fact that the short-term export response was disappointing. Second, there is the obvious consideration that if Turkey (or any other country) could obtain imports without exports, it would be deflationary. Thus if Turkey from 1958 on could have had her actual level of imports with her 1958 level of exports, the net effect would have been deflationary as contrasted with the actual course of events. However, Turkey would have been unable to borrow more without increasing export EERs, as other countries were not willing to finance an import surplus of the implied size. Export-EER alterations were thought necessary to restore prospects of eventual export growth. Even if Turkey had received an initial foreign credit enabling the increase in imports, it would have been a once-and-for-all increase. The import flow would have had to be reduced once the initial credit was exhausted, with attendant inflationary pressures at that time.

Thus it seems reasonable to conclude that: (1) the increased flow of imports was an important factor in enabling the achievement of price stability; (2) altering import EERs, by absorbing domestic purchasing power, was at least as important a deflationary factor as the increased flow of imports; (3) since the imports were financed by foreign credits, altered export EERs were not essential to the attainment of price stability in the short run; but (4) alteration of export EERs was essential if the flow of imports was to be maintained over an extended period of time, which was necessary for continuation of price stability over the longer run.

III. *The Stabilization Program and the level of economic activity*

The years 1959 to 1962 were slow-growth years for the Turkish economy, and there is little doubt that recession was experienced over much of the period. In this section, the magnitude, timing and determinants of the level of economic activity over the period are examined.

The magnitude and timing of the recession

Data are woefully lacking for an adequate evaluation of the degree and timing of changes in the level of economic activity over the 1959-to-1962 period. Such data as are available suggest that the rate of growth leveled off in the first six to nine months after the August 1958 devaluation, and then increased rapidly. That was followed, however, by a sharp decline in the level of economic activity in the last half of 1960 and most of 1961.

The SIS estimates of national income at constant prices suggest overall growth rates of 3.8, 2.4, zero, and 6.4 per cent, respectively, for the years 1959 to 1962,[20] with income originating in manufacturing remaining constant over the three years 1959 to 1961. As indicated above, one factor accounting for the relatively slow growth rate over the period was undoubtedly the lackluster performance of the agricultural sector, from which income originating at constant prices actually declined.

There are few if any valid indicators of changes in the level of economic activity between quarters. Data on quarterly electric power and cement production reported by the EIU are given in Table IV-8 and indicate a slackening in the growth rate of power production and sharp fluctuations in cement production. The right–hand side of the Table gives the percentage change from the same quarter in the previous year. The power production data suggest that the two middle quarters of 1959 and the four quarters starting with the third quarter of 1960 were the periods of most pronounced slackening in growth, and also that the slackening was both longer and more pronounced in 1960–1961 than in 1959.

The figures of cement production show rather more marked changes. For cement, an import-substitute during the 1950's, production fell somewhat after the third quarter of 1958, rose rapidly from mid-1959 to mid-1960, and thereafter declined once again. The 1960–1961 decline is both steeper and of longer duration. Insofar as cement and power production can be taken as indicators of short-term changes in the level of economic activity, these data would suggest that the 1960–1961 recession was far more pronounced than that of 1959.

Annual production data tend to confirm this impression. As seen in Chapter I, real national income is estimated to have declined in 1961. Residential construction declined in 1959 and did not reattain its 1958 level until 1962.

---

20. See Table I-3, above.

Table IV-8

Quarterly power and cement production, 1956 to 1962

	Level of Production					Percentage Change from Previous Year				
	I	II	III	IV	Year	I	II	III	IV	Year
Power (million kwh)										
1956	524	494	496	536	2050	14	8	5	−2	6
1957	617	602	623	702	2544	18	22	26	31	24
1958	686	663	716	823	2888	11	10	15	17	14
1959	780	722	784	946	3232	14	9	9	15	12
1960	890	833	847	1011	3581	14	15	8	7	11
1961	947	863	940	1142	3892	6	4	11	13	9
1962	1095	1051	1108	1297	4551	16	22	18	13	17
Cement (thousands of metric tons)										
1956	188	356	320	396	1260	−18	19	16	41	19
1957	340	420	452	452	1664	81	18	41	14	32
1958	396	556	584	480	2016	16	32	29	6	21
1959	272	604	708	728	2312	−31	9	21	52	15
1960	452	768	748	752	2720	66	27	6	3	18
1961	352	760	848	748	2708	−22	−1	13	−1	−1
1962	504	848	888	848	3088	43	12	5	13	14

Sources: EIU, *op. cit.* (Note 1, Chap. II): *No. 18*, May 1956, p. 14; *No. 23*, August 1957, p. 13; *No. 27*, August 1958, p. 11; *No. 31*, August 1959, p. 11; *No. 35*, August 1960, p. 11; *No. 39*, August 1961, p. 10; *No. 43*, August 1962, p. 11; *No. 47*, September 1963, p. 14.

Other construction declined continuously from 1958 to 1961 and was well below its 1958 level in 1962. The textile industry apparently was also stagnant over the four-year period. Other industries generally show an increase in output in 1959, with stagnation or decline between 1960 and 1961.[21] The OECD interpretation was

> Manufacturing production was practically stagnant in 1958 but, under the impetus of renewed imports of raw materials and spare parts, made possible by the credits received in the framework of the 1958 Stabilization Programme, output rose by nearly 5 per cent in 1959. In 1960, the events leading up to, and immediately following, the revolution in May 1960 led to some hesitation on the part of producers and consumers which had a depressing effect on economic activity.[22]

It seems a reasonable conclusion that there were two separate recessions in Turkey. The first started with the devaluation and reached its nadir in the second quarter of 1959. Thereafter economic expansion resumed, especially in the last half of 1959 and the first few months of 1960. The second recession began in the summer of 1960, and reached its trough late in 1961. Since there was probably some slack in the economy in early 1960, the second recession was undoubtedly the more severe of the two, reflecting both a bigger downswing and a lower level of economic activity at the start of the decline. The greater magnitude of the downswing is evidenced both by the sharper and more widespread declines in production in different sectors of the economy and by the national income estimates for the period. The absence of quarterly data of course renders more precise measurement impossible.

Factors contributing to recession

Causes of the 1958—1959 slowdown. In the absence of data upon which more scientific tests could be based, any interpretation of the determinants of the level of economic activity within Turkey over the 1958-to-1962 period must of necessity be based on personal judgement. The 1958—1959 recession will be first considered.

It has already been seen (Table IV-3, above) that the shift in monetary policy was sharp and abrupt. Given its magnitude, the surprising thing is not that there was a recession but rather how mild the recession appears to have been. In this author's judgment the shift in monetary policy was responsible for the recession that did occur, and had it not been for some mitigating circumstances the monetary shift would have led to a deeper recession than was in fact realized. The increase in economic activity late in 1959 was

21. OECD, *Turkey, 1963*, p. 58; and OECD, *Turkey, 1961, op. cit.* (Note 42, Chap. III), p. 9.
22. *Ibid.*

attributable primarily to the abandonment of monetary stringency and the resulting change in expectations.

This view is consistent with Fry's estimates of the money supply-money income relationship and also with the apparent slowdown in construction activity. The really significant question is why the recession was so mild. Again, no quantitative answer can be given although several factors undoubtedly contributed. First, fiscal policy was expansionary: part of the reduction in investment (as reflected in the construction data) was probably offset by changes in government expenditures. Second, the shortage of imports prior to the second quarter of 1959 had retarded economic activity to some extent. In particular, a large influx of capital goods imports in 1959 and 1960 suggests that replacement demand for capital goods may have been relatively high. This demand probably offset part of the downward shift in private investment which would otherwise have occurred. Insofar as imports of capital goods required complementary domestic resources to complete the investment, the influx of imports was probably less depression-inducing than would otherwise have been the case.

Some observers have suggested in interviews that an additional factor contributing to the mildness of the first recession was the degree of wage and price flexibility in Turkey in the late 1950's and early 1960's. That is a difficult argument to assess. It is true that Turkish labor law at that time forbade strikes. However, there are no reliable data on either employment or wages with which to evaluate this argument. Of the 14 components of the price index which are available on a quarterly basis for the 1961-to-1962 period, eleven declined at least once, and many more frequently during the two-year interval,[23] which would suggest considerable flexibility.

Causes of the 1960–1962 recession. It is far more difficult to evaluate the factors contributing to the 1960–1962 recession than those for 1958–1959. As shown above, the available evidence indicates that the 1960–1962 recession was substantially more severe and protracted than its earlier counterpart. Yet as seen in Table IV-6 the simple model used to estimate aggregate excess demand shows that there was more expansionary stimulus to the Turkish economy in 1960 and 1961 than there had been in 1959.

Contemporary accounts attributed the recession to uncertainties following the May 1960 Revolution. Hoarding on the part of the peasants was particularly blamed for much of the difficulty:

> The economy at the moment is in the doldrums, and it looks as if the recovery will be both slow and painful. The root of the present trouble seems to be that the peasants are simply refraining from spending, with the result that business in the

23. Data from OECD, *Turkey, 1963, op. cit.* (Note 21), p. 59.

consumer goods sector has slackened off to such a degree that many of the big firms are living off their capital and cannot meet their wage bills, while the smaller firms are being forced to close down...[24]

The OECD view was similar:

The signs of a renewal of inflationary pressures and speculation, particularly after the vote in February 1960 on the 1960-61 budget at a greatly increased level of expenditure, were counteracted from the spring onwards by government policy to restrict the growth of public expenditure and by the spread of sales resistance and currency hoarding among the population, particularly the peasants. Consequently, demand for consumer goods, such as textiles, declined during part of the year...Hoarding of banknotes and, to a lesser extent, gold coins was a feature of 1960 and was the counterpart of the reluctance of consumers, particularly peasants, to buy...[25]

The available evidence on this hypothesis is mixed, however. The ratio of current GNP to the money supply, a crude indicator of the velocity of circulation, declined from an average of 8.84 in 1950–1954 to 7.59 in 1955–1957, rose to 8.85 in 1958 and 9.62 in 1959. Thereafter it fell to 9.27 in 1960 and 9.07 in 1961, rising to a peak of 10.16 in 1963. Then it gradually declined to 8.65 in 1969. One would expect a gradual decline in the income-money ratio as the Turkish economy becomes increasingly monetized. However, the data for the 1960-to-1962 period suggest a higher-than-average velocity of circulation, the opposite of that implied by the hoarding hypothesis.

If one inspects real consumption behavior over the period, there is a suggestion that consumption expenditures were somewhat below normal. If the percentage of consumption in GNP as given by SPO (Table I-1) is multiplied by real GNP, the resulting estimates of real consumption for the years 1958 to 1962 are:

Year	Consumption as a Per cent of GNP	Real GNP	Estimated Real Consumption
		(billions of TL at 1961 prices)	
1958	77	46.3	35.7
1959	77	48.1	37.0
1960	75	49.9	37.4
1961	74	49.1	36.3
1962	75	52.1	39.1

While these estimates are necessarily crude, they suggest that real consumption declined more than real income, which is consistent with the view that the recession resulted from the response to the political changes.

As seen in Table IV-3, the increase in the money supply was very small during 1960 and 1961. The behavior of the money supply undoubtedly contributed to the length and severity of the second recession. Indeed, the phe-

24. EIU, *op. cit.* (Note 1, Chap. II), *No. 37*, February 1961, p. 2.
25. OECD, *Turkey, 1961, op. cit.* (Note 42, Chap. III), p. 14.

nomenon from which it is tempting to draw conclusions is that the timing of the first and second recessions coincided almost exactly with changes in the rate of monetary expansion. The conclusion is highly plausible, and the behavior of the money supply was unquestionably important. What is not known, however, is whether during the 1960–1962 period the money supply remained stable as a matter of deliberate government policy or whether it remained stable in the absence of increasing demand for credit.[26]

There is no doubt that the Revolutionary government was committed to make the Stabilization Program work. Indeed, one of the reasons given for the takeover was that the NUC government could better carry out the Stabilization Program than had the Menderes government. The NUC substantially pared the budget submitted by the Menderes government. Rapid expansion of the money supply would not have been countenanced. Expectations based upon the commitment of the new government may well have contributed to recession. However, whether the actual behavior of the money supply was the result of passive adaptation to demand or of deliberate government policy is unknown.

The important question for present purposes is the degree to which the two recessions were related to the Stabilization Program. The picture in regard to the first recession is fairly clear: the abrupt shift in monetary policy and other deflationary pressures emanating from the Stabilization Program were the major factors in leading to it. That recession was very mild in relation to the sharp reversal in monetary policy. The rapid expansion in economic activity in the last part of 1959 and early 1960 is largely explained by the government's abandonment of the major monetary and fiscal elements of the program.

It is more difficult to say to what degree the second recession was linked to the Stabilization Program. Once expansionist policies had been resumed in 1959–1960, the shift back to the Stabilization Program undoubtedly led to a renewal of the recession. It is doubtful, however, whether the severity and intensity of the recession can be laid solely at the door of the resumption of the Stabilization Program. While the behavior of the money supply played a key role in prolonging and intensifying the second recession, that behavior may have been largely a passive response to money demand. Moreover, since the government could have expanded the money supply somewhat without imperiling price stability, part of the blame for the second recession must be attributed to the failure of the money supply to expand.

We conclude therefore that insofar as Turkey had to pay a cost in the form

---

26. The OECD declared that the commercial banks were in general highly liquid and that the demand for loans was "sluggish." OECD, *Turkey, 1961, op. cit.* (Note 42, Chap. III), p. 21.

of foregone output for the Stabilization Program, that cost lay primarily in the lower-than-average rate of growth in 1959 and 1960. The decline in real national income between 1960 and 1961 was neither necessary for the achievement of price stability nor a result of the Stabilization Program.

Short-run resource-allocational effects of the Stabilization Program. It has already been seen that the behavior of export earnings immediately after 1958 was disappointing. The longer-run results were much more satisfactory and are analyzed in Chapter VII. Here, focus is upon the short-run resource-allocational effects of the Stabilization Program. In the absence of detailed data, there are only three effects which deserve attention: (1) the composition of investment; (2) the behavior of construction; and (3) the productivity of factors of production.

The sharpest shift observable from annual data was that in the composition of investment. Table IV-9 gives the data.[27] By 1957 construction investment had increased to 76 per cent of total investment, with machinery and equipment down to 24 per cent. By 1960 construction investment (which fell in real terms) was 65 per cent of the total, while machinery and equipment had increased to 35 per cent. Real machinery and equipment investment increased fairly sharply. Imports of machinery and equipment virtually doubled between 1958 and 1959.

Simultaneously, the import content of machinery and equipment investment rose sharply after the Stabilization Program, while that of construction investment merely reattained its 1957 level. It was seen above that the machinery-and-equipment component of investment was hit much harder by import shortages in the mid-1950's than was construction. One effect of the Stabilization Program was to reverse the trend toward the increasing importance of construction investment.

The decline in relative importance of construction was, as just noted, accompanied by an absolute drop in construction activity in real terms. During the mid-1950's the increased share of construction had been accompanied by a drop in real machinery and equipment investment. A natural interpretation of this reversal is that the earlier import stringency had led to a non-optimal expansion in construction, which was counteracted with a reverse resource-allocational shift after the Stabilization Program. If there were bottlenecks limiting production in other sectors in the mid-1950's, the construction sector, relatively independent of imports, could have been the market into which resources flowed. If so, the easing of bottlenecks would have reversed the shift, thus leading to the downturn which actually occurred.

27. The data are not carried beyond 1960 because: (1) Gürtan's estimates terminate with that date, and (2) the TL value of imports changed after 1960, so that the import figures (in TL) are noncomparable. See, however, Table VIII-5, below.

Table IV-9

Investment composition and import composition of investment, 1957 to 1960

	1957	1958	1959	1960
A. (millions of TL, current prices)				
Construction investment				
Construction materials imports, c.i.f.	112	94	282	262
Domestic value of imports	324	261	528	505
Domestic materials	800	1289	1927	2043
Domestic value added	1800	2074	2159	2372
Total construction investment	2923	3624	4614	4921
Machinery and equipment investment				
Imports, c.i.f.	249	369	1061	1339
Domestic value of imports	628	894	1727	2115
Domestic goods	276	441	567	584
Total machinery and equipment	903	1335	2294	2699
Total Investment	3827	4960	6908	7620
B. (percentages)				
Composition of total investment				
Construction	76	73	67	65
Machinery and equipment	24	27	33	35
Imports (domestic value) to investment in:				
Construction	11	7	11	10
Machinery and equipment	70	67	75	78

Source: Same as Table II-10.

There is no way of testing this hypothesis with available data. The implicit deflators, calculated in the manner described in Table II-11, indicate a 14 per cent increase in the price of machinery and equipment from 1958 to 1960 compared with a 35 per cent increase in construction prices, thus reversing the increase in the relative domestic price of machinery and equipment of earlier years. To the extent that import liberalization accounted for the decrease in the relative domestic price of machinery and equipment, this would suggest that liberalization accounted for the change in investment composition.

The final resource-allocational effect is that on the productivity of resources. On this subject little evidence is available. Whatever changes did occur are obscured in the available annual data by the effects of recession. Contemporary observers however believed increased productivity to have been an important outcome of the Stabilization Program. The Industrial Development Bank of Turkey observed in its 1959 Annual Report:

Before application of the stabilization policy the limits of the industrial production of Turkey were determined by the existing industrial production capacity and especially by the possibility of supplying the need for raw materials, auxiliary materials and spare parts. During the year under review, however, the deciding factors in determining the volume of industrial production were especially the volume of demand and the ability of the industrial and commercial community to finance inventory formation...The fact that the sellers' market, which was evident before the inflation turned into a buyers' market and especially the competition of imported goods brought the question of quality improvement and lower cost of production to the foreground.[28]

The OECD placed more emphasis upon the facts that "the serious underutilization of productive capacity that had developed during the previous eighteen months was thereby corrected," and that imports of spare parts and raw materials enabled increases in output from existing capacity.[29]

All these resource-allocational effects undoubtedly emanated from the Stabilization Program and the increased flow of imports. But it is impossible to quantify even approximately the degree to which the productivity of resources was thereby increased.

IV. The optimality of the Stabilization Program

Although the costs in the form of recession of the Stabilization Program have been discussed above, the benefits in the form of an altered long-run growth path have not been. It is nonetheless still possible at this stage to ask the question: if Turkey was going to undergo such a program, could the package have been improved upon?

Evaluation is difficult because there were three separate goals of the program: (1) achieving internal price stability; (2) eliminating some undesirable effects of government policies upon the domestic economy; and (3) altering the nature of the foreign trade regime. Imposition of bank credit and government budgetary ceilings and the raising of SEE prices were primarily aimed at achievement of the first goal. Removal of the government's price control regulations was designed to undo some of the damage inflicted by government policy upon the domestic economy.[30] Altered EERs, debt rescheduling and the import liberalization financed primarily by foreign credits were in-

28. *Annual Statement,* Industrial Development Bank of Turkey, 1959, pp. 27–8.
29. OECD, *Turkey, 1961, op. cit.* (Note 42, Chap. III), p. 6.
30. Removal of the price control laws and price ceilings could have been undertaken at any date independent of the Stabilization Program. While their removal was highly desirable, it was not an integral part of the Stabilization Program, although failure to remove them at that date would have resulted in continued domestic black markets and other difficulties. They are therefore not considered further within this section.

tended to affect the nature of the foreign trade regime. An additional compli-
cation to analysis of the optimality of the program is the fact that the
monetary-fiscal components of the Stabilization Program were abandoned in
1959 and resumed in 1960 along with other policy changes undertaken by
the NUC government.

An important question is whether the dual objectives of price stability and
an altered trade regime should have been sought in the same package. Ob-
siously, unless the rate of inflation had been substantially reduced, no long-
run alteration in the trade regime could have been anticipated on the basis of
a fixed exchange rate. Thus if price stability had not been sought, some form
of flexible exchange rate would have been the only means whereby lasting
changes in the trade regime could have been effected. Speculation about the
pros and cons of continued inflation, with a constant real EER, seems futile
because the political consensus in Turkey seems to have been that the evils of
inflation far outweighed its benefits. The price-stability goal of the program
seems to have been more important politically than trade-regime alterations.

However, even though price stability was achieved, by setting a fixed
exchange rate Turkey left herself vulnerable to renewed foreign-exchange
shortages and overvaluation, as indeed occurred in the 1960's. Although
inflation was mild contrasted with that in the 1950's, the adoption of a fixed
exchange rate precluded use of the exchange rate as a means of attaining
continuous external balance. It can be argued that the costs of such preclusion might have been acceptably low had Turkey devalued again in the mid-
1960's. But the very fact of a fixed exchange rate created political pressures
making that difficult to do. Thus the effects of exchange-rate overvaluation in
the late 1960's can in a sense be blamed partly on the non-optimality of the
1958 Stabilization Program as it failed to include a mechanism for continued
exchange-rate adjustment.

Although such a mechanism would have been preferable, the Stabilization
Program did include a fixed exchange rate. To evaluate the program, therefore, the goals of price stability and an altered trade regime at a fixed-
exchange rate are accepted as the basis for evaluation for the remainder of
this section. We consider the optimality of each component of the package in
turn.

Little comment is required on the adjustment of SEE prices. Of course
SEE prices could have been increased without the remaining components of
the Stabilization Program, and one inflationary pressure in the situation
would have been reduced. However, given that SEE prices had not previously
been increased, a source of finance for the SEEs other than Central Bank
credits had to be found if inflation was to be reduced or eliminated at the
time the Stabilization Program was adopted. Given the situation of the SEEs
in August 1958, raising SEE prices was essential for the attainment of price
stability.

The other anti-inflation components of the Stabilization Program, budgetary and credit ceilings, require slightly more evaluation. There can be no doubt that the ceilings were stringent enough to bring inflation to a halt and to that extent, were eminently successful. If the ceilings were nonoptimal, it was in the other direction: the reversal of inflationary forces may have been too strong. Not only did monetary expansion cease, but other factors were deflationary: the doubling of import EERs led to a sizeable absorption of purchasing power and the requirement that funds be deposited at the time of import-license applications enhanced the effect. Thus with a constant money supply the demand for money to finance imports shifted upward and the volume of imports increased sharply without an off-setting increase in exports.

The best argument for the necessity of the zero-increase ceilings — which implied constancy of the money supply — is that any permitted rate of expansion might have led the administration to evade the ceilings, or at least to carry out whatever expansion was permitted at the earliest possible date. Then too there is the consideration that some readjustment, accompanied by recession, may have been essential after the near-runaway inflation of the preceding years.

On the opposite side, some permitted expansion in the money supply might have made the effects of the Stabilization Program less unpalatable to the government. If that had happened the renewed inflationary impetus of late 1959 might either have been smaller or nonexistent, thus rendering the recession of 1960—1962 less prolonged and severe or even reversing it.[31] Whether a smaller rate of increase in ceilings in 1958—1959 would have been sufficient to induce the government to maintain the Stabilization Program is integrally related to the question raised above as to the intentions of the government when it accepted the Stabilization Program, and no definitive answer is possible.

The Menderes government probably did not fully accept the goals of the Stabilization Program. If that is so, zero-increase ceilings were probably necessary if the Stabilization Program was to be imposed by foreign creditors and to achieve price stability. However, had there been a government in Turkey which fully accepted the goals of the program, it would probably have been preferable to expand the money supply by 1 or 2 per cent per quarter during the year after the adoption of the Stabilization Program. In view of

31. In view of the developments in 1960—1962, it is evident *ex-post* that monetary and fiscal policy ought to have been more expansionist. But insofar as the reasons for that recession lay in the downward shift in the consumption function and other phenomena associated with the change in government, the problem was one of general monetary-fiscal policy and did not have its origins in the Stabilization Program.

the deflationary effects of imports and their financing and the potential growth rate of the Turkish economy (as well as its increasing monetization), such an increase would still have represented a major shift from past monetary behavior and enabled the cessation of inflation with a smaller impact on the level of economic activity. That conclusion is highly debatable, however, and other interpretations are equally valid.

Turning now to the components of the Stabilization Program aimed at altering the trade regime, there can be little doubt about debt rescheduling. It really was necessary years before it occurred. It is virtually impossible to perform the mental experiment of rationalizing the trade regime in any way in 1958 without debt rescheduling.

The desirability of the foreign credits received by Turkey is another matter about which it would appear that conclusions can be reached. As seen above, it is doubtful if the reversal of speculative capital flows exceeded $100 million. Even though that response by itself would have enabled a temporary increase in the volume of imports, the increase would have been relatively minor in view of the level to which imports had fallen. Moreover, if import liberalization was to be achieved, credits were probably necessary to provide confidence that the liberalization could be continued for more than a very short period.

In the economic conditions of 1958 the marginal product of additional imports far exceeded the interest rate on foreign credits. Some of the credits, especially in late 1959 and early 1960, were probably unwisely used when the government renewed its expansionist policies, and under ideal management the credits would not have been fully expended by mid-1960. However, the large increase in imports which the credits permitted was important in several ways: (1) it virtually wiped out the premia associated with import licenses; (2) it was a significant factor in contributing to the deflationary pressure; and (3) insofar as it enabled increased capacity utilization and other ways of better utilizing existing resources, the direct productivity of the imports was very high.

The final component of the program, alteration of EERs, raises two questions. (1) To what extent were the new EERs optimal? (2) Could the way they were altered have been improved upon? The first question is the more difficult. As seen above, the nominal devaluation was 220 per cent. But even the effective devaluation (the change in the average PLD-EER) was 75 per cent, which is large by any standard. Certainly a smaller effective devaluation would have been less desirable: (1) as seen above, for many export commodities the new EER simply raised the lira equivalent of the international price to the domestic price; (2) available evidence suggests that a change of smaller magnitude would have left premia on import licenses for many commodities; and (3) given that the exchange rate was to be fixed, some allowance had to be made for the increase in the domestic price level that would follow the raising of SEE prices and other adjustments.

A larger effective devaluation might have been more desirable. A maximum would have been about TL 12 = $1.[32] We have seen that the actual alteration in EERs did not substantially affect the degree of discrimination against exports, as the ratio of the import EER to the export EER in late 1959 was almost the same as in the pre-1958 years. Partly, however, that was attributable to the implicit taxes on traditional exports and any larger effective devaluation would probably have necessitated higher export taxes on some of those commodities. Given the responsiveness of non-traditional exports and minerals to increases in real export EERs (see Chapter VII below), a somewhat greater devaluation could have increased the export response, perhaps sizeably. On balance, the actual EER changes were probably on the lower bound of the right order of magnitude, being sufficient to wipe out premia but not enough to offset discrimination against exports.

The manner in which the exchange rates were altered is another question. Exchange premia were altered so that the devaluation was *de facto* rather than *de jure*, and if Turkey was committed to a fixed exchange rate, the technique used to alter the rates led to a greater likelihood of one-sided speculation about future EERs than *de jure* devaluation would have. Moreover, while taxes on traditional agricultural exports are defensible on a variety of grounds, their use was certainly unwarranted for minerals, and even for other commodities their use led to speculative inventory withholding. Part of the disappointing performance of exports in the first years after 1958 was the result of the manner in which export EERs were changed.

The Stabilization Program must be judged on balance to have been a successful one. Its objectives and achievements were in a sense negative, in that the black markets, inflation, dislocations and import premia of the mid-1950's were largely wiped out. Whether from the situation of 1958 it would have been desirable to attempt more, i.e., to alter incentives drastically in favor of exports, is a matter of judgment. But evaluated in terms of its own goals, the Stabilization Program accomplished a great deal and the costs, in terms of domestic recession, appear to have been held within reasonable bounds.

32. This is the rate suggested by Okyar and Iren in Columbia School of Law, *op. cit.* (Note 14, Chap. I), p. 406.

Part Three

The Anatomy of the Regime in the 1960's

CHAPTER V

Planning and the trade regime in the 1960's

Whereas the Turkish foreign trade regime of the 1950's was largely independent of domestic objectives, that of the 1960's was closely interrelated with domestic economic policy. As indicated above, there was no conscious planning or coordination of economic policies in the 1950's, and economic goals did not closely interrelate with the nature of the trade regime except insofar as the expenditures undertaken were contributory to balance-of-payments stringency. Indeed, the lack of planning and coordination of economic policy was one of the criticisms leveled at the Menderes government in its last years and after its downfall.

When a new constitution was formulated under the Revolutionary government in 1960–1961, one of the key changes was that planning for social and economic development was defined as the duty of the State:

> Economic and social life shall be regulated in a manner consistent with justice, and the principle of full employment, with the objective of assuring for everyone a standard of living befitting human dignity.
>
> It is the duty of the State to encourage economic, social and cultural development by democratic processes and for this purpose to enhance national savings, to give priority to those investments which promote public welfare, and to draw up development projects. [1]

Further, the State Planning Organization was established as the planning organ within the constitution. Under the heading, "Development projects and the State Planning Organization," Article 129 reads:

> Economic, social and cultural development is based on a plan. Development is carried out according to this plan.
>
> The organization and functions of the State Planning Organization, the principles to be observed in the preparation and execution, and application and revision of the plan, and the measures designed to prevent changes tending to impair the unity of the plan, shall be regulated by special legislation. [2]

Thus development plans became central to government economic policy in the 1960's. Through the plans and their implementation, the foreign trade regime was much more closely related to other economic policies than it had been in the 1950's.

1. *Constitution of the Turkish Republic,* translated for the Committee of National Unity (Ankara), 1961, Article 41.
2. *Ibid.,* official translation, Article 129.

The purpose of this chapter is to examine the nature and evolution of economic policy in the 1960's and to evaluate the relationship between trade policy and domestic economic goals. The first section contains a brief description of the planning mechanism and its relationship to the execution of policy. The second section outlines the major characteristics of the Plans and examines the degree to which Plan targets were achieved. The third section is concerned with the role of the foreign trade sector within the Plans. Finally, the role of foreign aid, foreign indebtedness, and private foreign capital in the 1960's is considered.

I. The planning mechanism and execution of economic policy

The State Planning Organization (SPO), as stated in the constitution, is the government body assigned the responsibility for Plan preparation in Turkey. It is also given the duty of following up on the implementation of the Plan and advising on current economic policy. With one exception, the SPO does not have operational responsibilities and is advisory in nature.[3] But when the SPO's recommendations are adopted by the cabinet, as they must be before they become official policy, their impact is greater than that of most advisory organizations.

Since the inception of planning in the early 1960's, the SPO has drawn up two Plans: the First Five Year Plan (FFYP) covering 1963 to 1967, and the Second Five Year Plan (SFYP) covering 1968 to 1972.[4] The SPO prepares an Annual Program each year in which detailed annual plans are presented and the progress of the economy is monitored.

Although the SPO is not responsible for the implementation of policy except for matters coming under the purview of the Investment and Export Promotion Department,[5] it is empowered to monitor the actions of other government agencies with a view to determining the degree to which plan goals are carried out. In the late 1960's, for example, applications for licenses

---

3. The SPO itself has two closely interrelated bodies: the High Planning Council and the Central Planning Organization. The Central Planning Organization had three departments until 1967: Economic Planning, Social Planning, and Coordination. In 1967, a fourth department was added: Investment and Export Promotion. That department is operational, concerned with implementing export rebates and export and investment incentives. The Central Planning Organization is headed by an Undersecretary, who reports directly to the Prime Minister. The High Planning Council consists of the Prime Minister, the Undersecretary heading up the SPO, the heads of the original three Departments comprising the CPO, and three other members of the Prime Minister's cabinet.
4. At the time of writing, the Third Five Year Plan for 1973 to 1977 is being prepared.
5. Even these implementation functions were removed in 1971.

for capital goods imports had to be checked by the SPO to ensure that the proposed investments were consistent with the Plan before the license was approved. This power in itself gives the SPO considerable influence in economic policy.

II. The five year plans: goals and achievements

Overall goals

Prior to the FFYP a document, "Plan Objectives and Strategy," was prepared which laid forth the development goals to be achieved over the subsequent fifteen years. Although that document is relatively sparse in quantitative details, it set the two objectives which have remained fundamental in the FFYP and SFYP: (1) a target rate of growth of 7 per cent per annum and (2) continued development at the seven-per-cent rate without further foreign assistance, by 1977 at the latest:

> ...Turkey may reach a stage before the end of fifteen years and probably at the end of the second five years when she can continue her development efforts without being in need of exceptional external finance such as foreign aid.[6]

Foreign aid was counted upon to cover the gaps between investment and savings projected for the early years of the fifteen-year period.

The basic reasoning underlying the "Objectives and Strategy" was a straightforward Harrod—Domar capital-output-investment relationship. Although a few specific numbers were given for 1977, they were more in the nature of forecasts than of policy prescriptions. For example, the share of agriculture in GNP was expected to decline from 43.8 per cent in 1962 to 29.4 per cent in 1977, with increases in the shares of services and manufacturing from 12.8 and 9.8 to 26.3 and 15.6 per cent, respectively. An indication of the policies by which these forecasts or targets would be achieved was left to the Plans and the Annual Programs.

Although both Plans accepted the dual targets of the "Objectives and Strategy," there were differences between them in the choice of instruments to meet particular targets and also in the emphasis given to the public sector. As indicated in Chapter I, the 1965 elections brought the Justice Party under Prime Minister Demirel to power, whereas the Republican Peoples' Party (RPP) had ruled in a coalition government prior to that time. The FFYP, formulated under the RPP coalition government, placed slightly greater emphasis upon direct intervention in the economy and on the public sector's

6. FFYP, *op. cit.* (Note 20, Chap. I), p. 37.

role in development than did the SFYP. The SFYP by contrast leaned more toward the use of price incentives and reliance upon the private sector. Thus the FFYP declared:

> The private sector alone cannot realize all the conditions necessary for economic development. Economic development will be attained by accelerating investment and making basic changes in the structure and methods of production. These changes cannot be accomplished solely by entrepreneurs who adjust their activities according to market conditions... It is neither necessary nor possible to draw a definite line between the activities of the public and private sectors. The State should be authorized to regulate economic activities with a view to create the conditions required for the attainment of the objectives of the plan. The State should be in the vanguard of progress in the industrial sectors... [7]

Contrast this with the statements in the SFYP:

> The static and dynamic efficiency of the economy will be achieved mainly through the market mechanism...The State will insure price stability and minimise the deficiencies of the price mechanism through indirect means such as tax, credit, money and foreign trade policies...The policies to be adopted in the Second Plan period will enable the private sector to take over the development of manufacturing industry in the long run... [8]

Thus although both Plans accepted the fact of SEEs, the emphasis upon price incentives was greater in the SFYP period, while that upon direct government investments was greater in the FFYP.

The FFYP. [9]   Investment in the FFYP was to rise from 14.8 per cent of GNP to 18.3 per cent of GNP. This increase was to be accomplished by a rise in the average savings rate from 12.8 to 14.8 per cent and an increase in external financing from 2 to 3.5 per cent of GNP, with an estimated incremental capital-output ratio of 2.6. Government revenues were to increase from 24.7 to 27.5 per cent of GNP, while expenditures were to increase by the same amount, thereby implying that the increase in government investments would be financed by additional savings (including the surpluses of SEEs), and that private investment increases would be offset by increases in private savings.

Planned sectoral investments and income originating in those sectors in 1961 are given in Table V-1. Although the sector classifications are not entirely comparable, it is evident that heavy emphasis was placed upon infrastructure investments. As indicated in the FFYP,

---

7. FFYP, *op. cit.* (Note 20, Chap. I), p. 54.
8. *Ibid.* (Note 21, Chap. I), pp. 111−2.
9. Data given in this paragraph are drawn from *ibid.* (Note 20, Chap. I), pp. 104−117.

Table V-1
Share of sectors in national income and planned investments (percent)

Sector	Share of 1961 National Income	Share of Planned Investments
Agriculture	41.4	17.7
Mining	1.7	5.4
Manufacturing	14.8	16.9
Energy	0.6	8.6
Transport and communication	7.2	13.7
Services	21.4	6.6
Housing		20.3
Education	5.4	7.1
Other	8.0	3.7

Note: In the national income estimate, housing services are included in "Dwelling ownership."

Source: FFYP, *op. cit.* (Note 20, Chap. I), pp. 14 and 121, and *National Income, 1938, 1948–1970, Pub. No. 625,* SIS (Ankara), 1971. See Table I-3.

Sustained development implies that the production of basic goods and services should be geared to meet long-term demand. Due importance has therefore been attached to basic infrastructure investments (e.g., transport, energy, education, etc.).[10]

Other principles upon which sectoral development plans were based included: the prevention of bottlenecks, maintenance of output of raw materials and intermediate goods production in line with final demands, and the promotion

...of sectors producing export goods and those producing import-replacing goods. In view of the foreign exchange difficulties likely to occur during the plan period importance was attached both to expanding exports and promoting import-substitution.[11]

As will be seen below, considerably greater quantitative importance was placed upon import-substitution than upon export promotion.

Although the goals of the FFYP were not entirely realized, Turkish economic growth over the 1963-to-1967 period was satisfactory from any standpoint and considerably better than it had been in earlier years. Real GNP, which had been expected to be 40 per cent above the 1962 level, was 38 per cent above it in 1967. Agricultural production fell somewhat short of the target, increasing 17 per cent contrasted with a projected 24 per cent increase. Manufacturing production rose 63 per cent compared to the 73 per cent targeted increase. Output of the service sector grew somewhat more rapidly than planned.[12]

10. *Ibid.*, p. 117.
11. *Ibid.*
12. Targets: *Ibid.*; actual rates calculated from national income statistics.

Real investment increased considerably less rapidly than expected, especially in the early years of the FFYP. Private sector investments grew more rapidly than had been anticipated, whereas public sector investments fell short of plan targets. A higher fraction of private sector investment was directed toward residential construction and a lower fraction toward industry than had been anticipated.

Perhaps the biggest discrepancy between domestic targets and achievements at the macro-level was the failure of public revenues to keep pace with their expected increase. The rate of price increase remained relatively low despite that, averaging about 5 per cent annually.

The balance of payments proved even more of a bottleneck than had been forecast, despite an export performance better than that projected in the Plan. Export projections had been based upon estimated export earnings of $325 million in 1962, whereas actual exports were $381 million. Targeted exports for 1967 were $457 million contrasted with actual 1967 exports of $523 million. Moreover, an unanticipated source of foreign exchange earnings emerged during the FFYP period: the remittances of Turkish workers in Western Europe. Whereas Turkish workers in Western Europe had been relatively few in number in the early 1960's, their numbers rapidly increased in the mid-1960's. Thus workers' remittances were less than $1 million in 1963, $9 million in 1964, $70 million in 1965, $115 million in 1966 and $93 million in 1967.

Actual imports were very close to the planned level of $3,200 million for the five-year period as a whole, but their timing differed somewhat. Imports in 1963 were $688 million compared to the FFYP figure of $567 million;[13] while in later years imports were smaller than the projected figures except for 1966. Moreover, imports were kept near their projected level by greater stringency in the import regime than had been planned or desired.

The big discrepancy between balance-of-payments projections and realizations was in foreign aid. The planners had estimated a PL 480[14] inflow of $290 million over the five years, whereas it was actually $166 million. Consortium credits had been put at $1,573 million, whereas they actually were

13. Workers' remittances are recorded as an invisible current account transaction in Turkish balance-of-payments statistics, and are therefore reflected as one of the components in the difference between the trade balance and the current account balance. Workers' remittances were $273 million in 1970. See Appendix C. The 1963 import figure reflected, *inter alia,* huge imports in connection with the construction of the Ereǧli Steel Mill.

14. Under the Agricultural Trade Development and Assistance Act of 1954 (Public Law 480) and its subsequent amendments, the United States exports agricultural commodities and provides financing on terms more favorable than commercially-available rates, including loans in soft-currency.

$827 million. Thus the current account deficit proved to be smaller than anticipated by $485 million, but that was offset by a shortfall on capital account of $746 million in consortium aid and $124 million in PL 480. The shortfall in aid resulted from a variety of factors, to be discussed below, but the initial expectations on the part of the Turkish planners were probably overoptimistic under the best of circumstances.[15]

The SFYP. The SFYP covered the period 1968 to 1972. The basic goal of a 7 per cent growth rate in GNP was retained, as was the aim of reduced dependence upon foreign aid which was to fall from 2 per cent of GNP to 1.7 per cent of GNP over the five-year period. Emphasis upon industrial development intensified somewhat, as industrial output was projected to increase at an average rate of 12 per cent per annum. Private investment was expected to increase at an annual rate of 12.5 per cent, and public investment at 10 per cent, with private consumption increasing 5.1 per cent annually.[16] As indicated above, the shift in the share of investment and other changes in emphasis reflected the philosophies of the different ruling parties between the early and late 1960's. Other features of the SFYP were similar to the FFYP: a continued shift away from agriculture and toward industry, with a view to changing the structure of the Turkish economy; increased savings in the public and private sectors to raise the rate of capital formation; and emphasis upon import-substitution and export promotion for non-traditional goods.

At the time of writing, data are not available to compare the SFYP goals with achievements. During the first three years of the Plan, GNP increased by 6.7, 6.3 and 5.7 per cent (provisional SPO estimates) evaluated at 1965 prices, while agricultural production grew by only 1.9, 0.0 and 1.1 per cent, respectively. Failure to attain the overall target growth rate thus primarily reflects a relatively slow increase in agricultural output. In view of the relatively poor performance of agriculture over the first three years, the growth rates of other sectors were probably generally higher than the Plan targets.

In broad outline, the two Turkish Five Year Plans have been quite similar and have corresponded closely with actual government development policy. We turn now to an examination of the role assigned to the trade and payments regime within the two Plans.

15. For a more detailed evaluation of the FFYP, see: Wayne Snyder, "Turkish Economic Developments: the First Five Year Plan," *Journal of Development Studies*, Oct. 1969; Baran Tuncer, "Development of the Turkish Economy: An Experience in Planning," *Yale Economic Growth Center, Paper No. 112*, May 1971; and the SFYP, *op. cit.* (Note 21, Chap. I).

16. SFYP, *op. cit.* (Note 21, Chap. I), pp. 74 ff.

III. The role of foreign trade in the Plans

In the macroeconomic projections underlying each Plan, the chief role assigned to the foreign trade sector was that of meeting a projected savings-investment gap, especially in the early years of the fifteen-year horizon period. Beyond that, both Plans assigned three functions to the foreign trade sector: (1) to enable the importation of capital goods and inputs needed for the growth of the industrial sector through growth of foreign-exchange earnings; (2) to provide a mechanism (in coordination with other policy instruments) to foster the growth of new industries; and (3) to diversify the structure of Turkey's exports and to aim at rapid growth of industrial exports as one means of altering the structure of the Turkish economy.

Significantly, neither the Plans nor the "Objectives and Strategy" focussed upon Turkey's projected Common Market membership, despite the fact that the initial protocols for Associate Membership were already in preparation and signed in 1963. The only statement in the FFYP was that:

> The economic implications for Turkey of the Common Market, which were taken into account while preparing the plan, will also be carefully estimated in preparing annual programs.[17]

The SFYP was even less specific on the implications of the Common Market, referring to the need to "strengthen the Turkish economy to the desired level" during the preparatory period then in progress.[18]

Investment and raw materials requirements

In addition to the need for foreign assistance to meet the projected investment-savings gap, both Plans viewed growth in foreign-exchange earnings as necessary in order to provide a means of importing capital and intermediate goods required to attain the Plan objectives:

> A considerable increase in imports is to be expected as a result of development efforts. New investments and the maintenance of existing establishments will create a demand for capital goods...[19]

It was stressed in the FFYP that one criterion upon which new industries should be evaluated was their expected utilization of domestic, as contrasted with imported, raw materials in an effort to reduce the demand for imports. Moreover, criteria for import licensing were to be:

> Import programs will give priority to imports which contribute to the realization of

17. FFYP, *op. cit.* (Note 20, Chap. I), p. 460.
18. SFYP, *op. cit.* (Note 21, Chap. I), pp. 136–7.
19. FFYP, *op. cit.* (Note 20, Chap. I), p. 459.

plan targets. The import requirement of the industries concerned will be examined and fulfilled in the light of their implication for the plan.[20]

Again,

> The scarce foreign exchange resources will be directed to the economic activities which are directly related to economic development. The import of luxury goods will be avoided.[21]

This emphasis was borne out in the composition of imports projected under the two Plans. Table V-2 gives the actual composition of imports for the period 1961 to 1970 and the planned projections for the period 1963 to 1970. The planned figures are those given in the FFYP and SFYP. These figures were subsequently revised in the Annual Programs as evidence on actual imports emerged. In the FFYP the raw material requirements generated by the Plan were substantially underestimated. Imports of investment goods fell short of their planned levels due largely to the shortfall in investment. As Table V-2 indicates, SPO projections for the First Plan period were that raw materials imports would be less than investment goods imports in the early years of the Plan, reaching about equal magnitude in later years. In every year of both Plans to date, in fact, raw material imports have exceeded investment goods imports by sizeable margins. The planners took this into

20. *Ibid.*, p. 471.
21. SFYP, *op. cit.* (Note 21, Chap. I), p. 132.

Table V-2
Actual and planned import composition, 1961 to 1970 (millions of U.S. dollars)

	Investment Goods		Raw Materials		Consumer Goods	
	Planned	Actual	Planned	Actual	Planned	Actual
1961	–	185	–	208	–	116
1962	–	228	–	292	–	102
1963	241	254	235	332	71	102
1964	274	197	261	296	76	44
1965	296	197	300	313	85	62
1966	333	289	325	365	87	64
1967	363	260	363	380	94	45
1968	332	325	418	394	85	45
1969	350	251	460	431	90	119
1970	370	215	510	583	95	137

Note: PL 480 imports are not included.
Source: FFYP, *op. cit.* (Note 20, Chap. I) and SFYP, *op. cit.* (Note 21, Chap. I), for planned figures; and SPO, *Annual Programs* for actual figures.

account in formulating the SFYP, as can be seen by inspection of the altered relationship between investment goods and raw materials imports planned for the years 1968 to 1970. Even that was not enough, as imports of raw materials and intermediate goods generally exceeded Plan levels, while imports of investment goods fell far short of them.

Part of the strategy of the FFYP was to reduce drastically the level of consumer goods imports. In 1964, after the surge of imports in 1963, consumer goods imports were cut even below planned levels. The figures given for consumer goods imports are, as pointed out by SPO, misleading because of smuggling:

> During the last years of the [first] plan period, however, consumer goods of luxury nature which had been smuggled into the country began to appear in the markets of large cities. Therefore, the actual volume of consumer goods imports was higher than that indicated in the balance of payments.[22]

Fostering the growth of new industries

The second way in which the trade and payments regime was regarded as an instrument of development policy pertained to the industrialization objective. The strategy for industrialization was oriented toward import-substitution. To conserve scarce foreign exchange, it was declared in the FFYP that the list of items eligible for importation should be determined on

> ...the principle that goods of which internal production is quantitatively and qualitatively sufficient to meet internal requirements at fair prices should not be included...[23]

Similarly, goods for which there was some domestic production would be subject to import quotas and luxury goods would not be importable.[24] The SFYP reiterated the policy.[25]

Both Plans stressed the need for insuring that the choice of import-substitution industries should be based upon their long-term competitiveness, and that import restrictions and protection accorded to those industries should be of a temporary nature.

> Keeping in mind the necessity for the protection of newly established or developing branches of industry, imports will be restricted over a period of time specified in advance, when deemed necessary, and the possibility of importing goods outside the system will be avoided. This protection, however, will not be extended to the

22. *Ibid.,* p. 29.
23. FFYP, *op. cit.* (Note 20, Chap. I), p. 471.
24. SFYP, *op. cit.* (Note 21, Chap. I), p. 578.
25. *Ibid.,* p. 134.

branches of industry which are not likely to gain a competitive position in the future.[26]

In practice, there have been virtually no instances of reentering an item on the import lists once domestic production has been established. Even with regard to new industries, the long-term competitiveness criterion does not appear to have become operational. In the shipbuilding industry, for example, it was determined that "significant exports are out of the question in this sector,"[27] owing to "too much competition from foreign markets."[28] However, the principle enunciated for that industry was that "the demand for shipbuilding will be met domestically."[29] Similarly, many assembly industries were started during the FFYP. For a typical item — farm machinery — the SFYP stated that:

> ...the percentage of locally manufactured components of agricultural equipment and machinery will be increased on a large scale and, to that end, the development of those branches of industry which will manufacture domestic inputs will be encouraged.[30]

Objectives for other assembly industries were similar.

There can be little doubt that the two Five Year Plans were heavily biased toward import-substitution. In the FFYP balance-of-payments, considerations (aside from the estimated required foreign aid) were evaluated in the final chapter of the document, almost as an afterthought. Little stress was placed upon the need for growth of foreign exchange earnings. Requirements for foreign aid were estimated by the macroeconomic investment-savings gap projections.

By the time the SFYP was formulated, balance-of-payments difficulties were highly visible and the import-substitution strategy was intensified. The SFYP repeatedly noted the relatively high prices of Turkish manufactured products:

> The price of industrial goods produced in Turkey is usually higher than world prices. This question constitutes a problem which requires study and which must be solved quickly.[31]

Interestingly, one of the causes of these high prices was said to be "protective customs policies."[32] Yet other causes were the "excessively high import duties on investment goods, the high cost of basic industrial raw materials and

26. *Ibid.,* p. 134, see also p. 404.
27. *Ibid.,* p. 578.
28. *Ibid.,* p. 575.
29. *Ibid.,* p. 574.
30. *Ibid.,* p. 540.
31. *Ibid.,* p. 403.
32. *Ibid.*

services to the manufactures ..."[33] Quantitative restrictions were not mentioned. Concern with high costs was a factor motivating the altered treatment of duties upon imported capital equipment in 1968.

Thus in the FFYP, import-substitution was adopted primarily as a means of attaining the industrialization goal. By the time of the SFYP the motivation for stress upon import-substitution had shifted and stemmed much more from balance-of-payments difficulties.

Export goals and achievements

Both Plans revealed considerable pessimism about the prospects for increased foreign exchange earnings from traditional exports:

> Demand elasticity for Turkey's export goods is low. The studies made on this subject show that the elasticity of the main export products, mohair excepted, is near zero. It follows from this that no significant development can be expected in export of these goods and that a change in the composition of Turkey's exports is essential.[34]

33. *Ibid.*, p. 403.
34. FFYP, *op. cit.* (Note 20, Chap. I), p. 465. Inconsistently, the next paragraph went on to state that, "Since 1958, ... the wholesale price indices of foodstuffs and raw materials have shown a steady increase ... On the other hand, raw material prices have been falling on international markets. This, together with the rise in internal prices has impaired Turkey's competitive position on export markets as a primary product exporter." No action was recommended, however.

Table V-3
Export projections, 1963 to 1972, and actual exports, 1963 to 1970 (millions of dollars)

	Agricultural Exports		Mineral Exports		Industrial Exports		Total	
	Planned	Actual	Planned	Actual	Planned	Actual	Planned	Actual
1963	270	284	22	11	56	73	348	368
1964	291	312	22	15	61	84	374	411
1965	298	352	24	21	71	90	394	464
1966	329	379	24	23	73	88	427	491
1967	348	426	26	21	82	76	510	522
1968	409	405	31	26	100	66	540	496
1969	427	402	34	35	114	99	575	537
1970	445	n.a.	37	n.a.	133	n.a.	615	588
1971	465	–	40	–	160	–	665	–
1972	481	–	42	–	197	–	720	–

Sources: FFYP, *op. cit.* (Note 20, Chap. I), p. 469; SFYP, *op. cit.* (Note 21, Chap. I), pp. 32 and 100; *Yılı Programı 1971*, pp. 35–36.

The SFYP similarly stressed the need for structural change in the composition of export earnings, pointing out that,

> The export of agricultural products...which is more or less limited by foreign demand is estimated to register an increase of only 22.9 per cent [over the SFYP period] despite efforts to be made in this field. [35]

Insofar as either Plan stressed exports at all, the emphasis was on the development of new export products. In general, export performance was better than planned in the FFYP and below Plan levels from 1968 until 1970. This can be seen in Table V-3, where export projections and actual exports are contrasted. Throughout the FFYP agricultural exports did far better than had been anticipated in the Plan, whereas mineral exports did somewhat worse, particularly in the early years of the Plan period. The SPO classification of industrial exports is somewhat broader than that generally used, including most copper exports in particular. Until 1966 industrial exports grew more rapidly than had been anticipated in the Plan, but thereafter earnings from those commodities did noticeably less well than expectations.

Examination of the determinants of exports is left to Chapter VII, below. Here it need only be noted that the Plans placed relatively little reliance upon the development of traditional exports, and viewed export strategy as conforming to the overall strategy of industrialization of the Turkish economy. Even for industrialization, however, far less emphasis was placed upon export possibilities than upon import-substitution.

IV. The capital account and the foreign trade regime

As noted above, an important goal was the attainment of "self-sufficiency," the ability to continue 7 per cent growth without net receipts of foreign aid, by 1977. This goal was to be achieved through receipt of high levels of aid in the early years of the fifteen-year period which, it was expected, would induce a rising marginal and average domestic savings ratio. Aid in the early years was deemed essential, not only to make up the savings-investment gap, but also because of Turkey's relatively heavy debt-servicing obligations. Without aid in the early Plan years, debt servicing would have drained off sizeable resources from the development effort.

Debt service

Turkish debt-servicing obligations were thus integrally related to aid flows

35. SFYP, *op. cit.* (Note 21, Chap. I), p. 100.

Table V-4
Actual and planned capital flows, 1963 and 1964 (millions of U.S. dollars)

	1963	1964
Gross inflow		
planned	434	407
actual	216	187
Debt servicing		
planned	−148	−99
actual	−146	−141
Net inflow		
planned	286	308
actual	70	46

Sources: FFYP, *op. cit.* (Note 20, Chap. I), p. 467 and John White, *Pledged to Development,* Overseas Development Institute (London), 1967, p. 148.

and must be considered jointly with them. It was the conjunction of rapidly increasing import demands associated with the implementation of the FFYP and the failure of the net capital inflow to reach Plan levels that marked the transition to Phase II in 1964.

Table V-4 gives the basic data for 1963 and 1964. As can be seen, the gross capital inflow was less than half the planned level in each year. Given debt-servicing obligations, however, the result was a net inflow of one-quarter and one-sixth the planned amounts in the two years. Turkey's scheduled debt-servicing obligations for 1965 through 1967 were even greater than the 1963 and 1964 amounts. It became apparent that balance-of-payments difficulties would become massive and that the FFYP would be infeasible in the absence of some additional assistance. Finally, further debt rescheduling was agreed upon in the early months of 1965.[36]

The schedule of debt service in effect prior to rescheduling and the revised schedule are given in Table V-5. As can be seen, relief from debt obligations amounted to over $100 million in 1965, and an additional $115 million over the next two years. Additional loans, extended after April 1965, and loans that did not come under the purview of the revision led to heavier actual debt repayments and interest charges than were indicated in the revised amortization schedule. However, debt-servicing obligations in the 1966–1968 period were considerably less than had been anticipated, with a rising debt burden toward the end of the period. Even so, actual debt repayments plus interest amounted to $935 million over the period 1965 to 1970, compared to total export earnings of $3,098 million.[37] Thus by any standard, debt repayment

36. White, *op. cit.* (Table V-4), p. 149.
37. See Table V-6.

Table V-5
Debt service schedules, December 1964 and April 1965 (millions of dollars)

	Schedule as of 12/64			Schedule as of 4/65		
	Principal	Interest	Total	Principal	Interest	Total
1965	185	31	216	87	27	114
1966	143	28	172	94	76	101
1967	120	24	144	73	25	98
1968	82	26	108	91	31	122
1969	70	20	90	91	24	115
1970	55	15	70	88	21	109
1971–2014	597	163	760	709	166	874
Total	1253	307	1559	1232	300	1532

Source: White, *op. cit.* (Table V-4).

and interest charges constituted a sizeable burden upon the Turkish economy.

The debt repayment schedule makes the interpretation of Turkish foreign aid figures difficult, since the lenders considered that debt postponement constituted part of their net aid contribution. Thus it makes a considerable difference whether net or gross aid figures are used.

Aid flows [38]

Turkey's history of chaotic indebtedness led to considerable reluctance, particularly on the part of the Western European countries, to extend development aid at the outset of the FFYP. There appear to have been doubts about Turkey's ability to carry out a rational debt management program, much less embark upon a systematic development effort. Only the United States among the potential donors exhibited any enthusiasm for the FFYP, whereas the Turks had assumed that sizeable foreign assistance would be forthcoming in the early stages.

For a variety of reasons, among which the history of past indebtedness was prominent, a Consortium under the aegis of the OECD was formed to coordinate the contributions of all donors to the Turkish development effort. The Consortium started operations in 1963 coincident with the start of the FFYP. Throughout the period during which the plans have been in operation, the preponderance of foreign aid has come through the Consortium.

Turkey's relationship with the Consortium was by no means an easy one,

38. The material in this section on the development of the Consortium is drawn from White, *op. cit.* (Table V-4).

Table V-6
Gross and net aid flows, 1963 to 1970 (millions of U.S. dollars)

	1963	1964	1965	1966	1967	1968	1969	1970
Aid flows								
Consortium credits	169	145	169	175	161	145	106	217
Project credits	97	36	57	56	60	127	174	179
Commodity imports	94	32	29	17			41	83
Total flow	360	213	255	260	221	272	321	479
Debt service								
Interest	31	31	30	29	34	34	44	47
Principal	114	110	161	119	99	72	108	158
Total	145	141	191	148	133	106	152	205
Net Aid	215	72	64	112	88	166	169	274

Note: All data are from Turkish balance-of-payments figures.
Sources: 1963–1965, SFYP, *op. cit.* (Note 21, Chap. I), p. 28.
          1966–1967, *Yılı Programı 1968,* p. 59.
          1968–1970, *Monthly Economic Indicators,* Ministry of Finance, January 1972, p. 51.

especially in the early years. A major difficulty before 1965 was that Consortium aid to Turkey was made on an annual basis. From the planners' viewpoint, the fact that Consortium decisions as to aid in any given year were made in that year was worse yet. Thus the Turkish planners generally drew up their Annual Programs in a state of uncertainty about the amount of aid likely to be pledged.[39]

Data on the amount of gross and net aid received by Turkey are given in Table V-6. The high figure for 1963 reflects aid associated with the construction of the Ereğli Steel Mill and other once-and-for-all items. Similarly, the high 1970 figure reflects Consortium credits extended at the time of devaluation in August 1970. Only in those two years did net aid exceed 2 per cent of GNP. Project credits increased from $36 million to $179 million over the 1964-to-1970 period. Consortium credits by contrast reached a peak of $175 million in 1966 and declined to $106 million in 1969, rising again however to $217 million in 1970, under the special conditions just noted. PL 480 aid was not received in 1967 and 1968, and was important only in 1963 and 1970.

The steady increase in project aid indicates one of the reasons for both the slow pace of aid-giving in the early years of the FFYP and the lower-than-planned real investment levels: there simply were insufficient investment pro-

39. The problem was especially severe in 1964 when no pledges for 1964 were made until the very end of the year.

jects drawn up and ready to be implemented. While this factor was not the only reason for the shortfall of aid and investment levels in the early years of the FFYP, the SPO itself attributed the lagging investment performance in part to a lack of detailed projects.[40] Part of the increased volume of project credits in later years undoubtedly resulted from the government efforts early in the FFYP to improve project preparation.

Private foreign capital

Throughout the 1950's and 1960's the Turkish government attempted to attract private foreign capital. One of the aims of the 1958 Stabilization Program was to improve conditions so that private capital inflows might increase markedly. Also, while a goal of the fifteen-year perspective plan was to eliminate dependence on official capital, it was stated that private capital inflows would be welcome and relied upon even after 1977.

Despite official policy to encourage it, private foreign capital has not been a major factor in Turkey's foreign exchange receipts and balance-of-payments experience.[41] The total net private capital inflow from 1963 to 1969 was $51 million and there was a net outflow in all but two of those years.[42] Thus private foreign investment has played a very small role in Turkey's balance of payments or growth over the years, unlike official capital flows.

V. Relationship of trade and development policy

The intent of the planners at the outset of the FFYP was to use the foreign trade regime as an instrument of policy to help achieve Turkey's development goals. In that sense it was intended that the foreign trade regime be permissive in enabling the implementation of development policy. The FFYP emphasized import-substitution as a component of development policy, although the emphasis was qualified by recognition of the need for economic efficiency. Relatively little attention was devoted to ways and means of promoting exports, in part because the import demands projected by the Plan were expected to be covered by anticipated export earnings and aid flows.

A variety of factors soon altered the situation. Although foreign exchange

---

40. SFYP, *op. cit.* (Note 21, Chap. I), p. 15.
41. The one exception was private foreign investment in petroleum, which was sizeable in the late 1950's. The petroleum investments were encouraged by special legislation and not by the general law covering private foreign investment.
42. See Table I-6.

earnings exceeded expectations, import demands under the import regime as it was at the outset would have greatly exceeded available foreign exchange resources. Imports over the FFYP as a whole were held very close to projections, but the attainment of target levels was accomplished because of increased stringency of the import regime rather than because the initial projections were accurate.

Even if net aid had been forthcoming at somewhere near planned levels, some change in the import regime would have been required to restrict imports to levels consistent with foreign exchange availability. However, if net aid had reached planned levels, the import regime in 1964 and after would have considerably less restrictive than it was. The heightened exchange controls of the 1960's were in response to balance-of-payments difficulties rather than development goals, and emphasis upon import-substitution increased, not to attain the industrialization targets, but to offset unanticipated foreign exchange shortfalls. Hence a trade regime which started as permissive of development policy was quickly transformed into one which dictated the shape of development policy. While import-substitution would have been emphasized in any event, it is probable that more attention would have been given to "competitiveness" and to the criteria for selecting industries discussed in the Plans had it not been for the foreign exchange shortage which emerged as an impediment to the implementation of the development Plans. Development policy therefore quickly became shaped by the apparent dictates of the balance-of-payments rather than the converse.

CHAPTER VI

The import regime of the 1960's

As was seen in Chapter III, the import procedures and regulations existing prior to August 1958 were rescinded with the announcement of the Stabilization Program. Import Programs became the major regulatory instrument governing imports thereafter, and have remained so since then.

The purpose of this chapter is to examine the detailed workings of the Turkish import regime: the criteria used and intent of government officials in deciding upon the Import Programs, the procedures and regulations governing imports of various kinds, and the way in which the import regime functioned. Each of these three aspects forms the subject of a section below. But before turning to these subjects in detail, it will be useful to have an overview of the import regime, the subject of the first section.

I. The Import Programs and lists

Each Import Program has contained a statement of the procedures to be followed in applying for import licenses and a list of regulations governing importation. In addition each Program has itemized the commodities eligible for importation under each of two lists: the Liberalized List and the Quota List. Commodities not enumerated on either list are not legally importable.[1] Although there is no such thing, it is convenient to refer to commodities not included on an import list as being on the "Prohibited List."

The first Import Program was promulgated in September 1958, the second in February 1959, and the third in August 1959. Thereafter, Import Programs were issued semi-annually: from 1961 on they were issued early in January and July of each year. In 1969 import regulations and the Liberalized List were made valid for the full year so that only the Quota List was issued under the midyear Import Program.[2] The Import Programs have been consecutively numbered. Thus "Import Program No. 26" was issued in January 1971.[3]

1. Some items are designated by use, as, for example, "Articles required in connection with the production and assembly of tractors."
2. In 1971, the Quota List was also made valid for the full year. However, quotas were to be used semi-annually.
3. Each Import Program was published in the *Official Gazette* and reprinted by the Turkish Chambers of Commerce and Industry and the Union of Chambers. The titles have differed somewhat from time to time.

Quota List imports were generally about two-thirds the value of Liberalized List imports, though the ratio varied from time to time (see Table VI-3 below). The determination as to whether an item was eligible for importation at all, and if so on which list, was basic to the import regime. The Import Programs for Quota List items indicated the dollar value of licenses to be issued, and the procedures for allocation of those amounts then began. They involved determination of the amount of the quota going to the public and private sectors, and allocation of import licenses to individual private sector producers.

The value of imports of Liberalized List items was not indicated, as the intent was that licenses should be issued freely to all applicants. It will be seen below that this did not always happen, for a variety of reasons.

Between two-thirds and three-quarters of all imports entered directly under the Liberalized List and the Quota List. Other categories of imports were "Bilateral Agreement Imports" and "Self-Financed Imports." A Bilateral Quota List, published separately from the Import Program, enumerated the items eligible for importation from countries with which Turkey had bilateral trade agreements. Despite the fact that the list was published separately, the Liberalized List—Quota List distinction of the Import Program was still dominant, in that no item was eligible for importation under a bilateral agreement that was not included on one of the lists in the Import Program.

"Self-Financed Imports" were chiefly capital goods imported in connection with investments made under project aid. They were almost entirely for investments within the public sector and thus were government imports. Other "Self-Financed Imports" included PL 480 shipments and various miscellaneous items.

The key decisions made in formulating the Import Programs were: (1) the determination of which items were eligible for importation; (2) the designation of which eligible items should be on each list; and (3) the value of licenses to be allocated in each quota category. In addition, several other aspects of the Import Programs were important. The height of guarantee deposit requirements against license applications for items on each list was announced, and the period for which licenses were to be valid, the procedures to be followed in the event of delay and other administrative aspects of the system were spelled out.

In the latter part of the 1960's an additional feature assumed increasing importance: many categories of eligible imports on both lists became subject to "Ministerial approval." Enumeration on a list was no longer sufficient to insure importation of those items: approval from the designated Ministry had to be obtained first. It will be seen below that the requirement of Ministerial approval gave the government greatly increased control over the detailed allocation of import licenses.

II. The formulation of Import Programs

As indicated above, the Import Programs became the basic instrument in determining the import regime in 1958. The Import Programs retained their function when the SPO was organized, although the process by which they were formulated was altered as SPO assumed a larger role in their determination. Reference in what follows is to the period since 1962 when the Import Programs have been formulated in conjunction with the Plans and the Annual Programs.

There are many stages in the formulation of the Import Programs, and virtually all of them involve formal and informal consultations among many government ministries. There are almost no public records from these consultations, and the substance of the procedures probably varies with the fortunes and political influence of various cabinet ministers and other parties in the negotiating process. Thus any description of the formulation of the programs will fail to capture the degree to which political and subjective factors influence the process and in addition will make the procedures appear to be more cut-and-dried than they in fact are.

With that important caveat in mind, four stages of the process of formulating the Import Program can be distinguished: (1) the SPO projects import "requirements"; (2) those requirements are allocated globally among lists and financing sources; (3) a determination is made of which imported commodities are to be on each list; and (4) negotiations are carried out to determine the value of each Quota List item. Bearing in mind that these stages are not sequential and that the process really contains a fair amount of iteration, we consider each of the stages in turn.[4]

SPO projections of import requirements

The SPO starts by estimating import requirements by end-use: for consumption goods, investment goods and raw materials. These estimates are based upon the anticipated volume of investment (for investment-goods imports) and industrial production (for raw materials and intermediate goods). Consumption imports are projected primarily on the basis of past levels. Once these projections are established, the estimated amount of incremental import-substitution production in each category is subtracted from the totals, thus yielding estimates of net import requirements by end-use category. The value of "Self-Financed Imports" is then estimated. PL 480 imports are sub-

---

4. Except as otherwise indicated, the information contained in this section is based upon numerous interviews with persons associated with the process of formulating the Import Programs.

tracted from consumption-goods import requirements, and imports financed by project credits are subtracted from investment-goods import requirements. The resulting figures are taken as the control totals which the Import Program must satisfy.

Some iteration is involved even at this stage, since the value of imports projected under the Import Program must be reconciled with expected foreign-exchange availability. The totals in both this and the next stage are adjusted and recomputed to conform with foreign-exchange considerations. The Central Bank provides estimates of the amount of foreign exchange it expects to be available to pay for imports. However, since the SPO estimates the expected availability of foreign exchange from program aid and has some latitude in estimating the likely magnitude of imports financed by project credits, the Central Bank's estimates are not the sole determinant of the global total for the Import Program.

Allocation of end-use requirements among the import lists

The important operational decision is the value of imports to be permitted under the Quota List. It would appear in practice that this figure is initially determined as a residual, and later subject to iteration: (1) Liberalized List imports are projected on the basis of past trends, since (in principle) they are determined by market forces and hence presumably cannot be controlled (but see below, Section III); (2) the value of imports under Bilateral Agreements is generally stipulated in the agreements themselves and is taken as a datum; (3) the sum of imports under the Liberalized List and Bilateral List is then subtracted from total estimated end-use requirements (as reconciled with foreign-exchange availability) to yield the total value of imports to be allotted to quota categories. However, when estimates of Quota List import values become available after negotiations over the value of Quota List items, the estimate for the value of Liberalized List items is generally modified, as is the Quota List figure.

It will be seen below that the import projections by end-use have often differed from actual imports.[5] By contrast, imports by list as indicated in the Import Programs have generally been very close to the actuals. Since the lists are what is actually controlled, it is not surprising that projections of the lists agree much more closely with the actual results than do end-use projections. What should be noted is that the list totals have little significance for development goals. Thus the SPO's decision as to the value of Quota List imports does not give it effective control over end-use categories.

5. See below, Tables VI-2 and VI-3.

Determination of commodity composition of lists

Of major significance is the decision as to the commodities eligible for importation and their assignment to an import list. SPO generally sets the criteria for determining the lists, and decisions to alter the lists are made by the relevant ministries in consultation with the SPO. Usually an item appearing on a given list remains on that list until there is a reason for change; thus decisions are made at the margin, and commodities seldom jump back and forth between lists.

At the outset of the FFYP, the SPO set the criterion for inclusion on the Liberalized List:

> Goods of which internal production partly covers internal needs will not be included in liberalization lists and if already included, will be taken out... Import programs will give priority to imports which contribute to the realization of plan targets. The import requirements of the industries concerned will be examined and fulfilled in the light of their implications for the plan.[6]

Thus the Liberalized List was designed to encompass those commodities whose importation was deemed necessary for achievement of the development plan targets when domestic productive capacity was unavailable. The Quota List was designed to be more protective and restrictive, covering commodities of which there was some domestic production or which were deemed less essential to development, as in the case of most consumer goods. Thus vitamins and antibiotics were included on the Liberalized List, whereas coffee, cocoa and most other consumer goods were included on the Quota List.

The criterion for removing or transferring a commodity from a list gradually became centered upon domestic production considerations. Thus when domestic production of an item on the Liberalized List started, the producer appealed for the transfer of the commodity. The good was then transferred to the Quota List if it was determined that the new producer's capacity would be inadequate to meet domestic demand, or entirely removed from the list of eligible imports if the additional productive capacity was thought sufficient. Once domestic production had started, of course, producer pressure to delete an item from eligibility for importation was persistent.

In the Annual Programs prepared by the SPO, projected domestic production and demand figures are given for various sectors of the economy, as are export figures. Import projections are derived as a residual in the case of domestically produced goods, and from input-output coefficients for non-produced inputs. Those import projections cannot often be translated directly into the lists: for commodities on the Liberalized List, no values are

6. FFYP, *op. cit.* (Note 20, Chap. I), p. 471.

assigned to individual items; for commodities on the Quota List, the SPO figures are directly influential only if the import is used by just one sector.[7]

SPO's projections are nonetheless clearly a dominant element in determining the Import Program, even though the Annual Program figures are not precise guides. SPO's influence is generally acknowledged to be considerable; and it is undoubtedly in the Cabinet-level deliberations as well as the interministerial negotiations at lower levels that SPO officials are able to transform their Annual Program estimates into Import Program decisions.

Questions were asked in interviews with SPO officials as to how import values for individual commodities were estimated by SPO. The responses indicated that the basic mechanism was incremental projections: past import-output and import-investment relationships were applied to the projected increases in output and/or investment to yield import estimates.

In response to the suggestion that if all imports so estimated were exactly realized and all production targets met such projections would be self-fulfilling in perpetuity and the coefficients constant, officials answered that "shortages" did arise and that they quickly became aware of them. It was stated that in such instances the next Annual Program would take these shortages into account. When asked whether checks were ever made on differential disparities between landed cost and domestic selling prices of imports, SPO officials stated that such checks had not been made, although the magnitude of the disparities was generally known. It appeared on the basis of these responses that the basic projection technique was really a "materials balances" approach, and that price signals yielded by the economy were generally ignored.

The Import Program for the Liberalized List items is complete when the contents of the list are determined. The list itself contains several qualifications. It is specified for some Liberalized List items that permission of a particular Ministry is required before an import license application can be made. Some items are also subject to source-restrictions as, for example, goods eligible for importation only with AID funds.

The determination of Bilateral List imports is made essentially on the basis of which goods eligible for importation appear to be available from bilateral-agreement countries. The critical decisions for the Quota List are the value of quotas for each individual quota category.

Negotiations over the Quota List

Although the Annual Programs prepared by SPO indicate the value of imports expected by end-use category, by list and by sector, preparation of

---

7. H. Lubell, D. Mathieson, R. Smith and B. Viragh, *The Turkish Import Regime,* AID (Ankara), April 1968.

the Import Programs in conformity with the Annual Programs is the responsibility of the Ministry of Commerce. The process of determining the value of each quota item is complex and is conducted under the aegis of the Commerce Ministry, with SPO, the Central Bank, the Ministry of Finance, other government agencies and the Union of Chambers of Commerce and Industry taking part.

The Union of Chambers is a semi-official body to which all private sector firms having ten or more employees must belong. The Union represents the interests of its members in negotiations over quota values, while the Ministry of Finance represents the public sector enterprises. The Union and the Finance Ministry consult with their respective constituents prior to negotiations over specific quota values. Thus when quota-list negotiations take place the Union has consulted with its members and has received responses from them as to their expected import requirements.

There are two types of quotas, commodity-specific and user-specific. Commodity-specific quotas, such as electric motors of less than 60 horsepower, are further allocated between industrialists and importers. Industrialists are those using the quota-good in their own production process. Imports under licenses granted to industrialists cannot legally be resold. By contrast, importers are those who import for the purpose of resale without processing. Each quota value is subdivided into the amount to be allocated to industrialists and the amount for importers.

User-specific quotas are of two general types: (1) those covering the import needs of particular types of assemblers and manufacturers; and (2) investment-goods quotas. In the first category a quota is set aside for the importation of goods required in the production process. Firms operating under these quotas are subject to domestic content requirements. Two investment-goods quotas are set: (1) for private sector investments, and (2) for public sector investments. Goods imported under these quotas naturally require SPO approval to insure that the proposed investments are in conformity with plan objectives. For investment goods imported under those quotas, therefore, SPO has considerable influence over the direction of investment.[8]

The Import Program

As indicated at the outset, the stages discussed above take place simulta-

---

8. Many forms of machinery and equipment have individual quotas, so that the investment-goods quotas do not cover all investment goods. However, by the late 1960's SPO had power to grant duty-exemptions and other incentives to capital-goods imports when the purpose of the investment conformed with the Plan. Thus SPO could effectively influence virtually all investments. See Appendix A for an estimate of the value of the duty exemptions.

neously and considerable iteration is involved. The Import Program, when it emerges, consists of: (1) regulations and procedures for applying for import licenses; (2) regulations surrounding the use of import licenses and the clearing of goods through customs; (3) the Liberalized List (broken into two lists in recent years, with different guarantee deposit rates being the only distinction between the two), including an enumeration of goods on the List, an item-by-item specification of Ministerial permission requirements, if any, and indication for each item whether there are restrictions on the source of foreign exchange to be used for financing imports; and (4) the Quota List, indicating the value of licenses to be issued in each quota category, and its breakdown into industrialists' and importers' shares.

Once the Import Program is issued, persons wishing to import Liberalized List goods can, after obtaining Ministerial approval where necessary, apply to the Central Bank for an import license. Persons wishing to import a Quota List item begin the process of obtaining an allocation, to be described below. We turn now to the procedures and regulations governing the two types of imports. The functioning of the system, and the degree to which the Import Programs were realized, is then considered in Section IV.

III. Import procedures

Procedures for obtaining imports vary depending upon the list in which a good is included, the restrictions upon importation indicated in the list, and whether the would-be importer is in the public or private sector. This section focuses upon the procedures for private sector firms. Generally speaking, public sector quota allocations are administered by the Ministry of Finance. Public sector imports are not subject to guarantee deposit requirements except for AID-financed imports, and private sector spokesmen claim that generally the SEEs have a far simpler time obtaining their imports than do private sector firms.[9] No hard evidence is available upon this point, however. An effort was made to determine the fraction of all imports going to the public sector, but available data were not sufficient to enable an estimate.

Procedures for Liberalized List items are generally far simpler than for Quota List items, and are therefore considered first. Even at their simplest, however, import procedures are complex. The accompanying chart summarizes the procedures, and may be a useful reference throughout this section.

---

9. In the Import Programs, special quotas are set aside for "Emergency Requirements of SEEs" and "Emergency Requirements of Private Sector Enterprises." The SEE quotas have generally been twice those of private sector firms, despite the fact that the share of each in total production is about equal.

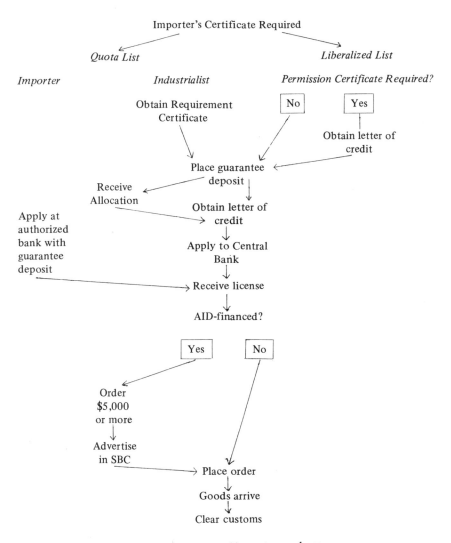

Fig. 3. Summary of import procedures.

The reader can refer to Tables A-11 to A-14 to gain an idea of which goods were in various categories.

Procedures for obtaining imports under the Liberalized List

As indicated above, some items on the Liberalized List require Ministerial approval prior to receipt of an import license. Others are eligible for importation only with AID funds. Special procedures are required for these goods. We first discuss the license allocations for those Liberalized List items which are not restricted in either way. Thereafter, the additional steps associated with AID financing or Ministerial approval are reviewed.

Unrestricted Liberalized List goods. Generally speaking, anyone having a "legitimate reason" to import a Liberalized List good can do so by following the procedures outlined here. First, no one is eligible to receive an import license unless he has an "Importer's Certificate." Such a Certificate is obtained from the local Chamber relevant for the importer's purpose: manufacturing firms are licensed by the Chamber of Industries whereas wholesalers are licensed by the Chamber of Commerce.[10] The Chambers' purpose in licensing is to establish that the applicant is a *bona fide* producer or wholesaler. The Importer's Certificate does not entitle the holder to select any item on the import list. Rather, it is restricted to the range of items relevant to the holder's business. The holder with such a Certificate is eligible to apply for any relevant item from any list.

Interviews with officials from the Chambers and with individual importers yielded the impression that obtaining an Importer's Certificate is straightforward and entails neither high costs nor long delays. Once an individual or firm holds such a Certificate, it is good for an indefinite period unless the holder is found guilty of violation of any import regulations. Thus it is a once-and-for-all procedure. However, the fact that Importer's Certificates are restricted to a given class of commodities implies that an individual importer cannot shift his imports around in response to demand shifts without an amendment to his Certificate. Thus if the domestic price of a given commodity rises sharply relative to landed cost, some wholesalers are ineligible to import it and may continue importing lower-profit items to which they are entitled while having their Certificates altered.

Once a new Import Program is announced, all individuals and firms holding Importer's Certificates valid for commodities on the Liberalized List can make application at any time for an import license (permit) from the Central Bank.[11] The applicant must give the description of the goods he wishes to import, the quantity of each item and the unit price. The applicant files his application, along with a guarantee deposit made at the local bank and then

10. Manufacturers and others importing only for their own use can use alternate procedures if they wish. In 1971 the Ministry of Commerce assumed responsibility for the issuance of Importer's Certificates.
11. Recall that Ministerial approval requirements and AID-financed imports are not yet being considered.

transferred to the Central Bank. The guarantee deposit rates for various categories of goods and at various points in time are given in Table A-8. The Central Bank then issues import permits in the amount applied for to the applicants, on a first-come first-served basis as foreign exchange is available. Generally speaking the fall and winter of each year are the peak export months, with delays in issuing licenses consequently tending to be shorter than during the late summer months. In addition to seasonal factors in export earnings, the general stringency of the foreign-exchange market can influence the delay encountered in receiving import permits. Thus in the early 1960's delays tended to be fairly short, but their average duration increased as the foreign-exchange situation became tighter.

It should be noted that despite the Annual Program figure for Liberalized List imports, licenses are actually issued for Liberalized List imports as foreign exchange becomes available. Thus any errors in forecasting foreign-exchange availability are compensated for by lengthening or shortening the delay in issuing an import license. Hence in the late 1960's when the excess demand for licenses was increasing rapidly, firms wishing to import Liberalized List goods made their applications early, and Liberalized List status did not assure would-be importers that they could import these goods. Also, the Central Bank generally refused to accept new applications in the last part of an Import Program period to prevent speculation against the new import lists.

Once received, an import permit is valid for six months unless an additional delay is required for manufacture to specifications, in which case it can be extended. In principle, if the import permit is not used within six months it is void, and 10 per cent of the initial guarantee deposit is forfeited. However, government officials and businessmen alike claimed in interviews that renewal of unused import permits was fairly automatic. Thus, at the cost of having resources tied up in guarantee deposits, individuals could "speculate" against the disappearance of a commodity from later Liberalized Lists. Some government officials interviewed claimed that the practice of speculating in import licenses, even if that speculation took place over a period of several years, was commonplace.[12] Indeed, a license once issued constitutes a valid claim against foreign exchange. Government officials complained that the practice of speculative holding of import licenses made new regulations difficult to enforce, particularly when a commodity was removed from the list of eligible imports.

12. With the very high guarantee deposits in the latter part of the 1960's, it is difficult to imagine that speculation was terribly great. However, it is conceivable that individuals held import permits from earlier periods, when guarantee deposits were considerably lower. Of course individual speculators would still have incurred the risk that the license would be invalidated, as per the law.

All Liberalized List imports must be financed under letters of credit. Estimates of the cost of letters of credit have ranged from 1.5 to 10 per cent of the c.i.f. value of the goods. (It should be noted that these costs have not been included in the EER calculations given below.) Once the import permit and letter of credit are in hand, the importer can place his order. The last step is clearing customs. In general, the customs' role is two-fold: (1) to ascertain that the imported items conform in every respect to the description on the import permit; and (2) to collect the duties and surcharges associated with importation.

The process of checking that the goods conform with those described on the import permit has been the subject of complaint at various periods. The consignment was supposed to conform not only in physical description but also in total volume and price to the amount on the import permit. Businessmen have cited in interviews instances where they had been able to obtain orders more cheaply than anticipated. Such a discrepancy was as difficult to clear as one in which the price had been underestimated. Of course one obvious purpose of the customs check is to insure that goods on the prohibited list are not imported clandestinely, either as unnecessary components of larger units, or in other disguised forms. Interviewees occasionally volunteered that they had imported an item to obtain only one component which itself was not legally importable. It is doubtful, however, whether such a practice was widespread.

The collection of duties and surcharges is straightforward, as far as available information indicates. One point should be noted, however. Importing was such a profitable activity that importers were frequently eligible for favored interest rates from the banks and for special classes of credit.[13] The availability of this credit ended at the point where goods cleared customs. Thus it was not infrequent for an importer to keep his goods in customs for considerable periods, since financing was provided through importers' credits. Although the cost to the importer was sizeable, it was less so than holding the goods, once through customs, since duties and surcharges raised the carrying cost of the goods by a high percentage.

Thus licensing procedures are virtually automatic for Liberalized List imports not subject to restriction. The chief difficulties have been with the high guarantee deposit requirements, and with uncertainty about delays in issuance of licenses. When adequate foreign exchange was available, goods on the Liberalized List were generally importable without great difficulty or high costs.

13. Fry, *op. cit.* (Note 30, Chap. II), p. 139.

Liberalized List imports subject to permission. When the approval of a government agency is required prior to issuance of an import license, an additional step is added to the licensing procedure. A "Permission Certificate" has to be obtained from the specified agency. Once such a Certificate is obtained, the other formalities follow the same lines as an unrestricted Liberalized List commodity.

Generally speaking, the intent of the Permission Certificate requirement is to restrict imports. Delays in obtaining Permission Certificates can occasionally be considerable, sometimes spilling over into an Import Program where the item is no longer eligible for importation. In most cases the effect of the additional certificate requirement is simply to lengthen the delay prior to obtaining a license. Sometimes would-be importers are told that the item they seek is available domestically. In those instances it is incumbent upon the applicant either to obtain letters from domestic producers stating they can not provide the item to the right specifications, or to purchase from a domestic source. Apparently the sort of difficulties associated with these stipulations varies considerably from one manufacturing sector to the next.

AID-financed Liberalized List goods.   Some Liberalized List goods were designated as "AID-only" and others as "partly-AID."[14] Liberalized List items designated "AID-only" could be imported only with AID funds subject to the restrictions on those funds. "Partly-AID" designations meant that the item could be purchased from the United States with AID funds or from other countries with free foreign exchange. Use of non-AID foreign exchange to purchase goods from the United States under "partly-AID" designations was not permitted.[15] Thus once a particular tranche of program aid was exhausted, importers' applications for permits for AID-financed imports were delayed until new AID funds became available. On rare occasions importers could file a new application designating an alternative source of supply, and receive their import license sooner than by awaiting approval of their AID-financed import application.[16]

AID-financed imports were subject to special formalities. First, U.S. Government regulations were that the minimum size shipment under AID financ-

---

14. The procedure changed late in the 1960's as program aid became relatively less important and as dollars received under AID were utilized early in the Import Program periods. For most of the 1960's AID-designations were an important part of the system. The episode provides an amusing instance of aid-tying resulting in smaller exports from the aid donor than would otherwise have occurred.
15. In principle, the Ministry of Finance could make special exemption in the case of emergency requirements. That seldom happened, however. It was the United States that requested that the AID-designations be removed.
16. Lubell *et al., op. cit.* (Note 7), p. 84.

ing was $5,000.[17] Thus a firm requiring spare parts or other items in smaller value was forced to stockpile the additional amount, to pool the order with another firm's, or to order from an alternative source of supply where there was no such requirement. Second, because the U.S. imposed certain requirements on AID-financed imports, customs checks were undertaken in greater detail than for non-AID financed goods. Third — the formality about which there was most complaint — the U.S. required that prospective importers advertise in the *Small Business Circular* (SBC) of the AID Office of Small Business. Advertising had to commence at least 45 days prior to the placing of an order. Importers were required under Turkish regulations to submit their specifications in English for transmittal to the SBC within twenty-five days after receipt of their import permit but not before. Thus the SBC-advertising requirement added at least a month and a half to the delay in obtaining imports.[18]

Procedures for Quota List items

The procedure for individual quota allocations is much more complex than the Liberalized List procedure. As with Liberalized List imports, an Importer's Certificate or other proof of a valid business interest is required, and once a permit is obtained the customs procedures are the same as for Liberalized List items. In between, the procedure differs considerably.

Potential importers must obtain a quota allocation before applying for an import license. As indicated above, potential importers indicate their prospective needs to their local Chamber of Commerce or Industry. The local Chamber representatives then meet under the auspices of the Union of Chambers. The conflict between importers and industrialists is resolved at that stage. Then regional claims are disentangled at the Union of Chambers level. The Union of Chambers represents the private sector in the negotiations for the determination of quotas. Once the quota list is published, firms apply through their Chamber for allocations. After receiving allocations, import license applications are submitted and the Central Bank issues licenses fairly automatically.

---

17. $5,000 became the minimum in 1965. Prior to that date it had been $1,000.
18. The requirement was most onerous on the private sector, since SEEs were not subject to guarantee deposit requirements. Even for the private sector, there were some ways of avoiding SBC advertising: having sole supplier status, exclusive representative status, buying from U.S. stockpiles, etc. A U.S. Government study drew a sample of firms actually winning bids from SBC advertising. Firms in the sample included IBM, General Electric, International Harvester, Dow Chemical, B.F. Goodrich, and General Motors. See Lubell *et al., op. cit.* (Note 7), p. 89.

Importers versus industrialists. As already mentioned, the Union of Chambers is an association of all the regional Chambers of Commerce and Industry. The regional Chambers are in turn subdivided into Chambers of Commerce and Chambers of Industry. Both are further subdivided into functional groups — tire manufacturers, for example, are called together under the auspices of the Chamber of Industry to provide estimates of their import needs. Similarly, an importers' group meets to estimate its demands for imported tires of types not domestically produced. The obvious potential for conflict between importers and industrialists has been fully realized: so much so, in fact, that what used to be a Chamber of Commerce and Industry has become two Chambers. The importers are of course interested in increasing the flow of resaleable goods into the country, in receiving foreign-exchange allocations themselves and in keeping finished goods on the list of eligible imports. Industrialists are by contrast interested in their own quotas of intermediate goods and raw materials and in reducing the importers' quotas to limit competition with their products.

The importers as a group lost out to the industrialists in the 1960's. This can be seen in Table VI-1, which gives the value of industrialists' and importers' quotas for various Import Programs. The user-specific quotas are not included; their inclusion would make the figures show even more vividly the increasing preponderance of the industrialists in the import license allocations. Thus in 1962 importers were allocated 48 per cent of the quota items; by 1970 they received only 23 per cent, and their total allocation had declined by 43 per cent.

Table VI-1
Importers' and industrialists' allocations, various Import Programs (thousands of dollars)

	Number and year of Import Program				
	No. 8 1962	No. 12 1964	No. 16 1966	No. 20 1968	No. 24 1970
Industrialists	15,420	16,017	21,339	23,614	27,046
Importers	14,125	10,181	11,316	10,027	8,135
Total	29,545	26,198	32,655	33,641	35,181
Percent to importers	48	39	35	30	23

Notes: a) Merino wool was included in the 16th and 20th Quota Lists, with quotas to industrialists of $12 million and $13.5 million. To maintain comparability over the period, merino wool was excluded from the sum of the industrialists' quotas.
b) Legally, PL 480 imports are an importers' allocation, but they are not treated in the same manner. Hence they are not included in the totals.
Sources: *Import Programs Nos. 8, 12, 16, 20* and *24* (see Note 3).

Allocation of quotas after publication of lists: Industrialists.   As indicated above, the public and private sector shares of individual quotas are worked out by the Ministries of Commerce, Industry and Finance and the Union of Chambers. When quotas are announced, some items are designated as being subject to the control of individual ministries. Industrialists apply for those items to the relevant ministry for a "Requirements Certificate." When no Ministry is specified, they apply to the local Chamber of Industry, which forwards the applications to the Union of Chambers.

The Chambers and practically all ministries base the allocation among industrialists according to the plant capacities of the applicants.[19] Requirements Certificates are issued in proportion to those capacities unless the value of all applications totals less than the quota, in which case applicants receive the amount requested. The amount allocated to each industrialist is shown on the Requirements Certificate which, when forwarded to the Central Bank (with guarantee deposit), is the basis upon which the import license is issued.

In contrast to Liberalized List goods, the Central Bank issues licenses against quota items fairly rapidly, as foreign exchange is budgeted for the purpose. Applications for licenses for Quota List imports can be made only once in each import period, contrasted with Liberalized List imports, for which application can in principle be made at any time and repeatedly if desired.

Allocation of quotas: Importers.   Once the import lists are published importers are given a month within which to file their requests for licenses (and a guarantee deposit) with an authorized bank. No application may exceed 20 per cent of the amount of a quota unless 20 per cent does not cover even one unit of the item subject to allocation.

The authorized banks forward the importers' applications to the Central Bank, which sums the value of requests by quota category. Should the sum of the value of imports requested from a given quota category fall short of the amount of the quota, each applicant is given an import permit for the amount he requested. In theory, when the sum of the value of the applications in a given category exceeds the quota amount, the Central Bank grants all applications by scaling them down proportionately so that the quota is exactly filled. Provisions are available for circumstances in which *pro-rata* rationing results in applicants receiving a license for less than the cost of a single unit of the commodity. If such licenses cover more than 50 per cent of the price, each recipient receives an incremental allotment sufficient to cover the purchase of one unit.

19. See below, Section IV, for the way in which the capacity criterion worked.

Bilateral agreement quotas. The items eligible for importation under Bilateral Agreements must be included on either the Liberalized List or the Quota List. Determination as to which items should be on the Bilateral List is made entirely on the basis of the goods available in the bilateral agreement countries. Generally speaking, it was and is considerably easier and quicker to obtain a Bilateral Agreement quota license than any other import permit. Importers who were interviewed claimed that the chief advantage of the Bilateral Agreement quotas was the ease with which licenses could be obtained, and hence that when a commodity was required quickly the Bilateral Agreement list was employed if possible.

Price checks

The applicant is required to indicate in each import-license application the nature of the commodity he wishes to import, its f.o.b. price and its c.i.f. price per unit. Each Import Program has contained a provision to the effect that "Imports will be made at the most suitable prices obtainable in the world markets."[20] In principle, imports were subject to *ex-post* price checks to insure that overinvoicing of imports did not occur. The price checks during the 1950's had, as seen in Chapter II, been vigorously carried out. By the 1960's, however, it was rare that individuals were investigated post-importation. When the government changed in 1971 it was widely believed that there had been overinvoicing during the 1960's and price checks were enforced with greater vigor than before. (See Section IV, below, for estimates of the evasion of the regime.)

IV. The functioning of the import regime

Given the intent with which Import Programs were formulated, it is of interest to consider how the system actually worked. Several questions are significant: (1) How close were actual imports to Import Program figures? (2) How did the composition of the lists change over time? (3) How did applications for import licenses under quotas compare with the quota values? (4) To what extent was the system evaded through over and underinvoicing and other phenomena? Finally, (5) what sorts of import EERs and premia on licenses resulted from the system? Each of these questions will be considered in turn.

---

20. *Import Program No. 15*, Article 24 (See Note 3).

Actual and program imports

Table VI-2 shows the planned composition of imports from 1964 to 1970. As can be seen, imports categorized as "investment goods" were approximately evenly split between the Liberalized List and the Quota List. The heavy dependence upon anticipated foreign aid can be seen in the large volume of investment–goods imports planned under the "self-financed" category, in which project aid was expected to constitute the largest component.[21] About two-thirds of raw materials imports were planned to originate from the Liberalized List and one-third from the Quota List. However, imports of crude petroleum, the largest single import category, were included in the Liberalized List, thus making the comparison for other products deceptive. As can be seen, the Programs allowed for virtually no increase in consumption-goods imports in the early years, and an absolute decrease after 1968. The consumption-goods totals conceal the fact that an increasing number of "non-essential" consumer goods were dropped from the import lists, while the size of the Liberalized List allocation for consumer goods reflects the growth of those consumer–goods imports deemed vital to health and education. Of course reduced utilization of PL 480 funds also cut the anticipated total of consumer-goods imports.

Unfortunately, no data classified by end-use are available on the actual composition of imports within each import list.[22] Table VI-3 gives the comparison of actual and programmed totals by list and by end-use.

The biggest single disparity between Import Programs and realized imports was in the "self-financed" category prior to 1969 (as reflected in the "other" column of Table VI-3). The disparity between planned and actual figures reflects the shortfall of project credits. Actual quota imports were very close to Plan levels in every year, as were Liberalized List imports.

The composition of imports by end-use was generally different from that planned, as was noted in Chapter V. In every year except 1967 imports classified as investment goods fell below planned levels, generally by substantial amounts. In large part, this once more reflected the lower-than-planned

---

21. These "self-financed" imports constitute the major part of the column headed "Other" in Table VI-3.
22. The SPO estimated the percentage of Liberalized List imports in each end-use category for 1961, 1964 and 1966. There were no projections of end-use for 1961. For 1964 and 1966, the actual percentage of imports in each category (with projections in parentheses) were cited in Lubell *et al., op. cit.* (Note 7), p. 13:

	Investment Goods	Raw Materials	Consumption Goods	Total
1964	23 (23)	70 (70)	7 (7)	100
1966	30 (30)	63 (60)	7 (10)	100

Table VI-2
Annual program imports, 1964 to 1970 (millions of dollars)

	Liberalized List	Quota List	Bilateral	Other	Total
1964					
Investment goods	55	55	25	145	280
Raw materials	168	64	28	20	280
Consumption goods	17	16	12	35	80
Total	240	135	65	200	640
1965					
Investment goods	65	72	30	127	294
Raw materials	158	79	25	29	291
Consumption goods	17	18	15	30	80
Total	40	169	70	186	665
1966					
Investment goods	78	105	27	110	320
Raw materials	157	108	40	20	325
Consumption goods	25	12	13	30	80
Total	260	225	80	160	725
1967					
Investment goods	100	105	15	120	340
Raw materials	215	100	60	0	375
Consumption goods	25	35	15	10	85
Total	340	240	90	130	800
1968					
Investment goods	100	95	17	120	332
Raw materials	235	120	63	0	418
Consumption goods	25	25	20	15	85
Total	360	240	100	135	835
1969					
Investment goods	80	100	35	150	365
Raw materials	260	120	60	0	440
Consumption goods	15	15	10	15	55
Total	355	235	105	165	860
1970					
Investment goods	110	91	20	154	375
Raw materials	270	110	70	0	450
Consumption goods	20	4	15	16	55
Total	400	205	105	170	880

Note: Planned figures given here do not agree with those in Table V-2. The plan figures in Table V-2 were taken from the Plans, whereas data in this table are from the Annual Programs.

Source: *Annual Programs,* State Planning Organization, various years.

Table VI-3
Comparison of program and actual imports, by list and by end-use (millions of dollars)

| | | A. By list | | | | |
		Liberalized List	Quota List	Bilateral	Other	Total
1964	Plan	240	135	65	200	640
	Actual	239	128	50	120	537
1965	Plan	240	169	70	186	665
	Actual	247	159	69	97	572
1966	Plan	260	225	80	160	725
	Actual	293	218	94	113	718
1967	Plan	340	240	90	130	800
	Actual	326	196	105	58	685
1968	Plan	350	250	100	135	835
	Actual	361	202	108	93	764
1969	Plan	355	235	105	165	860
	Actual	344	181	104	172	801
1970	Plan	400	205	105	170	880
	Actual	405	205	105	220	935

| | | B. By end-use | | | |
		Investment Goods	Raw Materials	Consumption Goods	Total
1964	Plan	280	280	80	640
	Actual	197	296	44	537
1965	Plan	294	291	80	665
	Actual	197	313	62	572
1966	Plan	320	325	80	725
	Actual	289	365	64	718
1967	Plan	340	375	85	800
	Actual	260	380	45	685
1968	Plan	332	418	85	835
	Actual	325	394	45	764
1968-to-	Plan	1052	1388	270	2710
1970	Actual	791	1408	301	2500

Note: The 1968-to-1970 figure is given in the 1971 *Annual Program.* 1969 data, in the 1970 Program, covered January–June only. Therefore, only the three-year total is available.

Source: *Annual Programs*: same year for planned imports; subsequent year for actual imports.

Table VI-4
Transition matrices, 100-commodity samples

1. Third to sixteenth import list

From:	Sample 1				Sample 2				Sample 3			
	L	Q	P	T	L	Q	P	T	L	Q	P	T
To: L	16	12	0	28	14	13	7	34	15	7	12	34
Q	4	46	0	50	4	32	15	51	3	24	9	36
P	2	20	0	22	1	5	9	15	0	6	24	30
T	22	78	0	100	19	50	31	100	18	37	45	100

2. Sixteenth to twenty-fourth import list

From:	Sample 1				Sample 2				Sample 3			
	L	Q	P	T	L	Q	P	T	L	Q	P	T
To: L	22	7	1	30	28	5	1	34	30	0	8	38
Q	4	39	3	46	3	36	4	43	4	34	12	50
P	2	4	18	24	3	10	10	23	0	2	10	12
T	28	50	22	100	34	51	15	100	34	36	30	100

Notes: L = Liberalized List
Q = Quota List
P = "Prohibited List"
T = Total

Source: *Semi-Annual Import Programs.*

level of project credits which were expected to finance investment-goods imports.

Throughout the 1960's raw materials imports (including intermediate goods) were consistently underestimated. It was projected in the FFYP that raw materials imports would be $1,485 million over the five years, constituting 44 per cent of total imports. As experience demonstrated that these figures were underestimates of the raw materials component of the lists, the Annual Programs revised the raw materials import projections upward and the investment-goods import projections downward. Thus the sum of the Annual Program raw materials estimates was $1,506 million. Despite that upward adjustment, actual raw materials imports were $1,681 million or 13 per cent greater than envisaged in the FFYP, and constituted 51 per cent of total imports during the Plan period.

Thus programmed imports by list were generally quite close to actual imports, save for imports financed by project credits. By end-use categories, however, raw material imports were considerably larger and investment goods imports smaller than had been planned.

Another feature of the outcome should be noted. The fact that Liberalized List imports came as close to program levels as they did does not reflect the accuracy of the planners' demand projections, since import licenses for Liberalized List imports were granted only as foreign exchange became available. Given that licenses under the Quota List were granted fairly rapidly, the value of Liberalized List licenses issued was in fact the residual in terms of Central Bank behavior. Insofar as estimates of available foreign exchange were accurate, the value of Liberalized List imports projected in the Import Programs was realized, as acceleration or delay in the issuance of licenses kept total Liberalized List imports at planned levels.

As foreign-exchange stringency developed in the mid-1960's several factors reduced the degree of freedom associated with Liberalized List imports. It became standard practice to cease processing import license applications for Liberalized List goods prior to the end of the program period. The motive for the cessation was generally "to avoid speculation about the next Import Program." Second, when foreign exchange was in short supply, license applications for Liberalized List imports were held until such time as foreign exchange became available, when they were treated on a first-come, first-served basis. Thus prior to devaluation in 1970 import licenses for Liberalized List goods were issued eight months after application. As these delays developed it was evident that the freedom which the Liberalized List was designed to provide had severe restrictions surrounding it.

In addition to delays in and cessation of licensing, other restrictions began to pervade Liberalized List imports. The ministerial permission requirements have already been mentioned. Guarantee deposit requirements against applications for Liberalized List imports were generally higher than those for Quota List imports. Moreover, many items on the Liberalized List could be imported only with AID funds, and hence only from the United States. Particularly given the high minimum import order under AID funds (not to mention advertising in the Small Business Circular and other administrative delays), the restriction against use of free foreign exchange for some Liberalized List imports caused difficulties in many instances.

In interviews with producers using imported intermediate goods, one question that was asked was whether the producers preferred that their imports be on the Liberalized List or the Quota List. In 1965 most responders indicated relative indifference, claiming there were advantages and disadvantages to each. By 1969 however most expressed the view that Quota List classification was preferable since one could then be more or less assured that foreign exchange would be available and licenses would be forthcoming quickly once quota allocations were determined.

Composition of the lists

Given the growth of the Turkish economy and the altered structure of its imports, due both to structural changes and to the import control system, no general description in terms of the value of imports on each list or by end-use can accurately convey the evolution of the import regime under the import lists. Indeed, the commodity-specific nature of the lists make such a macro-view deceptive.

In an effort to characterize the microeconomic aspects of the import control system it was decided to trace the fate of samples of individual commodities. In this section, a report is given on the results from the 1960 to the 1971 import lists.

It was initially decided to choose three samples of commodities, one from an early import list, one from a middle import list, and one from a recent list, and to examine their treatment over time. The choice of three time periods seemed necessary because use of an early list would fail to reflect commodities entering the lists at later dates; use of a later list would ignore commodities which had been dropped from earlier lists. Perhaps the best description of the degree of complexity of the lists and their evolution is the difficulty encountered in attempting to formulate and characterize the sample.[23] The efforts made in that direction and such results as can be gleaned from them are reported in the first part of this section. In the second part a smaller sample of commodities, taken from tariff schedules, is discussed.

Three one-hundred commodity samples. The three Import Programs from which samples were drawn were the Third (August 1959), Twelfth (January 1964), and Twenth-sixth (January 1971). Determination of the items to be included was done by random number drawings: the first determined the page, the second the location of the commodity on that page.

Once the sample items were determined, it was planned to go over the lists for Import Programs 1 through 5, 12, 16, 22, 24 and 26. It was expected that on the basis of the samples one could characterize the evolution of the system: the number of items which moved from the Liberalized List to the Quota List, the number from either list to the "Prohibited List," and the values of permissible imports of quota items at various dates.

The task was considerably more complex than had been anticipated. Mean-

---

23. I am heavily indebted to Ashok Kapoor, who spent many thankless hours trying to make sense out of a difficult assignment.

ingfully tracing the fate of any import-good category proved difficult, and characterizing the results for each 100-commodity sample grossly oversimplifies what actually happened.

Some examples will illustrate. The third item drawn in the first sample, Quota Number 197, "Miners' Lamps," combined BTN codes 83.07 and 85.10. In the Third Import Program, $5,000 was allocated to importers' quotas from free foreign exchange, and $5,000 from bilateral agreement countries' quotas. Over the next several Programs this same item was on the Liberalized List. In the Twelfth Import Program however 83.07 disappeared from the import list while 85.10, "Miners' Lamps and Parts Thereof," was on the Liberalized List. In the Sixteenth Import Program, 85.11 was Quota No. 307, allotting $20,000 to industrialists and $10,000 to importers for the category "Electric Lamps for use in Industrial Establishments and Laboratories," while 85.10, "Miners' Lamps", was on the Liberalized List. Item 85.11 was omitted from all lists thereafter, implying that imports were now prohibited, while item 85.10 was on the Liberalized List. Many of the commodities drawn in the sample presented difficulties of a comparable nature in terms of classification.

An even more serious problem arose with items such as the fourteenth category drawn in the first sample. That item, BTN code 48.08, was "Paper for Filter Appliances." A total quota allocation of $450,000 was split between importers and industrialists, while another $50,000 was at the disposal of a ministry. In the Fourth and Fifth Programs, 48.08 was lumped with several other commodities to form one quota number. By the Twelfth Import Program, 48.08 had its own quota (112) again. By the Twentieth Import Program, however, Quota Number 163 contained 48.08.10 and 48.08.90, "Paper Pulp Filter — Mass Plates Containing Asbestos Fibers" and "Other," with an allocation to importers of $5,000. No other part of 48.08 appeared on any list. In this and many other cases part of the quota item initially indicated became ineligible for importation, whereas part of the item remained eligible. In some instances the situation was further confounded as an initial four-digit code became subclassified into several six-digit codes, each of which was grouped with commodities from other four-digit codes to form a new quota number. An additional difficulty resulted from the following practice: in drawing commodities from the second and third sample it often happened that no comparable commodity had appeared on earlier lists. This resulted from: (1) the introduction of new intermediate goods to the lists as the items for which domestic productive capacity developed increased, and (2) the use of detailed itemized subcategories, crossing over four-digit classifications in later Programs with no comparable practice in the earlier ones.

Thus in the following characterization of the three samples it must be borne in mind that a considerable element of judgment had to enter into each categorization. Any characterization of the samples, moreover, vastly oversimplifies what really happened.

Table VI-4 presents transition matrices for each of the three samples. Part 1 gives the change in status for each commodity in each sample between the third (pre-planning) and sixteenth (early planning) import list. Of the 78 items from the Quota List chosen in the first sample (third import list), at least some parts of 46 of the commodity classifications were still on a Quota List in the Sixteenth Import Program. Obviously, since the sample was drawn from the third list, no items on the "Prohibited List" were chosen, which explains the zeros in the last column of the sample 1 figures. Twenty-two of the 100 items appearing on the third import list did not appear on any list by the Sixteenth Import Program. Twelve items which were quota items in the third list were on the Liberalized List in the Sixteenth Program. The results differ somewhat for the second sample, drawn from the Twelfth (1964) Import Program. Thirty-one of the items from the Twelfth Program had not appeared in the Third Program, and nine did not appear in the Sixteenth. The fact that an item appeared on the Twelfth Program and neither on the Third nor the Sixteenth indicates that there were some items on each import list which did not recur or recurred only infrequently.

Only 15 items from sample 2 were on the "Prohibited List" in the Sixteenth Program, contrasted with 22 from the first, reflecting the fact that the second sample was chosen for a date which was much closer to the Sixteenth Program. That is, many items from the Third Program which were dropped from an import list were dropped before the Twelfth Program; thus, choosing a sample from the Twelfth Program failed to pick up those items. The third sample was chosen from the 1971 import list which, post-devaluation, was somewhat more liberal than earlier lists had been. That factor, plus the continuing addition of intermediate goods to the import lists as domestic production required new goods, combined with the fact that 1971 categories were of much more detailed nature, explains why there were 45 items on the twenty-sixth import list which did not appear on the third.

Part 2 of Table VI-4 gives similar data for the fate of commodities in the three samples between the sixteenth and twenty-fourth import lists. The increased importance of the diagonal elements reflects the greater fluctuations in the treatment of commodities in the early days of planning. By the late 1960's changes between import lists tended to be somewhat smaller. Thus between the third and sixteenth import lists, 12, 13, and 7 items, respectively, subject to quota in the three samples were transferred to the Liberalized List, whereas between the Sixteenth and Twenty-fourth Programs, 7, 5, and 0 items, respectively, were so transferred. Similarly, most of the items from the first sample which were destined for the "Prohibited List" reached it by the Sixteenth Program; only 6 new items were added to the

"Prohibited List" from the first sample between the Sixteenth and Twenty-fourth Programs.

The transition matrices fail fully to reflect the extent of the increasing use of the "Prohibited List": (1) since all three samples were drawn from import lists, any item continuously prohibited could not be drawn (but see below, where a sample is taken from the Tariff Code); and (2) for many of the items which continued on the lists, only a subcategory of the original classification was eligible for importation in later Programs.

Some evidence of this can be gleaned from classification of the commodities in each sample. Five categories reflect, at least roughly, increasing specificity of an eligible import class. They are, in order of increased restrictiveness: a four-digit category; a six-digit category; a four-digit category containing an "only" or a "for use only by"; a six-digit category containing one of the same restrictions; and a "for use only...subject to ministerial permission" category. The "use-only" categories are by items such as "Rollers for Textile Machines Only." Examples of the "only" part of a classification were cited above.

The breakdown of the number of items in each group in the three samples is as follows:

	4-digit	6-digit	4-digit restricted	6-digit restricted	use/ permission
Sample 1	34	51	3	11	1
Sample 2	23	38	11	21	7
Sample 3	8	48	16	9	19

As can be seen, only one item chosen from the Third Import Program was in the most restricted category, and 85 per cent of all items were in the first two, least restrictive, categories. By the Twelfth Program seven items were in the most restricted category, and 61 per cent were in the least restricted groups. By 1971, the Twenty-sixth Program, 19 items were in the use/permission category, and only 56 per cent were in the least restrictive categories. The "use" categories of course reflect the increasing shift of the Import Programs to heavier and heavier emphasis upon intermediate and other producers' goods.

When the samples were initially drawn it was hoped to trace the value of eligible imports over subsequent Programs to gain some idea of the increasing restrictiveness of the regime. Thus it was hoped that one could estimate the value of the 100 items included in the first sample in 1959 and over subsequent Programs. This proved to be impossible because of the detailed nature of the commodities included in the lists and an inability of find a comparable classification in actual import statistics. All that could be done was to estimate by sample the value of import quotas for those goods that remained in

Table VI-5
Value of items subject to quota at both ends of interval, sample groups
(thousands of dollars)

	First Comparison		Second Comparison	
	Value of Quotas 3rd Program	Value of Quotas 16th Program	Value of Quotas 16th Program	Value of Quotas 24th Program
Sample 1	29,810	5,905	5,665	2,942
Sample 2	18,550	2,781	16,316	9,381
Sample 3	7,555	3,165	5,756	7,167

Source: *Semi-Annual Import Programs.*

quota categories over various periods. As can be seen from the transition matrices this computation covered 46 per cent of the first sample for the period 1959 to 1966 and 39 per cent of the sample for 1966 to 1969. The coverage was even smaller in the second (32 and 36 per cent) and third (24 and 34 per cent) samples. Nonetheless, in the absence of any better indicator the value of quotas for those items which remained on Quota Lists is of some interest. Table VI-5 gives the results of the computations. As can be seen, the value of permissible imports for quota items fell sharply between the Third and Sixteenth Programs, and declined a further 50 per cent between the Sixteenth and Twenty-fourth Programs if judged by the first sample. Of course items subject to quota at an initial but not as a terminal date are excluded from the sample, so that the value of the quotas in the Sixteenth Import Program contrasted to the Third is not the same as that of the Sixteenth contrasted with the Twenty-fourth. Of Items worth $5,905,000 in the Sixteenth Import Program Quota Lists, products worth $240,000 were ineligible for importation or were on the Liberalized List in 1969. The fact that a few items did shift from the Quota List to the Liberalized List makes it impossible to infer the total change in values of quotas, although it is probably reasonable to guess that the "Prohibited List" dominated.

The narrowing of eligible import categories is clearly reflected in the sharp reduction in values of permissible imports, especially between the Third and Sixteenth Programs. As already pointed out, new items were added to the later import lists. It is evident therefore that given the slow growth of total imports over the period, sizeable shrinkage in other import categories had to occur to finance the addition of new import categories.

A sample from tariff categories.   To supplement the information from the import list samples (as well as to estimate EERs), a sample of commodities was chosen from the Tariff Schedules. Details on the means of sample selection are given in Appendix A, while Tables A-11 to A-14 detail some of the results.

It was possible, with some first approximations, to designate tariff items as consumer goods, intermediates and raw materials, investment goods, and imports competing with domestic production, although the procedure was necessarily rough. The same difficulties arose as with the import list samples: only part of a given category would be eligible for importation (designated by

Table VI-6

Distribution of import goods by use and list

	1962			
	L	Q	P	T
Consumer goods	5	9	22	36
Intermediate goods	17	18	12	47
Capital goods	7	1	6	14
Imports competing with domestic goods	3	4	6	13
Total	32	32	46	110
	1965			
	L	Q	P	T
Consumer goods	5	7	24	36
Intermediate goods	19	16	12	47
Capital goods	5	5	4	14
Imports competing with domestic goods	2	5	6	13
Total	31	33	46	110
	1968			
	L	Q	P	T
Consumer goods	4	7	25	36
Intermediate goods	14	17	16	47
Capital goods	4	7	3	14
Imports competing with domestic goods	2	5	6	13
Total	24	36	50	110

Notes: L = Liberalized List
          Q = Quota List
          P = "Prohibited List"
          T = Total
Source: Appendix A.

a P-prefix in the Appendix tables), the ambiguity of some categories, the fact that some items were split between two lists, etc. The reader can see the mass of different categories by inspection of the Appendix Tables.

Table VI-6 summarizes the data for 1962, 1965 and 1968. The gradual shift toward Quota Lists (as domestic production began) and the "Prohibited List" (as domestic production was deemed adequate to meet domestic demand) is evident. The intermediate goods which were eliminated from the eligible import lists were generally already fabricated in Turkey. Part of the shift toward the "Prohibited List" is obscured by the behavior of the capital goods category, where more commodities were made eligible for importation in later years (with appropriate ministerial approvals of investment plans). Six of the capital goods were not on an import list in 1962 whereas only three were missing by 1968. Of a total of 97 commodities in other categories, 40 were prohibited in 1962, 42 prohibited in 1965, and 47 prohibited in 1968.

Thus as expected, the "Prohibited List" appears more important in a sample drawn from tariff classifications than in a sample drawn from import lists. Moreover, the shift in eligible imports away from finished consumer goods toward raw materials, intermediate goods and capital goods is apparent. The results of the mechanism and its effects on the economy are examined in Chapters VIII and IX below.

Detailed allocations under Quota Lists

As seen above, the amount allocated to each quota item was specifically determined in the Import Programs. A natural question is the degree to which these amounts were adjusted to reflect the relative strength of excess demand for different imports. But little information on the procedures followed in allocating values to individual quotas is available. Some things can be inferred however by inspection of the value of applications for each quota number relative to the value of the quota.

Several Union of Chambers publications provide some data, although they are far from complete. Reports are available only for the Eighth Import Program (1962),[24] the Eighteenth Import Program (1967),[25] the Twenty-first Import Program (1968),[26] and the Twenty-third Program (1969).[27] The

24. Türkiye Ticaret Odaları, Sanayı Odaları ve Ticaret Borsaları Birliği, *8. Kota Sanayici Tahsislerinin Tevziati* (Ankara) Mart 1962.
25. Türkiye Ticaret Odaları, Sanayı Odaları ve Ticaret Borsaları Birliği, *XVIII. Kota Sanayici Kotalari Tevziati Durumu* (mimeograph) Mayis 1967.
26. Türkiye Ticaret Odaları, Sanayı Odaları ve Ticaret Borsaları Birliği, *XXI. Kota Sanayici Kotalari Tevziati Durumu* (mimeograph) Ekim 1968.
27. Türkye Ticaret Odaları, Sanayı Odaları ve Ticaret Borsaları Birliği, *XXIII. Kota Sanayici Kotalari Tevziati Durumu* (mimeograph) Ocak 1970.

reports are on private sector allocations and cover only those quotas allocated by the Union of Chambers at the time the report was published.

Several interesting sidelights can be gleaned from the 1962 report, which is the only one containing a text explaining some aspects of the allocations. It was stated, for example, that there were six quota groups for which allocations could not be made, since additional information was required about the "needs and capacities" of industrialist applicants. All but one of these was an assembler's quota, the other being a quota for animal fats and oils for use in edible oils factories. Of the 155 quotas listed, allocations had been made for 139. A variety of reasons had prevented determination of allocations for the remainder. In one case (quota 114) the allocation was under the control of the Ministry of Industry. In another case (quota 141) it was stated that allocations had not yet been made pending reexamination of applications. In yet other cases the size of the applications exceeded the available quota by exorbitant amounts and it was stated that the situation had to be examined and studied before an allocation could be made. Thus against a private sector quota of $25,000 for pumps, applications had amounted to $163,671; for machine tools (quota 184) applications were for $380,000, contrasted with a $75,000 allocation to the private sector. It can be seen in Table VI-7 that

Table VI-7

Ratio of value of license applications to licenses issued by quota categories 1962, 1967, 1968, 1970 (number of quota categories)

Ratio of Value of Applications to Value of Licenses Issued to Private Sector								
Allocations	0	Less than 1	1 to 1.99	2 to 3.99	4 to 9.99	10 to 19.99	Over 20	Total
1962								
$25,000 or less	9	20	8	16	15	1	0	69
Over $25,000	1	10	25	20	14	0	0	70
1967								
$25,000 or less	2	9	22	21	21	14	4	93
Over $25,000	2	4	13	25	29	14	5	92
1968								
$25,000 or less	0	5	19	31	25	18	11	109
over $25,000	0	3	11	15	20	20	13	82
1970								
$25,000 or less	8	3	15	28	29	17	15	115
over $25,000	0	0	12	13	23	10	23	81

Source: Union of Chambers, documents cited in footnotes 24–27.

such discrepancies became commonplace later in the 1960's, but they were apparently rare in 1962.

Although providing only a partial picture of excess demands, the reports give some indication of the characteristics of the system. Table VI-7 gives the data. For each of the Import Programs covered and for each of the quota items, the value of applications by the private sector as a multiple of the value of licenses allocated to it was computed. Such a statistic does not give an indication of actual excess demand since firms undoubtedly applied for more imports than they actually desired. However, applicants were required to place guarantee deposits against their applications. As such, applying for quotas did involve costs to the applicants.

Table VI-7 can be read as follows. In 1962 sixteen quotas of $25,000 or less were allocated where applications were between two and four times the value of the quotas. Only one small quota (under $25,000) was oversubscribed by a factor of ten or more, while none of the larger quotas were oversubscribed by that amount; there were ten quota numbers against which no applications were filed. There were 30 others for which applications were less than the value of the quota, thus indicating that applicants received the full amount of their applications.

Several aspects of the evolution of the import regime can be inferred from Table VI-7. First, despite the increasing reliance upon ministerial permissions, the number of quotas, and especially of small quotas, increased over time.[28] Second, the fraction of small and large quotas that were heavily oversubscribed increased over time, reflecting the increasing stringency of the import regime. Thus in 1962 only one of 139 quota items was oversubscribed by a factor of ten or more. By 1970 (predevaluation) 65 quotas out of 196 were oversubscribed by at least that multiple. At the other end of the scale, 52 per cent of all quotas were either undersubscribed or oversubscribed by a factor of less than two in 1962: by 1970 only 19 per cent were in that category.

---

28. The increasing number of quotas reflected the greater fragmentation of importable items as domestic production capacity was developed. The number of quota categories, by Import Programs, was as follows:

Import Program number	Date	Number of Quota Categories
5	1960	215
8	1962	261
12	1964	322
14	1965	392
16	1966	418
18	1967	454
20	1968	474

These totals, compared with the total number of quotas indicated in Table VI-7, also give an idea of the fraction allocated by the Union of Chambers.

Third, even with heavy excess demand for many quotas in the later part of the 1960's, there were some undersubscribed quotas. It thus seems irrefutable that premia on different quota items must have varied widely (see Section V, below). Thus in 1970 applicants for three quota items received the full amount they applied for, while applicants for 38 items received less than one-twentieth of their applications.

In interviews with SPO officials, inquiry was made as to whether information about the value of excess demand in any given category or the disparity between landed cost and domestic price of an import was employed in determining detailed quota allocations. The response was negative: it was felt that "speculative and other short-term influences" were too great to provide reliable bases for changing the relative size of different quotas. As indicated above, the general view was that physical shortages became known when present and were taken into account in the allocation of quotas for subsequent periods.

Evasion of the regime

No analysis of the way the import regime functioned would be complete without consideration of the extent to which extra-legal and illegal means of subventing the Import Programs were practiced. Three factors must be considered: (1) the degree to which resale of imports actually occurred; (2) the extent of faked invoicing; and (3) the prevalence of smuggling.

Resale of imports. As indicated above, industrialists could not legally resell their imports. However, there were several means by which resale occurred. Indeed, since new firms in an industry were to be given a quota initially on criteria rather different from established producers, there were reported to be many instances of entrepreneurs "going into business" for the purpose of obtaining imports and reselling to larger firms. Even some small established firms found it more profitable to sell their imports at an appropriate price to larger firms rather than to produce themselves.

One perfectly legal means of resale was for a small producer to ask a large producer to place his order together with the larger establishment's. The purpose of permitting this practice was to enable the small producer to get a better price on his import order than was thought possible with a very small allocation. A producer with a small quota would approach a larger firm, asking that his small quota be pooled with the larger quota for purposes of importing the item in question. The larger firm would readily agree. When the consignment arrived, the small firm could claim that the larger house had violated their understanding; the consignment was not what the small firm required or could use regarding quality, technical specifications, or other matters. The small firm would claim damages and state that the matter could be settled in court. The larger firm, seemingly anxious to repair whatever damages it had incurred, would then settle the matter by paying the importer the value of his foregone income from the imports and retain the imported goods for his own use.

Other means of resale were also devised. (There are even reported instances where the local Chambers organized resale markets.[29]) Thus although there was a legal restriction upon the resale of industrialists' quotas, resale was in fact fairly frequent.

Faked invoicing. All applications for import licenses had to contain descriptions of the goods to be imported, the quantities of each and their unit prices. It has already been seen that although price checks were legally in force they were not seriously enforced during the 1960's. There is considerable evidence that substantial under-invoicing of imports in fact occurred, as import licenses were issued in value terms so that more could be imported and both duties and surcharges avoided.

A detailed study of the phenomenon during the period 1963 to 1969 has been made by Cahid Kayra.[30] Kayra undertook a detailed reconciliation of Turkish and partner-country trade statistics, including adjustments for transport costs, differences in the timing of imports and other factors. On the basis of his detailed computations he then provided estimates of the actual value of imports flowing through official channels. Some of his detailed findings are of interest and illustrate the possible magnitude of faked invoicing.

Synthetic fibers are a case in point and Table VI-8 presents Kayra's results. For each five-digit fiber class, Kayra summed the exports to Turkey, as reported by members of the Common Market, and contrasted them with the Turkish records. As can be seen, the discrepancy is substantial: suggesting that less than 10 per cent of the value of Turkish imports of these items was officially recorded in the customs category. Kayra calculated the savings in customs duties made by such under-invoicing. His results are given in the last column of Table VI-8. Thus, in importing $3,500,000 of SITC No. 266.21 (discontinuous or unspun fiber) in 1968, Turkish importers saved $1,544,000 in customs duties by declaring only $412,000 as imports. Kayra then proceeded to examine unit value figures for these countries. The unit value derived from Turkish trade statistics was $681 in 1968 compared with $1,025 for Germany, $1,403 for Greece, and $1,278 for Spain. In 1969 the disparity

29. Lubell *et al., op. cit.* (Note 7), p. 95.
30. Cahid Kayra, *Türkiye'nin Dış Ödelemler Dengesi Tahminleri Üzerinde Düşünceler,* Boğazici Üniversitesi (mimeograph), January 1972.

Table VI-8
Turkish synthetic fiber imports, Turkish and Common Market records
(thousands of dollars)

SITC No.	Year	Turkish Import Figures	Partner Country Export Figures	Difference	Customs Taxes Saved
266.21	1968	412	3500	3088	1544
	1969	111	2833	2722	1360
266.22	1968	–	291	291	145
266.23	1968	234	4992	4758	2855
	1969	74	3675	3601	2160

Source: Kayra, *op. cit.* (Note 30), Table 30.

between Turkish unit-value figures and those of other countries was slightly greater. A similar pattern was found for other groups.

Considering the probable magnitude of under-invoicing (at most 50 per cent) and the disparity in recorded imports, it can be presumed that synthetic fibers (which were on the Quota Lists and generally commanded high premia — see Table VI-11 below) were both under-invoiced and imported under licenses other than those issued directly for those goods. Thus part of the restrictiveness of commodity-specific licensing (and the "Prohibited List") was undoubtedly offset by under-invoicing and erroneous classification of imports into eligible import commodities.

Kayra estimated the value of Turkish imports for the period 1963 to 1969 on the basis of his detailed study of partner country trade statistics. His results, given in Table VI-9, indicate that actual imports by Turkey were an average of about $60 million over recorded imports in the years 1963 to 1965, implying underinvoicing of about 10 per cent. And the magnitude of the phenomenon increased sharply thereafter, reaching over $190 million in 1969.

Table VI-9
Official statistics and Kayra's estimates of imports, 1963 to 1969 (millions of dollars)

	1963	1964	1965	1966	1967	1968	1969
Turkish trade statistics	688	537	572	718	685	764	801
Kayra's estimates	748	577	645	815	836	882	993

Source: Kayra, *op. cit.* (Note 30).

Many goods were imported by the public sector or financed with project credits and therefore were presumably not significantly under-invoiced. For private sector imports, therefore, the magnitude of underrecording of imports was substantial by any standard.

There can be little doubt that under-invoicing and falsely classifying imports made the import regime less restrictive than it would have been in the absence of those practices. However, it will be seen in Section V that despite the leakages in the system the premia accruing to import licenses were substantial.

Smuggling. By its nature, smuggling is a more difficult activity to try to quantify than is faked invoicing, and all that can be done is to provide impressionistic evidence. For a variety of reasons, it would appear that smuggling was concentrated on consumer goods. First, most consumer goods were not legally importable, and are, by their nature, difficult to misclassify into an eligible import category. Second, there have generally been very high disparities between foreign and domestic prices of consumer goods, so that smuggling of those items was probably more profitable than smuggling other categories of goods.

From personal experience, the author can report finding an incredible variety of imported goods not eligible for importation on the shelves of local groceries and in the windows of various shops: canned American salted peanuts, gum, foreign cigarettes, German phonographs, Nabisco crackers, German and American baby food, and so on. As mentioned in Chapter V, smuggling was so widespread that its existence was officially acknowledged at the end of the FFYP. There is every reason to believe that in the early years of the SFYP, smuggling activity grew as the stringency of the import regime increased. Beyond the fact that sale of smuggled goods was fairly open and that prices of black-market merchandise were generally well known, it is impossible to estimate the magnitude of the phenomenon.

V. Import EERs and premia: the 1960's

As seen in Chapter IV, the 1958—1960 devaluation did not result in any significant change in the ratio of import EERs to export EERs. In this section the course of import EERs throughout the 1960's is traced, and the premia accruing to license recipients are estimated for 1968.

Import EERs

Details of the method of computation of EERs are given in Appendix A.

In addition to basic tariff rates which were altered in 1964, several surcharges and the discriminatory component of the production tax led to sizeable differentials between the c.i.f. price and the landed cost of an import, and the c.i.f. price-cum-duty and landed costs of imports.

Table VI-10 gives the import EERs for the 1960's based on Tables A-11 to A-14 and also presents PLD-EERs. EERs were deflated by use of the home goods price computed on a 1958 base. A higher PLD-EER implies a more depreciated exchange rate for the category of goods in question.

All categories of imports became cheaper in real terms during the 1960's. Relative to home goods, imported capital goods were almost 30 per cent cheaper in 1969 than they were in 1960, even taking into account duties and surcharges. That was of course partly the result of the removal and postpone-

Table VI-10

Import EERs and PLD-EERs, by end-use category of imports, 1960 to 1969
(TL per dollar c.i.f. price)

	Capital Goods	Intermediate Goods	Imports Competing with Domestic Production	Consumer Goods
EERs				
1960	12.11	13.25	21.22	18.66
1961	12.55	13.25	21.22	18.66
1962	12.54	13.12	18.96	15.78
1963	12.99	13.57	19.41	16.23
1964	12.99	13.57	19.41	16.23
1965	15.50	14.79	23.01	17.75
1966	15.50	14.79	23.01	17.75
1967	15.29	15.24	23.46	18.20
1968	12.26	16.15	21.98	18.79
1969	13.16	17.05	21.98	19.69
PLD-EERs				
1960	10.35	11.32	18.13	15.95
1961	10.54	11.13	17.83	15.68
1962	10.03	10.49	15.17	14.70
1963	9.84	10.28	14.70	12.30
1964	10.14	10.60	15.16	12.68
1965	11.48	10.96	17.04	13.14
1966	10.61	10.13	15.76	12.16
1967	10.09	9.65	14.85	11.52
1968	7.52	9.91	13.48	11.64
1969	7.44	9.63	12.96	11.12

Notes: a) For definitions of categories of imports, see Appendix A.
          b) PLD-EERs are 1958 TL per dollar c.i.f. price.
Source: Appendix A.

ment of duties upon capital goods in the late 1960's. However, imports competing with domestic goods became relatively cheaper by the same proportion, while imported consumer goods were 31 per cent cheaper in terms of home goods in 1969 than they were in 1960. The price of imported intermediate goods in terms of home goods fell only 15 per cent from 1960 to 1969. Thus, whereas capital goods and raw materials and intermediate goods imports had similar EERs in the early 1960's, intermediate goods imports became relatively more expensive in the late 1960's.

This shift in the structure of EERs reflects the SPO's desire to increase the fraction of foreign exchange allocated to capital goods imports. As noted above, raw materials and intermediate goods imports were consistently above planned levels in the mid-1960's, while capital goods imports were below desired levels. The remission of duties and surcharges on capital goods imports was therefore designed to alter the relationship between the two import classes.

It is more difficult to determine the reason why the EERs for imports competing with domestic production retained their parity with capital goods during the 1960's. The absolute differential between the capital goods and the other two classes was of course high at the start of the period. Thus even without allowing for price deflation there was little movement in the EER of imports competing with domestic output over the 1960's. It fell somewhat in the early years, and rose thereafter. Another factor should be considered, however, and that is that the EERs were calculated from the sample of commodities eligible for importation. It is quite possible that the increasing use of the "Prohibited List" as more and more goods were domestically produced resulted in a bias in the estimate of import EERs for consumer goods and import substitutes. Inspection of the list of goods included in each sample suggests that there was some bias toward retaining the commodities with relatively lower EERs on the eligible list. Thus the EER estimates can in no way be interpreted as the degree of protection afforded to the two categories of goods.

Import premia

As indicated above, there was considerable activity in the resale of imports and import licenses, both legally and otherwise. Even for Liberalized List items, the fact that delays in receipts of licenses could be protracted meant that the domestic price of such imports could exceed landed cost by more than the normal distributors' markup. For items on the Quota List, the detailed, firm-specific allocations resulted in an even greater potential for resale, as well as a divergence between landed cost and the domestic price.

Detailed estimates of the premia accruing to license recipients are available only for 1968. The only available evidence for earlier years is based upon the author's interviews with businessmen and observers. Interviews with businessmen were conducted by the author in 1965, 1967, 1969, 1970 and 1971. Businessmen not only were asked what the then-prevailing prices on import licenses were, but also were queried as to their recollection of premia for earlier periods. The responses were necessarily impressionistic, but were surprisingly consistent between interviews and over time. The consensus appeared to be the following.

Premia for licenses in the 1955-to-1958 period ranged up to TL 20–25 per dollar, or eight times the parity rate. The resale market all but disappeared after devaluation in 1958, and premia on licenses were negligible up to 1962. Premia reemerged for some items by 1963, but it was rare that they were more than TL 1 to 2 per dollar. By 1964 however (as foreign aid failed to reach anything near Plan levels and imports rose in response to Plan expenditures) premia jumped to a range of TL 4–6 per dollar, representing 40–66 per cent of the c.i.f. cost of imports, but a far smaller percentage of landed cost (because of duties and surcharges on imports). Premia remained within the TL 4–6 range in 1965 and 1966, but rose to TL 7–9 per dollar, almost 100 per cent, by 1967. They were considerably higher by 1968, and the variation in price among import categories increases sharply. The average price of import licenses in 1968 and 1969 ranged from TL 9 to TL 15 per dollar, or 100 to 166 per cent above the c.i.f. price. Premia were substantially reduced after devaluation in 1970, and there was little reported resale of licenses at the end of 1970.

While the emerging picture is necessarily impressionistic, it is useful in putting the 1968 situation in perspective. An excellent set of data for 1968 exists with which to evaluate the relationship between c.i.f. prices, landed cost and import premia. In the summer of that year Professor Ahmet Aker of Robert College (now Boğazici Üniversitesi) conducted interviews with numerous firms in the Istanbul area. He sought to obtain comparable data on the c.i.f. prices, landed costs and wholesale prices of identical commodities, and succeeded in obtaining comparable price quotations at all three levels for 74 commodities, representing 8.6 per cent of Turkey's total import bill. In his judgment these figures were reliable.

Table VI-11 reproduces his price data. As can be seen in the next-to-last column, there was a sizeable variation in the relationship between wholesale prices and landed costs.[31] Some commodities, such as lanolin and synthetic thread, sold in the wholesale market at little above their landed cost. Of

---

31. The estimate of landed costs includes the duties, surcharges and production taxes levied upon imports, but does not include the costs of guarantee deposits and letters of credit.

Table VI-11
Import prices, landed costs and wholesale prices, 1968

Commodity	TL per Unit			Ratio		
	Import Price c.i.f.	Landed Cost	Whole-sale Price	Landed Cost to Import Price	Whole-sale Price to Landed Cost	Whole-sale Price to Import Price
Pigs' bristles	58.35	80.60	475.0	1.38	5.89	8.14
Dates	0.06	0.13	6.5	2.17	49.10	108.33
Unroasted coffee	7.34	13.31	36.0	1.81	2.90	4.90
Black peppers	7.19	15.14	29.0	2.10	1.91	4.03
Cloves	7.62	13.20	23.5	1.73	1.78	3.08
Henna	2.94	5.83	11.0	1.98	1.89	3.74
Shellac	6.97	13.65	16.0	1.95	1.17	2.29
Gum arabic	2.77	6.29	13.5	2.27	2.15	4.87
Lard	2.33	3.92	12.0	1.68	3.06	5.15
Lanolin	6.46	10.88	12.0	1.68	1.10	1.86
Hint oil	3.23	4.85	9.5	1.50	1.96	2.94
Cocoa oil	3.17	5.33	60.0	1.68	11.26	18.93
Sunflower oil	2.53	4.25	5.9	1.68	1.39	2.33
Oleic acid	2.64	4.40	5.5	1.67	1.25	2.08
Cocoa beens	3.87	8.29	40.0	2.14	4.83	10.34
Copra oil	8.14	18.72	32.0	2.30	1.71	3.93
Whiskey	9.70	29.92	85.0	3.08	2.84	8.76
Portland cement	0.09	0.15	0.2	1.66	1.33	2.22
Gas oil	0.30	0.70	0.8	2.33	1.14	2.67
Motor oil	0.19	0.56	0.8	2.95	1.42	4.21
Vaseline	1.94	3.18	5.0	1.64	1.57	2.58
Sulphuric acid	0.25	0.44	1.0	1.76	2.27	4.00
Zinc oxide	2.42	3.88	5.5	1.60	1.42	2.27
Titanium oxides	3.99	6.10	8.5	1.53	1.39	2.13
Sodium hydrosulfide	3.50	5.08	7.5	1.45	1.48	2.14
Sodium bicarbonate	0.50	0.79	1.4	1.58	1.77	2.80
Sodium carbonate	0.44	0.62	1.2	1.41	1.93	2.73
Potassium carbonate	1.71	2.73	3.7	1.60	1.36	2.47
Trichlorethylene	1.50	2.23	3.5	1.49	1.57	2.33
Pure methyl alcohol	2.41	3.86	4.5	1.60	1.17	1.87
Acetone	1.68	2.93	3.5	1.74	1.19	2.08
Printing inks	8.22	12.18	60.0	1.48	4.92	7.30
Tall oil	1.74	2.44	5.5	1.40	2.25	3.16
Synthetic rubber	3.86	6.45	42.0	1.67	6.51	10.88
Tires	10.62	21.94	25.0	2.07	1.14	2.35

Table VI-11 (continued)

Commodity	TL per unit			Ratio		
	Import Price c.i.f.	Landed Cost	Whole-sale Price	Landed Cost to Import Price	Whole-sale Price to Landed Cost	Whole-sale Price to Import Price
Inner tubes	10.50	21.69	80.0	2.07	3.69	7.62
Natural cork	1.67	2.11	5.0	1.26	2.37	2.99
Cords of synthetic continuous fiber	9.37	22.47	35.0	2.40	1.56	3.74
Continuous silk fiber	8.01	19.21	29.0	2.40	1.51	3.62
Synthetic thread	14.25	34.19	35.0	2.40	1.02	2.46
Silk thread	8.32	19.96	40.0	2.40	2.00	4.81
Synthetic textiles	23.31	35.70	175.0	1.53	4.90	7.51
Merino wool	11.20	14.11	30.0	1.26	2.13	2.68
Synthetic fibers	8.92	13.47	47.5	1.51	3.53	5.33
Artificial fibers	3.87	6.98	52.5	1.80	7.52	13.56
Jute fiber	2.89	3.64	5.5	1.26	1.51	1.90
Jute yarn	3.75	8.12	11.0	2.17	1.35	2.93
Quilting material	0.50	0.78	2.5	1.56	3.21	5.00
Iron + steel bars or con-cretes which have I profile	1.03	1.71	2.5	1.66	1.46	2.43
Iron + steel bars or con-cretes which have H profile	1.00	1.67	3.0	1.67	1.80	3.00
Magnetic sheets	1.20	2.27	2.9	1.89	1.28	2.42
Thick and thin pipes made of cast iron	4.30	7.47	35.0	1.74	4.69	8.14
Unplated pipes, diameters to 3 fingers	2.41	4.46	4.5	1.85	1.01	1.87
Plated pipes, diameters to 3 fingers	2.17	3.01	9.0	1.39	2.99	4.15
Zinc	3.07	5.37	22.0	1.75	4.10	7.17
Air pumps	254	417	2000	1.64	4.80	7.87
Refrigeration units	990	2080	3000	2.10	1.44	3.03
Lathes	1179	1930	8500	1.64	4.40	7.21
Cutting machinery	2898	4746	6500	1.64	1.37	2.24
Typewriters	432	697	1375	1.61	1.97	3.18
1–2 HP electric motors	87	137	300	1.57	2.19	3.45
3–10 HP electric motors	300	475	750	1.58	1.58	2.50

Table VI-11 (continued)

Commodity	TL per unit			Ratio		
	Import Price c.i.f.	Landed Cost	Whole-sale Price	Landed Cost to Import Price	Whole-sale Price to Landed Cost	Whole-sale Price to Import Price
Vacuum cleaners	371	822	1500	2.22	1.82	4.04
Distributors	38	50	275	1.31	5.50	7.24
Automatic telephone	32	61	250	1.91	4.10	7.81
Wire telephone parts	36	68	190	1.89	2.79	5.28
Loudspeakers	25	37	60	1.48	1.62	2.40
Small tractors	7654	12,227	50,000	1.60	4.09	6.53
Medium tractors	13,912	22,297	62,500	1.60	2.80	4.49
Large tractors	32,808	52,582	67,500	1.60	1.28	2.06
Passenger cars	16,152	41,902	57,500	2.59	1.37	3.56
Motorcycles	1428	2841	5000	1.99	1.76	3.50
Kilowatt hour meters	29	63	190	2.17	3.02	6.55

Source: Data kindly provided by Professor Ahmet Aker.

course landed cost itself was considerably above the c.i.f price, but none-theless there were no premia associated with the importation of these com-modities. For many commodities, however, premia were substantial. For thirty-one commodities in the sample — almost half — the premium exceeded the landed cost of the import. There were only four commodities in the sample where the wholesale domestic price of the item was less than double the c.i.f. price. The landed cost estimates relative to the c.i.f price estimates accord closely with the EER estimates given in Appendix A whenever items are found in both samples. But confirming the impressions given by excess demand for licenses, there was little relationship between the height of the EER and the domestic wholesale price of the commodity. Distributors, sub-ject to only 31 per cent duties and surcharges, sold domestically for more than seven times the c.i.f. price, for example. Passenger cars, subject to 159 per cent duties and surchanges, sold for about 3½ times their c.i.f. price. Thus the premia on import licenses varied considerably from commodity to com-modity, as expected under a quota system. And the tariffs and surcharges absorbed different fractions of the domestic/foreign price differential in the various commodity categories.

To obtain an estimate of the importance of the premia relative to duties and surcharges, the 1967 value of imports of each commodity in the sample was obtained. The value of the premia as given by Aker was then computed under several assumptions as to what mark-up would yield a normal rate of return. Three mark-up rates were used: 20, 50 and 100 per cent. The results of the computations were:

	(millions of TL)
Value of imports in the sample, c.i.f.	547
Landed cost of imports	1,443
Wholesale value of imports	3,568
Premia:	
20 per cent markup	1,836
50 per cent markup	1,404
100 per cent markup	682

The average EER for the sample was thus TL 23.76 = $1 contrasted with the official rate of TL 9 = $1. This EER is slightly above the rate calculated in Appendix A. The premium, however, equalled TL 30.21, TL 23.1, or TL 11.22, depending upon the assumption made about the normal mark-up. That would vary from one product to another, but in this author's judgment a 50 per cent mark-up is probably the best estimate. On that basis, a dollar's worth of imports cost the importer TL 23.76, and his return from it was TL 58.75, giving him an average windfall gain, or premium, of TL 23.11 per TL 9 of licenses received.

Thus by 1968 the premium on import licenses was considerably in excess of the duties and surcharges imposed upon imports. Industrialists receiving import licenses for intermediate goods imports were, in effect, subsidized by the amount of the premium they received, and protected by the amount of the EER plus the premium on imports competing with their own production. The premia associated with final outputs were at least as high as those on intermediate goods, and frequently were much higher. For domestic producers of those goods, therefore, the protection afforded through quantitative restrictions considerably exceeded that through tariffs and surcharges. Quantitative restrictions were thus of much greater importance than price interventions in providing incentives for import-substituting production.

The resource allocational and growth effects of these powerful incentives for import-substitution will be examined in Chapters VIII and IX. First however, attention must be devoted to the differential incentives for exports and their effects, the subject of Chapter VII.

The Determinants of Turkish Exports

It has already been seen that there were strong differential incentives in favor of import-substituting production in both the 1950's and the 1960's. In the 1950's the disincentives to export were the consequences of currency overvaluation and the resulting premia arising from import stringency. In the 1960's these differential incentives were partly the result of deliberate government policy, although that policy itself was based to a considerable extent upon pessimism about the potential for export growth. Even in the 1960's, however, part of the differential incentive against exports was unintended, in the sense that import stringency was greater than had been planned; and the premia on imports were therefore higher than had been anticipated or intended by the planners. The resource-allocational effects of the differential incentive to export are examined in this chapter. First, an overview of the behavior of exports over the period 1950 to 1971 is presented, and the structure of export earnings is examined. Next, government domestic policies, which are very important for understanding the determinants of both the production and the volume of exports of certain commodities, are discussed. Thereafter the behavior of individual export commodities is analyzed. Finally, estimates of the effects of exchange-rate policy on export earnings are presented.

I. Behavior and structure of exports, 1950 to 1971

Export earnings

Table VII-1 presents annual data on the dollar value of Turkish exports, Turkey's share of world exports, and the share of Turkish exports in Turkish GNP over the 1950-to-1971 period. Turkey's exports rose to $396 million in 1953, representing 0.54 per cent of world exports. Turkey's exports had declined to $247 million by 1958, and Turkey's share of the world market had fallen by more than half, to 0.26 per cent. Turkey did not reattain her 1953 export earnings until 1964, when exports reached $411 million, although her share of world exports in that year was barely above the 1958 level. Turkey's exports then grew at almost the same rate as world exports from 1964 to 1967; thereafter, Turkey's share fell to 0.21 per cent in 1970, although exports had risen in absolute value to $588 million.

Table VII-1
Turkey's exports and share of world exports, 1950 to 1971

	Turkish Exports (millions of U.S. dollars)	World Exports (millions of U.S. dollars)	Turkish Exports as a Share of:		
			World Exports (%)	GNP	
				Official (%)	EER-adjusted (%)
1950	263	55,200	0.47	7.1	7.1
1951	314	74,800	0.42	7.2	7.2
1952	363	72,400	0.50	7.1	7.1
1953	396	73,400	0.54	6.6	6.7
1954	335	76,400	0.44	5.5	5.7
1955	313	83,220	0.38	4.2	4.4
1956	305	92,600	0.33	3.5	4.0
1957	345	99,300	0.35	3.2	3.6
1958	247	94,800	0.26	1.8	2.8
1959	354	100,600	0.35	2.1	5.6
1960	321	112,600	0.29	3.4	5.7
1961	347	117,800	0.29	5.8	5.8
1962	381	124,100	0.31	5.7	5.7
1963	368	136,100	0.27	4.8	4.8
1964	411	152,700	0.27	5.0	5.0
1965	464	165,400	0.28	5.2	5.2
1966	490	181,300	0.27	4.7	4.7
1967	523	190,600	0.27	4.5	4.6
1968	496	212,900	0.23	3.9	3.9
1969	537	243,500	0.22	3.8	4.2
1970	588	280,300	0.21	3.3	4.5
1971	677	312,600	0.22	3.7	4.7

Notes: a) EER-adjusted exports as a share of GNP were calculated by multiplying dollar export values by the weighted average EER for exports. The adjustment is made to reflect the actual earnings of exporters as a proportion of GNP.
b) Export data do not entirely agree with the data in Table I-6. The source of the discrepancies is not known.

Sources: Turkish and world exports from *International Financial Statistics,* various issues. Turkish exports in TL from *Statistical Yearbook,* SIS 1968; and *Yılı Programı,* State Planning Organization, 1971.

Accompanying the Turkish loss of share in world markets, the TL value of exports as a percentage of GNP declined from 7.1 per cent in 1952 to 3.7 per cent in 1969, according to official Turkish figures on the TL value of exports. But these official figures are misleading, especially for the period 1956 through 1960, as dollar receipts were converted into TL at the official *de jure* exchange rate. To adjust for this, dollar export earnings were multiplied by the weighted export EERs to obtain a more meaningful estimate of income accruing to exporters in Turkey. The next-to-last column gives the official figures, and the last column of Table VII-1 gives the export share of current GNP when the TL value of exports is based upon EERs rather than the official exchange rate. As can be seen, even with that adjustment exports fell from 7 per cent of GNP in the early 1950's to 3.8 per cent of GNP in 1958, rose to 5.8 per cent of GNP in 1961, and declined thereafter to 3.9 per cent of GNP in 1968.

In keeping with the delineation of Phases in Chapter I, several subperiods can be distinguished. (1) From 1953 to 1958, exports declined precipitously in dollar value, in volume, and as a percentage of GNP. The true magnitude of the decline during the 1950's was probably even greater than the data in Table VII-1 suggest, as the bilateral debt-payment trading agreements (see Chapter II) undoubtedly led to an overstatement of the value of export earnings.[1] (2) Exports rose and the Turkish share of world trade rose after the devaluation in 1958, as did exports as a percentage of GNP. The relative levels of the early 1950's were by no means reattained, however. (3) The rate of expansion of export earnings decreased after 1965, and the share of Turkish exports in world trade and in Turkish GNP once again resumed its decline, which continued until 1968–1969. Thus, even using the export EERs to value export earnings in TL, 1968 exports were 3.9 per cent of GNP, contrasted with 5.6 per cent and more in the early 1960's. Turkey's share of world trade had declined yet more sharply, from 0.35 per cent in 1959 to 0.21 per cent in 1970.

Composition of exports

Table VII-2 gives data on the structure of Turkish exports. Tobacco and cotton have been the largest foreign-exchange earning commodities. They jointly accounted for about 40 per cent of total foreign-exchange earnings from exports. Cotton exports increased markedly both in relative and in absolute importance, whereas tobacco exports declined relatively as a source of foreign exchange. Four additional commodity groups are important in Turkish exports: hazelnuts (filberts); dried fruit (raisins and figs); and two minerals, chrome and copper. The relative importance of the minerals has declined over time, whereas that of the fresh and dried fruit and nuts has increased. Turkish exports of fresh fruit began increasing rapidly in the late 1960's.

1. It will be recalled that the bilateral debt repayment agreements enabled Turkey to export at above-world prices.

Table VII-2
Structure of Turkish exports, 1952 to 1970, selected years (millions of U.S. dollars)

	1952	1956	1960	1964	1967	1970
Commodity group						
Cereals	93.4	28.2	6.6	6.0	1.6	1.5
Fresh fruit	1.4	2.3	2.2	3.6	8.3	10.3
Dried fruit	15.7	19.9	29.8	30.5	31.6	30.8
Hazelnuts	18.4	29.8	39.2	50.2	84.3	87.0
Livestock products	5.7	5.7	13.5	20.5	17.6	27.7
Lumber	2.9	1.2	1.2	1.3	1.9	3.8
Animal feed	6.5	12.3	10.6	17.4	n.a.	n.a.
Mohair	5.7	9.5	9.5	5.9	8.9	3.8
Cotton	69.1	26.4	46.1	92.3	131.5	171.3
Tobacco	62.1	93.6	65.5	90.1	118.0	78.5
Olive oil	0.0	0.0	0.0	3.8	6.8	0.0
Sugar	0.2	0.8	16.5	19.9	n.a.	n.a.
Minerals	46.5	48.0	31.4	26.8	37.9	54.4
Other	35.3	27.3	48.6	42.5	74.3	119.4
Total	362.9	305.0	320.7	410.8	522.7	588.5

Note: Sugar and animal feed are included in other exports for 1967 and 1970.
Sources: 1952 to 1964, *Economic and Social Indicators – Turkey,* USAID, April 1965.
          1967 and 1970, *Economic and Social Indicators – Turkey,* USAID, August
          1972.

Although Turkey has a wide variety of export products, most of them are agricultural commodities. Thus 87 per cent of Turkish exports originated in agriculture, 8.1 per cent in minerals, and 4.9 per cent in manufactures in 1968. Although some agricultural commodities, e.g., citrus fruits, represent "non-traditional" exports, the bulk are traditional.

Table VII-3 gives data on Turkey's share of the world export markets for her major exports. Turkey was at one time the world's leading exporter of chrome, but her share has declined sharply over the years. Turkish exports of copper constitute a very small fraction of world exports, and the Turkish share has decreased over time. Of all Turkey's exports, there are only three for which Turkey's share exceeds 15 per cent: raisins, figs and hazelnuts. Thus it is doubtful whether Turkey has any significant monopoly power for more than 85 per cent of her export earnings. The structure of Turkish exports in this regard is decidedly more favorable than that of many developing countries. Although the share of Turkey's three top export commodities in Turkish exports (about 55 per cent) is about average for the developing countries, Turkey's share of her markets is generally low,[2] and most Turkish

2. Michaely computed a coefficient of export concentration of 0.397 for Turkey in

Table VII-3
Turkey's share of world markets, various years (percentage of world exports)

	1953	1957	1960	1963	1966	1969
Chrome	18.0	20.0	11.0	9.9	10.5	12.3
Copper	1.0	0.7	0.6	0.5	0.6	0.5
Cotton	n.a.	2.0	2.1	3.6	6.0	5.5
Figs	n.a.	n.a.	n.a.	n.a.	65.9	69.7
Hazelnuts	n.a.	n.a.	n.a.	n.a.	47.1	66.7
Mohair	0.0	–	0.4	0.3	0.1	0.1
Olive oil	1.1	n.a.	0.1	8.9	2.2	9.1
Citrus fruit	n.a.	0.1	0.3	0.4	0.6	1.0
Raisins	n.a.	16.7	23.6	16.4	16.5	18.2
Tobacco	n.a.	12.0	7.5	5.1	9.2	7.1

Note: Data for chrome, copper and figs represent Turkey's share of world production, not of world exports.

Sources: Minerals: *Statistical Summary of the Mineral Industry,* Great Britain, Directorate of Colonial Geological Surveys, various issues. Agricultural Commodities: *Trade Yearbook,* FAO, various issues. Shares for figs and hazelnuts from *World Agriculture Production and Trade,* USDA, Foreign Agricultural Service, February and September 1971.

exports are commodities for which there is reason to believe that the income and price elasticities of demand are reasonably high.

Geographic distribution of exports

Table VII-4 gives data on the share of exports going to various trade blocs: the EEC countries, the EFTA countries, the United States, the CMEA countries, and others. About one-third of Turkey's exports are destined for the EEC, which Turkey plans to join. As indicated in Chapter I, Turkey signed the initial protocol in 1963 but received little more than tariff-quota preferences until 1970. Thus the preferences extended by the EEC countries through 1970 did not affect the volume of Turkey's exports to the EEC, since tariff quotas simply allowed for reduced duties on a given quantity of exports.

The EEC and other Western European countries are Turkey's natural major trading partners, as Table VII-4 indicates. They jointly account for over half of Turkey's exports. The United States has been a sizeable market for

1954, compared to coefficients of 3.11 for developed countries and 0.558 for underdeveloped countries. Michael Michaely, *Concentration in International Trade,* North-Holland (Amsterdam), 1962, pp. 11–12 and 16.

Table VII-4
Geographic distribution of Turkish exports, 1950 to 1971 (percentage of total exports)

	EEC Countries	EFTA Countries	U.S.	CMEA Countries	Other
1950	34.7	24.5	16.9	6.8	17.0
1951	40.3	14.5	21.3	7.9	16.0
1952	47.4	13.3	16.0	5.6	17.8
1953	35.8	12.3	20.5	7.3	24.1
1954	28.9	14.1	17.4	16.5	23.2
1955	34.1	14.4	15.5	21.9	14.1
1956	34.0	15.1	19.6	19.6	11.6
1957	31.3	15.4	26.0	18.4	8.9
1958	34.7	13.8	19.5	22.6	9.4
1959	39.5	14.9	18.0	11.6	16.0
1960	33.5	17.4	18.3	12.2	18.6
1961	37.1	17.7	18.8	8.6	17.8
1962	40.5	9.9	19.6	7.0	23.0
1963	38.0	24.5	13.5	9.6	14.4
1964	33.5	23.6	17.8	9.2	15.9
1965	33.9	18.0	17.7	14.7	15.7
1966	35.0	18.8	16.4	15.2	14.6
1967	33.7	16.9	17.8	16.7	14.9
1968	33.1	17.1	14.6	18.1	17.1
1969	40.1	15.0	11.0	17.0	16.8
1970	39.5	17.7	9.6	13.8	19.4
1971	39.3	19.5	10.1	12.0	19.0

Note: Totals do not always add to 100.0 due to rounding.
Sources: *Yearbook of International Trade Statistics,* United Nations, various issues; and
          Economic and Social Indicators – Turkey, USAID, 1965 and 1972.

Turkish exports, although in recent years the U.S. share has declined substantially.

Perhaps the most striking feature of Table VII-4 is the marked fluctuations in the share of the CMEA countries in Turkey's exports. The changes in shares accord closely with the delineation of Phases indicated above. In Phases II and III bilateral agreements have increased in absolute and relative importance for Turkey's exports. The share of CMEA countries has been considerably smaller during Phases I and IV.

Turkey has used bilateral trade agreements to sell her exports when they have not sold well on the free international market. Thus the dollar and physical volume figures for exports of given commodities do not accurately reflect the true "competitiveness" of the Turkish export position in any given

Table VII-5
Average prices received for exports under bilateral agreements, 1964 to 1968

Commodity	Unit Price (dollars per ton)		Percentage of Exports under Bilateral Agreements	
	Bilateral	Other	Quantity	Value
Chrome	23.56	20.86	32.29	35.01
Cotton	614.36	567.43	11.03	11.83
Hazelnuts	1149.61	1098.37	17.46	18.13
Hides and skins	1293.23	886.22	35.37	44.40
Mohair	1970.39	1959.76	56.54	56.67
Oilcakes	78.72	76.62	12.70	13.00
Raisins	319.44	317.37	25.24	25.37
Tobacco	1470.11	1314.87	14.80	16.27

Source: Can, *op. cit.* (Note 3), p. 18.

commodity, since a frequently used mechanism was to sell the "surplus" under bilateral trading agreements.

In addition to bilateral agreements made with CMEA countries, Turkey has had bilateral agreements with Egypt, Israel and Yugoslavia. Exports under those agreements (included in "other" in Table VII-4) accounted for 8.1 per cent of exports in 1955, 3.9 per cent in 1960, and declined in relative importance during the 1960's.[3]

Thus bilateral agreements were more important quantitatively in the 1950's, and there are no data available on prices and quantities under the agreements for that period. Some idea of the quantitative effects of bilateral agreements upon the export statistics for individual commodities in the 1960's can be gleaned from the data in Table VII-5. The first two columns give the average unit price of exports over the period 1964 to 1968, under bilateral agreements and for free foreign exchange. As can be seen, average prices received under bilateral agreements ranged from 45 per cent above world market prices for hides and skins to virtual parity with international prices for mohair. These five-year averages obscure a great deal of year-to-year variation. For example, prices for chrome sold under bilateral agreements averaged 13 per cent above prices for sales in convertible currencies. From 1964 to 1968, however, the annual percentage differences were −2, 2, 17 and 6 and 18 per cent, respectively.[4] Similarly, the percentage by value of chrome

3. Tevfik Can, *Anlaşmali Memleketler ile Olan Diş Ticaret İlişkileremiz,* Ek. 1-A, DPT 936-IPD 298, August 1970.
4. Obtaining meaningful unit value comparisons on the import side is far more difficult than it is for the export commodities. Can did, however, obtain some data. The prices (dollars per ton) of Turkish imports under bilateral agreements and from

exported under bilateral agreements was 26, 29, 24, 42, and 54 per cent, respectively, of total chrome exports in each of the five years. Other commodities show similar fluctuations.

There is every reason to believe that the bilateral agreements of the 1950's resulted in even larger discrepancies in unit values than in the 1960's. The prevalence of "switch deals," the general uncompetitiveness of Turkish exports, and the larger percentage of total exports taking place under bilateral agreements in the 1950's (not to mention the debt-repayment arrangements discussed in Chapter II) all indicate that the data on individual commodities were significantly affected by the extent of trade under bilaterals. This should be borne in mind when interpreting the data on individual commodities presented in Section III.

II. Government policies affecting exports

Government policies affecting a wide range of exports are examined in this section. First, attention is given to exchange-rate policy and its interaction with domestic price policies. Second, the practice of "price registration" and "price inspection" is discussed. Third, export licensing procedures are examined. Finally, government policies affecting non-traditional exports are analyzed.

In addition to policies affecting a wide range of exports, there were many domestic policies affecting specific export commodities. Those policies are examined below, when the behavior of individual export commodities is discussed.

Exchange rate policy

Table VII-6 summarizes the exchange rates applicable to different categories of export transactions in the 1953-to-1971 period. As can be seen, the

convertible currency countries were:

	Bilateral	Convertible
Iron bars (Thomas)	73	67
Iron bars (SM)	79.5	73
Steel sections	99–108	91
Sodium bicarbonate	51–53	49
Polyethylene	385–405	363–374
Zinc chromate	570	530–550

Data are from *ibid.*, p. 9. Thus the evidence suggests that import and export prices have probably been inflated by about the same proportions.

Table VII-6
Export EERs, PLD-EERs, and export–import EER differentials, 1953 to 1971

	Export EERs		PLD-EERs (1958 prices) Ratio		
	Traditional	Non-Traditional	Traditional	Non-Traditional	Export-to-Import EER
1953	2.80	3.92	5.83	8.17	–
1954	2.85	4.48	5.28	8.33	0.57
1955	2.89	4.50	4.82	7.50	0.56
1956	2.91	5.00	3.93	6.76	0.58
1957	2.94	5.00	3.27	5.56	0.47
1958	5.14	9.00	5.14	9.00	0.33
1959	6.77	9.00	5.69	7.56	0.47
1960	9.00	9.00	7.69	7.69	0.55
1961	9.00	9.00	7.56	7.56	0.55
1962	9.00	9.00	7.20	7.20	0.60
1963	9.00	9.00	6.82	6.82	0.58
1964	9.00	9.62	7.03	7.51	0.58
1965	9.00	9.69	6.67	7.18	0.51
1966	9.00	10.09	6.16	6.19	0.51
1967	9.02	9.72	5.71	6.15	0.50
1968	9.02	10.28	5.53	6.31	0.53
1969	9.37	10.31	5.45	6.00	0.55
1970	12.15	15.12	6.66	8.29	0.57
1971	13.20	16.50	6.19	7.10	0.58

Note: PLD-EERs were computed by dividing nominal EERs by home-goods prices until 1968. Thereafter the percentage increase in the wholesale price index was linked to the home-goods price index.

Sources: Appendix A for 1953 to 1969. Appendix C for 1970 and 1971.

weighted PLD-EER for traditional exports declined by 44 per cent between 1953 and 1957, and then rose 32 per cent above the 1953 level by 1960. It gradually declined during the 1960's, reaching 93 per cent of its 1953 level in 1969. For traditional exports, the 1970 devaluation brought the real exchange rate back only to its 1965 level. Non-traditional exports have fared somewhat better: except during the early 1960's, the EER has been above that for traditional exports; the PLD-EER declined somewhat less for non-traditional exports before 1958 and again during the 1960's; and the 1970 devaluation resulted in a greater increase in the PLD-EER for non-traditional exports[5] than for traditional exports.

The last column of Table VII-6 gives the ratio of the weighted export EER

5. See Appendix C, below, for details.

to the import EER over the period. Except for the 1957 to 1959 period, the relationship between the TL receipts for exports and the TL cost of imports has been remarkably constant, ranging between 0.5 and 0.6. Although the import EER does not measure the full differential incentive toward import-substituting production – because quantitative restrictions meant that the domestic price could be above landed cost and because new import-substituting production was protected by removing the commodity from the list of eligible imports – the fact is that the structure of taxes and duties on imports resulted in a substantial disparity between incentives for export and those for import-competing production, even without regard to the effects of quotas and import prohibitions. Despite the 1958 devaluation, there was little change in the ratio of export and import EERs between the 1950's and the 1960's. There was if anything a greater differential in the 1960's than in the 1950's.

Under optimal resource allocation, the incentive for import-substituting and export production would be equal at the margin.[6] Even if one interprets the non-traditional export EER as the marginal rate, it is evident that exchange-rate policy has led to a wide and persistent differential in incentives over the entire twenty-year period. Despite the fact that economic policy was much more closely coordinated with development goals in the 1960's than in the 1950's, discrimination against exports has been about the same throughout the two decades.

In subsequent efforts to trace the resource-allocational effects of the trade policies, the fact of the relative constancy of incentives should be borne in mind. There has been no time during the period under review when there have not been substantially greater rewards for home market production than for exports. As such, the export response examined below is one that occurred when disincentives were reduced or increased: there are no observations of what would have happened under equal incentives, or for that matter, under greater incentive for export than for import-substitution.

Price inspection and price registration

The practice of price registration during the 1950's was discussed in Chapter II. In essence, registered prices for various exports during the 1950's became minimum prices at which exports were permitted. It has already been seen that these prices, although designed to "protect exporters" and to prevent capital flight, undoubtedly led to the preclusion of some exports and the diversion of others to "switch deals" with Eastern Europe.

---

6. This statement holds even with monopoly power in trade, since optimal export "taxes" would appropriately equalize marginal incentives.

Price registration continued in the 1960's although it appears that the actual administration of the system was less onerous than the "minimum export prices" of the 1950's. For some commodities, e.g., chrome, price registration and related price policies continued to be unrealistic, with a continued loss of markets for Turkey.

The intent of price registration in the 1960's was:

> ...for the purpose of obtaining information in advance with a view to the conditions of exportation, facilitating the pursuance of commodity and price policy, avoiding artificial fluctuations, warning the exporters in regard to differences noticed in the prices of the same export commodities at the same time, as well as furnishing the persons concerned with information when and if required.
>
> During the process of registration, the authorities provide standardization of prices registered, making allowance for qualitative differences, of any commodity to be exported to any monetary area...[7]

The list of commodities for which registration was required prior to exportation was:[8]

Tobacco
Dried figs (processed and natural—scrap-paste)
Live animals
Pistachio nuts
Bran
Any and all kinds of oil-seed cakes
Fresh fruits, preserves and products
Wine
Shrimp and other marine products
Fresh fish, preserves and other products
Black and green olives (brine included)
Carpets
Souvenir items
Handicrafts
Woolen and cotton textiles
Clothing and wearing apparel, ready made
Colognes
Turkish delights and sugar candies
Meat and meat products

For most of the commodities on the list registered prices appear to have been set at reasonable levels, in contrast to the 1950's. While the practice of price registration was by no means a dead letter, the deleterious effects upon exports were undoubtedly much less than before, which was due both to the reduced scope of the requirement and to its more benevolent administration.

7. "Regulation Concerning Foreign Trade Affairs," Part I, Article 5, *Official Gazette, No. 12040,* July 5, 1965.
8. *Ibid.,* lists I and II.

Those commodities not subject to price registration requirements were still subject to a price declaration by the exporter at the time of shipment. The declarations submitted by exporters were subject, in principle, to *ex-post* inspection, and the authorities were empowered to require the exporter to surrender additional foreign exchange if the selling price was deemed unrealistically low. In practice, exporters were rarely confronted ex-shipment about their export prices in the 1960's, and interviews with exporters did not yield complaints about price inspections. However, such a set of administrative procedures undoubtedly created some uncertainty at the margin and could not have encouraged Turkish producers to be overly zealous in attempting to invade new export markets.

Export licensing

Export licenses were required for a variety of commodities throughout the 1953-to-1970 period. Ministerial permission was needed to obtain an export license in those cases, and licenses were not necessarily granted automatically. The relevant ministries were charged with: "...regulating offers and demands within domestic and foreign markets, avoiding speculation, and giving consideration to the conditions of local and foreign markets and to the requirements of this country."[9] Thus virtually all cereals required export licenses prior to exportation. Nuts, raisins, several metal ores, all articles containing precious metals and stones, and margarine were subject to export licensing, as were various other commodities from time to time.[10]

Export promotion policies

As seen above, import EERs were considerably above export EERs throughout the 1950-to-1970 period. This occurred despite the fact that premia were accorded to exports during the 1950's and export rebates were employed after 1963. The operation of the premium system was examined in Chapter II and therefore need not be dealt with here. In a sense, the premia as well as the rebates constituted a measure reducing the differential against exports rather than an export promotion measure. Rebate rates are given in Appendix A, and their net effect on EERs is included in Table VII-6.

The export premia of the 1950's and the rebates of the 1960's were the most significant export incentives, or partial offsets to disincentives, in the Turkish foreign trade regime. Here we focus upon those miscellaneous government policies that affected exports.

9. *Ibid.,* Article 6.

10. Meat exports rose sharply after the 1970 devaluation, and the domestic price of meat increased drastically. Meat exports were then banned.

On the books, there were a few export incentives in addition to the rebate system operative during most of the 1960's. By and large, those incentives began in the mid-1960's and like rebates assumed somewhat greater importance toward the end of the decade. Even then they were generally quantitatively unimportant, both in their effect upon EERs and in the total receipts of exporters, and hence deserve only brief mention here. These measures included: (1) export credits at subsidized rates of interest; (2) attempts at export promotion; (3) an increased probability of receiving favorable treatment when dealing with government officials if one were exporting; and (4) an import replenishment scheme.

Export credits.   Turkish interest rates have been regulated by legal ceilings imposed upon the banks. Since these ceilings have been below market-clearing interest rates, credit rationing has resulted. The statutory interest rate ceilings remained constant from 1961 to 1968. Loans for financing agriculture and exports were set at a 9.0 per cent nominal rate of interest, which with taxes and other charges was actually a 13.5 per cent nominal interest rate. Loans for other purposes were made at the nominal rate of 10.5 per cent, which was 15 per cent including taxes. Thus exporters were provided with a subsidy of about 1.5 per cent on the interest cost of their loans. Several features of the banking system, however, prevented the lower interest rate from having much effect. Most important was that the banks had little incentive to lend at these rates, given the excess demand for loans. Consequently, there were generally hidden charges which absorbed the difference in interest rates and perhaps even raised the actual rate of interest above the legal maximum when loans were made at subsidized rates.[11] Given the fact of credit rationing, moreover, additional exports did not automatically entitle exporters to additional credit at the subsidized rate. Thus it is doubtful whether the 1.5 per cent interest rate differential, even when it existed, did more than channel some funds to firms which were, at any event, exporting.

The government abolished the transaction tax and stamp duties on export financing operations in the fall of 1968, and reduced the nominal interest rate on export credits from 9 to 6 per cent. This constituted a reduction in the effective nominal rate of interest from 13.5 per cent to about 9 per cent. The export credit scheme was not quantitatively important even in its amended form. Central Bank credits extended for export financing purposes rose from TL 30 million in 1961 to TL 120 million in 1965 and TL 388 million in 1969, representing 1.4, 1.2, and 2.0 per cent, respectively, of all Central Bank credits,[12] and 0.8, 2.9 and 8 per cent of exports in those years. Given the

---

11. See Fry, *op. cit.* (Note 30, Chap. II), pp. 142 ff. for a fuller discussion.
12. *Monthly Bulletin,* Central Bank, October-December 1971, pp. 18–21.

small amount of Central Bank credit extended for export financing, it is unlikely that export credit subsidization constituted more than a very small incentive to exports at the margin.

Export promotion. The second export measure was directed toward promoting Turkish exports abroad, but this promotion was done on a very small scale. Individual businessmen found it difficult to obtain foreign exchange (except by paying the 50 per cent foreign travel tax) for purposes of foreign promotion of their products, and little was done at the government level. Although an Export Promotion Agency was established in the mid-1960's, its budget was very small and its primary function until 1967 was to administer export rebates. Despite expert recommendations and pleas from private exporters, efforts at export promotion were very limited. For example, the annual budget for promotion of hazelnut exports was $40,000, all of which was spent in the United States.[13] Thus government provisions for export promotion efforts in the 1960's would have to be judged relatively insignificant compared with the incentives for import-substitution.

One indication of the failure to adopt serious export promotion measures was inaction with regard to export standards. It was widely recognized that Turkish exports could be aided considerably if grading and quality standards were adopted and enforced by the government. But despite repeated technical advice to establish such standards, the government took little action. Many exporters claimed that their markets were spoiled by competitors with inferior or low quality products. Complaints about low quality were heard frequently in interviews both with Turkish exporters and with foreign importers of Turkish goods. The failure of the government to take positive action was symptomatic of its general policy toward exports.

Favored treatment to exporters. The next export incentive, a heightened probability of favorable government treatment in connection with administration of government regulations, is difficult to evaluate. Except that exports were deemed a "priority" sector and investments in industries that planned to export were accorded the same treatment as "priority" import-substituting investments, there was no legal provision for favored treatment of exporting firms. In interviews, however, some exporters claimed that if they could cover marginal costs in exporting it was worth their while to do so because they would receive slightly preferential treatment on other matters. This was undoubtedly more important for non-traditional exporters than it was for the exporters of traditional commodities, but even then preferential treatment was generally a relatively small incentive.

13. *Turkish Exports: Problems and Opportunities,* USAID (Ankara), 1967, p. 12.

Import replenishment. There was no scheme under which exporters could replace imports used in the production of goods for export before 1968. When import shortages limited production, the absence of an import replenishment scheme constituted a sizeable deterrent to exports.

In 1968 an import replenishment scheme was adopted under which a special quota of $2 million was set aside for import replenishment.[14] The amount allocated remained at $2 million even in 1970, and was under the control of the State Planning Organization.[15] Immediately after the introduction of the scheme, exporters of non-traditional goods declared the scheme to be inadequate on the grounds that paperwork, delays, and the relatively small amount of the quota meant that the scheme would not serve its purpose. They requested, through the Union of Chambers, an automatic 30 per cent retention of their export earnings instead.[16] The request was not acted upon, and the $2 million quota remained the only source of replenishment.

Either because it was too new or because of paperwork and other factors, exporting firms generally regarded the import replenishment scheme as being of little value. As with other export incentives the scheme was probably of use only to a few firms and did not constitute an across-the-board incentive for exports.

The picture that emerges in general is that little was done by the government to encourage exports during the 1960's. Although measures such as the reduced export interest rate were taken, they were generally far less strong than comparable measures to encourage import-substitution industries. By and large, government policies designed to encourage import-substitution provided far more powerful incentives than those aimed at increased export earnings. This general impression is reinforced when consideration is given to measures surrounding individual export commodities, to which we now turn.

III. Behavior of individual export commodities

In addition to the generally greater incentives for import-substitution than for exporting, a number of government policies specific to individual commodities further affected the relative attractiveness of exporting. In this section the features of the foreign trade regime as they influenced export commodities and the domestic policies with which those features interacted are examined, along with other institutional factors relevant to the analysis. The major export commodities — tobacco, cotton, hazelnuts, chrome, and copper

14. Decree No. 6/10649, September 13, 1968.
15. Decree No. 6/12856, January 5, 1970.
16. EIU, *op. cit.* (Note I, Chap. II), *No. 4,* November 1968, p. 7.

— are considered first. Thereafter, some minor export commodities are discussed.

Tobacco

Table VII-7 gives basic data on Turkish production, exports and position in the world tobacco market. Taking the averages of 1950 to 1952 and comparing them with the 1967-to-1969 period, Turkish production increased by 72 per cent over the 17-year interval, while exports increased by 47 per cent in volume. Foreign exchange earnings from tobacco thus grew at an average annual rate of 1.39 per cent.[17] Since world trade in unmanufactured tobacco grew by 70 per cent over the same time period, Turkey's share of the world tobacco market declined somewhat, falling from 9.6 per cent in the 1950-to-1952 period to 8.3 per cent in 1967 to 1969.

Although Turkish tobacco is not a perfect substitute for other tobaccos, Bulgarian and Greek tobaccos are major competitors, averaging almost twice the volume of Turkish exports. The last two columns of Table VII-7 give the ratios of Turkish export prices to the Greek and American export prices, respectively, as given by the IMF.

The very high ratios of the Turkish prices to the Greek and American prices in the 1953-to-1959 period reflect several factors: (1) the mechanism for debt repayment under bilateral trading arrangements with the Western European countries (discussed in Chapter II) under which foreign importers had to accept high Turkish prices if they wished to receive even partial repayment for their loans; (2) the large share of trade with Eastern European countries whose average prices paid were higher than prices in Western countries during those years; and (3) the relatively high prices charged by Turkey in the 1953-to-1959 period.

Domestic agricultural price policies are an important determinant of Turkish tobacco exports.[18] For domestic production of manufactured tobacco products, there is a State Monopoly. The State Monopoly inspects the tobacco crop each year and makes each farmer an offer of a price for his crop, taking into account the quality and condition of the harvest. The offer is open and there is no time limit upon its acceptance.

Meanwhile private merchants who buy tobacco only for the export trade

---

17. The irregular growth of tobacco export earnings can be seen by the poor fit of the regression equation:

$$ET_t = 66.2(1.0139)^t$$

where ET are millions of dollars of tobacco exports, and $t = 1$ in 1950. $R^2 = 0.167$ and the standard error of the time trend is 0.004.

18. This section draws on Forker, *op. cit.* (Note 24, Chap. II).

Table VII-7
Tobacco production and exports, and Turkish share of world market

	Produc-tion	Exports	Exports/ Produc-tion	World Exports	Turkish Share of World	Ratio: Turkish Price to Price in	
	(thousands of metric tons)		(%)	(thousands of metric tons)	Exports (%)	Greece	U.S.
1950	93	51	55	570	8.9	0.81	1.04
1951	89	58	65	620	9.4	0.92	0.85
1952	92	57	62	550	10.4	0.87	0.81
1953	118	72	61	610	11.8	1.14	0.83
1954	102	64	63	634	10.1	1.16	0.89
1955	120	60	50	679	8.8	1.08	1.03
1956	117	61	52	689	8.9	1.19	1.09
1957	123	88	72	733	12.0	1.18	1.01
1958	115	56	49	707	7.9	1.16	0.97
1959	129	67	52	723	9.8	1.14	0.87
1960	139	58	42	775	7.5	0.97	0.70
1961	101	88	87	846	10.4	0.87	0.60
1962	90	91	101	821	11.1	0.72	0.69
1963	132	45	34	895	5.0	0.81	0.90
1964	194	57	29	1008	5.7	0.96	0.96
1965	132	68	52	969	7.0	0.89	0.80
1966	164	85	52	921	9.2	0.86	0.72
1967	182	92	50	992	9.3	0.83	0.71
1968	163	81	50	968	8.4	0.82	0.64
1969	147	71	48	1000	7.1	0.86	0.65
1970	138	74	54	n.a.	n.a.	0.68	0.53

Source: Production and exports from SIS. World exports from *Trade Yearbook*, FAO, various issues; price data from *International Financial Statistics*. Data for 1970 and 1971 from *Economic and Social Indicators – Turkey*, USAID, 1972.

can also bid for the crop, and do so after the State Monopoly offers have been made. Thus the State Monopoly's offer in effect sets a floor under the export price. When the State Monopoly ends up purchasing more of the crop than it uses it can either add to inventories or sell at a loss. When the latter has occurred, "the merchants complained bitterly."[19] Forker concludes that, "Essentially the State Monopoly acts as a benevolent price leader that does not retaliate, but ... has adequate resources to cover its mistakes."[20]

The Monopoly has exported over the years, although the magnitude of its exports is not known. Forker obtained data for the period 1961 to 1965:

19. Forker, *op. cit.* (Note 24, Chap. II), p. 25.
20. *Ibid.*

over that five-year interval exports were 20,000 metric tons greater than merchants' purchases had been over the period. Most striking in this regard was 1962, when the monopoly price of TL 11.75 per kilogram exceeded the export price of TL 9.72 per kilogram. The price paid by merchants was TL 11.52. However, merchants purchased 39.1,000 metric tons, whereas exports were 91,000 metric tons. Thus the very low relative price of Turkish tobacco in 1962 (Table VII-7) may reflect the State Monopoly's distress sales of the commodity rather than other factors.

Data are not available to indicate the fraction of the crop sold under bilateral trading arrangements, nor the inventory holdings of either merchants or the State Monopoly over the entire period. Given the State Monopoly's price policies, there must have been sizeable fluctuations from year to year in both inventories and distress sales to Eastern Europe. For the period 1964 to 1968, for which Can's data are available, exports to bilateral-agreement countries ranged from 12 to 18 per cent of the value of Turkish exports.[21]

Forker points out that tobacco production has increased more rapidly than domestic consumption plus exports. He further notes that "the monopoly practice of pricing the high-quality high-cost tobacco at a higher level than the world market will bear, and the low quality at a lower price than the market will bear is encouraging the exportation of lower quality Turkish (oriental) tobacco."[22] His calculations indicate that the Tobacco Monopoly's intervention in the domestic market represented an annual subsidy of almost 8 per cent of the value of the crop for the 1962-to-1966 period.[23]

These considerations taken together suggest that domestic price support for tobacco and the behavior of the State Monopoly have been the key determinants of the quantity and value of Turkish tobacco exports. Given the ability of the State Monopoly to sustain losses, it is hardly surprising that tobacco exports appear to have been little affected (except perhaps by short-term speculative behavior) by fluctuations in the real exchange rate or by the 1958 devaluation. As will be seen below, there is no statistical evidence that tobacco exports have been influenced by changes in the real exchange rate, nor by changes in the domestic-export price relationship.

Cotton

Table VII-8 presents data on Turkish production and exports of cotton, as well as the domestic and export prices of cotton. As can be seen, cotton production has increased rapidly over the period since 1950. Turkey has

21. Can, *op. cit.* (Note 3), Ek. II-A.
22. Forker, *op. cit.* (Note 24, Chap.II), p. 48.
23. *Ibid.,* p. 52.

Table VII-8
Cotton production, exports, and prices, 1950 to 1971

	Production (thousands of metric tons)	Exports (thousands of metric tons)	Export Price (TL/kg)	Domestic Price (TL/kg)
1950	118	76	2.56	2.85
1951	150	56	3.86	3.74
1952	165	70	2.77	2.41
1953	139	101	2.19	2.00
1954	142	60	2.44	2.41
1955	157	52	2.45	3.00
1956	165	35	2.13	3.02
1957	135	61	1.92	4.30
1958	180	35	1.82	4.32
1959	195	97	1.52	4.60
1960	175	80	5.41	5.04
1961	212	89	5.61	5.08
1962	245	105	5.02	4.87
1963	257	146	5.23	4.88
1964	326	168	5.23	4.76
1965	326	190	5.08	4.73
1966	382	259	4.83	4.58
1967	396	248	5.18	5.05
1968	435	252	5.47	4.95
1969	387	235	4.92	4.59
1970	400	202	6.71	8.60
1971	n.a.	313	9.52	9.28

Note: Export data from the UN and those from SPO do not agree. For 1963, the UN gives cotton exports as 134,000 metric tons. SPO data were used for the 1960's to obtain data for recent years.

Sources: Production data 1960-to-1969, *Indices of Agricultural Production 1960-to-1969*, USDA, ERS-Foreign 265, April 1970. 1950-to-1959 data provided to the author by USDA. 1970, *Economic and Social Indicators—Turkey*, USAID, 1972. Exports 1950-to-1962, *Yearbook of International Trade Statistics*, UN, various issues. 1963-to-1970, *Yıllık İhracat* 1961-to-1966 and 1967-to-1970. Export Prices, *Monthly Bulletin*, Central Bank, various issues. Domestic Prices, *Statistical Yearbook*, SIS, various issues.

almost tripled the volume of cotton exports and dollar earnings of cotton over the period, increasing her share of world cotton exports from 2 per cent in 1957 to 6 per cent in 1967—1969. Thus earnings from cotton exports grew at an average annual rate of 4.5 per cent.[24]

24. The regression equation is $EC_t = 6.0 \ (1.045)^t$, with $R^2 = 0.27$ and the standard error of the trend, 0.017.

Whereas tobacco was Turkey's largest single export in the 1950's, cotton was the biggest foreign-exchange-earning commodity in the 1960's. Unlike tobacco, the volume of cotton exports declined markedly in the middle 1950's, and cotton exports appear to be quite sensitive to changes in the real exchange rate.[25] Domestic consumption of cotton products has increased markedly, and there is no evidence of any accumulation of stocks. Thus in contrast to tobacco, increases in cotton exports require increases in domestic production or diversion of production from domestic to foreign consumption.

There appears to have been considerably less price intervention in the domestic cotton market than has been true for other major Turkish exports. A Union of Sales Cooperatives, essentially a government organization with voluntary producer membership, is the vehicle by which price intervention could occur, but Forker estimates that prices set by the Union have either been below market clearing prices or there has been no intervention price set during most of the years in the period under review.[26] Thus conditions in the cotton market have been primarily determined by market forces rather than government intervention.

Hazelnuts

Table VII-9 provides data on the performance of hazelnut exports in the period since 1950. Hazelnut exports have doubled in volume, and export earnings have tripled as the international price of the nuts has risen. The average annual growth of export value was thus 8.0 per cent.[27] As can be seen, there are sharp year-to-year fluctuations in production which have been smoothed on the export side by government intervention.

The hazelnut sales cooperative, Fiskobirlik, is similar to the cotton sales cooperative in its organization. About half the growers belong to it, although purchases are also made from non-members. The government determines the support price for the crop and lends the cooperative sufficient funds to purchase all hazelnuts offered at that price. A minimum export price is also set at the same time. Losses on export sales are not financed by the government. Forker estimates that price intervention for the first half of the 1960's amounted to a 7 per cent subsidy to hazelnut growers.[28]

Although Turkey's share in the hazelnut market is large, there is considerable evidence that the demand for hazelnuts is price-elastic. They are a close

25. See below, Section IV.
26. Forker, *op. cit.* (Note 24, Chap. II), p. 34.
27. The regression equation is $EH_t = 5.16(1.0798)^t$, with $R^2 = 0.89$ and the standard error of the trend, 0.0065.
28. Forker, *op. cit.* (Note 24, Chap. II), p. 52.

Table VII-9
Hazelnut production, exports, and prices, 1950 to 1971

	Production (thousands of metric tons)	Exports (thousands of metric tons)	Exports (millions of dollars)	Prices		
				Domestic (TL/kg)	Export (TL/kg)	Ratio
1950	23	27	18.6	n.a.	n.a.	n.a.
1951	91	22	18.0	2.26	2.42	0.93
1952	73	26	18.4	2.19	2.00	1.09
1953	40	29	22.3	2.32	2.16	1.07
1954	115	31	25.0	2.75	2.48	1.11
1955	26	44	43.9	3.83	2.82	1.36
1956	65	24	29.5	3.91	3.54	1.10
1957	73	40	44.4	2.82	3.07	0.92
1958	100	32	27.6	4.33	2.63	1.65
1959	90	52	43.1	6.62	2.34	2.83
1960	59	42	39.2	8.76	9.06	0.97
1961	70	36	43.4	10.87	10.53	1.03
1962	90	44	56.0	12.30	11.56	1.06
1963	91	42	42.4	11.58	11.71	0.99
1964	16	49	50.2	9.54	9.25	1.03
1965	68	60	61.7	9.57	9.52	1.01
1966	190	56	53.2	9.58	9.46	1.01
1967	70	74	84.2	10.24	10.43	0.98
1968	132	65	75.9	10.95	10.82	1.01
1969	170	83	107.7	12.17	11.80	1.03
1970	225	46	87.0	12.84	15.97	0.80
1971	n.a.	65	81.3	14.53	17.17	0.85

Note: Export data are for shelled nuts; production data are for unshelled. Forker
estimates that about 90 per cent of the crop is exported.

Sources: Production and export data: same as Table VII-8. Price data from Forker, *op.
cit.* (Note 24, Chap. II); and *Monthly Bulletin,* Central Bank, various issues.

substitute for other nuts and are purchased primarily for baked goods, where substitution possibilities as well as changes in ingredient proportions are sensitive to relative changes in input prices. Forker points out that hazelnut export earnings have been positively correlated with the volume exported, as is evident from Table VII-9. Demand for hazelnuts, moreover, has apparently become more price elastic in the 1960's than it was in the 1950's.[29]

Given this, the government's policy of withholding supplies from the export market in good crop years is open to question. There have been years in

29. *Ibid.,* p. 32.

which the minimum export price has been set well above international levels. Thus in the fall of 1966, with a record crop, a high minimum export price apparently adversely affected sales.[30] Despite Turkey's share of the market there is evidently no reason why other countries cannot develop hazelnut production should Turkey over-use her short-term monopoly position. With price-elastic demand, it is difficult to understand the need for active government intervention to smooth year-to-year fluctuations in exports to the degree that has been undertaken.

As with tobacco exports, government intervention policies have been the major determinant of export volume and value, and market forces have not been permitted to operate freely in the hazelnut market. As such, it has not been exchange rate policy *per se* but rather domestic price policy and minimum export prices that have determined the behavior of hazelnut exports.

Raisins and figs

Raisins and figs constitute the bulk of Turkey's dried fruit exports. As indicated in Table VII-3 the Turkish share of the raisin market is sizeable, and Turkey has more than half the world's exports of figs.

Table VII-10 gives the basic data on production and exports of raisins and figs. Export earnings from raisins have increased at an average annual rate of 4 per cent.[31] As can be seen, raisins are approximately three times as important a source of foreign exchange earnings as are figs. Data on export value and volume for figs are unavailable prior to 1954; the average annual rate of growth of export earnings over the 16-year period was 4.9 per cent.

Since 1964, export prices for raisins — effected through the relevant sales cooperative — have been set on the basis of a trade agreement between Turkey, Greece and Australia, with cooperation from Californian growers. Price intervention by the cooperative in the domestic market has amounted to an annual average subsidy of 8 per cent to growers, according to Forker's estimates. Forker estimates that production is responsive to price increases and that the intervention program has resulted in "more production and more burdensome and costly stocks..."[32] Thus domestic production has not limited exports, which have been determined primarily by government policies with respect to export prices.

Fig exports are a relatively small fraction of total production, which has tripled since the early 1950's. Although there has been subsidization of fig

30. *Turkish Exports: Prospects and Problems,* USAID (Ankara), 1967, pp. 12 and 25.
31. The regression equation estimated for the time trend of the value of raisin exports is: $ER_t = 4.6(1.0398)^t$, with $t = 0$ in 1950, $R^2 = 0.46$ and the standard error of the time trend, 0.010.
32. Forker, *op. cit.* (Note 24, Chap. II), p. 52.

Table VII-10
Production and exports of dried fruit, 1950 to 1971

	Raisins			Figs		
	Production (thousands of metric tons)	Exports (thousands of metric tons)	(millions of dollars)	Production (thousands of metric tons)	Exports (thousands of metric tons)	(millions of dollars)
1950	69	80	21	86	n.a.	n.a.
1951	52	35	11	107	n.a.	n.a.
1952	68	44	11	118	n.a.	n.a.
1953	64	33	7	105	n.a.	n.a.
1954	65	53	11	107	12	3.3
1955	40	33	8	100	16	3.6
1956	100	48	15	121	16	3.6
1957	53	59	19	137	17	4.2
1958	65	49	18	155	17	3.6
1959	100	61	18	156	15	2.0
1960	67	82	23	145	35	6.9
1961	85	64	16	204	24	4.9
1962	90	69	16	210	30	5.7
1963	60	66	17	208	27	5.9
1964	73	52	17	206	25	6.1
1965	120	66	21	210	29	7.0
1966	75	68	22	215	28	6.7
1967	93	72	23	232	32	7.2
1968	103	75	23	215	32	7.0
1969	80	77	23	215	28	6.8
1970	n.a.	70	21	214	29	7.2
1971	n.a.	89	22	n.a.	32	8.6

Sources: Physical exports and production from *Trade Yearbook*, FAO, various issues; export values from *International Financial Statistics*, International Monetary Fund (Washington); *Annual Foreign Trade Statistics*, SIS; and *Yearbook of International Trade Statistics*, United Nations.

production, Forker estimates that the intervention levels have generally been below market levels since 1961, and hence that intervention has not significantly affected the fig market.[33] Evidently little attempt has been made to develop fig exports into a year-round activity: fig exports have as yet been realized only during the processing season. This has led to a loss of a fraction of the crop due to labor shortages and to a poorer export performance than could have been realized had attempts been made to smooth out export sales

33. *Ibid.*, pp. 48 ff.

during the year. Also, given Turkey's high share of world exports, it is significant that little by way of promotional work has been done. Expert opinion seems to be that had greater attention been paid to quality standardization, marketing and smoothing out the seasonal pattern of exports, Turkish exports of figs could have been much greater than their actual levels.[34]

Chrome

Of all Turkey's major exports, chrome has had the worst performance. Earnings from chrome exports decreased at an average annual rate of 4.4 per cent over the period 1950 to 1969.[35] As indicated in Table VII-3, the Turkish share of the world chrome market was 18 to 20 per cent during the 1950's, declined to a low of 9.9 per cent in 1963, and rose thereafter to 12.3 per cent in 1969.

Table VII-11 gives data on the production and exports of chrome. Many factors, both domestic and international, have contributed to its poor performance. During the late 1950's the minimum export price for chrome was substantially above world market levels. Moreover, as seen in Chapter II, lack of transport equipment and failure to obtain imports even for replacement of machinery and equipment led to high costs at the mines, so that production and exports declined. On the international front, new low-cost sources of chrome were developed in other countries, and aluminum and stainless steel were substituted for chrome in many of its uses.

In the early 1960's the Turkish export prices were again set above international levels, with further losses in Turkey's share of the world market. Chrome was one commodity for which price registration practices did adversely affect exports in the 1960's. Internal rail charges for exportable chrome became a major problem, as the price of shipping a ton to port was $13 per ton compared with production costs of $10 a ton at high-cost mines and a unit export price of $20 (see Table VII-11).[36]

By the late 1960's there were some increases in investment in the mining sector. The first signs of revival in chrome output came in 1969. Output even then was still only 651 thousand long tons, contrasted with an average annual production of 785 thousand long tons in the 1957-to-1958 period. There is no evidence that the decline in production was associated with a decrease in economic reserves. On the contrary, Turkish reserves continue to be among the richest and largest in the world.

34. *Turkish Exports*, USAID, *op. cit.* (Note 30), pp. 13–14.
35. The estimated regression equation for the time trend was:

$$ECH_t = 21.2 \ (0.955)^t, \text{ with } t = 0 \text{ in 1950. } R^2 = 0.26; \text{ standard error} = 0.018.$$

36. *Turkish Exports*, USAID, *op. cit.* (Note 30), p. 23.

Table VII-11
Chrome production and exports

	Production (thousands of tons)	Exports (thousands of tons)	Exports (millions of dollars)	Unit Price (dollars per ton)
1950	415	348	10.7	30.7
1951	588	497	16.5	33.3
1952	763	617	22.9	37.1
1953	637	668	28.2	42.2
1954	531	351	15.4	43.9
1955	634	551	19.8	35.9
1956	820	632	23.3	36.8
1957	900	562	21.4	38.1
1958	512	508	15.5	30.5
1959	382	301	8.9	29.6
1960	471	380	11.5	30.3
1961	396	383	9.9	25.8
1962	461	344	8.5	24.7
1963	397	209	3.7	17.7
1964	406	346	7.0	20.2
1965	588	450	8.7	19.3
1966	503	501	10.3	20.6
1967	365	309	7.1	23.0
1968	400	381	9.6	25.2
1969	651	389	12.8	32.9

Note: Tons are long tons.
Sources: *Statistical Summary of the Mineral Industry, op. cit.* (Table VII-3); and *International Financial Statistics,* various issues.

Although it is difficult to document, it appears that the entire range of governmental policies has contributed to the failure of chrome exports to expand. It is perhaps suggestive of this that neither the FFYP nor the SFYP contained any discussion of the decline in chrome exports. In the FFYP, it was projected that chrome exports would increase from the estimated level of 400,000 metric tons in 1962 to 500,000 metric tons in 1967. In the SFYP chrome exports were projected to remain constant at 500,000 metric tons per annum throughout the Second Plan period. Domestic production was expected to increase at an average annual rate of 3.1 per cent but (without explanation) the entire increment was expected to be absorbed by domestic demand. Given the perceived foreign exchange stringency at the time the SFYP was formulated, it is remarkable that little consideration was given to increasing chrome exports.

Copper

Although copper export earnings have grown at an average annual rate of 4.3 per cent, overall export performance has been relatively poor, especially in view of world market conditions.[37] As seen in Table VII-3 the Turkish share of the world copper market has fallen from 1 per cent to 0.5 per cent since the mid-1950's. Table VII-12 gives the basic data.

Most of the growth in export earnings can be seen to have originated from

Table VII-12
Copper production, exports, and prices, 1950 to 1970

	Production (thousands of tons)	Exports		International Price (dollars per 100 pounds)
		(thousands of tons)	(millions of dollars)	
1950	11.5	6.2	2.5	22.38
1951	17.3	7.4	8.1	27.58
1952	23.0	16.4	14.9	32.68
1953	26.9	22.2	11.9	31.55
1954	24.8	15.5	7.2	31.34
1955	23.4	15.5	8.8	44.53
1956	24.3	18.9	17.0	40.52
1957	24.0	14.4	8.6	27.02
1958	22.2	12.5	6.5	24.72
1959	23.5	26.8	6.9	29.68
1960	25.8	18.5	12.7	30.70
1961	19.7	8.1	4.8	28.69
1962	25.4	14.2	8.9	29.23
1963	24.4	9.9	5.9	29.26
1964	27.7	21.1	10.2	43.84
1965	28.3	28.0	17.2	58.72
1966	28.5	19.6	24.8	69.22
1967	28.7	15.5	16.6	51.10
1968	31.5	14.9	13.7	56.09
1969	29.5	7.0	5.9	66.51
1970	29.0	5.0	4.9	64.17

Note: Tons are long tons.
Sources: Production and export data from *Statistical Summary of Mineral Industries,*
          op. cit. (Table VII-3). International price is the U.K. wholesale price, *Inter-*
          national Financial Statistics.

37. The fitted time trend is $ECO_t = 6.4(1.043)^t$, with $t = 0$ in 1950, $R^2 = 0.20$, and the standard error of the trend, 0.021.

a more favorable international price rather than significant increases in export volume. As with chrome, high freight charges have been a problem for copper exports. Similarly, production stagnated in the late 1950's and early 1960's due to high domestic costs relative to international prices.

Part of the decline in copper exports in the late 1960's was offset by increased domestic refining of copper and exports of manufactured copper. As of 1970, however, the increase in manufactured copper exports was not sufficient to offset the decline in copper exports. Considerable emphasis was placed on the development of a domestic refining industry in the SFYP, and some observers believe this will result in sizeable expansion of manufactured copper exports in the 1970's. Despite that, the diagnosis as of 1971 must be that the performance of copper exports was as poor, relative to international market conditions, as that of chrome.

Minor exports

In addition to the commodities discussed above, Turkey has a variety of minor exports, many of which have considerable export potential. Among these products are lumber, wool, olive oil, minerals other than those discussed, fresh fruits and vegetables, processed foods, and a variety of manufactured and handicraft products.

The picture that emerges from any review of export policy is that government policy in general has not incorporated measures that would encourage the development of these products as a rapidly growing source of foreign exchange. This is true both of exchange-rate policy and of other sorts of actions that might enable rapid growth of export earnings. For example, Turkey's mineral wealth is much greater than current production and export figures reflect. Government policy has generally favored public ownership and development of mineral resources, yet many government-owned economic mineral reserves have not been exploited. Turkey's proved reserves of borate ores, for example, are the second largest in the world, and world consumption of borates is increasing at an average annual rate of 10 per cent. Yet Turkey's exports remain at about $5 million per year. Technical surveys have suggested that a four-fold increase in borate production could be accomplished in a relatively short space of time if the managerial, organizational and capital resources were available for the purpose. Yet despite applications by private firms to enter into joint ventures with foreign companies for the purpose of investing and developing mineral production, government action was not forthcoming.

World demand for lumber is also increasing rapidly, and the Anatolian plain is clearly an area with a comparative advantage in lumber products. Turkey's annual timber growth potential is about the same as Finland's, yet

Turkish exports have averaged around $2 million per year, contrasted with Finland's $550 million (excluding paper).[38] Investments in sawmills, plywood and other fabricating facilities have been estimated to yield high rates of return, yet efforts to develop these resources have been relatively small to date.

Turkey's proximity to Europe and the Mediterranean climate of southern Turkey suggest a strong comparative advantage in fresh and processed fruit and vegetable exports.[39] Citrus fruit exports averaged around $2 million in the early 1960's, rising to $10 million by 1969. Similarly, processed food exports rose from $10 million in the early 1960's to $20 million in 1969. As will be seen below, there is considerable evidence that these exports are sensitive to changes in the effective exchange rate.

With or without appropriate exchange-rate policy, other sorts of government actions could have facilitated the growth of minor export industries, but they were not forthcoming. The lack of standardization of grades has been a frequent headache for Turkish exporters, and even those whose quality control has been adequate have found themselves suspect, given the failure of their compatriots to conform to similar standards. Considerably more could have been done to assist the many small producers of given commodities to organize export development and promotion. This is particularly true in the case of export crops and the agricultural processing industries. As with exchange-rate policy, government actions with respect to import-substituting industries were much more strenuous than those for promotion of new exports.

IV. The determinants of exports

As seen in Section III, direct government actions have frequently been the dominant determinants of export performance, especially for the major agricultural commodities, the export prices of which have not been reflected either to domestic consumers or to domestic producers because of intervention. It is nonetheless worthwhile to examine the degree to which Turkish exports have been responsive to exchange-rate policy. To examine this question, a simple model was tested statistically for a variety of exports.

In theory, as Turkish resources increased the transformation curve shifted outward. Given the outward shift, the relative growth in export supply would

38. Turkey's standing forests are about half those of Finland, but with appropriate conservation practices weather conditions would yield higher growth.

39. Wool and olive oil are two other commodities whose export performance could have been considerably better. Turkey's share of the world market is very small in each, and there is ample opportunity for increase in production and exports.

be a function of the price received for a given commodity relative to the price of home goods. While such a specification is obviously too simple to capture all aspects of export determination, it nonetheless has the advantage of focussing directly upon the role of the commodity-specific PLD-EER as a determinant of export earnings.[40] Of course such a model is invalid for those commodities where Turkish exports were large enough to affect the world price significantly. But as seen above this was probably true only of figs, tobacco and hazelnuts. And for hazelnuts the possibility of substitution with other nuts raises a question as to the degree of monopoly power held by Turkey.

As a proxy for the outward shift in the transformation curve, two variables were used: (1) for agricultural commodities an index of total agricultural production was used as the "capacity" variable; (2) for other exports time was used as a proxy. An index of agricultural production was developed in the following manner: the U.S. Department of Agriculture provides price weights (at international prices) for each major agricultural commodity,[41] and employs those prices to devise an index of agricultural production during the 1960's. Estimates of physical output by specific agricultural commodities were obtained for the 1950's, and the outputs were then multiplied by the price weights to devise a continuous index for the 1950-to-1969 period. That index was used throughout the regression analysis.

Since weather conditions lead to large fluctuations in agricultural production, the use of an agricultural production index as an indicator of the shift in the transformation curve has an additional advantage. Since weather factors affect commodity production generally, an agricultural production index reflects weather variation and provides a good measure of total domestic capacity for agricultural commodities.

The relative price variable was constructed as follows. When a dollar export price series was available, it was multiplied by the effective exchange rate appropriate to the commodity, and the resulting product was then divided by the index of the price of home goods (from Table I-5). Thus if an increase in the relative price of an export commodity generated an increase in the quantity exported, the sign of the relative price coefficient would be positive.

In general, physical quantities of exports were employed as the dependent

40. It was initially anticipated that a variable to reflect the state of domestic excess demand should also be employed, since that variable would reflect the net shift in excess supply. The percentage rate of inflation did prove to be significant but not quantitatively important. It was finally dropped from the regressions, since better fits resulted from logarithmic estimation, and negative observations could not be used.

41. *Indices of Agricultural Production, 1960—1969,* USDA Economic Research Service, Foreign Regional Analysis Division, ERS-Foreign 265, April 1970.

variable except in cases where no appropriate physical unit was available, as with minor exports. In those cases the dependent variable was in units of millions of U.S. dollars. Since the logarithmic form of the regression generally differed little from the arithmetic and had the decided advantage that the coefficients are easier to interpret, logarithmic estimates were used in all cases.

International prices are assumed given and the dependent variable is in physical units, so that the coefficients on the price terms indicate the percentage increase in exports resulting from a 1 per cent increase in the real domestic price of the export commodity. Thus a zero coefficient implies that the quantity exported is not affected by the real price of the export (PLD-EER multiplied by the international price), and a positive coefficient is the percentage increase in export earnings resulting from a 1 per cent increase in the PLD-EER, the foreign price assumed given.

One other factor should be noted. The Turkish export season for agricultural commodities covers the last quarter of one calendar year and the first quarter of the next. Therefore, in addition to estimating the supply response based upon annual observations, an effort was made to determine exports from the fourth quarter of one calendar year to the third quarter of the next. Such a construction was not possible for all exports, although quarterly foreign exchange earnings were available for a number of major agricultural export commodities. For those commodities the constructed fourth-to-third quarter annual export earnings figure was used as the dependent variable. To take the 1959 crop as an example, exports from October 1959 to September 1960 were the dependent observation; 1959 agricultural production and the prevailing real price of the commodity as of December 1959 were the independent observations. When it was impossible to construct such a dependent variable according with the export season, agricultural production lagged one year was used as an alternative independent variable.

Table VII-13 gives the results of the computations. The first column indicates the commodity and the units of the dependent variable. The "seasonal" dependent variable is export earnings from that commodity in millions of dollars, fourth quarter of one year to third quarter of the next. The second column indicates the number of years for which data were available. All variables except for time were estimated in logs. Pf.EER/PH is the foreign price of the commodity times the EER for that commodity divided by the price of home goods. Standard errors of the coefficients are given in parentheses.

As expected, the results for chrome, copper, hazelnuts and tobacco reflected no influence of the PLD-EER. In the case of the minerals, minimum export prices, domestic transport charges and other government policies determined export performance. As can be seen, the coefficient on time is

Table VII-13
Estimated export response to real exchange rate changes

Independent Variable	No. of Years	Independent Variables				
		Agricultural Production	Lagged Agricultural Production	Time	$\dfrac{\text{Pf.EER}}{\text{PH}}$	R^2
Chrome exports						
tons	19			−1.5 (0.12)	−0.12 (0.12)	0.29
dollars	19			−0.36 (0.18)	−0.23 (0.19)	0.41
Copper exports						
tons	19			0.65 (0.17)	−0.01 (0.22)	0.10
dollars	18			−0.07 (0.15)	0.57 (0.21)	0.35
Cotton exports						
tons	19	3.33 (0.41)			1.14 (0.34)	0.80
seasonal	15	3.47 (0.66)			0.99 (0.60)	0.73
Hazelnut exports						
tons	17	1.83 (0.50)			0.04 (0.09)	0.67
tons	17		1.78 (0.37)		−0.05 (0.08)	0.75
Minor exports						
dollars	19	1.19 (0.30)			0.81 (0.40)	0.51
seasonal	15	1.80 (0.24)			1.34 (0.26)	0.86
Mohair exports						
tons	19	−3.09 (3.82)			3.05 (1.24)	0.36
tons	19		−2.35 (3.30)		2.92 (1.21)	0.35
Olive oil exports						
tons	10	9.14 (6.75)			5.39 (6.04)	0.23
tons	10		1.13 (6.91)		8.21 (6.37)	0.30
Raisin exports						
tons	17	0.61 (0.50)			0.17 (0.11)	0.59
tons	17		0.91 (0.37)		0.10 (0.09)	0.68
Tobacco exports						
tons	19	0.42 (0.30)			−0.01 (0.17)	0.12
tons	19		0.45 (0.26)		−0.04 (0.16)	0.17

negative for chrome and insignificant for copper. In neither estimate where the physical quantity of exports is the dependent variable is the relative price coefficient significantly different from zero. The coefficient on relative price for dollar copper export earnings probably reflects the influence of the autonomously determined foreign price on total export earnings.

The coefficient of the relative export price for tobacco exports is also insignificantly different from zero, and even agricultural production (in either form) is insignificant. Given government price intervention policies and Turkish monopoly power in the export market, the results are hardly surprising. The picture for hazelnuts is similar: the PLD-EER does not appear to have affected the quantity exported. In view of the government's direct intervention in the hazelnut export market, it seems clear that direct intervention, and not price policy, determined exports.

For cotton, where government intervention has been minimal, agricultural production and the relative export price are both highly significant. The results suggest that a 1 per cent increase in the real exchange rate led to a 1 per cent increase in export earnings from cotton exports. The sharp decline in cotton exports in the mid-1950's and the rapid growth in cotton exports in the 1960's can thus be attributed largely to exchange-rate policy.

"Minor exports" were defined to be all exports except those for chrome, cotton, hazelnuts, raisins, tobacco and wheat (since wheat was a major export in the early 1950's and not exported in the 1960's). The dollar value of exports had to be used as the dependent variable, and observations were constructed by subtracting the value of the major exports from total export earnings in each year. Minor exports averaged about $100 million in the 1950's and ranged from $133 million to $192 million in the 1960's. Given that commodities such as figs and copper are included in minor exports, the response of the commodity group as a whole to real exchange-rate changes is high. The "seasonal" dependent variable performed better; but upon either estimate, a 1 per cent increase in the real exchange rate resulted in more than a 0.8 per cent increase in minor export earnings. On a 1969 base, this would imply an increase in minor export earnings of $1.9 million in response to an increase of TL 0.1 per dollar in the exchange rate. These results must of course be interpreted with care, but they reinforce other available evidence. There probably is considerable scope for export diversification and growth along non-traditional lines with appropriate exchange-rate and government policies.

Two minor exports for which data were available were olive oil and raisins. Exports of olive oil were negligible before 1960. The production pattern remains bi-annual: a good crop year is followed by a very poor one. Since olive oil does not, therefore, conform to the fluctuations in agricultural production, it is hardly surprising that the agricultural production variable proved insignificant. Given the few degrees of freedom, the estimated coefficient of the relative export price is not significant. For what it is worth, however, it is large.

Raisin exports had a positive coefficient on the relative export price variable, although it was insignificant. Given government intervention, the surplus stocks of raisins in Turkey, and other factors, the result is not surprising.

Thus it would appear that except for cotton, Turkey's major exports have probably been determined primarily by government domestic policies and interventions in the export market rather than by the nature of the trade regime itself. For cotton (where intervention is less pronounced) and for minor exports, the picture is very different. Exports of cotton and those of a variety of smaller commodities appear to have been considerably influenced by exchange-rate policy.

The general picture that emerges is one of strong bias toward import-substitution in both exchange-rate and domestic policies. An important question is what would have happened had Turkish policy been export orientated, or at least geared to equal emphasis on export promotion and on import-substitution. The fact is that cotton exports and minor exports grew much more rapidly than did earnings from commodities subject to government intervention. That happened despite the sizeable disparity in EERs between minor exports and imports and the consequently greater price incentives for expansion of domestic import-competing production. Failure to develop minerals exports, predominantly produced by SEEs, is perhaps most telling in this regard, since there can be little argument about market potential for those commodities.

What would have happened under an alternative government policy orientation is conjectural by its nature. Available evidence, however, suggests that Turkish export potential has not been given a chance. Insofar as pessimism about export prospects has influenced the government's decision to focus upon import-substitution there is little empirical support for such pessimism and a considerable amount of evidence that export prospects might, under appropriate policies and incentives, be fairly bright.

Part Four

Resource Allocational and Growth Effects
of the Regime in the 1960's

CHAPTER VIII

Microeconomic effects of the trade regime

One can make a number of qualitative predictions from economic theory about the effects of a trade regime such as that of Turkey. (1) There are bound to be differences among industries in the social return to factors of production employed in them. (2) The criteria for obtaining import licenses and permission to import capital goods will lead to differences in efficiency among firms. (3) The method of allocating import licenses is likely to lead to underutilization of capacity and general excess costs of production. (4) Subsidizing capital goods imports will induce substitution of capital for labor, at least for firms receiving permission to import capital goods. This will have implications for employment and income distribution.

In this chapter an attempt is made to ascertain the quantitative importance of each of these effects in Turkey during the latter half of the 1960's. That period represents a time when the trade regime was fairly stable (although the premium on import licenses was increasing over time) and when Turkey was in Phase II. It is also a period for which data are available to a more satisfactory extent than is true for the earlier experience with Phase II in the 1950's.

In Section I, estimates of Domestic Resource Costs (DRCs) for various activities are presented to provide evidence as to the variation in economic costs arising between industries and firms. In Section II the excess costs of production associated with the system are evaluated. In Section III the effects of the trade regime upon employment, factor proportions and income distribution are examined.

This chapter is concerned with the effects of the trade regime and its interaction with domestic policies upon individual firms and industries. In Chapter IX estimates will be provided of the macroeconomic effects of the trade regime upon economic growth.

I. Domestic resource costs

From 1953 until the time of writing, there have consistently been differential incentives to producers within Turkey. The result has been biased incentives, not only away from export activities but also among import-competing activities. During the 1950's most of the differentials in incentives were the outcome of the measures taken by the government in response to the excess demand for imports that resulted from maintenance of a fixed exchange rate in the presence of inflationary pressures. After 1962 the import regime was much more consciously geared to fostering import-substitution. Although the average differential between export and import EERs remained approximately constant over the entire period, variations in nominal and effective rates of protection among different activities increased considerably in the 1960's. Increased use of such instruments as the "Prohibited List" meant that the protection afforded by duties and surcharges, as in the 1950's, became relatively less important than other protective devices. By the late 1960's the premia on import licenses varied enormously between commodity categories.

Differences in costs between industries and firms

One would expect significant disparities in the economic costs of various activities to result from such highly protective measures. Two sorts of disparities can be distinguished: (1) production would have higher opportunity costs in some industries than in others; and (2) firms within the same industry might produce at varying levels of efficiency.

Differences in opportunity costs between industries can result, with protection, because of the differential degree of total protection afforded to different industries. With differential protective levels, all the factors that determine a country's comparative cost structure, the capital and skill-intensity of the industry, the industry's location relative to the source of its inputs and their transport costs, technology, scale, and so on, affect the economic costs of the industry.

Differences in efficiency between firms in the same industry will not result from protection if the means used to grant protection enable competition among firms and expansion of highly profitable firms. In Turkey, however, the nature of quantitative restrictions and other controls both prevented competition and restricted the ability of firms to expand when they wished: (1) the availability of imported inputs limited output for those firms requiring imported inputs on the quota lists – which included assemblers' quotas and manufacturers' quotas (see below); (2) most new investments (as seen in Chapter VI) required imported capital goods which were subject to quota allocation and required the SPO's permission.[1]

---

1. Not only was SPO approval generally required, by the late 1960's, but the value of the investment incentives – postponement or reduction of duties upon imported capital goods – was so high that few firms would carry out their investment plans without receiving the SPO's dispensation from the duties.

Assemblers' and manufacturers' quotas were used to allocate imports of intermediate goods in most of the new import-substituting industries. These quotas, allocated on a firm-specific basis, were not item-specific but user-specific. By 1970 there were thirteen assemblers' quotas (covering tractors, vehicles, radios, typewriters and other import-substituting assembly production) amounting to $11.9 million, and forty-one manufacturers' quotas (covering production of such items as tires, transformers, washing machines, industrial furnaces, paints, light bulbs, electric motors, and so on) whose value was $10.4 million. All import licenses under these quotas required Ministry of Industry certificates for firm-specific allocations.[2]

Thus for firms requiring imported inputs subject to quota allocations there was little opportunity for competition, since output was virtually determined by the size of the quota allocation. Similarly, expansion of low-cost firms could not be undertaken automatically and was generally disapproved if excess capacity existed in the industry or if it was anticipated that demand would not expand by enough to warrant additional capacity. Even when expansion of an industry was deemed warranted, attempts were made to be "fair" and to allocate investment-goods import licenses *pro-rata* with applications for expansion. Since intermediate goods import licenses were allocated in proportion to firms' capacities,[3] there were incentives for all firms in the industry to apply for investment goods import licenses, for the penalty for not doing so was likely to be a reduced share of the quota allocation.

Measuring economic costs

Under optimal resource allocation, all industries and firms in a country will produce to the point where the domestic marginal rate of transformation (DMRT) between any two commodities equals the international marginal rate of transformation (IMRT). In the absence of monopoly power in international trade, and ignoring intermediate goods for the moment, the IMRT equals the ratio of international prices between pairs of commodities. In the absence of distortions in the domestic market, the ratio of domestic prices would equal the DMRT.

The domestic price ratio cannot be used in the presence of distortions, and an alternative measure, domestic resource cost (DRC), provides a better indicator. It is designed to provide an empirical estimate of the DMRT by adjusting domestic prices to reflect the opportunity costs of producing various commodities. Thus elements of monopoly rent must be removed from domestic prices when there are domestic monopolies. When there are distortions in

2. *Official Gazette, No. 13391,* January 5, 1970.
3. See Section II, below.

factor markets, adjustments must be made so that the social opportunity costs (shadow prices) of factors of production employed in each activity are reflected.

To allow for the presence of intermediate goods, the DRC measure (as with domestic and international price ratios under perfect markets) becomes a value-added measure. Thus the DRC of a given activity reflects the DMRT of producing value-added.

In empirical measurement, DRCs are computed per dollar of international value-added, and the IMRT between pairs of activities is thus one. Inequalities in DRCs therefore reflect the facts that DMRTs and IMRTs are unequal and that there is a consequent non-optimal resource allocation. The wider the difference between DRCs, the greater the disparity between IMRTs and DMRTs. Thus if one activity has a DRC twice as high as another, the implication is that had the first activity not been undertaken and had the resources been employed in the second activity, these resources would have produced twice as much foreign exchange earning or saving as under the existing allocation.[4]

A crucial assumption is that industries or activities could expand or contract at relatively constant costs. While such an assumption is sometimes unwarranted, it is valid for data from plants in developing countries where the investments could be duplicated and where the unit of observation is an integral investment project.

Of course there are numerous empirical difficulties that lead to imperfection in the measurement of DRCs. Even in a country with perfectly competitive markets and no impediments to international trade, one would not expect exact equality of all DRCs at a point in time, for dynamic adjustments could be taking place and errors in measurement could be made. But in such a country one would not be able to observe persistent wide differences in DRCs, since competition would provide a mechanism where low-cost firms could expand and high-cost firms would contract.

Sources of DRC data for Turkey

Estimates of Turkish DRCs in the late 1960's are available from several sources. The data are presented in Table VIII-1, but before analyzing them, differences between the methods of computations used in the different

---

4. For a fuller exposition of the DRC measure and its properties, see Anne O. Krueger, "Evaluating Restrictionist Trade Regimes: Theory and Measurement," *Journal of Political Economy,* January/February 1972; and Michael Bruno, "Domestic Resource Costs and Effective Protection: Clarification and Synthesis," *Journal of Political Economy,* January/February 1972.

Table VIII-1
Summary of estimates of DRCs and sectoral DRCs (TL per dollar)

Sector	Item	Date	DRC	Sector DRC Mean	Sector DRC Variance
Food and beverages				14.11	46.06
	Food sector average	1968	14.76		
	Food sector excluding tea and sugar	1968	10.17		
	Alcoholic beverages	1968	24.66		
	Dried figs	1968	8.01		
	Raisins	1968	7.92		
	Hazelnuts	1968	8.55		
	Canned food	1968	17.55		
	Olive oil	1968	11.34		
	Tea	1968	16.11		
	Sugar	1968	31.50		
	Meat	1968	10.17		
	Tomato paste	1965	13.40		
	Tomato canning	1969	9.30		
Textiles				13.48	43.77
	Sector average	1968	12.78		
	No. 20 yarn	1968	9.20		
	Striped cotton fabric	1968	9.93		
	Export cloth	1968	12.17		
	Silk printing fabric	1969	3.30		
	Cotton textiles	1968	12.15		
	Woolen textiles	1968	14.94		
	Cotton fiber	1968	8.55		
	MA 88 cloth	1968	21.17		
	Serge cloth	1968	22.07		
	Canvas top for vehicles	1966	1.79		
	Nylon textiles	1966	negative		
	Air filter for vehicle	1966	20.27		
	Particle board	1969	12.50		
Forest products				10.44	n.a.
	Sector average	1968	10.44		
Leather products				10.24	n.a.
	Driver seat for vehicle	1966	10.24		
Paper products				23.69	67.40
	Sector average	1968	15.48		
	Kraft paper	1965	31.90		

Table VIII-1 (continued)

Sector	Item	Date	DRC	Sector DRC Mean	Sector DRC Variance
Rubber products				45.59	890.49
	Sector average	1968	15.93		
	Hoses for vehicles	1966	78.49		
	Weatherstripping for vehicles	1966	23.68		
	Tires 1	1966	13.45		
	Tires 2	1966	26.98		
	Truck tires	1965	81.40		
	Passenger tires	1965	79.20		
Plastic				37.05	843.90
	Plastic	1965	66.10		
	Plastic bags	1969	8.00		
Chemicals				14.56	16.92
	Sector average	1968	14.40		
	Rayon	1968	16.11		
	Synthetic fiber	1968	10.35		
	Nylon	1965	11.00		
	Sodium phosphate fertilizer	1965	negative		
	Ammonium nitrate fertilizer	1965	negative		
	Citric acid	1969	11.00		
	Paints	1966	22.96		
	Vehicle battery	1966	16.13		
Cement				14.80	6.26
	Sector average	1968	13.68		
	Factory 1	1966	15.71		
	Factory 2	1966	16.75		
	Factory 3	1966	16.36		
	Cement plant	1969	11.50		
Stone and clay products				10.62	n.a.
	Tiles	1968	10.62		
Glass and ceramics				10.80	28.34
	Sector average	1968	11.52		
	Glass windshield	1966	8.30		
	Car outside mirror	1966	21.76		
	Rear view mirror	1966	4.91		
	Glassware	1965	7.90		
	Windowglass	1965	10.40		

Table VIII-1 (continued)

Sector	Item	Date	DRC	Sector DRC Mean	Sector DRC Variance
Iron and steel				13.68	29.70
	Sector average	1968	16.47		
	Billets	1968	15.93		
	Rods	1968	20.43		
	Tin plate	1968	13.95		
	Grey iron castings	1969	2.80		
	Steel billets	1968	12.50		
Iron and steel products				93.87	43,737.12
	Vehicle body	1966	15.79		
	Springs	1966	23.67		
	Car exhaust system	1966	17.43		
	Car frame	1966	15.92		
	Iron products factory	1966	negative		
	Soft drink caps	1969	49.90		
	Vehicle fenders	1966	13.90		
	Tail gate	1966	55.97		
	Tail gate chain	1966	11.10		
	Hinges	1966	15.17		
	Bolts and nuts	1969	719.80		
Other metal products				14.17	22.89
	Vehicle gas tank	1966	15.00		
	Vehicle tools	1966	12.12		
	Brake drum	1966	15.63		
	Hand brake assembly	1966	15.00		
	Windshield frame		16.94		
	Copper products	1966	23.28		
	Radiator	1965	14.00		
	Radiator	1966	17.03		
	Brake and clutch lining	1969	6.60		
	Water and gas meters	1969	6.10		
Machinery and parts				21.81	139.37
	Sector average	1968	13.60		
	Vehicle wiring harness	1966	7.40		
	Vehicle lamps	1966	7.86		
	Horn assembly	1966	15.00		
	Cooling unit	1965	21.40		
	Electric motor	1965	31.90		
	Electric cables	1965	46.00		
	Refrigerator	1968	15.00		
	Refrigerator	1969	27.70		
	Washing machine	1969	32.30		

Table VIII-1 (continued)

Sector	Item	Date	DRC	Sector DRC Mean	Sector DRC Variance
Transport equipment				27.78	278.88
	Assembler 1	1966	26.42		
	Assembler 2	1966	55.48		
	Assembler 3	1966	14.74		
	Motorcycle engine	1969	14.50		

Note: A negative DRC means that the foreign-exchange cost of the inputs (direct and indirect) exceeds the foreign-exchange value of the output.

Sources: Data for 1965 are from Anne O. Krueger, "Some Economic Costs of Exchange Control: The Turkish Case," *Journal of Political Economy,* October 1966. Data indicated as 1966 are from data compiled by the USAID Mission, Ankara, in the summer of 1966. Data for 1968 are from: Necati Özfırat, "Competitive Ability in the Manufacturing Industries and the Structure of Cost," *Pub. No. SPO 754, Economic Planning 267, SPO.* Data for 1969 are from Anne O. Krueger, *Turkish Domestic-Foreign Price Relationships, 1969,* mimeograph (Ankara), 1969.

sources should be mentioned. The 1965 and 1969 data are similar in that all estimates are based on the assumption that firms operate at full capacity, and that all capital — equity plus debt — earned a shadow return of 20 per cent. The 1969 data, however, differ from the 1965 data in two regards: (1) They were all drawn from loan applications which had been approved and where one criterion for extending a loan was that the DRC not be too high. Thus there is something of a downward bias in the 1969 estimates. By contrast, the 1965 data consisted both of loan applications at a time when no such criterion was used and of existing firm experience (projected to full capacity utilization) and loan project information. (2) The 1969 data did not contain a breakdown of the firms' domestically purchased inputs into tradeable and home goods whereas the 1965 data did. For 1969, therefore, DRCs were computed on three alternative assumptions: a) all purchased inputs were tradeable at TL 9=$1; b) all domestically purchased inputs were home goods; and c) all purchased inputs were tradeable at TL 15=$1. Assumption (c) is perhaps the most realistic, and the one used in the data for Table VIII-1. But it should be noted that the rank correlations between DRCs computed on the three alternative bases all exceeded 0.95. The only significant difference was that some 1969 observations indicated foreign exchange losses (negative foreign exchange saving) when computed on the basis of assumption (a).

Data for 1966 were obtained by USAID personnel in the summer of 1966 and are based upon interviews and questionnaires with over 150 Turkish firms. These data were derived entirely from existing firms' actual operations. No adjustments were made for differing rates of return upon capital, varying degrees of capacity utilization, and the like. Thus the data really represent the TL value added at market prices divided by the foreign exchange saved or earned when direct and indirect utilization of foreign exchange in inputs is taken into account.

The 1968 data are also based upon actual operating experience. Their chief drawbacks are that no adjustment was made for varying profit rates and that indirect imports utilized in production were not subtracted from international value-added estimates. The net effect is probably to bias the 1968 estimates downward. For example, the refrigerator estimate for 1968 (under Machinery and Parts) is TL 15 per dollar and that for 1969 is TL 27.7 per dollar. Although inflation may have affected the estimates slightly, the 1968 estimate allowed a zero return on capital, and the 1969 estimate allowed a 20 per cent rate of return. Moreover, indirect imports used in production were netted out of international value added in the 1969 estimates and not in the 1968 ones. While there is no way of knowing whether the same refrigerator producer was evaluated in the 1968 and 1969 data, adjusting the 1969 data to a zero profit base and adding indirect imports into foreign exchange saved accounts for over 95 per cent of the difference between the two estimates of DRCs. It was not possible to contrast the sources of differences to the same extent in all other cases, but the relationships between the various sources of data generally appear consistent over the range of commodities observed.

Variations in DRCs

In Table VIII-1 the date after each activity denotes the source of the estimate, as indicated in the notes to the table. There is wide variation in DRCs among industries and activities. Despite the fact that the four sources did not provide estimates on an entirely comparable basis, all four sets of estimates show this wide variation.

The last two columns of Table VIII-1 provide an unweighted mean of all the estimates for each sector and the variance of DRCs around the sectoral means. The sectoral means and variances should be interpreted with extreme care, since negative DRCs (where the international value of the inputs exceeded the international value of the output) could not be included in the estimates. The chemicals sector, for example, has a relatively low mean DRC. Yet out of nine estimates for that sector, two activities showed negative international value-added. Because these two observations were not included in the computation of the mean and variance for chemicals, both numbers appear low. Similarly, the presence of an extreme observation, given the small number of activities for which estimates are available in each sector, seriously influences the mean and variance. Thus iron and steel products contain nuts and bolts, which were computed to have a DRC of 791.80. The mean for the sector therefore is above all but that observation, although an iron products factory had a negative DRC in 1966 and was therefore excluded from the sectoral mean.

We now consider the evidence. DRCs for the food and beverage sector have been relatively low (with a few notable exceptions). If one assumes that TL 15 = $1 was close to an equilibrium exchange rate during the latter half of the 1960's, all subsectors except sugar, alcoholic beverages (which were a State Monopoly and whose DRC is therefore difficult to interpret since the 1968 estimates are not adjusted for different levels of profitability), tea and canned food were clearly export industries. The DRC for meat products should be especially noted. It is a sector in which Turkey probably has a vast unrealized export potential. There has been a sizeable, mostly illegal, export of meat products over Turkey's eastern border, and the Turkish internal price of meat is below the international price. Government policies aimed at keeping the domestic price of meat down have been a major factor in discouraging the development of meat exports.

In food products, as in other sectors, the variation in DRCs appears to be of about the same order of magnitude as the differences in incentives between export and import-competing producers. Thus figs, raisins, hazelnuts and tomato canning all had DRCs below ten while sugar (an import-substitution industry) had a DRC in excess of 30. The only DRC estimate in the food and beverage sector that appears inconsistent with the export-import-substitution generalization is that for canned food 1968. That estimate is well above those for tomato paste and tomato canning, which are the two predominant forms of food canning. Most observers believe that food canning is an industry in which Turkey has relatively low economic costs, and where exports could be developed profitably under an alternative trade regime. The cause of the high figure in this sample is not known, but it is possible that the 1968 estimate did not adjust for disparities between the domestic and international price of tinplate. For canning, the fact that domestically-produced tinplate was priced at about three times the world level effectively precluded the development of canned-food exports. It is also possible, of course, that a high-cost firm was the basis for the estimate of the canned food DRC.

Like the food sector, the textile sector appears generally to have relatively low DRCs, but there are several exceptions. The 1966 study indicated a negative foreign-exchange saving for nylon textiles, and both serge and MA 88 cloth had DRCs above TL 20 per dollar in 1968. The coexistence of low-cost and high-cost firms in the same sector is consistent with *a priori* expectations about the effects of the trade regime.

Other sectors, where there are very few observations but for which DRCs appear to be reasonably low, are forest products, leather products, and stone and clay products. As seen in Chapter VII there is some independent evidence suggesting that these sectors may have considerable export potential, which tends to corroborate the low DRC estimates.

The picture is rather different on the import-substitution side. The iron and steel sector was generally high cost. In the 1968 study iron and steel was found to be the highest-cost sector. While some of the high costs may have been attributable to start-up activities of the industry, some of the firms in the sample had been operating for extended periods. Iron and steel products show the widest variation in DRCs. Many of the items included in that sector are parts and components for vehicles, but other items exhibit equally high variation. The bolts and nuts DRC is reflected in the sectoral average and variance. Even omitting bolts and nuts, however, the average DRC for iron and steel products is TL 24.3.

Machinery and parts, transport equipment, paper, plastic, rubber and chemicals are other sectors where many of the activities are import-substitution oriented. As can be seen, some DRCs have been negative, implying that there have been negative foreign exchange savings in import-substitution. That is especially true for fertilizer, where the transport cost of importing raw materials exceeds the transport cost of importing the finished product.

The wide variation in DRCs on the import-substitution side is indicative of the degree to which encouragement of import-substitution has been indiscriminate. Some activities clearly were economically sound investments, whereas others were extremely high cost. That happened not only between different production lines, but also in the same production line. Tires, within the rubber products sector, are a case in point. The two 1966 DRC estimates, made on a comparable basis, indicate a DRC of 13.5 for one firm and 27 for another. There can be little doubt that the production of tires at a DRC of 13.5 would have been economically justified and profitable under optimal resource allocation whereas production at a DRC of 27 would not have been. Yet under the trade regime and investment regulations both firms were able to survive.

Another factor should also be noted. Among the import-substitution activities, some would have been viable exports under appropriate incentives. Yet the high cost of inputs from other domestic industries (where importing the input was infeasible because of the "Prohibited List") effectively precluded the possibility of developing export markets. The cases of tinplate and canned food have already been cited, and there were many similar instances. Thus in some cases import-substitution was not only high-cost in itself, but it also had indirect costs, given the use of the "Prohibited List," in preventing the development of exports in other industries.

It is evident that under an alternative and economically more desirable set of incentives Turkey could have achieved a considerable increase in net foreign exchange availability for the same level of investments and resources devoted to the manufacturing sector. The unweighted average of sectoral DRCs from the data in Table VIII-1 was TL 23.5 per dollar. A more selective import-substitution policy and increased incentives for efficiency resulting from competition could certainly have reduced the average substantially. Estimates of the increased output which could have been achieved will be presented in Chapter IX. They are based upon data from sectoral averages. When interpreting those results it will be important to bear in mind that the sectoral data themselves conceal a great deal of variation among subsectors and among firms.

II. Excess real costs of the system

In addition to expecting a restrictionist trade regime to result in wide variations in costs of different activities, one would also anticipate that a system such as the Turkish would impose excess real costs on virtually all firms operating under the regime. Several types of excess costs are identifiable: (1) entrepreneurial time and energy; (2) additional clerical staff required to handle paperwork; (3) expenses, such as airplane trips to the capital, associated with obtaining import licenses; (4) costs associated with the effects of the regime on inventory levels; and (5) excess capacity resulting either from inability to obtain imports or from incentives to overbuild resulting from the trade regime.

The first three costs are extremely difficult to quantify, and their importance is hard to estimate. Entrepreneurship is generally regarded as a scarce resource in developing countries. If entrepreneurial energies and efforts are devoted to obtaining import licenses, the drain on the scarce resource clearly constitutes a cost of the import regime. Likewise, insofar as firms must hire additional bookkeepers, clerks and office staff to handle the paperwork associated with obtaining licenses, the firm's costs are increased by the import regime.

There is no evidence available with which to evaluate the magnitude of the costs incurred in obtaining import licenses. Even interviews failed to yield any firm estimates. Some businessmen stated that they would be willing to pay about 10 per cent above landed cost if items could be domestically produced, since they could save that much by avoiding the licensing process. However, there is clearly an important difference in the magnitude of cost-saving, when the source of supply of one item shifts from the foreign to the domestic market and when all items shift or when licensing procedures are simplified for all items.

The last two components of excess costs, inventory and underutilized capacity, can be evaluated to some extent. In this section, these two components are considered. It should be borne in mind, however, that the costs incurred in obtaining licenses are unknown, but certainly are of some importance.

Excess inventory costs

Incentives to hold large stocks of imported goods originated from several factors: (1) for Liberalized List goods there was uncertainty as to a) the length of delay in issuing licenses in the future, b) whether goods would continue on the Liberalized List or be eligible for importation at all, and c) the date at which licensing would be suspended for the current import period; (2) for Quota List items a) there was the consideration that only one order could be placed during each six-month period — so that inventories had to be sufficient to cover until the next importing period, and b) there was the possibility that imports might be prohibited at a future date as higher-cost, lower-quality domestic capacity came onstream; (3) for both Liberalized List and Quota List imports, the domestic premium was rising rapidly in the latter half of the 1960's, so that investment in inventory for resale or own use was likely to be profitable; and (4) throughout much of the 1960's there was discussion of possible devaluation. Stamp taxes and other charges for imports were increasing, so that expectations of profitability of investment in inventories of imported foods were further enhanced. Excess demand for imported goods therefore made inventory accumulation profitable despite the high guarantee deposit requirements.

The import regime, of course, prevented firms from attaining their desired stocks of imported goods. There were cases where low inventory holdings led to excess production costs due to plant shutdowns or production delays, and other cases where firms incurred the costs of holding higher inventories than they would have under a liberalized import regime.

Thus it was not simply the aggregate level of inventories of imported goods, but the composition of the inventories that led to excess costs. Sometimes very high costs were incurred as a penalty for inadequate inventories. In several cases reported in interviews, bulky materials such as carbon black and copper tubing were air-freighted into Turkey after special permission had been obtained to do so a month or more after the plant had ceased production. Resort to the black market was probably fairly frequent and entailed not only the costs of production delays but also those of inferior-quality items and non-standardized inputs.

There is no means of quantifying the costs incurred by firms whose inventories of imported inputs were suboptimal. However, there is some evidence to suggest that despite the import regime firms were generally successful in avoiding those costs by holding considerably larger inventories than they would have considered optimal had imports been liberalized. Interviews, a sample of firms' balance sheets, and data on the ratio of investment in inventory to total investments in Turkey compared to other countries all suggest the same result. Interviews with industrialists provided some impressionistic evidence. Businessmen in firms with foreign parent companies were especially vocal on the subject of inventory costs. It was generally claimed that a West European producer would hold inventories adequate for about two months' production, at an average interest cost of 8 per cent. The Turkish counterpart, by contrast, would hold inventories adequate for an average six months' production, at an interest cost of 14 per cent. For domestic producers, the Turkish rate of inflation probably equated the real interest rate with that in Europe. Even so, the real costs associated with an average inventory level three times as high as that incurred under a liberal trade regime certainly constituted, at least in part, an excess real cost of the system. Firms which might otherwise have exported were, of course, at an even greater disadvantage as long as the exchange rate, and foreign prices, remained stable, as the 14 per cent interest charge then constituted a true cost disadvantage.

A sample of thirty-two Turkish firms' balance sheets, as of the close of each firm's 1969 fiscal year, provides some additional information.[5] From each firm's balance sheet, the value of raw materials and other goods used in production — but not its holding of semi-finished and finished products — was calculated. In addition, each firm's net fixed assets were taken. The weighted average ratio of inventories of inputs to net fixed assets was 0.4655, and the unweighted average was 0.5175, thus implying that for the sample firms' inventory investment was approximately half as large as investment in fixed assets.

Data on the composition of gross domestic capital formation in various countries tend to confirm impressions from the sample and from interviews. Table VIII-2 provides estimates of the ratio of investment in inventory to fixed capital investment for a sample of countries. The average ratio for the three years 1966 to 1968 was used, since inventory investment can show sizeable year-to-year fluctuations. As can be seen, Turkish investment in stocks in the three years averaged 15 per cent of investment in fixed capital. That ratio is more than twice that of all countries in the sample except that of Japan and Spain.

Although the high Turkish ratio of inventory to fixed investment cannot be attributed entirely to the trade regime (domestically produced goods were

5. The data were kindly provided by the Industrial Development Bank of Turkey. All firms in the sample had applied for loans from the bank, and most had received them.

Table VIII-2
Ratio of investment in stocks to fixed investment, various countries, 1966 to 1968

Country	Ratio	Country	Ratio
Australia	0.080	Israel	0.030
Belgium	0.036	Italy	0.038
Brazil	0.074	Japan	0.135
Chile	0.081	Korea	0.060
Denmark	0.049	Netherlands	0.054
France	0.069	Spain	0.107
Germany	0.025	Turkey	0.152
Greece	0.021	United Kingdom	0.030
		United States	0.065

Note: a) Data for Brazil are for the 1965–1967 period.
b) These data cover *all* inventory investments in all sectors and are therefore not comparable with data from firms' balance sheets.

Source: SPO data for Turkey; *Yearbook of National Accounts Statistics,* United Nations, 1969, country tables for other countries.

part of inventory accumulation, too) there can be little doubt that the import regime was a contributing factor in Turkey's high figure. Unfortunately, Turkish estimates of inventory investment do not go back before 1963. It is therefore not possible to contrast the figures during Phase II with the figures from earlier years.[6] Nonetheless, the very high Turkish figure combined with interview impressions and sample data suggests that inventories were probably substantially higher as a result of the trade regime than they would otherwise have been.

Underutilized capacity

Import-substitution policies are usually paradoxical: undertaken to reduce dependence upon imports for final consumption, they can increase dependence upon imports of raw materials and intermediate goods. When import-substitution industries are established they require imports to sustain the flow of production. In the event of "foreign-exchange shortage" not only does final consumption decline, as it would have done in the absence of import-substitution policies, but employment and domestic production can decrease due to the absence of intermediate goods and raw materials required more or less in fixed proportions to the production process. Planners can find themselves on the horns of a dilemma. If intermediate goods necessary for current

6. The average ratio of inventory to fixed capital investment was 0.136 for the period 1963 to 1965.

production are permitted, then capital goods imports to expand capacity are reduced, and the growth process is inhibited. One possible outcome is the underutilization of existing capacity, due to unavailability of imported intermediate goods.

There is no doubt that the Turkish planners were caught in this particular dilemma: as seen in Chapter VI, raw materials imports were systematically underforecast and had to be successively increased. To the extent the flow of raw materials was permitted, the cost was the failure of capital goods imports to rise as rapidly as they would have otherwise. Insofar as raw material imports were restricted to permit additional capital goods imports, excess capacity in existing firms could develop.[7]

In addition to the possibility of excess capacity arising because of smaller-than-desired flows of imports, another factor was important in Turkey and makes estimation of the degree of excess capacity very difficult. It was seen in Chapter VI that import licenses were allocated among industrialists upon the basis of their capacity. Thus incentives were created by the import-licensing system to build additional capacity even if existing capacity was underutilized.[8] Failure to expand when other firms were obtaining capital goods import licenses and expanding could result in a reduced share of the market even if existing capacity was underutilized.

Thus, not only could underutilization of capacity arise because of inadequate raw material imports, it could also result from firms' deliberate over-expansion. Either way, the costs of the excess capacity are clearly attributable to the trade regime.

Difficulty arises because the license-allocation procedure led not only to idle capacity but also to overstating actual capacity. Table VIII-3 gives data reported to the Union of Chambers on capacity utilization for 1966, 1967 and 1969, the only years for which data are available. For each quota number against which license applications were made, the Union reported actual levels of output and capacity. The first column gives the number of quota allocations under which reported capacity utilization was less than 10 per cent. In 1968 18 quotas, or 12 per cent of the quota numbers for which estimates are available, were destined for industries reported working at less than 10 per cent of capacity, and 65 per cent were destined to firms reported operating at less than 50 per cent of capacity. The figures are comparable for 1965 and

---

7. It should be noted that excess capacity, in the sense used above, implies that producers would expand output at existing input-output prices if they were free to purchase their desired amounts of all inputs at those prices. Other forms of physical excess capacity that would occur as the result of unprofitability of additional production at prevailing prices are not included in the analysis.
8. Jagdish Bhagwati and Padma Desai, *India Planning for Industrialization,* Oxford University Press (London), 1970, pp. 326–7, analyze the same phenomenon for India.

Table VIII-3
Data reported to Union of Chambers on capacity utilization, 1966, 1967, 1969

	Per cent of Capacity Reported Utilization by Applicants						
	Less than 10	10–25	25–50	50–75	75–90	More than 90	Total
	Number of quotas allocated						
1966	18	28	49	27	7	17	146
1967	23	35	43	21	6	13	141
1969	23	40	38	23	9	15	148

Notes: a) No definition of capacity is given by the Union of Chambers. They give two entries: (1) total capacity, and (2) capacity utilized in the year indicated. The ratio of the two was computed for the entries in this table.
b) The number of quotas is less than in Table VI-7 because some quotas had multiple uses and no physical measure of capacity was given.

Source: Same as Table VI-7.

1967, with a slightly higher fraction working at less than half of capacity.[9]

If these data were accepted at face value, they would indicate serious underutilization of capacity. While some industries might have been operating below capacity due to strikes or inadequate demand, that explanation cannot cover half the recipients of quota allocations. However, as indicated above, incentives were present to overstate capacity.[10] Once an entrepreneur's capacity was certified, he could sell his equipment and remain eligible for import licenses. Thus in some cases the same physical capacity could be counted two or three times. Moreover, incentives were present to overstate the physical capacity of actually operating equipment.

It is thus difficult to place much credence in the evidence based upon import-license data. Other available evidence suggests that there was excess capacity in some sectors, but that it was not nearly as widespread as the Union of Chambers' data indicates.

In the summer of 1966, at a time when import shortages were believed to be resulting in excess capacity, an AID team undertook an extensive study of the problem. Their conclusions were as follows:

9. Capacity measures are given by the Union of Chambers in physical units, so no meaningful weighting of sectors was possible.
10. A story, told by a friend, may illustrate. A man imported some machinery in the early 1960's. His machinery was inspected and his capacity certified. He then sold the machinery for more than he paid for it. He continues to get import licenses: his profits on resale in each period prior to August 1970 exceeded the initial cost of the machinery.

> The interviews indicated that despite the problems of the import system — and they were and are many — most producers were able to obtain the essential imported supplies needed to operate their factories. Not all firms were operated at or near capacity, but those that were not generally limited to industries which used very large amounts of imported materials relative to their output. This was particularly the case with the assembly industries...Other branches of industry which were adversely affected were wool textiles (which use imported merino wool), canning, and plastics, all of which depend heavily on imported materials...

> On the basis of more recent discussions, there is little reason to believe that the situation has changed radically...Although the total level of imports has decreased since 1966, the level of raw materials necessary to maintain total production has not, except for steel products which are now being supplied from Ereğli Steel Mill...[11]

In interviews with businessmen conducted during 1965, 1967, and 1969 this author found only two cases of plant shutdowns and several instances where finished goods — less one or two parts — had to be stockpiled pending receipt of imports. Relatively few interviewees commented upon underutilization of capacity as being a problem, although many complained of having to purchase from small firms at high prices. Similarly, time series production data do not provide any evidence of widespread, persistent, excess capacity.

It seems reasonable to conclude that the import regime led to some overbuilding of capacity and idle capacity in some heavily import-dependent sectors. By and large, however, businessmen avoided the costs of plant shutdown and underutilization by incurring heavy inventory costs.

III. Employment, factor proportions, and income distribution

As seen in Chapter VI, the EER for capital goods fell in the latter half of the 1960's. The decline in the rate was the result of increasing use of "investment incentives," which essentially consisted of the partial or total exemption from or postponement of duties and surcharges otherwise payable on imports. Thus by 1969, with an official exchange rate of TL 9 = $1, a capital good import subject to 50 per cent duty would have cost the importer in excess of TL 18, combining stamp tax, surcharges and production tax, but would have cost him as little as TL 10 if granted total exemption from duties. Thus for those receiving SPO approval of their investment projects, the implicit subsidy on capital goods imports was sizeable.

In theory, subsidization of capital goods imports can have several effects: (1) capital-intensive industries will become relatively more attractive investment alternatives than labor-intensive industries; (2) entrepreneurs who can

---

11. Lubell *et al., op. cit.* (Note 7, Chap. VI), pp. 96–97.

obtain the subsidy will substitute capital for labor; and (3) there will be a substitution of imported capital goods for domestic capital goods. As a consequence, in a competitive market one would expect the equilibrium wage to be lower and less growth in domestic capital goods industries than would otherwise have occurred. When wages are determined by non-market forces, one would expect that employment opportunities would grow less rapidly than they would in the absence of subsidization of capital goods imports.

The labor market was not free in Turkey. Minimum wages were in effect throughout the 1960's, and the real wage increased at an average annual rate of 2.9 per cent between 1963 and 1969.[12] Thus increases in the real wage would have led to some incentives to substitute capital for labor even if the real price of capital goods had remained constant. As it was, the real price of capital goods imports fell on average about 4.5 per cent per annum. Thus employment and factor proportions were the combined result of the trade regime and of domestic policies with respect to labor. Insofar as the effects predicted by theory are concerned, a rough approximation would be that about two-thirds of any shift probably resulted from the trade regime, and about one-third from domestic labor policies.

In this section the microeconomic aspects of employment and factor proportions and their effects upon income distribution are examined. In Chapter IX estimates of the overall employment effects are presented.

Employment and factor proportions

Several pieces of background information will be useful to the reader. Throughout the 1960's Turkey had an excess supply of unskilled labor. It is estimated that 9.5 per cent of the urban labor force and 9.9 per cent of the rural labor force were unemployed in 1967.[13] The impact of unemployment is cushioned, to some degree, in two ways: (1) a large number of Turkish workers are employed in Western Europe, and particularly in Germany;[14]

12. Data are from Duncan R. Miller, "Labor Force and Employment: An Overview," in Duncan R. Miller (ed.), *Labor Force and Employment in Turkey,* USAID, mimeograph (Ankara), 1970, p. 33.
13. SFYP, *op. cit.* (Note 21, Chap. I), pp. 148–9.
14. As of 1970, over a half million Turkish workers were employed in West Germany. In 1965, 9.7 million persons were employed in agriculture out of an economically active population of 13.5 million, leaving a non-agricultural labor force of 3.8 million. Even allowing for labor force growth after 1965, the half million Turks working abroad represent well over 10 per cent of the Turkish non-agricultural labor force. Although Turkey could be placed in an exceedingly difficult situation in the event of a severe recession in Western Europe, the governments have been cooperating to smooth the flow of workers and to avoid the disruptions that could result with sharp changes in European employment opportunities. For an excellent analysis of some aspects of the Turkish workers in Germany, and differential productivity and learning behavior of Turkish workers in the two countries, see Terry D. Monson, *Migration, Experience-Generated Learning and Infant Industries: A Case Study of Turkey,* Ph.D. thesis, University of Minnesota, March 1972.

and (2) family ties are usually sufficiently strong so that the unemployed are supported by their families and thus are not as adversely affected as would otherwise be the case.[15]

In addition to an excess supply of unskilled labor, the number of college graduates in Turkey expanded very rapidly during the 1960's. With relatively few exceptions there was an abundant supply of highly trained manpower. By contrast, however, persons with middle-level technical skills were generally in short supply.[16] In such specialities as glass-blowing, die-casting, repair and maintenance jobs and middle-level technical personnel of virtually every variety, the absence of persons with appropriate skills constituted a major problem.[17]

Changes in relative factor prices.   Table VIII-4 presents data on the prices of domestic and imported capital goods and on the industrial wage. Ideally, of course, one would like data on the cost of capital services rather than on the cost of capital goods. However, insofar as any data are available they do not suggest any significant changes in the nominal interest rate nor in the return to capital in the period under review; moreover, any changes which did occur were undoubtedly small contrasted with changes in the real price of capital goods.

The first column of Table VIII-4 gives the average daily wage in manufacturing, which more than doubled between 1960 and 1969. The second column gives the TL cost for a dollar's worth of imported capital goods as calculated in Appendix A. Of course, to the extent that the international price of capital goods rose, the EER provides an underestimate of the increase in the domestic price of imported capital goods. However, changes in international prices since 1960 have probably been small relative to changes in the PLD-EER. Column 3 gives the implicit GNP deflator for the manufacturing sector, taken as a proxy for the price of domestically produced capital goods. Column 4 gives the average price of capital goods and column 5 the wage relative to the weighted price of capital goods. The wage rose relative to the price of both types of capital equipment, especially in the latter half of the

15. In the summer of 1971 the author was on the campus of the Middle East Technical University and witnessed 4,000 men applying for eight janitorial and ground maintenance positions. All were healthy, well-fed, and reasonably dressed. Workers applying at the Labor Exchange for permission to go to Western Europe are of similar appearance. The large numbers of applicants attest to the severity of the unemployment problem, while the fact of the family system indicates how that problem can exist without greater unrest.
16. For an analysis of this phenomenon and the reasons for it, see Anne O. Krueger, "Rates of Return to Turkish Higher Education," *Journal of Human Resources,* Fall 1972.
17. See the discussion in the SFYP, *op. cit.* (Note 21, Chap. I), pp. 161 ff.

Table VIII-4
Wage rates and capital goods prices

	Wage Rate (TL per day)	Capital Goods Prices		Weighted Capital Goods Price (1965=100)	Wage Relative to Capital Goods Price
		Imported (TL per $)	Domestic (1961=100)		
1955	6.87	4.10	38	32	2.15
1960	14.11	12.11	92	82	1.72
1961	14.88	12.55	100	85	1.75
1962	15.73	12.54	103	86	1.83
1963	17.21	12.99	108	91	1.89
1964	19.07	12.99	110	96	1.98
1965	20.66	15.50	114	100	2.07
1966	22.66	15.50	121	106	2.14
1967	24.75	15.29	124	114	2.17
1968	27.47	12.26	124	118	2.33
1969	33.98	13.16	132	124	2.74
1970	37.40		139	133	2.81

Sources: 1) Wage rate: average daily wage rate of workers in manufacturing covered by social insurance, Social Insurance Institute, *Statistics Annual,* 1955–1969.
2) Imported capital goods EERs from Appendix A.
3) Domestic capital goods: Implicit deflator for the manufacturing sector was taken and linked in 1961 and 1965.
4) Capital goods price: for 1962–1970, implicit deflators from *Yılı Programı,* 1971 were used. Before that, imported and domestic prices were weighted by their share in machinery and equipment investment.

1960's, and the price of imported capital goods fell sharply relative to the price of domestic capital goods after 1965. We consider first the evidence on use of imported and domestic capital equipment, and thereafter examine the evidence on substitution of capital for labor.

Imported versus domestic capital equipment. There are two ways in which one would expect the ratio of imported to domestic capital goods to be affected by the trade regime: (1) the price of imported capital goods relative to the price of domestic capital goods would induce greater use of the cheaper kind, and (2) the availability of foreign exchange for capital goods imports, in the presence of excess demand under quantitative restrictions, would determine the volume of imported capital goods.[18] The first effect is relatively straightforward and would occur in all sectors of the economy, although investment in some sectors would become relatively more attractive than in

18. It should be recognized in what follows that underinvoicing and other phenomena associated with the trade regime might lead to serious problems with the data.

others depending upon the ratio of imported to domestic capital equipment employed in each sector. The second effect is more complex. Within each sector, firms may purchase more domestic capital equipment when they are unable to obtain import licenses. In addition, investment may shift to sectors relatively less dependent upon imported capital equipment as domestic savings are available for the purpose.

McCabe and Michalopoulos investigated the combined effects of foreign exchange availability and relative prices of imported and domestic capital investment for the years 1950 to 1963.[19] As a proxy for the availability of foreign exchange, they used the amount of foreign credit received by Turkey in each year. The use of that proxy seems reasonable since foreign credit, especially in the 1950-to-1963 period, consisted largely of suppliers' credits and project aid, both of which are generally used to purchase imported capital goods.

Their regression equation, and results, were:

$$\log(I_m/I_d) = 2.40 - 0.03 \log(P_m/P_d) + 0.26 \log(R_e/R_d) - 1.60D$$
$$\quad\quad\quad\quad\quad (0.04) \quad\quad\quad\quad (2.57) \quad\quad\quad\quad (-6.51)$$

$$R^2 = 0.89 \quad\quad F = 28$$

where I_m/I_d is the ratio of investment in imported to domestic capital equipment (given the unavailability of capital stock figures), P_m/P_d is the ratio of the price of the two kinds of equipment, R_e/R_d is the ratio of external credit to internal credit (the volume of bank loans) and D was a dummy for the post-devaluation years (1959 to 1963).

The McCabe-Michalopoulos results suggest that a 1 per cent increase in foreign credits resulted in a 0.26 per cent increase in the ratio of imported to domestic capital equipment invested. The results are what one would have expected, especially for the period covered by their study, with foreign exchange availability being an important determinant of capital goods imports.

The fact that the relative-price variable is not significant may be the result of the inclusion of the dummy variable for the years after 1958. Since the 1958 devaluation constituted the major change in the relative price of imported capital goods, that variable probably picks up most effects of the relative price changes.

In addition to the McCabe-Michalopoulos results, additional evidence on the effects of the import regime on investment composition can be gained by inspection of the behavior of construction investment relative to total investment over the period. As seen in Chapter II, plant and equipment investment

19. James McCabe and Constantine Michalopoulos, "Investment Composition and Employment in Turkey," *Discussion Paper No. 22,* AID, October 1971.

Table VIII-5
Composition of investment, 1959 to 1969

	Construc-tion (millions of TL)	Machinery and Equipment (millions of TL)	Total (millions of TL)	Construction (% of total investment)	Machinery and Equipment (% of total investment)
1959	4,397	2,294	6,691	65.7	34.3
1960	4,817	2,699	7,516	64.1	35.9
1961	4,917	2,926	7,843	62.6	37.3
1962	5,292	3,420	8,712	60.7	39.3
1963	6,569	3,508	10,077	65.2	34.8
1964	7,381	3,186	10,567	69.8	30.2
1965	8,466	3,301	11,767	71.9	28.1
1966	10,399	4,754	15,153	68.6	31.4
1967	11,931	5,331	17,262	69.1	30.9
1968	14,015	6,416	20,431	68.5	31.4
1969	16,656	6,718	23,374	71.2	28.7

Note: SIS data are not consistent with Gürtan's data given in Table II-10 and IV-9 for years for which the series overlap. The source of the discrepancy is un-known.

Source: *National Income 1970, op. cit.* (Table I-2), Table 6.

in Turkey is much more heavily dependent upon imports than is construction investment. Data for the period 1953-to-1958 were given in Table II-10. Table VIII-5 gives data for subsequent years.

It will be recalled that investment in plant and machinery fell from 30.6 per cent of total investment in 1953 to a low of 23.6 per cent in 1957, rising to 26.9 per cent in 1958. As can be seen, the absolute and relative increase in the importance of machinery and equipment investment rose until 1962, reaching 39.3 per cent of total investment in that year. Thereafter investment composition once again shifted toward heavier emphasis upon construction investment. The import stringency of 1964–1965 is clearly reflected in the data, as the share of construction increased to its levels of the mid-1950's. With renewed project credits in 1966–1968, investment in machinery and equipment again increased, but by no means reattained its relative importance of the early 1960's.

The timing of the changes in importance of construction in total invest-ment coincides remarkably closely with the delineation of Phases of the trade regime in Turkey. During Phase II, in both the 1950's and 1960's, invest-ment became increasingly oriented toward those sectors requiring relatively few imported capital goods. During Phase IV of the early 1960's investment shifted toward plant and machinery, despite its price, relatively higher than in the Phase II episodes. It would appear that the availability of import licenses has been relatively more important than the relative price of imported capital equipment, although both factors have influenced the composition of investment.

Capital-labor substitution. The fact that quantitative restrictions on capital goods imports may have offset part or all of the desired substitution between types of capital equipment does not rule out the possibility of substitution of capital for labor on the part of those firms fortunate enough to receive capital goods import licenses and duty exemptions. As seen above, two factors were operative here: the price of imported capital goods fell in real terms, and the real wage rose.

It is difficult to estimate how much substitution of capital for labor in fact took place because the large change in relative factor prices occurred in the late 1960's and the latest available *Census of Manufactures* is for 1963. Demirgil undertook a variety of tests on data for the public sector for the periods 1939–1963 and 1949–1963 and found some statistical evidence of capital-labor substitution,[20] although productivity growth dominated the data.

McCabe and Michalopoulos extended their analysis to investigate the relationship between the labor share of value-added and the ratio of imported capital goods investment to total investment. They used the wage share, in the absence of better data, as a proxy for the labor intensity of each sector. Their data were cross-section data from the 1963 *Census of Manufactures*. Their results were:[21]

$$W/V = 0.43 - 0.20(I_m/I)$$
$$R^2 = 0.10 \qquad F = 6.1$$

where W/V is the labor share in value added, and I_m/I is the share of imported equipment in total equipment investment. In their model, the coefficient on the term I_m/I reflects the difference between the labor shares in processes using domestic and imported capital equipment.[22] Substituting the

20. Demir Demirgil, "Factors Affecting the Choice of Technology in Turkey and Implications for the Level of Employment," in Miller (ed.), *op. cit.* (Note 12).
21. McCabe and Michalopoulos, *op. cit.* (Note 19), pp. 6–8.
22. The total capital share is a weighted average of the capital coefficients corresponding to the two types of capital stock: $(1 - W/V) = K_m/K (1 - b_m) + (1 - K_m/K) (1 - b_d)$, where b_d and b_m are the labor shares in the two processes. By manipulation, the percentage difference in the capital-labor ratio of two sectors $(\Delta L/K)/(L_m/K_m)$ is:

$$\left(\frac{b_d/(1 - b_d)}{b_m/(1 - b_m)} - 1 \right) \times 100 .$$

results of the regression estimate, they estimated that the labor share in value-added was 43 per cent in processes using domestic capital goods and 23 per cent in processes using imported capital equipment. Thus if wages are equal across sectors, employment would be twice as great per unit of investment in domestic capital equipment as it would be in foreign.[23]

Both the McCabe-Michalopoulos data and the Demirgil data are for the period ending in 1963. With the amount of structural change in Turkey between the earlier years and the 1960's, their results do not necessarily reflect the degree of capital-labor substitution during the 1960's. In the absence of recent Census data, Öngüt investigated the extent of capital-labor substitution on the basis of information from investment projects financed by the Industrial Development Bank of Turkey.[24] He found that businessmen generally regarded the choice of technology as given, although

> ...it is also quite likely that because investors do not have an incentive in adopting labor-intensive techniques, they do not explore the availability of less expensive, less modern and more labor absorbing equipment.[25]

There was considerable evidence, however, that substitution was possible in a variety of ancillary operations. There was a "marked tendency to replace labor with automatic machinery" for those operations.

Öngüt found that in cases where a variety of techniques were available to choose from, the capital-intensive technique was invariably chosen. In one case, a firm with an existing plant and 600 employees wished to double their capacity. Investment was 50 per cent greater than in the earlier, labor-intensive factory, and employment was 106 workers, contrasted with the 600 in the older factory. The present value of the two alternative expansion patterns was computed under alternative assumptions. Including all investment incentives and evaluating both investments at existing prices, the present value of the capital-intensive factory was TL 7.1 million, and that of the labor-intensive factory TL 6.14 million. Excluding investment incentives and adjusting capital goods imports to a shadow rate of foreign exchange of TL 15 = $1, both projects had negative present values although the labor-intensive project was the more attractive of the two. With wages constant (contrasted with a projected 10 per cent annual rate of increase upon which the firm had based its expansion plans), no investment incentives, and the shadow exchange rate, the present value of the labor-intensive project was TL

23. McCabe and Michalopoulos also found that output per man was lower with use of domestic capital equipment, but that total value-added per unit of investment would be higher.

24. İbrahim Öngüt, "Economic Policies, Investment Decisions, and Employment in Turkish Industry," in Miller (ed.), *op. cit.* (Note 12).

25. *Ibid.,* p. 93.

5.6 million while that of the capital intensive project was negative at minus TL 0.5 million. Öngüt noted that the choice of the labor-intensive project would have created more than 500 additional jobs, since the foreign exchange saved on the project by choice of the labor-intensive technique would have been used to import other capital goods, with additional employment opportunities thereby created.[26]

In Chapter IX estimates of the employment effects of import-substition for the manufacturing sector as a whole will be given, based upon existing capital-labor ratios in each sector. It should be borne in mind that the substitution of capital for labor which might occur within each sector is not included in the estimates and that therefore the macroestimates probably underestimate the total employment effects of the trade regime and import-substitution policies.

Income distribution

There can be little doubt that the Turkish trade regime resulted in nonoptimal resource allocation with consequent losses in the attainable bundle of goods and services available for society's utilization. One defense sometimes given for nonoptimality in the economic efficiency sense is that income distribution may be altered in socially desired ways which cannot be attained by first-best measures.

In Turkey, as in many developing countries, one of the development goals has been a "fair distribution of income."[27] In this section consideration is given to the income-districutional effects of the Turkish trade regime. It will be seen that by and large the trade regime altered income distribution only within groups, and that the alteration which did occur was generally questionable on social grounds. Thus Turkish trade policies were non-optimal on both efficiency and equity grounds.

Evidence on Turkey's income distribution is so fragile that any inferences drawn with respect to changes over time would be perilous. Nonetheless, there are strong *a priori* grounds for believing that the effects of Turkey's trade regime on overall income distribution have probably been slight. Moreover, such effects as did result were probably in the nature more of redistribution within the middle and upper income groups than of a transfer between groups.

Export versus import-competing interests. In an exchange-control regime with currency overvaluation, theory predicts that potential exporters

26. Öngüt, *op. cit.* (Note 24), Table 1.
27. FFYP, *op. cit.* (Note 20, Chap. I), p. 43.

will be adversely affected relative to those whose interests lie in import-competing production. In Turkey, however, the major exporting interests are in agriculture and mining. The effect for agriculture of any redistribution away from exporting interests that might have resulted from currency over-valuation was largely offset by the government's price policies toward agriculture. As seen in Chapter VII, price intervention by the various state agencies and cooperatives resulted in severing the relations between the real exchange rate and the price received by farmers for wheat, tobacco, figs, raisins and hazelnuts. For those commodities, which constitute the bulk of agricultural exports, the chief determinant of prices was the nature of the price support program and not the real exchange rate.

For agriculture as a whole the evidence suggests that its term of trade improved gradually from 1950 to 1953, and remained fairly constant until about 1968, the latest year for which data are available.[28] Thus neither on *a priori* grounds nor on the basis of agriculture's terms of trade is there any evidence to suggest that agriculture suffered relative to industry. Within agriculture, it is probably the case that the farmers of the coastal plains, producing the citrus fruit, cotton, olive oil, vegetables, etc., suffered relative to what their position would have been under a unified exchange rate. However, there was some offset in that (1) those commodities were subject to more favorable exchange rates in the 1950's than were the traditional commodities, and (2) in the late 1960's the export rebates partially compensated for the overvalued exchange rate. Even taking these factors into account, however, agricultural income and output in the coastal region was less than it would have been under different exchange rate policies: agricultural exports from the coastal areas were highly responsive to price changes (as seen in Chapter VII), and the DRC of output expansion in that region would have been relatively low. Since the fertile coastal region has a per capita agricultural income well above the Turkish average, agricultural incomes may have been slightly more evenly distributed as a result of discrimination against exports, but the effect was very small and more than offset by government subsidies on grains.

The second export sector in which adverse income distributional consequences might have been expected was the mining sector. There can be little doubt that mining activity was stagnant and even declining in response to the erosion of the real exchange rate. However, in terms of the personal income distribution it is not clear that there would have been any effect: most mining enterprises are state-owned. During the 1950's Central Bank credits covered most of the SEE deficits, with the result that the incidence of the losses was spread over the entire community. Although a more rapid expansion of

28. Nur Keyder, "Türkiye'de Tarımsal Reel Gelir ve Köylünün Refah Seviyesi," *METU Studies in Development,* Fall 1970, p. 38.

mining activities might have led to greater employment in that sector, the effect thereof could not have been significantly different from that of growth of other sectors.

Thus the groups that theory suggests would lose through currency overvaluation were fairly well protected through the government's absorption of the losses that would otherwise have resulted. In the absence of these domestic policies, the efficiency losses resulting from currency overvaluation and suboptimal levels of production for export would have been accompanied by redistribution from agriculture and mining. Since the same income distribution could have been achieved by higher export EERs, a unified exchange rate would have achieved superior resource allocation without adverse effects on income distribution.

The groups that theory predicts would gain from currency overvaluation and exchange control are the import-competing producers and the recipients of import licenses. Many of the apparent gains were unreal here, as businessmen entered into import-competing production activities who would have entered into production of manufactured goods for export under alternative exchange-rate policies. Moreover, under a unified exchange rate, there would have been considerably greater imports of finished goods than in fact occurred. Importers who received windfall gains on their import licenses would otherwise have had a greater volume of business.

As seen in Chapter VI, there was a significant and important conflict between importers and industrialists. The conflict was natural and real, although it centered over which group was to receive the gains. New import-substitution firms received import licenses as soon as they emerged, and therefore obtained the premia associated with those import licenses. Such a development came at the expense of the importers who had previously dealt with the commodity. Thus importers of television sets, for instance, were forced to find another line of business or to close down when domestic production of television sets started. Because importing was such a profitable undertaking, the losses experienced by the importers were large. Some responded by starting their own import-substituting enterprises. Others contracted their operations, and changed the type of goods imported as new domestic production capabilities arose.

The importers were sometimes able to slow down the rate at which goods disappeared from eligible import lists, but they were unable to stop it. The economic and political power of the importers declined gradually throughout the twenty-year period and conversely, that of the industrialists gradually rose. By 1970 it was evident that the power of the importers was largely spent and that the industrialists as a group had gained the ascendancy.

Functional shares.   It is likely that the incidence of the trade regime on functional income distribution was small and was felt primarily through changes in distribution within groups rather than between them. The importer-industrialist conflict was one such case and has already been discussed.

During the 1950's the share of those on fixed salaries declined. Indeed, the FFYP declared that one of the major detrimental effects of the 1950's was that of altering the income distribution in an "unjust" direction.[29] That effect, however, was the result of inflation rather than of the trade regime.[30]

Probably the largest effect of the trade regime was on the distribution of labor income. As will be seen in Chapter IX, the import-substitution industries generally paid higher wages, required skilled workers, and offered fewer employment opportunities than did the traditional and export-oriented industries. Minimum wage legislation also contributed, since the import-substitution firms, being large and visible, could evade it less easily than the smaller, relatively labor-intensive traditional firms.

The consequent increase in demand for skilled workers undoubtedly raised the wages of those men relative to those of the unskilled. The fact that demand for unskilled labor rose more slowly than under an alternative trade regime probably meant fewer employment opportunities, rather than lower wages, in the presence of minimum wage legislation.

The incidence of fewer employment opportunities for unskilled workers was on the urban unemployed and those in rural areas who would have migrated if employment had been available. Insofar as there would have been more migration, per capita incomes in the agricultural sector might have been higher had urban employment increased more rapidly.[31] Regardless of whether it was the urban unemployed or potential migrants who were adversely affected, the income-distributional effect was to increase the labor income accruing to one group and reduce the labor income going to another. Without quantitative evidence to estimate the magnitude of the increase in skilled workers' incomes and the elasticity of demand for unskilled workers, it is not possible to estimate whether labor income increased or decreased. With the two changes in offsetting directions, however, it is likely that any change in aggregate labor income was relatively small.

29. FFYP, *op. cit.* (Note 20, Chap. I), p. 22.
30. Even in 1971, many Turks cited the fact that some people made large fortunes from the trade regime in the 1950's as one of the greatest evils of that period. It is likely that the gains accrued to those already in the upper income group at the expense of others in that group who were adversely affected by economic policy. Redistribution was primarily among sources of profit, rather than between functional groups.
31. The disparity between urban and rural living standards appears to have narrowed. The ratios of urban to rural per capita income were: 1950, 6.0; 1955, 5.7; 1960, 4.8; and 1965, 5.1. Merih Celasun, "Prospective Growth of Non-agricultural Employment in Turkey," in Miller (ed.), *op. cit.* (Note 12), p. 159.

Public sector versus private sector.   Both the administration of the trade regime and import-substitution policies somewhat favored the public sector at the expense of the private sector. Most important was the degree to which public and private firms had differential access to scarce foreign exchange. Public sector firms were probably at an advantage in obtaining import licenses because of their relatively greater representation on committees responsible for allocating foreign exchange. In the 1950's, SEEs were often exempt from paying surcharges and duties on their imports; even when they were not, the duties and surcharges frequently were left unpaid, as the SEEs were unable to meet their financial obligations. As was seen in Part Two, the SEEs were not required to pay the new *de facto* exchange rate for almost a year after August 1958 and continued to obtain their imports at TL 2.80 per dollar while the private sector was paying TL 9 per dollar.

In the 1960's SEEs were not subject to guarantee deposit requirements, whereas private sector firms were. Also, the fact that much of the heavy import-substitution investment was undertaken by the public sector led to a direct increase in the relative importance of SEEs.

But none of these effects need necessarily have resulted from the trade regime or from import-substitution policies. SEEs could have been subjected to the same treatment as private firms with no alteration in the nature of the regime. It seems more reasonable to interpret the treatment of the SEEs as the result of deliberate government policy: since the import regime was there anyway, it was one of the instruments used to attain the government's goals with regard to the relative importance of the two sectors.

In summary, the subsidization of capital goods imports combined with rising real wages due to domestic policies created a bias toward use of imported machinery and capital-intensive processes. Except for the relative wages and employment opportunities of skilled and unskilled workers, there is little evidence that the income distribution was significantly affected by the trade regime, as government policies with respect to agriculture offset the effects that might otherwise have occurred.

CHAPTER IX

Macroeconomic Effects of the Trade Regime

During the 1950–1970 period, Turkey's growth rate was well above the average for all LDCs. Despite year-to-year fluctuations and changes in the growth rate between various subperiods, the average annual rate of growth was a healthy 5.7 per cent. Even so, Turkey's per capita income in 1970 was the lowest in Europe. All Turkish governments since 1950 have made a rapid increase in per capita income a major goal.

Not only was Turkey's per capita income low relative to that of her European neighbors, but as experience with planning progressed in the 1960's, bottlenecks to growth appeared: foreign exchange shortage and inadequate savings and capital formation were the most prominent.[1] In addition, discussion about the conflict between employment creation and growth began toward the end of the 1960's.[2]

Despite Turkey's relatively favorable growth rate, a natural question is how much more rapid growth might have been. In terms of this study, the question can be formulated in terms of a consideration of Turkish growth under the quantitative-restriction, import-substitution regime compared with the growth that could have been achieved under alternative policies.

Estimates are made in this chapter of the losses in the manufacturing sector incurred in the 1960's by overemphasis upon import-substitution. It is shown that alternative strategies could have resulted in significant increases in the rate of growth of manufacturing output and value-added at both Turkish and international prices, reduced import requirements for both new investment and for intermediate goods, a reduced incremental capital-output ratio, and greatly increased employment opportunities for the same level of investment. Section I describes the method of analysis and Section II provides the results.

Mention should first be made of the experience of the 1950's. The fact that the focus is upon the 1960's does not imply that the trade regime did not incur sizeable costs in the 1950's. On the contrary, they were probably greater.

Data for the 1950's are inadequate to attempt to estimate the growth-rate costs of the regime in a manner comparable to that undertaken here for the

1. SFYP, *op. cit.* (Note 21, Chap. I), pp. 46-7.
2. See the papers in Miller (ed.), *op. cit.* (Note 12, Chap. VIII).

Table IX-1
Five-year averages, real GNP and investment, and ICORs, 1951 to 1971

	Average in Annual Growth in GNP (percentage)	Average Annual Investments as Percent of GNP	Average Annual ICOR
1951–1955	6.1	13.0	2.13
1952–1956	4.7	13.5	2.87
1953–1957	4.2	13.5	3.21
1954–1958	3.1	13.8	4.45
1955–1959	5.7	14.1	2.47
1956–1960	5.1	14.4	2.82
1957–1961	3.4	14.8	4.35
1958–1962	3.4	14.8	4.35
1959–1963	3.8	15.2	4.00
1960–1964	4.1	15.2	3.71
1961–1965	4.2	15.4	3.67
1962–1966	6.5	16.0	2.46
1963–1967	6.5	16.8	2.58
1964–1968	6.3	17.0	2.72
1965–1969	6.5	17.8	2.82
1966–1970	6.7	18.6	2.90
1967–1971	6.5	18.8	2.94

Source: For 1951–1968: Fry, *op. cit.* (Note 30, Chap. II), p. 30. For 1968–1971: Fry,
          "Reply," *Economic Journal,* June 1972.

1960's. Fortunately Fry has already derived some important empirical relationships at an aggregate level, and his results are significant in the present context.

Using five-year moving averages of investment and GNP Fry calculated investment as a fraction of GNP, the fractions of public and private investment in total investment, and the incremental capital-output ratio (ICOR). He then tested two hypotheses: (1) changes in the rate of growth of GNP (at 1961 prices) are explicable in terms of changes in the investment-GNP ratio and its composition between public and private investment; and (2) there was a significant difference in the growth rate between the 1950's and the 1960's.

Fry's data are reproduced in Table IX-1. The ICOR rose steadily until 1954–1958, fell sharply in 1955–1959 and 1956–1960, reattained its peak in 1957–1961 and 1958–1962, and thereafter declined until 1962–1966, rising gradually again in the late 1960's. By contrast, investment as a fraction of GNP rose fairly steadily throughout the two-decade period.

Fry concluded that:

No significant changes occured in the trends in total, public and private investment as proportions of GNP...There was a highly significant change in the trend in GNP itself measured at 1961 prices...[3]

Thus changes in the ratio of investment to GNP do not explain the changes in the growth rate over the period. Using the Chow test, Fry found that there was a highly significant difference between the 1950's and the 1960's. He dates the point of the changes as 1957–1961 and concludes that the change

...would seem to have been a result of a change in the incremental capital-output ratio (and not in the trend in the proportion of investment to GNP).[4]

Fry attributes the significant change in the growth rate to a reduction in the ICOR. Since 1961 was the year of the altered structural relationships, Fry concluded that the change can be attributed to the onset of planning. Two questions arise with respect to that diagnosis: (1) planning did not take effect until 1963 and there were undoubtedly lags before it could affect the growth rate; and (2) the ICORs are moving averages, reflecting events of earlier as well as terminal years. Since the change in the real exchange rate and the reduction of inflation preceded the start of planning, it seems reasonable to attribute some part of the change to those events. It is difficult to isolate the effects of the trade regime in the 1950's from those of inflation. Even so it can be argued that the resource misallocational and growth effects of inflation were felt primarily through their effects on Turkish trade and payments. Certainly a very high fraction of the effects of policies in the 1950's was attributable to the trade regime and its consequences, as Turkey was heavily dependent upon trade and the effects of the deterioration in her payments position were severe.

Although Fry's finding of significant structural change at the point 1957–1961 is highly suggestive, it is by no means conclusive. Alternative efforts to measure the effects of trade policies on growth in the 1950's are thwarted by lack of data. We then turn to the 1960's.

I. Estimating alternative growth patterns

It is always difficult to provide quantitative estimates of the changes that would have occurred under different alternatives, and more so when discussing alternative growth patterns. One means of doing so would be to provide a

3. Fry, *op. cit.* (Note 30, Chap. II), pp. 29-30.
4. *Ibid.*, p. 31.

fully specified model of the structural relations in the Turkish economy.[5] However, not only are the data lacking to accomplish such a task, but the sorts of policy alternatives we wish to consider — a more liberal trade regime, equalized incentives for export promotion and import-substitution, and an export-oriented growth strategy — are so far outside the range of observations on the Turkish economy that one would have little confidence in the resulting estimates even if data were available.

A significant change in incentives would obviously have a large number of effects. As seen in Chapter VIII, many high-DRC firms would either increase their efficiency or would contract, so that some excess costs of production would be eliminated for all firms. As a consequence the capital and labor coefficients for individual sectors would alter. Greater competition might lead to yet further changes. And the mix of products within industries would undoubtedly alter, with the relative importance of various sectors also shifting.

Not all of these effects can be estimated, and yet they may be very important. Here we content ourselves with a simpler approach which can provide insights into possible orders of magnitude on inter-industry shifts, although there is no basis for estimating changes in coefficients for individual industries that might occur. To limit the analysis still further, we focus only on manufacturing and shifts within it that might have arisen under alternative policies.

Before providing details of the method of estimation, it will help the reader to have an overview. The procedure essentially amounts to comparing planned manufacturing investment and growth with what would have happened under alternative allocations of the same total investment in manufacturing. The alternative allocations are hypothetical and designed to approximate what might have happened had growth been oriented somewhat less toward import-substitution and if approximately equal incentives had been given for the development of manufactured exports and import-substitution.

The analysis is restricted to manufacturing industries for several reasons. Under any conceivable growth strategy, manufacturing would be the leading growth sector. Given this fact, a strategy entailing less emphasis upon import-substitution would necessarily imply development of manufactured exports. Rapid growth of manufacturing appears to have been a goal of economic policy, so that it would make little sense to examine a strategy that placed

5. There are several dynamic planning models for Turkey but they are not suitable for analysis of the kinds of questions posed here. See Charles Blitzer, Hikmet Çetin and Alan Manne, "A Dynamic Five Sector Model for Turkey, 1967–82," *American Economic Review,* May 1970; and Charles Blitzer, *A Perspective Planning Model for Turkey: 1969–1984,* Stanford University Research Center in Economic Growth, mimeograph, August 1971.

less emphasis upon manufacturing growth. An alternative growth strategy would undoubtedly have resulted in considerable expansion of non-manufactured minor and traditional exports, such as lumber and livestock. Analysis of the potential of these factors would require detailed study of each sector in Turkey, as well as of export markets. Markets have been shown to exist for Turkish manufacturing and data are available, and Turkey's manufactured exports generally constitute negligible fractions of their world markets. Finally, inspection of the manufacturing sector alone provides very conservative estimates of what could have been achieved under alternative growth patterns, especially since parameters for individual industries are assumed unchanged.

The assumption that manufacturing investment would have been the same with no change in investments in other sectors implies that the use of infrastructure — electricity, transport, and so on — would have been the same under each pattern of manufacturing growth. To the extent that import-substituting industries actually had higher (or lower) infrastructural requirements than other manufacturing industries, the estimates of the adverse growth-rate effects of the import-substituting pattern will be understated (or overstated).

Identification of investment patterns under alternative growth strategies

The important question in the absence of a structural model is the identification of investment allocations that would have corresponded to different growth strategies. We seek to estimate what would have happened had growth been less import-substitution oriented and had incentives to manufacture for export been equal.

The main question is, what would have been "reasonable" allocation patterns in contrast to that which actually prevailed? Attempting to identify potential export sectors and quantifying the amount by which they might have grown would be the best way of reaching an answer to this question, if there were a sound scientific means of identification and quantification.[6] Most such means, however, contain a large arbitrary and subjective element. Two significant facts provide a way out of the impasse. First, import-substitution sectors were generally allocated a much higher share of new investment than their share of existing capital, value-added, and output. Although every manufacturing sector clearly has both potential export- and import-competing sectors, a strategy oriented less toward import-substitution would surely have

6. Consideration was given to estimating sectoral DRCs and maximizing international value-added from new manufacturing output subject to the volume of investment actually undertaken and the availability of foreign exchange for capital goods and for intermediate-goods imports. Neither foreign exchange constraint was binding and thus all investment was allocated to one sector, a clearly unsatisfactory solution.

allocated more new investment to the established sectors and less to the newer industries. Second, the import-substitution sectors generally had higher ICORs than the established industries.

These two considerations enable identification of plausible alternative investment patterns: (1) a strategy oriented less toward import-substitution would have been one where each sector was allocated new investment in proportion to its share of the initial manufacturing capital stock; and (2) each sector would be allocated new investment in proportion to its initial share of domestic manufacturing value-added. By using a base year (1963) when considerable import-substitution had already occurred, the allocation of new investment according to share in capital stock corresponds to a growth strategy less heavily oriented toward import-substitution than the actual, although considerable further import-substitution would still have occurred. That pattern will be described as "moderate import-substitution" (MIS). Allocation of new investment in accordance with value-added shares would have resulted in some import-substitution growth but less than MIS. It thus approximates what might have happened had incentives been equalized for export promotion and import substitution. This will be called "balanced export promotion and import substitution" (BEPIM).

The two growth alternatives represent identifiable allocation patterns. They both give heavier weight than the Plans did to those industries where Turkey apparently has the greater comparative advantage. Both patterns imply at least as rapid a growth of the overall manufacturing sector as was envisaged by the policy makers. Thus if the hypothetical alternatives had enabled more rapid growth of manufacturing, income, and employment, those alternatives would presumably have been preferred to the actual pattern, oriented toward import-substitution. Several questions are relevant: Taking the amount of investment in manufacturing as given, how did the rate of growth of manufacturing value-added compare with that which would have occurred under MIS or BEPIM with the same total investment, when value-added is evaluated at Turkish prices? Further, how does the actual growth rate compare with that which would have been experienced under the two alternatives evaluated at world prices? Then, what would have been the import content of investment and how does that compare with the actual import content? What would intermediate goods imports have been, compared to what they actually were? What would the ICOR in manufacturing have been, compared to what it actually was? And what would employment in manufacturing have been?

Method of estimation

The basic observed variables, considered as equal under the planned growth pattern and the two alternatives, are as follows:

e_j employment per million TL of value added in the jth sector

k_j the ICOR of the jth sector in value-added terms

m_j imports of intermediate goods per unit of output of j

n_j imports of capital goods per unit of investment in j

q_j ratio of Turkish value-added price to world value-added price of j

v_j ratio of value-added to output at Turkish prices in j

The variables for which estimates were derived, under each of the three growth alternatives, are:

E_j^i employment in j under the ith allocation strategy

I_j^i investment in j under the ith allocation strategy

IVA_j^i value added in the jth sector at world prices

K^i ICOR in value-added terms for all manufacturing

M_j^i intermediate goods imports in the jth sector under the ith strategy

N_j^i capital goods imports for investment in j under the ith strategy

P_j^i output in the jth sector at Turkish prices

V_j^i value-added in j at Turkish prices under the ith strategy

where i superscript refers to alternative allocations. These are denoted by

a the allocation in the plan

b BEPIM

m MIS

Under any allocation pattern, by definition:

$$E_j = e_j V_j \tag{1}$$

$$V_j = I_j / k_j \tag{2}$$

$$P_j = V_j / v_j \tag{3}$$

$$IVA_j = q_j V_j \tag{4}$$

$$M_j = m_j P_j \tag{5}$$

$$N_j = n_j P_j \tag{6}$$

and totals for all manufacturing sectors can be obtained by summing the both sides of each equation over j.

Letting the period for which output patterns are observed be denoted by a superscript 0,

$$I_j^b = \sum_k I_k^a \left[V_j^0 / \sum_k V_k^0 \right] \tag{7}$$

$$I_j^m = \sum_k I_k^a \left[k_j V_j^0 / \sum_k V_k^0 k_k \right] . \tag{8}$$

Once solutions are found for (7) and (8), eq. (1) through (6) can be solved for the outcome under planned investment and the two hypothetical alternatives. But first, the sources of data and their reliability must be examined.

The data

It was decided to estimate the effects of alternative investment allocations for two separate time periods: the 1963-to-1967 period, corresponding to the FFYP; and the 1967-to-1972 period, corresponding to the SFYP. The basic data for each period were taken, insofar as possible, from the respective Plans, and the partitioning of manufacturing into subsectors followed that in each of the Plans.

A key problem was that of obtaining internally consistent estimates of the various parameters. At first it was thought that the ICORs implied in the Plans could be combined with actual investment and output data. But prices had changed, and the data were noncomparable in several other regards. It was therefore decided to utilize all data implicit in the FFYP and SFYP, treating the projected outputs in the Plans as the actual outputs. Thus all three patterns could be estimated, using the same parameters as actually used by the planners. The implied ICORs were derived by taking Plan estimates of investment and value-added changes between the base and terminal year. By using a five-year period as the basis of observation it was hoped that the effects of differences in timing of investments upon the observed changes in value-added would be minimized. These same ICORs were used for estimation of the attained rate of growth (really the planned rate of growth) and for the two alternative allocations. The ratios of value-added to output at Turkish prices were also implicit in the Plan documents and these were used in all sets of estimates. To the extent that the planners underestimated the costs of import-substitution, that bias is also contained in the results below.

Four needed parameters were not available from the Plans. These were employment per unit of output, import coefficients per unit of investment, import coefficients per unit of output, and the ratio of domestic value-added to international value-added.

Two sources were used to obtain import coefficients: (1) data on sectoral intermediate goods imports per unit of output were taken from the 1967 input-output table; and (2) data on import requirements per unit of investment in each sector were derived from the 1964 *Census of Manufacturing Industries.*[7] These data were the only ones available in both cases, and were

7. The *Census of Manufacturing Industries* provided data on gross additions to fixed assets during 1963, and the value of imported goods in machinery and equipment acquisitions. The ratio of imported machinery to total investment in buildings and plant and equipment was used.

assumed constant between the FFYP and SFYP. Employment coefficients were also obtained from the *Census of Manufactures*.

The most· difficult estimates to obtain were coefficients linking Turkish value-added per unit of output to international value-added per unit of output. The procedure finally adopted was to use data from Özfırat's study[8] for those sectors for which they were available, and to estimate an unweighted average of available estimates for those sectors for which Özfırat did not provide data. As seen in Chapter VIII, Özfırat's data probably underestimated the differences in the ratio of international to domestic value-added between the export and import-substituting sectors. As such, there is probably a downward bias in the estimate of the difference in international value-added that would have resulted under alternative strategies.

In general, estimates of the differences in growth rates between the alternative allocations are likely to be biased downward. Not only are they sectoral aggregates, thereby obscuring the differences within sectors between export-oriented and import-substituting activities, but the coefficients of each sector are assumed constant over the period of estimation. Any effects of the trade regime in altering capital intensities or in increasing capital and labor coefficients are obscured by the method of estimation.

Table IX-2 gives the coefficients used in the analysis. The first two columns give the ratio of imports to investment and to production in each sector. These coefficients were used for analysis of both Plan periods, although the data on imports of capital goods for investment relate to 1963 and the intermediate-goods import coefficients are for 1967. The absence on any alternative basis for estimating the coefficients for the periods separately dictated this decision.

The third column of Table IX-2 gives the ratio of international value-added to Turkish value-added in each sector. Again, these ratios were used for analysis of both periods. It should be remembered that these coefficients, like the import coefficients, obscure a great deal of intrasectoral variation. As such, the resulting estimates of the growth rate effects of import-substitution are undoubtedly underestimated, as the intrasectoral allocations tended toward the high-cost, high-import-content subsectors.

The next two columns give the implied ICORs (increase in value-added at Turkish prices per TL of investment in each sector) in the FFYP and SFYP. As can be seen, there was considerable fluctuation between the two periods and some coefficients are open to considerable question. Perhaps the most suspect sectors are wood products and rubber products, where the change between the two Plans is very great, and petroleum in the SFYP, where the low capital-intensity of the sector appears completely implausible. The trans-

---

8. Özfırat, *op. cit.* (Table VIII-1).

Table IX-2
Coefficients of the model

Sector	Import Coeff.		Ratio IVA/ DVA	ICOR		Employ- ment
	n_j	m_j		FFYP	SFYP	e_j
Food products	0.112	0.009	0.884		1.582	51.68
Beverages	0.168	0.019	0.364	1.149	2.132	16.85
Tobacco	0.143	0.004	0.750		0.905	16.78
Textiles	0.452	0.070	0.704	1.083	1.200	46.78
Footwear, wearing apparel	0.051	0.070	0.704			
Wood and cork products	0.133	0.021	0.862	3.704	1.572	76.98
Furniture and fixtures	0.055	0.021	0.862			
Paper and products	0.581	0.269	0.581	11.364	10.309	39.96
Printing and publishing	0.403	0.269	0.581		1.333	41.41
Fur and kaliber products	0.353	0.123	0.881	n.a.	5.000	47.53
Rubber products	0.531	0.441	0.564	0.891	2.415	56.33
Chemicals	0.611	0.307	0.625	5.495	2.659	28.74
Petroleum	0.847	0.151	0.721	n.a.	0.975	3.27
Non-metallic products	0.173	0.072	0.813	1.381	1.116	45.08
Basic metals	0.210	0.064	0.555	3.831	4.032	20.70
Metal products	0.080	0.158	0.637	1.087	1.420	36.57
Machinery	0.309	0.309	0.412	1.279	1.297	19.44
Electrical machinery	0.277	0.224	0.615	1.225	1.125	23.02
Transport equipment	0.076	0.252	0.324	0.629	0.568	51.71
Miscellaneous manufacturing	0.421	n.a.	n.a.	0.289	n.a.	n.a.

Sources: n_j's from 1964 *Census of Manufacturing Industries,* computed as the ratio of imported goods to total investment in each sector.

m_j's from 1967 input-output table, kindly supplied by SPO. They are exclusive of taxes paid on imports. IVA/DVA: all are from Özfırat, *op. cit.* (Table VIII-1), except fur and leather products, petroleum, metal products, machinery, and transport equipment. The latter, except petroleum, are based on data from the sources listed in Table VIII-1. The petroleum estimate was kindly provided by industry sources in interviews.

ICOR's: calculated by taking the ratio of increment in value-added to five-year investment in each Plan. FFYP, *op. cit.* (Note 20, Chap. 1), tables 84–86, pp. 185–6. SFYP, *op. cit.* (Note 21, Chap. 1), tables 197, 199, pp. 405, 407.

e_j's: ratios of employment to value-added for firms with ten or more employees, from *Census of Manufactures.*

Notes: The footwear and wearing apparel, furniture and fixtures, and printing and publishing sectors were included in the textile, wood products and paper sectors respectively in the 1967 input-output table and by Özfırat. Import coefficients for intermediate goods and the ratio of IVA to DVA are therefore the same for each pair of sectors.

In the SFYP, several sectors were disaggregated, and the subsector estimates were used in the computations. The sectors, subsectors, and ICORs were:

Non-metallic products	Ceramics	0.889
	Glass	1.116
	Cement	0.400
Metal products	Non-ferrous-metal	1.605
Machinery	Agricultural machinery	0.769
Electrical machinery	Electronics	0.937

The last three subsectors were calculated separately for the SFYP, with IVA/ DVA ratios of 0.623, 0.430, and 0.615, respectively.

port equipment ICOR also appears implausibly low, but the sector is dominated by repair activities, which may explain it.

Despite the probable margins of error in the ICORs it was decided to use all figures as given in the Plans, on the grounds that they were the data actually used in deciding upon an import-substitution strategy and are at least internally consistent. Selection of any alternative technique for estimation involved the difficulty that constant-price estimates of actual investment and output, by sectors, are simply unavailable. The bias that would be introduced by use of current-price data or choice of sectoral deflators was judged to be greater than any errors in the SPO data. It should be noted that the FFYP data were in 1961 prices whereas the SFYP data were in 1965 prices. Insofar as domestic prices of some sectoral outputs rose more rapidly than average, or as the price of manufactured goods changed relative to the price of the investment goods, the ICORs are noncomparable. Another factor, which in the author's judgment is probably not important, is that the implicit ICORs could have been influenced by the planned timing of investments within each period.

Thus the data are at best indicative of orders of magnitude. While they are undoubtedly subject to error there is little basis for believing that those errors are systematic, except that intrasectoral differences are obscured. We turn to consideration of alternative allocational patterns.

II. Growth under alternative allocations

Table IX-3 gives the actual investment allocation set forth in each Plan, and the two hypothetical allocations. As is evident from the table, the degree of disaggregation in the FFYP was considerably less than in the SFYP. Since in each period the hypothetical allocational procedures allotted investments in proportion to the sector's share of total manufacturing value-added or capital stock, the SFYP allocation was influenced by the outcome of the FFYP. The first and fourth columns of Table IX-3 give the actual planned investments in each sector. The second and fifth columns give the amount of the investment in each sector that would have resulted under the MIS allocation.

The third and sixth columns give the investment allocation that would have resulted had each sector been allocated a share of total investment (in manufacturing) in proportion with its initial-year share of manufacturing value-added — i.e., the export-oriented strategy implied by the BEPIM allocation. The sectors with below-average capital intensity receive a smaller allocation under the MIS allocation than under BEPIM. Thus food products and textiles, both of which have capital intensities well below the average, would

Table IX-3
Alternative investment allocations, FFYP and SFYP (millions of TL at 1961 and 1965 prices)

	FFYP			SFYP		
	Actual	MIS	BEPIM	Actual	MIS	BEPIM
Food				1850	3710	4047
Beverages	1034	2288	3452	320	679	550
Tobacco				190	1009	1923
Textiles and clothing	910	2017	3168	2400	3527	5071
Wood products	100	44	20	440	683	750
Paper				1850	1343	225
Printing	553	741	111	200	232	300
Hides and leather	–	–	–	150	435	150
Rubber				700	944	675
Plastic	254	69	131	235	151	200
Chemicals	2735	1759	545	4250	2002	1299
Petroleum	–	–	-	1150	1143	2023
Ceramics				40	52	100
Glass				240	258	400
Cement	304	294	363	950	586	500
Cement and baked clay products				60	104	450
Iron and steel	2133	2090	928	4200	3502	1499
Nonferrous metals				1500	1703	550
Metal products	238	465	726	1150	1110	1349
Machinery				1550	789	1049
Agricultural machinery	1068	174	232	150	100	225
Electric machinery				450	244	375
Electronics	244	65	91	150	81	150
Road vehicles				350	271	825
Railway vehicles	422	52	141	110	239	225
Shipbuilding				350	88	75
Other	94	31	181	–	–	–
Total	10089	10089	10089	24985	24985	24985

Source: Coefficients from Table IX-2. Actual investment allocations from FFYP and SFYP, *op. cit.* (Notes 20, 21, Chap. I). Alternative allocations computed according to eqs. (7) and (8).

have received a considerably larger investment allocation under BEPIM than under MIS. Sectors such as chemicals, which are heavily capital-intensive, would have received a considerably larger allocation under MIS than under BEPIM.

Under either hypothetical allocation, investment in the "traditional" sec-

Table IX-4

First Five Year Plan: Increase in value-added at Turkish and international prices under alternative allocations of investment (increase from 1962 in millions of 1961 TL)

Sector	Value-added at Turkish Prices			Value-added at International Prices		
	FFYP	MIS	BEPIM	FFYP	MIS	BEPIM
Food, beverages, and tobacco	917	2027	3060	811	1792	2705
Textiles and clothing	840	1861	2924	591	1310	2058
Wood and cork	27	12	5	23	10	4
Paper	49	65	10	28	38	6
Rubber	285	77	147	161	43	83
Chemicals	499	320	99	312	200	62
Nonmetallic products	220	213	263	179	173	214
Basic metals	557	545	242	309	302	134
Metal products	219	427	668	139	272	425
Machinery	832	136	181	343	56	75
Electrical machinery	199	53	74	122	33	46
Transport equipment	671	83	224	217	27	73
Other	325	107	626	162	53	313
Total	5641	5926	8523	3397	4309	6198

Source: Tables IX-2 and IX-3.

tors would have been considerably greater than under the actual investment pattern. The MIS allocation represents something of a halfway house: import-substitution could have proceeded fairly rapidly, although some additional exports would have been available from the traditional sectors.

Several features of individual sectors should be noted. Perhaps most important, the implied ICOR for the petroleum sector in the second Plan was improbably low. Given that the oil sector's share in manufacturing value-added was already 8 per cent in 1967, investment in petroleum under BEPIM would have exceeded planned investment, if the figures for the latter (column 4 of Table IX-3) are taken as valid. At the opposite side of the spectrum, tobacco products are a large manufacturing sector in Turkey, and the hypothetical allocations would imply unrealistically high growth rates for that sector, given the probable difficulties of developing an export market on such a scale.

We first consider the planned growth of manufacturing value-added, and contrast it with the growth that would have occurred under the alternative strategies, at Turkish and international prices. Table IX-4 gives the data for the FFYP and Table IX-5 gives the data for the SFYP. The first three col-

Table IX-5
Second Five Year Plan: Increase in value-added, by sectors, at Turkish and international prices, under alternative allocations of investment (increase from 1967 in millions of 1965 TL)

Sector	Value-added at Turkish Prices			Value-added at International Prices		
	SFYP	MIS	BEPIM	SFYP	MIS	BEPIM
Food	1170	2345	2558	1034	2073	2661
Beverages	150	318	558	55	116	94
Tobacco	210	1115	2121	158	836	1590
Textiles and clothing	2000	2938	4225	1408	2068	2947
Wood products	280	434	477	241	374	411
Paper	180	130	22	105	76	13
Printing and publishing	150	174	225	87	101	131
Hides and leather	30	87	30	26	77	26
Rubber	290	391	279	164	221	157
Plastic	180	116	153	102	65	86
Chemicals	1600	753	489	1000	471	306
Petroleum	1180	1173	2076	850	846	1496
Ceramics	45	59	112	37	48	91
Glass	215	231	358	178	188	291
Cement	470	289	249	305	188	162
Cement and clay products	150	260	1124	126	218	944
Iron and steel	1040	868	372	577	482	206
Nonferrous metals	280	318	103	174	198	64
Metal products	810	781	950	516	497	605
Machinery	1195	608	809	492	250	333
Agricultural machinery	195	130	292	84	56	126
Electrical machinery	400	217	333	246	133	205
Electronics	160	86	160	98	53	98
Road vehicles	616	477	1451	200	155	470
Railway vehicles	60	130	123	26	56	53
Shipbuilding	170	43	36	55	14	12
Total	13226	14471	19685	8340	9860	13578

Source: Tables IX-2 and IX-3.

umns in each table give the increase over the Plan period in domestic value-added at domestic prices in manufacturing under the actual and two hypothetical investment patterns. The last three columns give the increase in value-added in manufacturing at international prices under each pattern.

Turning to Table IX-4 first, it is evident that under the MIS pattern the increase over the five years in domestic value-added at domestic prices would have been 5.1 per cent greater than was planned with the FFYP allocation for the same total investment. At international prices the differential increase in value-added would have been considerably larger: 26.8 per cent. The differences in the implied average annual rates of growth of manufacturing were relatively small at domestic 1961 prices, but much greater at international prices. Thus the FFYP planned for an average annual manufacturing growth rate of 13 per cent, valued at domestic prices, while the MIS investment strategy would have resulted in an average annual rate of 13.8 per cent at those prices. Measured at international prices, however, the planned growth rate would come to 10.5 per cent per annum, whereas the MIS allocation would have yielded 12.5 per cent per annum.

The differences between the planned growth and the hypothetical results from the BEPIM strategy are much greater, both at domestic and at international prices. Figured at domestic 1961 prices the increase in manufacturing value-added over the five years would have been 56 per cent more under the BEPIM pattern than that indicated by the FFYP allocation for the same level of total investment in manufacturing. This would have implied an average annual growth rate of 16.9 per cent under the BEPIM pattern, contrasted with the planned rate of 13 per cent. The difference would have been greater yet at international prices; value-added according to the BEPIM allocation would have grown at an average annual rate of 17 per cent, contrasted with the planned 10.5 per cent rate, as the increment over the five years would have risen to 82 per cent more under the BEPIM allocation.

Before evaluating the behavior of individual sectors, it is worthwhile to examine the results of similar computations for the SFYP, given in Table IX-5. The results are much the same: an MIS pattern of investment over the period would have resulted in a 9 per cent greater increase in output at domestic prices and an 18 per cent greater increase in output at international prices. Far bigger gains would have accrued to the BEPIM investment strategy, as value-added could have grown by 46.5 per cent more at domestic prices and by 63.1 per cent more at international prices than under the planned allocation.

The implied average annual rates of growth of manufacturing value-added in the SFYP under the three alternatives are:

	SFYP	MIS	BEPIM
At domestic prices	11.1	11.8	15.2
At international prices	10.3	12.0	16.5

As in the FFYP, the BEPIM investment pattern would have resulted in considerably faster growth of manufacturing value-added than the MIS strategy, which in turn would have resulted in a higher rate of growth than the planned rate.

The alternative strategies would therefore have resulted in considerably lower ICORs for the manufacturing sector.[9] The implied ICORs in the two Plans under each strategy are:

	Plan	MIS	BEPIM
FFYP	1.85	1.70	1.18
SFYP	1.89	1.73	1.28

The potential gains from alternative strategies appear slightly greater in the FFYP than in the SFYP period. The reason for this is that the base-year weights in the SFYP already reflected the past import-substitution efforts. Even the BEPIM strategy in the SFYP period would have resulted in a heavier weight to import-substitution sectors than in the FFYP. Neither hypothetical alternative of course is an optimizing one, and bigger gains would be reflected in an optimizing model than in either alternative evaluated here. Nonetheless, the differences in manufacturing growth rates are considerable, and imply that the costs of import-substitution may have been a loss on the order of 5 or 6 per cent per annum in the rate of growth of manufacturing value-added. Given the downward bias in the estimates, the results are sufficient to indicate that Turkish manufacturing could have grown considerably faster under an alternative allocation strategy than in fact occurred.

Inspection of the behavior of individual sectors in Tables IX-3 to IX-5 suggests that a few sectors account for the major part of the differences. Investment in chemicals as an import-substitution sector was heavily emphasized in both Plans. Chemicals are highly capital-intensive, and their ratio of value-added at international prices to value-added at domestic prices is low. A shift from chemicals to less capital-intensive sectors would have increased manufacturing value-added even at Turkish prices, and still more at international prices. Other sectors heavily emphasized in the Plans were paper and steel. Their characteristics are similar to chemicals, with high capital intensities and low ratios of value-added at international prices to value-added at domestic prices. Most of the gains in output reflected in the computations could have been obtained by shifts out of those sectors.

Textiles, food products and metal products all appear to have reasonably low ICORs and relatively high ratios of value-added at international prices to value-added at domestic prices. Increased investment allocations to those sectors would have implied a faster growth rate.

Despite the very large size of the potential gains, the results may be questioned on the grounds that Turkey could not have absorbed or marketed

9. Note that the ICORs are well below those given in Table IX-1. The main reason is that the estimates here are for manufacturing only and do not include infrastructure investments.

abroad such large increases in output of food, textiles, and tobacco. For tobacco, the contention is undoubtedly valid. For food and textiles, there probably would have been ample export markets with reasonable pricing policies and a realistic exchange rate. For the implied growth of output in food and textiles is less than 20 per cent per annum even under BEPIM, and with Turkey's negligible share of world markets, rapid increases in exports should have been feasible. For the five years of the SFYP, the increment in value-added at international prices in food and textiles between the Plan investments and the BEPIM patterns was TL 1,627 and TL 1,566 million, respectively, or $181 million and $174 million. Although the growth rate of these exports would have been very high, their absolute values would not have been. Achievement of even these modest targets would have required access to markets. But Turkey's ties with the European Common Market and her proximity to the Middle Eastern countries put her in an excellent position in this regard.

It is of interest to test the sensitivity of the results to the role of textiles, food, and tobacco. To do this, the author posited a constraint on tobacco investment to its actual level in the SFYP, and constrained investment in textiles and food to only 10 per cent above Plan levels. The author then visually picked off an investment strategy, based upon ICORs, which would entail the same level of investment.[10] The result was an increase of TL 17,486 million in value-added at domestic prices and of TL 12,157 million in value-added at international prices, which is much closer to the BEPIM results than to the MIS. The interested reader can verify that elimination of TL 2,500 million investment in iron and steel and its reallocation would substantially increase the gains.

Import requirements under alternative allocations

It is evident that an investment strategy aimed at BEPIM could have resulted in a considerably higher rate of growth of manufacturing output. Given appropriate marketing efforts and incentives, the increment in international value-added could have resulted in a sizeable increase in manufactured exports, which in itself would have alleviated Turkey's foreign exchange difficulties by expanding Turkey's manufactured-export earnings. Such a strategy would have implied that the export sector would have become a leading-growth sector.

The import-substitution strategy also raised requirements of imports, both

10. The investment levels used, in the same order of sectors as given in Table IX-5 were (TL million): 2035, 320, 190, 2640, 1400, 300, 200, 750, 850, 200, 500, 1150, 600, 1430, 700, 700, 2500, 100, 4500, 1800, 400, 500, 200, 55, 53, and 12.

on capital goods account and for intermediate goods, above the levels that would have been required by either alternative strategy. Turkish planners regarded the economy's capacity to invest as limited by foreign exchange. As stated in the *SFYP,*

> ...one of the main structural impediments to economic growth in the past was the fact that the foreign trade sector...could not keep up with the general economic development...When development and industrialization accelerate, the ability to increase the import capacity will be a very important factor in determining the growth rate...[11]

Chapter VI demonstrated how import demand for raw materials and intermediate goods generally exceeded the Plan estimates, with the result that capital goods imports were generally held to levels below those anticipated in the Plans. To the extent that foreign exchange did constitute a binding constraint upon the rate of investment it is of interest to calculate the imports that would have been required under an alternative investment strategy.

To do this, the import coefficients given in Table IX-2 were utilized to estimate what the incremental import requirements, both for capital goods and for intermediate goods, would have been under planned and hypothetical strategies. The results are given in Table IX-6.

For intermediate goods imports, MIS would have required 36 per cent less imports of intermediate goods, at 1963 coefficients, in the FFYP and 22 per cent less imports in the SFYP than the actual allocation. A BEPIM strategy would have required 26 per cent less intermediate goods imports in the FFYP and 6 per cent fewer imports in the SFYP than the planned strategy, although more imports would have been required than under MIS. When it is recalled

11. SFYP, *op. cit.* (Note 21, Chap. I), pp. 47–8.

Table IX-6
Import requirements under alternative growth strategies (millions of TL)

	Capital Goods	Intermediate Goods
FFYP (1961 prices)		
Plan	3656	1911
MIS	3332	1214
BEPIM	2788	1423
SFYP (1965 prices)		
Plan	8966	4321
MIS	7909	3383
BEPIM	7888	4070

Source: Text and Tables IX-2 to IX-5.

that manufacturing output and value-added grow much faster under BEPIM than under MIS, it is clear why import requirements are greater under the first than under the second. What is surprising is that increments of 82 per cent and 63 per cent, respectively, in value-added over the planned levels in the two Plans could have been sustained with a reduction in total intermediate goods imports.

For capital goods the picture is similar. A BEPIM pattern would have utilized 24 per cent fewer imports than the actual investment pattern during the FFYP, and 12 per cent fewer during the SFYP. This result is the more striking because of the relatively high import content of investment in textiles (see Table IX-2).

If foreign exchange availability was the binding constraint on the level of investment, these results would imply that investment could have been increased by about 50 per cent during the FFYP, with no change in the level of imports when both intermediate goods and capital goods import requirements are taken into account. In the SFYP, investment could have increased by about 30 per cent with no change in imports.

Thus the import-substitution strategy actually pursued was import-intensive, at least over the period of the FFYP and SFYP. In every sense therefore BEPIM strategy would have dominated: with the same level of investment, manufacturing growth could have proceeded at an average annual rate about 6 per cent above that planned, valued at international prices. If in addition investment in manufacturing had been increased by 25 per cent with an export-oriented strategy, the rate of growth of manufacturing value-added could have been doubled, with no change in total import requirements above the levels foreseen in the Plans. With additional output from export-oriented sectors, moreover, foreign exchange earnings could have increased substantially, permitting larger imports.

Employment effects of alternative strategies

Table IX-7 gives estimates of new jobs created under each investment allocation for the two Plans. MIS would have resulted in about 37,000 more jobs in the FFYP and 93,000 more jobs in the SFYP than the actual investment pattern. BEPIM would have created 70 per cent more new jobs, or 138 thousand more than the actual strategy in the FFYP and 50 per cent more (or over 200,000) than that of the SFYP.

Viewed against a non-agricultural labor force of about 3.7 million and implied urban unemployment of 462,000 in 1965,[12] the additional employment potential of the BEPIM strategy is impressive.

12. *Ibid.*, p. 149; and *Census of Population,* 1965.

Table IX-7
New jobs created by alternative investment patterns (thousands of jobs)

Sector	FFYP			SFYP		
	Plan	MIS	BEPIM	Plan	MIS	BEPIM
Food				60.4	121.2	132.2
Beverages	38.5	85.1	128.5	2.5	5.3	4.3
Tobacco				3.5	18.7	35.6
Textiles and clothing	39.3	87.1	136.8	93.6	137.4	197.6
Wood products	2.1	0.9	0.4	21.6	33.4	36.7
Paper				7.2	5.2	0.9
Printing and publishing	1.9	2.6	0.4	6.2	7.2	9.3
Hides and leather				1.4	4.1	1.4
Rubber	16.1	4.3	8.3	16.3	22.0	15.7
Chemicals	14.3	9.2	2.8	46.0	21.6	14.1
Petroleum				3.8	3.8	6.8
Ceramics				2.0	2.6	4.9
Glass	9.9	9.6	11.9	9.7	10.4	16.1
Cement				24.8	15.3	13.2
Cement and clay prod's.				6.8	11.8	51.1
Iron and steel	11.5	11.3	5.0	21.5	18.0	7.7
Nonferrous metals	8.0	15.6	24.4	9.6	10.9	3.5
Metal products				29.6	28.6	34.7
Machinery	16.2	2.6	3.5	23.2	11.8	15.7
Agricultural machinery				5.3	3.6	8.0
Electrical machinery	4.6	1.2	1.7	9.2	5.0	7.7
Electronics				3.6	2.0	3.6
Road vehicles				5.2	11.3	10.7
Railway vehicles	34.7	4.3	11.6	3.1	6.7	6.4
Shipbuilding				11.9	3.0	2.5
Total	197.1	233.8	335.3	428.0	520.9	640.4

Source: Data from Tables IX-2 to IX-4.

Since investment is assumed to be the same under each strategy, the labor-capital ratio would have increased in the same proportion as the increase in the number of new jobs.

All computations thus indicate that Turkey's trade regime and the associated import-substitution strategy had considerable growth-rate costs over the period of the two Five Year Plans. To the extent that foreign exchange was a binding constraint, the import-substitution strategy made it more so, and if investment was limited by foreign-exchange availability, investment could have been substantially increased by a different strategy. Even within the planned investment level the rate of growth of manufacturing value-added could have been increased by about one-third and employment opportunities could have grown even more.

The data are of course indicative only of orders of magnitude, and the alternatives considered are not optimizing ones. There were undoubtedly sub-sectors within each sector which would have been included in an optimal strategy. Given the downward biases inherent in the data, there can be little doubt that the growth-rate cost of the strategy was high. The alternative export-oriented strategy would have required a considerable change in Turkey's economic orientation, but that change would have been in line with Turkey's stated intent to enter the Common Market as well as with its objective of a more dynamic and progressive industrial sector. An export-oriented strategy would not have been confined to textiles, metal products and food products but could have permeated each industrial sector. There is thus every reason to believe that the static losses associated with import-substitution discussed in Chapter VIII were fully reflected in Turkey's growth rate during the 1960's.

CHAPTER X

Conclusions

Since 1953, Turkey's trade and payments regime has never been fully liberalized. The degree of restrictiveness has been modified with changes in the instruments used for control and with alterations in the manner that existing controls were exercised. And the purposes that the payments regime was intended to serve have been altered from time to time.

When controls were first imposed in the early 1950's they were intended to suppress the emerging balance-of-payments deficit. The "planlessness" that characterized the Menderes Government pervaded the payments-control mechanism, and the increasing restrictiveness of the regime before 1958 was largely the unintended outcome of measures taken as *ad hoc* responses to declining foreign exchange earnings and increasingly limited borrowing opportunities.

The Turkish experience of 1953–1958 probably has little relevancy for other countries. The inflation, SEE deficit, inflation cycle into which Turkey plunged was the outcome of particularly unfortunate economic policies. The causes of the cycle were obvious at the time, and it was the deliberate refusal of the Prime Minister and those about him to accept economic realities that led to the difficulties. The only pertinent lesson from all this may be that political leaders are free to disregard whatever they wish, at least in the short run.

The Stabilization Program of 1958 was as drastic as the inflationary cycle that preceded it — and, unlike the 1953–1958 experience, it is instructive for other situations. For the episode provides an instance of a country's transformation from rapid inflation to price stability. That transformation was accomplished primarily through a sharp shift from rapid expansion of the money supply to gradual contraction. A huge increase in the flow of imports and the deflationary effects of net revenues from foreign trade taxes augmented the primary effect of the shift in the rate of expansion of the money supply.

The transition to price stability was not painless, although the evidence seems to indicate that had the Stabilization Program not been reversed in 1959 the reallocation of resources that was necessary after the dislocations of the mid-1950's might have been accompanied by a very short-lived and mild recession. The abandonment of the Stabilization Program in 1959 meant that when it was resumed after the Revolution in May of 1960 a second recession ensued, which was intensified if not prolonged by political uncertainties.

The second major lesson emerging from Turkey's experience with the Stabilization Program is that there appears to be a substantial lag in the response of exports to an altered incentive structure. Exports did not increase markedly after the adoption of the Stabilization Program, even if allowance is made for the fact that export EERs were not immediately increased by the full amount of the nominal devaluation. But exports grew rapidly from 1959 to 1964, reversing the downward trend of earlier years. In view of the fact that there were no changes in export incentives after the Stabilization Program until 1963 (and then the only change was the introduction of export rebates, which did not assume importance until the latter half of the 1960's), the resumed growth of export earnings must be attributed largely to the altered export EERs which were a part of the Stabilization Program.

As seen in Chapter VII, there are many commodities produced in Turkey which are either exports or potential exports for which domestic policies pursued by the government essentially determine production and distribution. (1) Many agricultural commodities are subject to domestic price supports which are unrelated to international prices at the prevailing exchange rate. In addition, consumer prices are often set. The Turkish excess supply of those commodities is thus a function of the price paid to producers and that paid by consumers, and not of the relevant EER. (2) Minerals are generally produced by SEEs which have not been forced to behave as profit maximizers. The minerals sector has generally not responded to export incentives.

When evaluated in the context of those domestic policies, the export response to the altered PLD-EERs in the early 1960's was really quite sizeable. The regression estimates given in Chapter VII (Table VII-13) suggest that cotton, mohair, olive oil and minor exports, the commodities in which government intervention policies have not been dominant — have exhibited considerable responsiveness to altered real EERs. A 1 per cent increase in the PLD-EER of each commodity has led to at least a 1 per cent increase in the quantity exported. Since Turkey has little or no monopoly power for any of those products, that implies at least a 1 per cent increase in foreign exchange earnings from them in response to a 1 per cent increase in the PLD-EER.

There are a number of reasons for believing that those estimates of export responsiveness understate Turkish export potential. But the experience of the 1960's should be discussed first. It is important to note that the Import Programs, introduced as the control mechanism for imports in the Stabilization Program, were employed throughout the 1960's as the regulatory instrument for imports, although the purposes the regulations were designed to achieve altered. At first the Import Programs were seen as a means whereby the payments-arrears situation of the 1950's could be prevented from recurring. The initial intent was of course that imports would gradually be transferred to the Liberalized List so that the regime would become less and less restrictive over time.

The purposes which the Import Programs were designed to serve altered markedly when planning started. They became a major instrument for encouraging domestic production, particularly of import-substitutes. The "Prohibited List" emerged as an indiscriminate device for granting protection to any new industry. But there was no mechanism for making protection temporary.

As industrialization progressed, the lists of eligible imports became increasingly complex. New categories of intermediate goods were added to the lists and imports with domestic substitutes were deleted. To gain better control over the uses to which imports were destined, ministerial permission requirements were added to import licensing procedures.

The outcome was that the Import Programs, initially intended as a means of liberalizing the import regime, were gradually transformed into one for restricting it. To complete the transformation, the Liberalized List was, by 1969, regarded by many as at least as restrictive as the Quota List. Thus inspection of the mechanism by which a trade regime is administered tells little about the restrictiveness of that regime. The Turkish mechanism has remained the same for a period of more than a decade, while the restrictive content of that mechanism has altered substantially.

The side effects of the import regime upon excess capacity, inventory holdings and the capital-labor ratio were discussed in some detail in Chapter VIII. The evidence indicates that the excess costs of production resulting from the system were probably sizeable, especially in view of the limited degree to which quantification of those effects is possible. But those excess costs appear to have been small as compared with the costs of indiscriminate encouragement of new firms and industries.

The direct and indirect effects of the incentives provided by the import regime resulted in the emergence of a wide range of DRCs within and between industries. As the data in Table VIII-1 show, DRCs ranged from very low to extremely high. Of the number of factors undoubtedly contributing to this wide variation, several were probably especially important. (1) As emphasized repeatedly, the protection afforded by the "Prohibited List" was indiscriminate in the extreme, and precluded competition from abroad at any price. (2) The mechanism for allocating the Quota List imports essentially determined firms' market shares at each point in time. (3) Since few capacity additions could be undertaken without imports, government control over new investments was achieved through the import regime and, in the late 1960's, through administration of sizeable investment incentives. That control resulted in an inability of relatively low-cost firms to expand as much as they otherwise would have and thereby provided sheltered positions to less efficient firms.

In addition to the observable losses associated with the trade regime, there is the important question as to the sort of growth Turkey could have achieved had the growth strategy been less import-substitution oriented. An attempt was made in Chapter IX to answer that question. "What-would-have-happened-if" estimates are always open to debate, but the assumptions made in Chapter IX are fairly conservative. By accepting each sector's coefficients as given, an important part of the gains that might have accrued with a development strategy more oriented toward growth of exports was omitted from the analysis. For example, Turkish industry developed in a sellers' market atmosphere, devoid of pressures to become internationally competitive. Under an alternative strategy, competitive pressures would have been greater. The relative inattention to quality control among Turkish producers may be another example. In a more open economy, there might have been greater efforts in that direction. Similarly, Turkey has had relatively little indigenous research and development. This too might have been stimulated had Turkish producers been forced into greater competition with their European counterparts.

Even without taking potential gains of this type into account, one sees that the estimates of Chapter IX indicate that a BEPIM, or even MIS, growth path could have resulted in a sizeable increase in the rate of growth of manufacturing output and employment, a reduction in the ICOR, reduced import demands for any level of output, and increased export earnings. The estimated magnitude of the gains is impressive, and the results clearly suggest that such an alternative strategy could better have achieved the goals of Turkish policy-makers than did the development path actually chosen.

In response to the results of the analysis in Chapter IX, most Turkish economists and planners would probably regard the export-oriented alternative as having been infeasible. The widely held view in Turkey is that Turkish manufacturing exports simply cannot compete in international markets. The conclusion reached in Chapter VII and the magnitude of the potential gain estimated in Chapter IX make that argument doubtful. But no decisive proof can be given unless a genuine and sustained effort is made to compete in international markets. It may well be, though, that Turkish producers' inability to compete is more the result of the trade regime than the cause. The extreme disincentive to export, in favor of the handsome rewards for import-substitution during the past decade, is enough to make one wonder whether a rational, profit-maximizing entrepreneur would have found it in his self-interest to attempt to develop a sizeable export business.

Turkey's decision to enter the Common Market makes the question of her potential growth under an alternative, export-oriented development strategy an extremely important one. Given her past import-substitution orientation, there are two factors to be considered. The first is the manner in which a transition to an export-oriented strategy is effected. The second is the nature of the gains that might be achieved once the transition is accomplished.

The results of Chapter IX shed some light on the second factor. For all the evidence of Chapters VI to IX indicates that, satisfactory as Turkey's growth performance has been, it could be substantially improved if some of the excess costs of indiscriminate import-substitution were avoided in the future and her export potential were realized.

The problem of transition will be much more difficult. Over the past two decades new industries have been built up regardless of their long-run potential in response to the incentives provided to them. Many of the firms in these new industries would be confronted with difficult problems of transition.

Those problems have not been considered here because analysis has been centered upon past developments. The lesson of those developments is that the benefits from an altered growth strategy will more than compensate for the costs of that transition.

APPENDIX A

CALCULATION OF EERs

The method of calculating EERs is necessarily determined by the availability of data. In this appendix the sources and methods used to make the necessary computations are described, and the detailed data underlying the aggregate figures are presented. The order of presentation is: exports, imports, invisibles and capital transactions.

Exports

The task of calculating EERs for export commodities was broken into two periods: 1953 to 1960, and 1961 to 1969.[1] The reasons for this division are inherent in the nature of the trade regime. Prior to 1960, a multiple exchange-rate system was the basic means by which incentives were accorded to various export categories. After 1960, there was no longer a multiple exchange-rate system, and differentials among export categories emerged primarily because of the export rebate system.

Table A-1 gives the estimates of the EERs for exports between 1953 and 1960. For most major export commodities, such as tobacco and cotton, estimates of the EERs were obtained in a straightforward manner: they were the rates prevailing in the year in question, and were not frequently altered. For "marginal exports," however, the situation was rather different. While the rates were as indicated, the number of commodities to which these rates applied varied from time to time. Thus the class of exports eligible for the high rates both increased and decreased over time, as did the rates applicable to them. It was not possible to obtain detailed lists of the commodities eligible for the "marginal export rates" for the 1953-to-1958 period. When data were available for a specific "minor" export (such as meerschaum pipes, olive oil, etc.) these rates are presented separately. Thus while it would be this author's judgment that textiles, for example, were subject to the marginal export rates given in Table A-1, there is no documentation for that view.

The bottom part of Table A-1 gives weighted EERs for exports for broad commodity classes and for exports as a whole. Weights for individual commodities within a class were derived by taking the total 1956 value of exports

1. Estimates of EERs for 1970 and 1971 were made on a much cruder basis, due to the absence of detailed data. They are presented in Appendix C.

Table A-1
Export EERs, 1953 to 1960 (TL per dollar equivalent of foreign currency)

	1953	1954	1955	1956	1957	1958	1959	1960
Individual commodities								
Raisins	2.80	3.30	3.53	3.69	4.00	5.60	9.00	9.00
Fresh fruit	2.80	2.80	4.90	5.60	5.60	9.00	9.00	9.00
Dried figs	2.80	2.80	3.08	3.22	3.36	5.60	9.00	9.00
Chrome	2.80	2.80	2.80	2.80	2.80	4.90	9.00	9.00
Cotton	2.80	2.80	2.80	3.78	3.78	9.00	9.00	9.00
Olive oil	2.80	2.80	2.80	2.80	5.60	9.00	9.00	9.00
Meerschaum pipes	3.92	4.48	4.90	5.60	5.60	9.00	9.00	9.00
Tobacco	2.80	2.80	2.80	2.80	2.80	4.90	5.60	9.00
Mohair	2.80	2.80	3.50	3.50	4.48	9.00	9.00	9.00
Hazelnuts	2.80	2.80	2.80	2.80	2.80	5.60	9.00	9.00
Copper	2.80	2.80	2.80	2.80	2.80	4.90	9.00	9.00
Weighted EERs								
Minerals	2.80	2.80	2.80	2.80	2.80	4.90	9.00	9.00
Traditional crop exports	2.80	2.85	2.89	2.91	2.95	5.14	6.77	9.00
Cotton	2.80	2.80	2.80	3.78	3.78	9.00	9.00	9.00
Mohair	2.80	2.80	3.50	3.50	4.48	9.00	9.00	9.00
Fresh fruit	2.80	2.80	4.90	5.60	5.60	9.00	9.00	9.00
Marginal exports ($)	4.30	5.18	4.90	5.60	5.60	9.00	9.00	9.00
Marginal exports (EPU)	3.92	4.48	3.92	4.48	4.48	9.00	9.00	9.00
Marginal exports (other currencies)	3.50	3.72	4.20	4.20	5.20	9.00	9.00	9.00
			3.50	3.50	3.50			
Weighted export rate	2.84	2.89	2.96	3.15	3.17	5.87	7.61	9.00

Notes:　a) From 1953 to 1957, specific premia were extended in varying amounts to raisins and figs. These were converted to *ad valorem* rates by taking the estimated *domestic* wholesale price as given in *Fiat İstatistikleri 1949–1965, Pub. No.562,* SIS (Ankara), 1968. The estimates are therefore quite rough.

b) For chrome, export retention rights of 100 per cent of f.o.b. value were extended in 1956 and abolished in 1957. Their value was not included in the calculation.

c) A 35 per cent premium on cotton exports was extended in the summer of 1956, removed in the fall of 1956 (when it was suspected that switch deals were taking place) and reimposed during the 1957 export season. It is included in the EERs for both years.

d) Retention rights of 1 to 15 per cent of f.o.b. exports, for own-use only, were extended during 1957 to hazelnut and tobacco exports. The value of these rights is not included in the calculations.

e) Weights are derived by taking the percentage of the respective export commodities of the value of the total group in 1956 exports. The value of exports included in the group was $228.6 million, contrasted with total exports in that year of $305 million. Omissions include livestock and feedstuffs, and a variety of miscellaneous, generally agricultural and mineral. For marginal exports, the EPU rate was used, since no data were available on the fraction of exports eligible for the marginal rate going to each currency area. The minerals category includes copper (7.5 per cent) and chrome (10.2 per cent). Traditional crop exports include raisins (6.7 per cent), dried figs (1.6 per cent), tobacco (40.9 per cent) and hazelnuts (13.0 per cent).

Sources:　Data are compiled from various sources. The most important was the *Annual Report on Exchange Restrictions,* International Monetary Fund (Washington), various years. Selected price quotations were also found in the *Quarterly Reports,* EIU, and other sources.

of commodities for which rates were available, and then taking the fraction of that value represented by the commodity in question. Thus in 1956 copper exports were $17.1 million and chrome exports were $23.3 million. To obtain the weighted rate for mineral exports, the effective exchange rate for copper was multiplied by 0.423 and that for chrome by 0.577. A similar method was used to obtain the overall export EER.

Multiple exchange rates were not in use for exports during the period 1961 to 1970, and the main forms of differential incentives for exports took the form of export rebates.[2] The law enabling export rebates was passed in 1963.[3] Several decrees subsequently modified the operation of export rebates, extending and altering their coverage. The basic rate-setting mechanism throughout the period was to grant temporary rates which would be applicable until a rate was established. Once a rate was established, it could be altered upon petition of exporting firms, and firms which had received smaller temporary rates were entitled to collect the difference, while firms which had received more than their permanent rate were obliged to refund the difference.

The stated intent of allowing rebates was to offset taxes and duties paid by exporters on their production and inputs. A question thus arises as to whether the export rebates constituted an export incentive or simply an offset to a previously existing export disincentive. The issue is inherently muddy: (1) insofar as rebates were a genuine repayment of taxes and duties, they constituted a genuine incentive to exports only if home goods and import-substituting producers were subject to the same taxes; (2) insofar as rebates exceeded the amount of taxes paid they constituted a genuine differential incentive to export regardless of whether import-substitutes and home goods were subject to similar taxes.

The second issue is troublesome only because it is not possible to obtain estimates of the subsidy component of rebates. The law enabling rates, and the subsequent decrees determining them, were so worded that only actual taxes and duties paid were to be rebated. However, (1) rebate rates were set by inspection of the tax and duty components of costs of one or several large firms in an industry and if other firms had a differential tax incidence, the rebate rates could contain an element of subsidy to some firms; (2) rebate rates were set as a percentage of the f.o.b. price, so an increase or decrease in that price could result in a subsidy or failure to offset the taxes paid, even if the initial rebate rate had been an exact tax offset; and (3) many Turkish producers claimed in interviews that despite the wording of the Rebate Law rebate rates were in fact set in a manner designed to enable a firm to cover its

---

2. There were, in addition, other incentives described in Chapter VII. The value of these incentives is not included in the estimate of export EERs.
3. Law No. 261, June 27, 1963.

costs and earn 5 per cent on gross export sales, independent of the actual taxes paid.[4] Whether this last was so is vigorously contested by Turkish officials; however, inspection of the rebate rates below will suggest that there must have been some element of the profitability calculus in the rate-setting decision, at least for some exports.

The first issue, whether home-goods and import-substitutes' costs were equally taxed, is the more important, and the more difficult question to answer. Most of the rebated taxes (production tax, import and associated duties, stamp and financial taxes) applied to all transactions, not simply to exports. However, the incidence of these taxes could differ between firms and between industries. On net, agricultural output was subject to less taxation than was industrial output. Thus it could be argued that there was already a differential incentive, in favor of agricultural exports at least. In terms of industrial output, there is no *a priori* basis for believing that Turkish taxation discriminated in any systematic way between import-substitutes, exportables and home-goods. Hence we conclude that on balance export rebates probably did constitute a differential incentive, both in their tax rebate component and in any subsidy that was in fact granted. It must be remembered though that there were undoubtedly differentials between industries. The conclusion is at best a rough-and-ready first approximation.

Table A-2 gives the rebate rates in effect at various points for which the data are available. No rebate rates had been set for 1964 (except the provisional rates) for commodities other than textiles. By 1967 rates had been raised on a number of items, and some new items had been accorded definite rates. A far larger list of commodities had been accorded specific rates by 1969, of which the items listed are just a small sample. A variety of unprocessed agricultural products were also accorded rebates by that date. The rates varied widely, from 9 per cent for olive oil to 49 per cent for boric acid; some individual textile and clothing rates, not included in Table A-2, were even higher.

Table A-3 gives the value of exports in each category eligible for rebates, the amount of rebates actually paid, and the rebates paid as a per cent of exports. The categories for 1964 to 1966 are not entirely comparable with those for 1968 and 1970, and except for textiles, food products, and a few other well-defined classes, comparisons for individual categories between periods should be made with care. The totals are comparable for both periods,

4. The law and decrees stated that rebate rates were to be determined in such a way that taxes and duties paid were to be refunded in an amount permitting firms to earn 5 per cent on their gross export sales. The wording of the law was that rebates might cover *less* than full taxes paid although it is not so certain that this was what happened in practice. But government officials obviously could not have worded the law otherwise without violating GATT rules.

Table A-2

Rebate rates on representative commodities, by year, 1964 to 1969 (per cent of f.o.b. price)

	1964	1967	1968	1969
Temporary rates				
Agricultural commodities	0.0	5.0	–	–
Manufactured commodities	10.0	15.0	–	–
Negotiated rates				
Textiles				
Thick combed yarn	4.6	4.6	15.08	15.08
Thick carded yarn	3.2	3.2	13.48	13.48
Unbleached cotton fabrics	21–23	36–40	46.00	46.00
Towels	18.9	24.4	34.40	34.40
Woolen yarn	10.5	20.0	33.30	33.30
Mens' nylon socks	23.5	23.0	33.00	33.00
Non-textiles				
Chrome concentrate	–	13.0	13.00	24.81
Copper cables	–	37.3	47.30	47.30
Window glass	–	12.9	25.67	32.11
Olive oil	–	–	–	9.10
Tomato paste	–	–	–	23.06
Leather products	–	–	–	18.50
Boric acid	–	–	–	49.29
Iron and steel	–	–	–	28.84
Electric lamps	–	–	–	35.43
Cement	–	–	–	45.58
Plastic	–	–	–	38.87

Sources: *Resmi Gazete, Nos. 11712,* May 26, 1964, *12713,* June 30, 1967, and *12887,* April 30, 1968; *Yatırımların ve İhracatın Teşviki ve Uygulama Esasları,* SPO, 1969, *Pub. No. DPT 773-TUD:4].*

in the sense that they include all exports subject to rebate. Some commodities ineligible for rebates in the early years became eligible at later dates, though. Thus the coverage of the rebate system increased vastly. This is most apparent between 1968 and 1970. In 1969, a variety of unprocessed agricultural products, including cotton (10 per cent), tobacco,[5] raisins (37 per cent), and fresh fruits and vegetables (11.3 per cent) became eligible for rebates. Whereas eligible exports accounted for 2.5 per cent of all exports in 1964, they constituted 5.3 per cent of exports in 1967 and 29.5 per cent in 1969.

Although it would be preferable to employ the specific rebate rates actual-

5. Rebates of TL 2.8 million were reported against exports of TL 4.2 million of tobacco. That figure is far below the value of tobacco exports, and the basis for the number is not known.

Table A-3

Rebates and exports of commodities eligible for rebates, 1964 to 1970 (values in thousands of TL)

	1964			1966			1968			1970		
	R	X	%	R	X	%	R	X	%	R	X	%
Food	1,877	33,985	5.5	3,334	43,599	7.6	3,736	28,596	13.1	25,953	266,727	9.7
Beverages	—	—	—	230	2,303	10.0	364	2,149	16.9	1,116	8,718	12.8
Textiles-clothing	5,539	22,629	24.5	4,641	9,978	46.5	22,399	51,539	43.5	56,661	210,115	27.0
Wood products	448	4,479	10.0	2,796	27,266	10.3	1,043	10,181	10.2	7,630	33,518	22.8
Paper	—	—	—	—	—	—	2,574	4,832	53.3	2,502	3,278	76.3
Hides and leather	1,131	11,323	10.0	59	772	7.6	565	1,325	42.6	9,962	39,124	25.5
Chemicals	—	—	—	166	1,885	8.8	10,594	45,233	23.4	46,211	149,799	30.8
Glass	—	—	—	324	2,261	14.3	592	3,950	15.0	1,478	4,728	31.2
Ceramics	—	—	—	—	—	—	69	481	14.3	115	513	22.4
Cement	—	—	—	—	—	—	48	105	45.7	9,542	36,819	25.9
Iron and steel	20	203	9.9	5,323	28,700	18.2	43	287	15.0	152	523	29.1
Other metals	—	—	—	127	1,108	11.5	14,400	95,441	15.1	29,055	165,785	17.5
Metal products	—	—	—	707	2,341	30.2	83	412	20.1	4,337	8,846	49.0
Machinery	—	—	—	—	—	—	298	672	44.3	4,532	8,982	50.4
Electric machinery	—	—	—	—	—	—	154	648	23.8	464	1,434	32.4
Electronics	—	—	—	—	—	—	155	94	164.9	—	—	—
Transport equipment	—	—	—	—	—	—	—	—	—	260	850	30.6
Railroad equipment	—	—	—	—	—	—	—	—	—	—	—	—
Rubber products	—	—	—	—	—	—	—	—	—	—	—	—
Gift items	111	1,111	10.0	544	5,459	10.0	756	6,720	11.3	2,889	13,340	21.7
Miscellaneous	2,724	27,308	10.0	5,354	73,516	7.3	—	—	—	658	3,294	20.0
Agricultural products	—	—	—	—	—	—	—	—	—	70,438	651,928	10.8
Total	12,117	103,602	11.7	27,547	219,548	12.5	57,873	247,832	23.3	288,588	1,732,899	16.6

Notes: a) Categories for 1964 and 1966 do not exactly correspond to those for later years. The miscellaneous category in 1964 and 1966 includes many of the items left blank, including a large category, "mining products."
b) Figures do not always add to totals. The source of the discrepancy is unknown.
c) R = value of rebates; X = value of exports; % is the implied rebate percentage.
d) The average rebate rates for 1965, 1967, and 1969 were 9.7, 9.9, and 14.6 per cent, respectively.

Sources: 1964, 1966 and 1970, data kindly supplied by SPO; 1968, *1970 Yılı Programı*, p. 527.

ly in force in making EER estimates, some weighting system is required. Thus in the absence of data on the value of exports in each detailed rebate category, the percentage numbers given in Table A-3 are used in making EER estimates for the 1961-to-1969 period. Since there were undoubtedly some minor differences in the timing of exports from the timing of rebate payments, use of the rebate rates derived from the data in Table A-3 undoubtedly results in some error. However, inspection of the year-to-year fluctuations in rebates as a per cent of exports in each category suggests that with the possible exception of the very small export categories the changes in percentages from year to year conform rather closely to the general trends in rebate rates indicated in Table A-2.

Table A-4 gives the EERs for various categories of exports for 1961 to 1969, as implied by the rebate rates, and also gives the weighted EERs for traditional, non-traditional, and total exports, based on the rebate rates im-

Table A-4
EERs for exports, 1961 to 1969 (TL per dollar f.o.b.)

	1961	1962	1963	1964	1965	1966	1967	1968	1969
Traditional exports									
Tobacco	9.00	9.00	9.00	9.00	9.00	9.00	9.00	9.00	9.90
Cotton	9.00	9.00	9.00	9.00	9.00	9.00	9.00	9.00	9.90
Figs and raisins	9.00	9.00	9.00	9.00	9.00	9.00	9.00	9.00	10.17
Chrome concentrate	9.00	9.00	9.00	9.00	9.00	9.00	10.17	10.17	11.25
Other traditional	9.00	9.00	9.00	9.00	9.00	9.00	9.00	9.00	9.00
Weighted traditional export EER	9.00	9.00	9.00	9.00	9.00	9.00	9.02	9.02	9.37
Non-traditional exports									
Fresh fruit and vegetables	9.00	9.00	9.00	9.00	9.00	9.00	9.00	9.00	9.99
Processed foods	9.00	9.00	9.00	9.49	9.37	9.68	9.42	10.17	9.60
Textiles	9.00	9.00	9.00	11.21	12.05	13.18	11.65	12.91	12.04
Paper products	9.00	9.00	9.00	9.90	9.90	9.90	13.31	13.79	12.04
Glass	9.00	9.00	9.00	9.90	9.78	10.29	10.31	10.35	11.61
Metal products	9.00	9.00	9.00	9.90	9.90	11.72	10.24	10.81	11.90
Weighted non-traditional export EER	9.00	9.00	9.00	9.62	9.69	10.09	9.72	10.28	10.31
Weighted export EER	9.00	9.00	9.00	9.04	9.04	9.06	9.06	9.09	9.96

Note: Weights used were the value of exports of the commodity group in 1967 as a per cent of all exports included in the calculation. Of $522.7 million of exports in 1967, $454.4 million were included in these groups. Traditional exports (94.2 per cent) are slightly overweighted by this procedure.

Sources: Table A-3 and text of Appendix A.

plied by Table A-3. The weights used were the value of exports in 1967 for each export category as a per cent of the total value of exports included in the computations. The year 1967 was employed as a base for weighting because the commodity distribution of exports in that year was judged to be reasonably representative of the average structure of Turkey's exports during the 1960's. The nominal EERs given in Table A-4 are those employed throughout the text when measuring differentials in incentives between various commodity groups.

Import EERs

The computation of EERs for imports is inherently more difficult than that for exports. Not only were there multiple exchange rates over part of the period, but at various times tariffs, production taxes, guarantee deposits, stamp duties and port taxes were also imposed on the several categories of imports. In the middle and late 1960's some categories of imported capital goods were eligible for deferred payments or reduced schedules of duties and other surcharges at a subsidized rate of interest.

For some components of these charges, fairly complete information is available. For other components the data are far less adequate, and considerable judgment had to be used in deriving the estimates. Before discussing the method for estimating the EERs for import categories then, it will be useful to discuss the nature of the problems involved and the procedures used to analyze the various components of the TL cost of a dollar of imports.

Tariffs. Early in 1954 Turkey switched from specific to *ad valorem* tariffs on virtually all imports. No effort was made to estimate the *ad valorem* equivalent of tariffs prior to 1954, and hence the estimates of import EERs start with that year. Few tariff rates were altered between 1954 and 1964, but a major revision of the Turkish tariff structure was undertaken and effected in that year, and the set of duties imposed then remained in force with few rate modifications.

Both the 1954 and 1964 tariff schedules were obtained for the computation of the tariff component of EERs.[6] It proved impossible to trace the changes, generally stated to be few and highly infrequent, in tariff rates between 1954 and 1964, or after 1964. Thus while there is reason to believe that there were very few changes, whatever changes occurred are not taken

6. 1954 tariff rates were obtained from T.C. Başvekalet, "İstatistik Umum Müdürlüğü," *Gümrük Giriş Tarife Cetveli, Neşriyat No. 365* (Ankara), 1956. 1964 tariff rates were obtained from Law No. 474, "Import Customs Tariff, 1964," from the *Official Gazette, No. 11711,* May 25, 1964, as translated by Türk Argus Ajansi.

account of in the estimation of tariff rates. It is not believed that this omission is of significance.

More important perhaps is that the tariff categories do not correspond with the import classifications for which data are available. Thus the import categories on which tariffs are based are much more detailed than the categories for which value of imports is reported. Thus a weighting system for tariffs proved to be impossible.

As an alternative, it was decided to go through the 99 chapters of the tariff code, selecting items from each chapter containing commodities which Turkey imports. The basis of selection was primarily the author's judgment as to the relative importance and representativeness of the individual items. Some chapters cover a much higher value of imports than others, and more items were included from those chapters than from others.

The tariff rates for the selected items were then collected from the 1954 and 1964 tariff schedule. Each specific commodity category was then, somewhat arbitrarily, assigned to one of four groups: consumer goods; producers' raw materials and intermediate goods; capital goods; and imports with domestic substitutes. The last category cuts across the other three, but was deemed useful to indicate the height of protection accorded to domestically produced import-competing goods.

An unweighted average of the individual rates for each group was taken as representative of the functional grouping. Table A-5 lists the specific commodity categories selected in the sample, gives the tariff rates applicable to them from the 1954 to 1964 tariffs, and indicates the commodity class to which the item was assigned. Names of the commodity groups have generally been considerably shortened, with the name adopted being designed to provide an idea of the contents of the group. As can be seen, the allocation of items to the four categories is of necessity rather arbitrary: some items designated consumer goods are clearly also imports with domestic substitutes, and there are many cases where an item has more than one category of end-use (e.g. locks).

Altogether, 111 commodities were selected for the sample: there are 37 items designated consumer goods, 47 producers' intermediates and raw materials, 13 import-substitutes, and 14 capital goods.

Every effort was made to make the sample as representative as possible, and inspection of other categories does not suggest any obvious bias in the sample. It must be recalled that the absence of any meaningful quantity weights somewhat biases the resulting tariff averages, although the direction and magnitude of the bias is unknown. The tariff rates given in Table A-5 are those used for estimating EERs and are employed, by category, to get estimates of the unweighted tariff rates used below.

Table A-5
Sample of import commodities chosen, 1954 and 1964 tariff rates, and commodity class
to which assigned

BTN Code and Name	Class	Tariff Rate	
		1954	1964
5.10 Ivory	CG	10	20
7.06 Root and tuber vegetables	CG	50	25
8.01 Tropical fruit	CG	100	75
9.01 Coffee unroasted	CG	75	75
Coffee roasted	CG	100	100
9.02 Tea	CG	75	100
9.04 Pepper	CG	100	100
10.01 Wheat	CG	50	15
13.01 Dyeing raw materials	RM	100	100
15.12 Hydrogenated fats and oils	RM	60	60
17.01 Beet and sugar cane	CG	100	150
18.01 Cocoa beans	RM	10	50
19.03 Macaroni and pastas	CG	50	50
20.05 Jams	CG	150	75
21.05 Soups	CG	100	75
22.03 Beer	CG	150	100
23.04 Oil cakes	RM	15	15
25.03 Sulphur	RM	20	75
25.19 Magnesium carbonate	RM	25	25
25.24 Asbestos	RM	25	15
26.01 Metallic ores	RM	5	5
27.01 Coal	RM	10	60
28.04 Hydrogen	RM	50	50
28.06 Hydrochloric acid	RM	15	40
28.09 Nitric acid	RM	5	40
28.19 Zinc oxide	RM	10	20
28.26 Tin oxides	RM	15	15
28.39 Nitrates and nitrites	RM	5	20–25
29.06 Phenols	RM	25	25
29.14 Monoacids	RM	100	50
29.38 Vitamins	CG	5	5
31.02 Nitrogenous fertilizers	CG	35	35
32.03 Synthetic tanning materials	RM	25	40
24.01 Soap	CG	100	50–60
35.02 Albumin	RM	30	30
36.03 Blasting fuses	RM	50	100
37.02 Photographic film	CG	35	35
38.05 Tall oil	RM	15	35
39.02 Polymerization products	RM	50	50

Table A-5 (continued)

BTN Code and Name	Class	Tariff Rate 1954	1964
40.01 Natural rubber	RM	50	40
40.11 Rubber tires	MS	30	40
41.02 Tanned leather	RM	45	90
42.02 Leather travel goods	CG	100	150
43.03 Articles of furskin	CG	100	200
44.15 Plywood	RM	40	50
45.03 Natural cork articles	RM	35	50
46.02 Woven plaiting materials	RM	40	50
47.01 Paper pulp	RM	5	15
48.05 Corrugated paper, paperboard	MS	60	60
48.16 Packing containers	RM	100	75
50.04 Silk yarn	RM	40	40
51.04 Woven fabrics, man-made fiber	MS	100	150
53.11 Woven fabrics of wool	MS	80	100
54.01 Raw flax	RM	20	20
55.04 Carded and combed cotton	RM	20	20
55.06 Cotton yarn	MS	60	60
56.04 Man-made discontinuous fibers	MS	50–75	30
56.06 Yarns of man-made fibers	MS	100	100
57.03 Unspun jute	RM	5	5
58.05 Narrow woven fabrics	MS	100	100
60.01 Knitted fabric	MS	100	100
61.02 Womens' outer wear	CG	150	100
62.02 Linen (bed, table, etc.)	CG	100	100
64.05 Footwear	CG	100	100
65.05 Hats and headgear	CG	70	70
66.01 Umbrellas	CG	100	100
67.04 Wigs	CG	100	100
68.13 Asbestos articles	RM	25	75
69.02 Refractory bricks	RM	40	40
69.05 Roofing tiles	MS	75	50
69.10 Sinks, wash basins	CG	100	100
70.05 Common plate glass	MS	50	50
71.12 Jewelry	CG	20	20
73.07 Forged iron and steel products	RM	15	15
73.14 Iron and steel wire	RM	15	30
73.26 Barbed wire	RM	25	40

Table A-5 (continued)

BTN Code and Name	Class	Tariff Rate 1954	1964
73.32 Bolts and nuts	MS	35	50
74.07 Copper tubes and pipes	RM	10	40
74.17 Copper cooking and heating items	CG	40	50
75.03 Nickel plate	RM	20	25
76.08 Aluminum structures	KG	15	50
77.02 Magnesium rods, bars, etc.	RM	5	5
78.04 Lead foil and strip	RM	40	40
79.05 Zinc roofing material	RM	30	50
80.03 Tin plate, sheet, strip	RM	5	10
82.02 Saws	RM	25	50
83.01 Locks	CG	50	75
84.06 Internal combustion engine	KG	5	35
84.15 Regrigeration equipment	KG	10	60
84.22 Lifting, loading machinery	KG	5−10	50
84.31 Paper-making machinery	KG	5	30
84.37 Textile machinery	KG	5	35−40
84.45 Metal working machine tools	KG	5	50
84.63 Vehicle parts	KG	5	30
85.20 Electric filament lamps	CG	50	50
85.25 Insulators	RM	35	50
86.06 Railway rolling stock	KG	10	30
87.01 Tractors	KG	25	30
87.02 Buses and autos	KG	40	60−76
88.02 Airplanes	KG	5	0−5
89.01 Ships	KG	50	50
90.07 Photo cameras	CG	30	60
90.17 Medical instruments	RM	15	35
90.27 Meters	KG	25	50
91.01 Watches	CG	25	75
92.01 Pianos	CG	15	50
94.03 Furniture and parts	CG	80	100
96.05 Cosmetic articles	CG	100	100
97.02 Dolls	CG	100	100
98.03 Fountain pens	CG	60	75
98.08 Typewriter ribbons	CG	40	75

Note: Abbreviations for class are: CG, consumer goods; KG, capital goods; RM, raw materials and intermediate producers' goods; MS, imports with domestic substitutes.

Sources: T.C. Başvelaket, "İstatistik Umum Müdürlüğü," *Gümrük Giriş Tarife Cetveli, Neşriyat No. 365* (Ankara) 1956; and Law No. 474, Import Customs Tariff, 1964 *Official Gazette No. 11711,* May 25, 1964, as translated by Türk Argos Ajansi.

Municipality tax. Municipality taxes have been levied against imports throughout the period under consideration. The municipality tax has been constant, at 15 per cent of the customs duty charged against imports. Thus an import subject to a 50 per cent tariff was also subject to a municipality tax equal to 7½ per cent of the c.i.f. price.

Wharf tax. A wharf tax is, and has been, levied upon the sum of c.i.f. price, tariff, municipality tax, and other costs of landing goods (opening a letter of credit, stamps, storage charges, etc.). The rate of tax was 2½ per cent of the sum of all previously noted costs until 1966 and has been 5 per cent since that time. Thus for a commodity with miscellaneous costs equal to 10 per cent of c.i.f. price, a commonly accepted estimate, the wharf tax would be:

$$WT = w\left[p_f\left(1.10 + 1.15\,t\right)\right]$$

where WT is the wharf tax levied, w is the rate of wharf tax, p_f is the c.i.f. price of the good, and t the tariff rate. Despite the low nominal rate of the wharf duty, it generally exceeded the municipality tax, because of its much larger base. With a tariff rate of 20 per cent, for example, the municipality tax was equal to 3 per cent of the c.i.f. price, and the wharf tax equal (with the estimate of 10 per cent of c.i.f. price for miscellaneous charges) to 3.3 per cent at a $2\frac{1}{2}$ per cent rate and 6.6 per cent at the 5 per cent rate of c.i.f. price. In computing effective exchange rates for imports, no attempt was made to estimate the magnitude of other landing costs. Its magnitude cannot be more than 0.25 per cent prior to 1966 and 0.5 per cent of the basic exchange rate thereafter. This omission does not affect the relative EERs between different import categories, but does result in a slight understatement of the differential between import and export EERs.

Production tax. A major source of revenue in Turkey is the *İstihsal Vergisi,* generally referred to as the production tax (sometimes called expenditure tax). It is levied both on imported goods (on the basis of landed cost, including all previously indicated charges) and on domestic output. The production tax is levied against four basic lists:

(I) Primary Products. Imports and domestically produced raw materials (many of which are really intermediate goods) are subject to the same rate of tax, on landed cost and producers' sale price, respectively.

(II) Some Finished Products. For commodities on List II, the rate of tax, on the same basis as for List I, is the same for imports and domestically produced products.

(III) Coffee, Cocoa, Beverages and Glucose. Imported and domestically produced commodities are taxed at the same rate.

Table A-6
Production tax lists and schedules in effect, 1964

List I – Primary Products

Cement, bricks, and other heat resisting materials	12.5%
Iron products (rails, bars, wires, etc.)	12.5%
Iron and steel (pig iron and steel ingots)	20.0%
Copper (ingots, bars, sheets, strips, profiles, etc.)	30.0%
Other metals or minerals including sulfur	30.0%
Petroleum products	
Flash point below 30°C	TL 450 per ton
Flash point 30°–55°C	TL 240 per ton
Flash point over 55°C	
for 80% refined before cracking	TL 230 per ton
for 20% refined before cracking	TL 230 per ton
light oils	TL 50 per ton
L.P.G.	TL 50 per ton
Synthetic rubber	20%
Plastic	40%
Furs	75%
Bones and horns	75%
Precious stones	75%
Paper and pulp	
With over 70% wood	15%
Other	20%
Glass	20%
Textiles	
Animal yarns	
wool yarn	20%
other yarn	36%
Vegetable origin	
jute, sisal, manila	15%
cotton yarn	18%
others	36%
Electricity (domestic and hotels excluded)	TL 0.01 per kwh
Gas	TL 0.015 per M^3
Miscellaneous tariff nos.	
05.14, 13.02, 27.12, 27.13	18%
Toilet products and parfums	30%
Soap (except ordinary)	15%

List II – Finished Products

Ammunition, explosives and arms	25%
Matches	TL 0.60 per 1,000
Vehicles	
Bicycles (except childrens')	20%
Motorcycles	20%
Trucks (small)	25%
Passenger cars	25%

Table A-6 (continued)

Vehicles (continued)	
Chassis with engines	15%
Chassis without engines	10%
Watches and clocks	
Gold plated	40%
Silver plated	30%
Others	20%
Radios, record players, etc.	
Record players, combinations and tape recorders	30%
Battery powered radios	18%
Radio receivers	20%
Gramophones	25%
Photographic equipment and film	18%
Ceramic products	20%
China products	40%

List III — Coffee, Cocoa, Beverages and Glucose

Coffee	TL 5 per kg
Cocoa and cocoa products	30%
Beverages *not* produced by the Monopoly Administration	
Beer	TL 0.4 per liter
Champagne	TL 15 per liter
Other wine	TL 0.2 per liter
Whiskey	TL 30 per liter
Glucose	TL 0.5 per kg.

List IV — Imported Products

Products from cement or other heat resisting materials	10%
Metal products	
Machines (to be established)	10%
Other machines	18%
Bicycles (childrens' only)	15%
Other metal products	25%
Rubber products	25%
Plastic products	35%
Paper products	15%
Glass products	18%
Textiles	
Jute, sisal and manila products	12.5%
Others in List I	18%
Fur products	60%
Products made from horns and bones	60%
Products from precious stones	60%
Coffee products	25%
Cocoa products	25%
Miscellaneous (tariffs 28.02, 28.42, 28.54, and 28.58)	15%

Source: Data supplied by Professor Wayne Snyder.

(IV) Imported Products. Only imported products on this list are subject to tax, on the basis of the landed cost (c.i.f. price, tariff, municipality tax, miscellaneous costs, plus wharf duty).

The production tax for Lists I to III is levied at the same rate on imports and domestically produced goods in the same category. But elements of extra protection against imports nonetheless exist. Since the tax is levied upon landed cost, the tariff and other import taxes are in fact cascaded. And some

Table A-7

Domestic production tax, import production tax, and custom collections, 1952 to 1969
(millions of TL)

	Domestic Production Tax Revenues	Import Production Tax Revenues	Custom Duties	Value of Domestic Production	Value of Imports	(1) as % of (4)	(2) as % of (5)
	(1)	(2)	(3)	(4)	(5)	(6)	(7)
1952	162	225	191	1,490	1,556	10.8	14.3
1953	187	220	203	1,839	1,491	10.0	14.8
1954	220	200	214	2,248	1,339	9.8	14.9
1955	282	212	247	2,578	1,393	10.9	15.2
1956	343	170	193	3,290	1,140	10.4	14.9
1957	453	191	187	4,157	1,112	10.8	17.2
1958	453	295	249	5,418	882	8.3	33.4
1959	506	711	551	6,586	1,315	7.6	54.1
1960	506	681	575	6,886	2,214	7.3	30.8
1961	506	660	612	7,577	4,585	6.6	14.4
1962	618	837	737	8,323	5,599	7.4	14.9
1963	685	883	796	9,462	6,216	7.2	14.2
1964	705	744	948	10,475	4,878	6.8	15.2
1965	908	895	1,155	11,742	5,193	7.7	17.2
1966	1,144	1,061	1,413	13,727	6,522	8.3	16.3
1967	1,302	1,167	1,366	16,006	6,219	8.1	18.8
1968	1,558	1,199	1,332	17,760	6,937	8.8	17.3
1969	1,688	1,058	1,131	20,497	7,273	8.2	14.5
1970		1,150	1,275				

Notes: a) Value of domestic production is given by the Ministry of Finance.

        b) Not all imports are dutiable. NATO infrastructure, PL 480, and a variety of other miscellaneous categories are exempt from duty. However, figures on the amount of dutiable imports are not available for the entire period, so total imports were used for these computations.

Sources: 1952–1964 Ministry of Finance, General Directorate of Revenues, *Budget Revenues Bulletin No. 14,* Fiscal Year 1964, p. 124 (cols 1, 4, and 6), p. 130 (cols 2, 3, 5, and 7), 1965 to 1970. Tax receipts from *Social and Economic Indicators,* AID, 1971.

items on Lists I to III are almost exclusively imports and are thus taxed at rates above those applying to most domestic products.

There is no discrimination against imports, even for items on List IV, except insofar as the above considerations hold, or as the rates applicable to imports are above the average rate charged against domestic production, or if the commodity is domestically produced. Thus if an item on List IV were taxed at the average rate of all domestic products and there were no domestic production, the only discriminatory effect of the production tax would be the cascading of the tariff.

In addition to the conceptual difficulties just mentioned, production tax rates were revised substantially in 1956, 1963, and 1964, and only the lists and rates applicable for 1962 and 1964 are available (although the lists have not since been significantly altered).[7]

Table A-6 gives the lists applicable since 1964.[8] Table A-7 gives data on collections from the import production tax, domestic production tax, customs duties, and comparable value-added figures for the period 1952 to 1969. As can be seen, the import production tax has yielded revenue over the years about equal to that from customs duties. Until 1964, moreover, import production tax revenues were generally slightly in excess of the domestic production tax revenues as far as absolute figures go, and have throughout constituted a considerably higher percentage of the taxable base. Thus part of the import production tax constituted additional protection against imports. It should be particularly noted that the amount of production tax levied against a dollar of imports increased automatically whenever the tariff, stamp duty or other charge against that import increased, since the production tax was levied against landed cost of the import in question.

The problem lies in separating the protective component of the production tax from that part offsetting taxation on domestic production. There is no perfect solution to the problem, and the one adopted here is at best only a first approximation. The production tax was levied only on imports of items on List IV, and thus constituted additional protection against imports. The entire amount of the production tax was treated as an additional duty.

For commodities on Lists I, II, and III, only the cascading component of the import production tax was regarded as adding to the EER. Thus for a commodity subject to a 20 per cent production tax levied on landed cost (including stamp duties, wharf charges, etc.) of twice the c.i.f. price, the protective component of the production tax is taken as equal to 20 per cent of the c.i.f. price, although the production tax as a per cent of c.i.f. price was

7. The lists and rates in effect in 1962 were found in I. Kızıklı *et al., Gümrük Giriş Tarifesi*, pp. 63 ff. There was little difference between these and the 1964 rates given in Table A-6. Some production tax rates were altered in 1970.
8. I am indebted to Professor Wayne Snyder for supplying these data.

40 per cent. While this procedure is somewhat arbitrary, no feasible method was found for a closer approximation to the protective component of the tax. It probably understates the protective content of the production tax for many imported items, and hence the resulting estimates of EERs are under-estimates.

Stamp duty.   Turkey levied a 5 per cent stamp duty on the c.i.f. value of imports in 1963. This duty was increased to 15 per cent in 1967, and to 25 per cent in 1969. It was reduced in August 1970 to 10 per cent. Unlike the wharf, municipality and production taxes, no cascading was involved as this duty was levied on the c.i.f. price of the imports.

Guarantee deposits.   Since 1953, when a 4 per cent guarantee deposit was required with import license applications, there have been guarantee deposit requirements of varying heights and complexity. Guarantee deposit requirements never exceeded 10 per cent of the c.i.f. value of the goods for which import license application was made until 1962.[9] Thereafter, the

9. An exception was the eight-month period following devaluation in 1958. See Chapter III, above.

Table A-8

Guarantee deposits required, by list, 1958 to 1970 (deposit as per cent of value of application)

	Quota List		Liberalized List	
	Importers	Industrialists	List I	List II
1958	20	–	–	–
1959	10–15	–	10	–
1960	10	–	10	–
1961	10	–	10	–
1962	10	–	10	–
1963	10–20	10	10–30	–
1964	30	10	30	30
1965	30	10	70	100
1966	30	10	70	100
1967	30	10	70	100–125
1968	30	10	70	100–125
1969	50	20	90	120–150
1970	50	20	90	150

Notes: a) Guarantee deposit requirements against AID-financed goods were lower than the ratios indicated here.
b) From 1966 on, there were a few goods subject to lower rates than those indicated.

Source: Data supplied by SPO.

height of the guarantee deposit rates and the complexity of the guarantee deposit schedules increased rapidly.

Table A-8 gives the rates required, under various categories, for the period since 1958. As can be seen, guarantee deposit requirements varied between the Quota List and the Liberalized List, as also between industrialists and importers. By 1964 the Liberalized List had been split into two, with separate guarantee deposit rates for each list, and additional rates applied to imports financed by AID licenses as well.

There are two problems with estimating the tariff equivalent of the guarantee deposits. First, there is the question of the interest foregone while guarantee deposits were tied up. That problem is not very difficult. The second problem, however, is considerably greater: the implicit cost of the guarantee deposit varied not only with the foregone interest, but with the length of time for which the guarantee deposit was held.[10] Thus in 1966 the time for which the guarantee deposit was held was generally about 5 months, whereas by 1969 the guarantee deposit frequently was for 8 months or longer, as delays increased in the issuance of import licenses.

10. It also varied with the ratio of the value of license applications to receipts. No way could be found, however, to estimate variations in cost due to this factor.

Table A-9

TL cost of $1 c.i.f. of imports for various guarantee deposit requirements, 1953 to 1970

Period	Guarantee Deposit Rate (per cent)	Length of Deposit (months)	TL Cost per Dollar	Per cent Tariff Equivalent
1953 and 1954	4	3	0.003	0.1
1955 to 1958	10	5	0.014	0.5
1959 to 1962	10	3	0.027	0.3
1963 to 1964	10	4	0.036	0.4
	20	4	0.072	0.8
	30	4	0.108	1.2
	40	4	0.144	1.6
1965 to 1968	10	5	0.045	0.5
	30	5	0.135	1.5
	70	5	0.315	3.5
	100	5	0.450	5.0
	125	5	0.563	6.3
1969 to August 1970	20	8	0.144	1.6
	50	8	0.360	4.0
	90	8	0.405	4.5
	120	8	0.864	9.6
	150	8	1.080	12.0

Sources: Table A-8 and text.

It is difficult to obtain anything other than an impressionistic basis for estimating the average length of time from the data guarantee deposits were made until the date of importation. The time period included the period during which the import license application was pending as well as the time between the placing of an order after receipt of import license and the time the commodity arrived in customs. Table A-9 gives the estimated TL costs per dollar of c.i.f. value of imports for various guarantee deposit rates and elapsed time between license application and receipt of imports. The estimate of the average length of time for which guarantee deposits were held at the Central Bank is given in the third column. Throughout the period since 1958 the borrowing rate in Turkey fluctuated between 12 and 15 per cent. The 12 per cent rate is used here to estimate the foregone interest (or borrowing costs) of the guarantee deposit requirements. The rates obtained in the final columns are those used below to compute EERs for various import categories.

Capital goods imports.   Starting in 1964, a special provision was enacted (as part of Law 474 which revised customs duty rates) under which persons wishing to import capital goods could in some circumstances apply for and receive permission to pay customs duty, municipality tax, wharf tax and production tax (but not stamp duty) in five annual installments, subject to a 5 per cent rate of interest on their outstanding obligations. Since that interest rate was well below the borrowing rate, the provision when effective meant that the actual cost of duties and charges on capital goods imports was lower than their nominal value.[11]

To be eligible for the deferred payment of import charges the would-be importer had to have his investment approved as being in accord with the relevant Five Year Plan. In practice most capital goods were imported under this provision, as the likelihood of obtaining a license for importation of goods judged not to be in accord with the development Plans was small. No data are available to indicate what fraction of all capital goods were imported under this provision, but the fraction was undoubtedly very high. In the absence of more detailed information, it is assumed that all capital goods were imported under the deferred payment scheme.

The value of the deferred payment can be computed as the difference between the duties presently payable (without deferment) and the present value of the repayment schedule discounted at 15 per cent. Thus per TL 100 of duties owed on capital goods import, TL 20 would be paid at the time of importation, TL 24 one year thereafter (TL 20 principal plus 5 per cent on TL

11. The provisions are cited in Muhittin Tanci, Polat Yalçıner, and Yavuz Kadıoğlu, *İçtihatli ve En Son Değişiklikleri Muhtevi Gümrük Kanunu ve İstatistik Pozisyonlarına Bölünmüş Gümrük Giriş Tarife Cetveli* (Ankara), 1968, pp. 109–23.

Table A-10
Gürtan's estimates of TL cost of $1 of capital goods imports, 1953 to 1960

	1953	1954	1955	1956	1957	1958	1959	1960
Construction goods	3.58	3.76	4.25	4.55	6.16	7.56	13.81	13.94
Machinery and equipment	3.22	3.48	4.02	4.72	5.97	6.30	11.59	11.79
Average	3.34	3.57	4.10	4.68	6.03	6.55	12.06	12.14

Source: Kenan Gürtan, untitled, mimeographed by SPO.

80), TL 23 the year later, etc. If these future payments are discounted at 15 per cent, the present value of the deferred payments is TL 84.77. Thus the deferred payment scheme represented a 15.2 per cent reduction in duties and charges (excep stamp tax) on imported capital goods.

At the same time as the law enabling postponement of duties payable on capital goods was effected, a provision was also enacted which enabled the authorities to waive duties on capital goods imports under specified conditions. No data are available on the value of capital goods imports for which duties were entirely waived. One obtains a distinct impression from interviews that until 1967 the provision was rarely used. Thereafter, however, the practice of waiving duties completely was believed to have become fairly general. In estimating the subsidy against duties and taxes upon capital goods imports in 1968, therefore, it was assumed that 75 per cent of all capital goods were admitted duty-free (although still subject to stamp tax), while the remaining 25 per cent were entitled to the postponement of payment of duties.

The reduction in tariffs and surcharges on capital goods started in 1964. For the period 1953 to 1960 a set of estimates of the total TL cost of foreign exchange for capital goods has already been prepared by Gürtan for the SPO. Since his estimates were based upon actual receipts by appropriate subcategories of capital goods (construction goods, and machinery and equipment separately), it was decided to use Gürtan's estimates of the TL cost of capital goods imports for the period prior to 1958.[12]

Import "exchange taxes" in the 1950's. As indicated in Chapter II, a se-

12. For other commodities, and for capital goods imports in the 1960's, the sample indicated in Table A-5 was used. Gürtan's estimates can be compared with the sample estimates for the 1950's:

	1954	1957	1959
Gürtan	3.57	6.03	12.06
Sample	4.13	5.38	12.55

These give some confidence in the method of estimating other EERs. See Note 2 to Tables A-11 to A-14.

ries of surcharges and "treasury taxes" were successively imposed upon various imported goods during the 1950's. In late 1953, non-cascaded taxes on a variety of "luxury" goods were imposed, ranging from 25 to 150 per cent of the c.i.f. price of the commodity. These surcharges remained in effect until August 1958.[13] A "Treasury Tax" of 40 per cent on foreign exchange purchases went into effect on March 1, 1957, and was removed in December 1958.[14]

On the import side, EERs were thus fairly constant between 1954 and 1957, save for negligible changes in the tariff equivalents of guarantee deposits and occasional additions to the list of commodities subject to surcharges or changes in the rates of surcharge. The rates of additional duty on selected imports can be inferred from the "surcharge" column of estimates of import EERs for 1954, given in Tables A-11 to A-14.

Estimation of import EERs. Tables A-11 through A-14 provide estimates of EERs for the four categories of import goods for 1954, 1957, August 1958, 1962, 1965 and 1968. The first eight columns provide data for each period not contained in earlier Appendix Tables, and the last six columns give the EERs prevailing at each point in time expressed as a percentage of the c.i.f. price at the official exchange rate. To obtain EERs in TL, the numbers in the last six columns of Tables A-11 to A-14 can be divided by 100 and multiplied by 2.8 prior to August 1958 and by 9 thereafter.

Thus, BTN No. 5.10 (ivory, Table A-11) carried a 10 per cent duty (from Table A-5) in 1954 and was subject to the municipality tax. Its EER was 114, or 1.14 times the official exchange rate of TL 2.80 per dollar, thus TL 3.10. In 1957, ivory was subject to the 40 per cent Treasury Tax, the same tariff rate, and a guarantee deposit requirement. Its EER was thus 1.56 times the official rate, or TL 4.37. In August 1958, ivory had virtually the same proportionate EER (the guarantee deposit requirement was reduced) but at the TL 9 = \$1 exchange rate, that equalled TL 13.86. In 1962, ivory was eligible for importation by industrialists under a quota, and the 40 per cent Treasury Tax had been removed, giving it an EER of 1.14 times the exchange rate, or TL 10.26. After 1962, ivory was not on an eligible import list.

For commodities not on an eligible import list in the 1960's EERs were

---

13. Data on the commodities included, and the rate of surcharge, were obtained from Ragıb Rıfkı Özgürel, *The Turkish Foreign Trade Regime and Decrees, List of Import and Export Articles and Regulations,* Ministry of Economy and Commerce, undated, p. 230.

14. *Annual Report on Exchange Restrictions,* International Monetary Fund (Washington), 1958, p. 293; 1959, p. 301. The 42 per cent figure appearing in the tables reflects the 40 per cent tax plus an estimated cost of guarantee deposits equal to 2 per cent of the c.i.f. price.

Table A-11

EERs for consumer goods imports, 1954 to 1968 (all expressed as per cent of c.i.f. TL price)

BTN No.	1954 Production Tax	1954 Surcharge	1957 Surcharge	1962 List	1965 List	1965 Stamp Duty	1968 List	1968 Stamp Duty	EER 1954	EER 1957	EER 1958 (Aug.)	EER 1962	EER 1965	EER 1968
5.10	–	–	42	QI					114	156	154	114		
7.06	–	–	42						161	203	201			
8.01	–	–	67	PQI	PQWP	6	PQI+W	17	220	287	260	220	197	212
9.01a	48	–	42	QW	QWP	6	QWP	17	238	281	179	239	250	266
b	56	–	42						276	319	316			
9.02	–	–	42	L	LIP	9			190	233	231	191	229	
9.04	–	–	67	QW	QW	6	QWI	17	220	287	260	220	227	242
10.01	–	–	42						161	204	201			
17.01	–	–	42						220	287	260			
19.03	–	–	42						161	204	201			
20.05	–	–	42						279	321	319			
21.05	–	–	42						220	263	260			
22.03	90	–	42						268	411	409			
29.38	–	–	42	L	LIAID	16	LAID	19	108	150	140	108	124	130
34.01	18	–	67						238	305	278			
37.02	8	–	92	PQI	PL1,PQ	7	PQIP	16	152	244	192	152	159	171
42.02	–	–	67						220	287	260			
43.03	222	75	117						517	559	482			
60.02	50	–	42						329	271	369			
62.02	40	–	67						261	328	301			

Table A-11 (continued)

BTN No.	1954 Production Tax	1954 Surcharge	1957 Surcharge	1962 List	1965 List	1965 Stamp Duty	1968 List	1968 Stamp Duty	EER 1954	EER 1957	EER 1958 (Aug.)	EER 1962	EER 1965	EER 1968
64.05	–	–	42						220	263	260			
65.05	–	–	42						185	227	230			
66.01	–	–	67						220	287	260			
67.04	–	–	42						220	263	260			
69.10	25	75	117	PQW					320	362	285	245		
71.12	–	75	117						201	243	166			
74.17	–	–	42						150	192	190			
83.01	–	–	42		PL2	10	PL2	20	161	204	201		201	215
85.02	–	–	42	LAID	PL2	10	PL2AID	30	161	204	201	161	171	195
90.07	7	25	67	PL	PL2	10	PL2PQW	20	170	212	185	145	214	229
91.01	10	50–75	92–117	QW	QWAID	11	QW	17	203	327	176	136	229	241
92.01	–	–	42	QW	QW	7	QW	17	120	162	160	120	168	182
94.03	–	50	92						247	289	237			
96.05	36	–	42						256	299	296			
97.02	–	75	117						220	337	260			
98.03	–	–	42	L	PQ1+W	7	PQW+I	17	173	215	213	173		212
98.08	–	–	42	QW					150	192	190	150	197	
Average consumer good EER:									218	267	247	175	197	209

Notes: See statement following Table A-14.
Source: See statement following Table A-14.

Table A-12
EERs for raw material and intermediate goods imports, 1954 to 1968 (all expressed as per cent of c.i.f. TL price)

BTN No.	1954 Production Tax	1954 Sur charge	1957 Sur-charge	1962 List	1965 List	1965 Stamp Duty	1968 List	1968 Stamp Duty	EERs 1954	1957	1958 (Aug.)	1962	1965	1968
13.01			42	PQW	PQW	7	PQW	17	220	263	260	220	227	242
15.12			42	PQWI	PL1	8	PQWI	17	173	215	213	173	182	194
18.03	33		67	QW	QWI	6	QI	17	147	214	287	147	202	240
23.04			42						120	162	160			
25.03	8		42		QWI	6	PQW	17	134	176	174		224	232
25.19	17		42	QI	QI	6	QI	17	132	174	172	132	137	
25.24	3		42	QI	QI	6	PQI	17	149	191	189	149	141	155
26.01	4		42	PQW	PQI	6			111	152	151	111	116	130
27.01			42						118	161	158			
28.04			42	L	PL2	10	PL2	20	161	204	201	161	171	185
28.06			42	L	L1	8	PL1	19	120	197	160	120	158	172
28.09			42	PQI	PQW	6	QI	17	109	150	148	108	156	170
28.19			42	L	L2	10	LI	19	114	156	154	114	136	148
28.26			42	L	L2	10	PL2	20	120	162	160	120	130	143
28.39			42	L	L1	8	L1	19	109	150	148	108	137	151
29.06			42	L	L2	10	L2	20	132	174	172	132	142	155
29.14			42	L	L2	10	PL2PQI	20	220	263	260	220	171	152
32.03			42	QWI	PQWI	6			132	174	214	132	156	
35.02			42	L	PL1	8	PL1	19	138	180	196	138	146	160
36.03			42	QI	QIP	5			161	204	190	161	226	
38.05	81	50	42	L	L2	10	L2	20	120	162	184	120	154	167
39.02	12		92	PQI	PL1AID	16	PLAID	20	293	235	190	243	187	270
40.01		25	22	LAID	PL2	10	PL1AID	25	174	196	166	184	170	189
41.02			67						180	223	160			
44.15			42						150	192	235			

Table A-12 (continued)

BTN No.	1954 Production Tax	1954 Sur-charge	1957 Sur-charge	1962 List	1965 List	1965 Stamp Duty	1968 List	1968 Stamp Duty	EERs 1954	1957	1958 (Aug.)	1962	1965	1968
45.03			42	QWI	QW	7	PQW	17	144	186	184	144	168	182
46.02			42						150	192	189			
47.01	18		42	QI	PL1P	8	PLPQI	18	126	168	166	126	151	164
48.16			42	PQWP					220	263	260	220		
50.04	45		42						195	236	235			
54.01	25		42						151	193	191			
55.04	27		42						154	195	194			
57.03	15		42	QI	QI	5	QI	17	123	165	163	123	129	143
68.13	17		42	QIW	QIW	5	PQIW	17	149	191	189	149	227	243
69.02	21		42	LP	L2P	10			171	213	211	171	191	
73.07	3		42	PQIP	Q1AID	11	PQI	17	123	165	163	122	133	143
73.14	3		42	LP	PL1P	9	QI	17	123	165	163	122	151	163
73.26	4		42						136	178	212			
74.07	4		42	PQI	PQIW	6	PQW	17	119	161	159	119	162	188
75.03	6		42	L	L2	10	L2	20	132	174	174	134	151	166
77.02	3		42	L	L2AID	16	PL2	20	111	111	163	111	127	131
78.04	15		42						165	209	205			
79.09	11		42						149	191	189			
80.03	3		42	L	L1AID	16	PL1AID	25	111	152	163	111	134	147
82.02	33		67	L	PQW	6	PQIW	17	165	232	205	165	208	223
85.25	20		42	QW	PQW	6	PQIW	17	164	206	204	164	191	207
90.17			42	L	L2AID	16	PL1AID	25	120	162	160	120	160	172
Average EER:									148	191	187	146	164	183

Note: See statement following Table A-14.

Source: See statement following Table A-14.

Table A-13

EERs, capital goods imports (all expressed as percentage of TL c.i.f. values)

BTN No.	1954 Production Tax	1954 Sur-charge	1957 Sur-charge	1962 List	1965 List	1965 Stamp Duty	1968 List	1968 Stamp Duty	EER 1954	EER 1957	EER 1958	EER 1962	EER 1965	EER 1968
76.08	30		42				Q	−67	150	192	190			139
84.06	11		42	LAID	PL2PQ1	1	PL2PQW	−28	121	161	159	129	159	133
84.15	21	75	115	PLAID	PL1P	−10	L1PPQI	−66	210	250	175	145	194	143
84.22	21		42	PL	PL2PQW	−4	PL2PQW	−53	131	174	171	131	187	142
84.31	19		42	PL	PL2AID	7	PL2	−30	128	170	168	128	169	136
84.37	19		42				PQI	−45	128	170	168			133
84.45	19		42		QWP	−8	PQW	−58	128	170	168		183	137
84.63	27		83	PLAID	PL2AID	−5	L2AID	−30	135	219	175	145	167	146
86.06	21		42				Q	−16	135	177	175			125
87.01	33		42		QW	−5	PQWP	−26	165	207	205		167	141
87.02	12	25–50	67–92	PL	PQW	−8	PQWP	−69	200	243	202	162	195	140
88.02			42	PQI	PQW	−2	PQWP	10	109	150	148	108	104	118
89.01			42				Q	−40	161	203	201			130
90.27	33		42	L	L2	−5	L2	−64	165	207	205	165	196	143
Average capital good EER:									148	192	179	139	172	136

Notes: See statement following Table A-14.

Sources: See statement following Table A-14.

Table A-14

EERs for imports competing with domestic production, 1954 to 1968 (all expressed as percentage of TL c.i.f. values)

BTN No.	1954 Production Tax	1954 Surcharge	1957 Surcharge	1962 List	1965 List	1965 Stamp Duty	1968 List	1968 Stamp Duty	EER 1954	EER 1957	EER 1958	EER 1962	EER 1965	EER 1968
31.02			42	LP	PQIPL	16	L1PQI	29	161	204	201	161	141	158
40.11	34		42	PLAID	PQIW	6	PQWP	27	173	214	212	182	193	221
48.05	37		42	PQ	PQI	6	PQIW	17	210	252	250	210	216	232
51.04	83		67		PL2AID	16	PL1PQ1	66	303	370	343		410	317
53.11	70	50	92						267	359	291			
55.06	48		67						221	288	261			
56.04	59		67	PQI					235	302	275	235		
56.06	83		67		PQI	5			303	370	343		309	
58.05	83		67	L	PL2PL1	9	PL1	19	303	370	343	303	312	330
60.01	83		92						303	395	343			
69.05	27		42						218	260	258	203		
70.05	41		42	PQW			PQI	17	203	245	247	180	208	225
73.32	36		42	PQW	PQW	6	PL2PQ	20	180	222	220	211	257	227
Average import substitution EER:									237	296	276			244

Notes: See next page.

Sources: See next page.

Notes: a) Symbols for the lists are:

        Q = quota list

        L = liberalized list

        P prefix = part of the category eligible for importation

        P suffix = commodity eligible for importation only with Ministerial permission

        AID = AID-financing only

        L1,L2 = Liberalized Lists 1 and 2 respectively

        I,W suffixes = Industrialist, Importers eligible to import the commodity.

      b) EERs computed as: $(1 + t_i + w + p_i + s + g_i)$,

        where t_i is the tariff rate, w is the combined wharf and municipality tax rate in effect, p_i is the component of the production tax discriminating against exports, s is the stamp duty, m is the municipality tax, and g_i is the tariff equivalent of guarantee deposit requirements.

        The wharf and municipality taxes were computed as $WT + MT = a + bti$ where WT is the wharf tax and MT the municipality tax. $a = 0.025$ until 1965 and 0.05 thereafter, $b = 0.17875$ until 1965 and 0.2075 thereafter. The relationship holds since $MT_i = ct_i$ and $WT_i = h(MT_i + t_i + 1)$, where c and g are the proportionate tax rates.

        The production tax was computed as $P_i(1 + t_i + W)$ for goods on List IV and $P_i(t_i + W)$ for Lists I to III.

      c) A blank for the 1960's indicates that the commodity was not on the eligible import list.

      d) The stamp duty column for the 1960's contains the stamp duty and also the guarantee deposit requirement's *ad valorem* equivalent. For capital goods imports, the implicit value of the subsidy is subtracted. Thus some capital goods imports are reported to have a net negative stamp duty.

      e) EERs for 1958 are expressed as a percentage of the c.i.f. price at the TL 9 = $1 exchange rate.

      f) Stamp duty rates were: 5 per cent from 1963 to 1965, 15 per cent from 1965 to 1968, and 25 per cent in 1969.

      g) December 1958 EERs can be computed from August 1958 EERs by subtracting 0.4, since the Treasury Tax was removed at that time.

Sources: Production tax rates from Table A-6.

        Tariff rates from Table A-5.

        1954 surcharge rates from Özgürel, *op. cit.* (Note 13).

        1957 surcharge rates from *ibid.,* with additions to reflect the 40 per cent general "Treasury tax" plus a 2 per cent guarantee-deposit-requirement equivalent.

        List classifications for 1962, 1965 and 1968 are from Import Programs, *Nos. 8* (1962), *14* (1965), and *20* (1968). (Note 3, Chap. VI.)

not calculated, since they would have been meaningless. The sole exception was capital goods imports for which special "investment goods quotas" had been set aside, so that failure to include a capital goods item on an import list did not necessarily imply that the product could not legally be imported.

The fact that some commodities in the sample were not legally importable in the 1960's and therefore excluded from the calculation of the mean EER for each commodity category imparts a bias to the sample means over time. For example, some import-substitute commodities subject to very high tariff rates were omitted from the 1968 import list, so that the calculated EER for that group actually declined from its 1965 value. However (1) in the event of a commodity not being included on a list, it was impossible to calculate any guarantee-deposit-requirement equivalent; (2) it becomes a moot question as to whether the import production tax rate applied; and (3) if the good had been eligible for importation, additional taxes might have been levied. It was decided in view of these considerations that the bias imparted by estimating the mean rate for goods actually eligible for importation was smaller than the bias that would have resulted from creating fictitious guarantee deposit requirements and otherwise making estimates of tax rates applicable to goods that actually could not be imported.

The average EERs for each import category, given in the last rows of Tables A-11 to A-14, are the unweighted means of the EERs for the commodities in the sample. As indicated above, no satisfactory set of weights could be found.

For the years between the dates for which data are presented, either (1) known changes in the trade regime were of an across-the-board nature, or (2) changes were very small or not known. Thus there is no evidence that any component of EERs for imports changed from 1954 until 1957, except for the production tax (for which data are not available) and for an insignificant change in guarantee deposit requirements. Between August 1958 and 1960 the only known change was the abandonment of the 40 per cent Treasury Tax, which reduced by 40 the EER for each commodity as measured in the tables, so that separate calculations did not have to be made. Between 1962 and 1963 the 5 per cent stamp duty was introduced. The 1954 tariff rates were assumed to continue in effect in 1964. From 1964 to 1965 changes reflect the altered tariff rates and the effect of their being cascaded by other charges. Between 1966 and 1967 the stamp duty was increased from 5 to 15 per cent. Between 1968 and 1969 the stamp duty rose from 15 to 25 per cent. These were across-the-board changes, and are reflected in the import EERs given in Table VI-10. There were undoubtedly small modifications in the system which are not reflected in those estimates. For example, the delay in obtaining licenses increased in 1969, and therefore the implicit interest cost of the guarantee deposit requirements increased. However, most such phenomena were variable even within given years, and it is doubtful that they would alter the EER estimates significantly even if a means were available for estimating their effects.

Invisibles and capital transactions

Fortunately, the structure of rates on invisibles and capital transactions has been far simpler than that on imports. Three categories of invisibles require separate treatment: tourism, workers' remittances, and interest and dividends on foreign capital. Capital flows have essentially been kept at a uniform rate at each point in time.

Tourism. All tourist transactions took place at the TL 2.80 = $1 rate until October 1956, when a TL 5.25 tourist rate was introduced applicable to foreign tourists' purchases of lira in Turkey. The selling rate for Turks' foreign travel was changed at that time to TL 5.75 per dollar.[15] The rate was unified at TL 9 = $1 in August 1958. That rate remained in effect for foreign tourists in Turkey until 1968. In 1961, however, Turks purchasing foreign exchange for travelling abroad were taxed at the rate of 50 per cent, making the EER TL 13.50. That rate remained in effect until August 1970. For foreign tourists, a special buying rate of TL 12 = $1 was introduced in March 1968.[16]

Workers' remittances. Until the 1960's so few Turks worked abroad that there were no special arrangements for their remittances. But by the mid-1960's Turkish workers abroad constituted an important source of foreign exchange earnings, and special provisions were made for their remittances. In 1965 it was decreed that Turkish workers who remitted their foreign exchange to the Central Bank could immediately receive 3 years' interest (not compounded) on their deposit, which could be withdrawn at any time. Thus the rate at which workers remitted was effectively TL 11.43, since the interest rate was 9 per cent. In 1968 the workers' remittance rate was increased to TL 12, as the interest rate was raised to 11.11 per cent. Thus the EER became 12 in 1968 and rose only to TL 15 with the August 1970 devaluation. This was done by continuing to prepay interest, and setting the workers' remittance rate at TL 10 per dollar.

One other feature of workers' remittances deserves mention: returning workers were entitled, under most conditions, to import a car when they

15. *Annual Report on Currency Restrictions*, International Monetary Fund (Washington), 1957, p. 279.
16. *Annual Report on Currency Restrictions*, International Monetary Fund (Washington), 1969, p. 470.

Table A-15
EERs on invisible and capital transactions, 1953 to 1969 (TL per dollar)

	Tourism		Workers' Remittances	Dividends and Interest	Other Invisibles	Capital Transactions
	Buying	Selling				
1953	2.80	2.80	2.80	2.80	2.80	2.80
1954	2.80	2.80	2.80	2.80	2.80	2.80
1955	2.80	2.80	2.80	2.80	2.80	2.80
1956	5.25	5.75	2.80	2.80	2.80–5.75	2.80
1957	5.25	5.75	2.80	2.80	2.80–5.75	2.80
1958	9.00	9.02	9.00	9.00	9.00	9.00
1959	9.02	9.04	9.00	9.00	9.00	9.00
1960	9.02	13.50	9.00	9.00	9.00	9.00
1961	9.02	13.50	9.00	9.00	9.00	9.00
1962	9.02	13.50	9.00	9.00	9.00	9.00
1963	9.02	13.50	9.00	9.00	9.00	9.00
1964	9.02	13.50	9.00	9.00	9.00	9.00
1965	9.02	13.50	11.43	9.00	9.00	9.00
1966	9.02	13.50	11.43	9.00	9.00	9.00
1967	9.02	13.50	11.43	9.00	9.00	9.00
1968	12.00	13.50	12.00	9.00	9.00	9.00
1969	12.00	13.50	12.00	9.00	9.00	9.00

Source: *Annual Report on Currency Restrictions,* International Monetary Fund (Washington), various issues.

returned to Turkey.[17] Since the car was legally resellable, either *de jure* or *de facto,* a sizeable profit could be made. To be eligible for the privilege, the workers (or other Turks working abroad) had to demonstrate foreign savings in the minimum amount of $800. Thus they had to show a Central Bank deposit of at least that amount. Since the profitability of importing a car was generally sizeable, the EER for the first $800 of remittances considerably exceeded the TL 11.43 or TL 12 rate. However, once minimum savings were deposited, the incentive to deposit additional remittances hinged only upon the prepayment of interest, and the marginal EER was considerably below the average. For present purposes, however, it is the marginal rate, above the minimum savings rate, which is used in estimation of the EER's.

   Profit and interest remittances, and foreign capital transactions.   Inter-

17. *Annual Report on Currency Restrictions,* International Monetary Fund (Washington), 1967, p. 622. In 1968, the importation privilege was slightly restricted in that the importer had to show he had owned the vehicle for six months.

est, dividends and profit remittances, as well as capital repatriation were blocked after World War II. A Law for the Encouragement of Foreign Investment was passed in 1951 which guaranteed that foreign investors coming under the scope of the law would be entitled to repatriate 10 per cent of the investment annually in the form of profits, interest, dividends or capital repatriation. The 10 per cent ceiling was removed in 1964. Virtually all private capital flows since 1951 have come under those provisions and hence remittances have generally been legal.[18] Both foreign loans and foreign investment required government approval, and once it was received, came under the scope of the Law.

The TL 2.80 exchange rate was in effect for these transactions until August 1958. In 1956 patents, royalties, licensing fees and capital transfers of foreign companies not coming under the provisions of the Law for Encouragement of Foreign Investment were made subject to the TL 5.75 exchange rate. Except for that category, however, capital transfers and remittances have been made at the official exchange rate throughout the period under study.[19] Table A-15 summarizes the EERs for invisible and capital transactions.

18. Companies earning more than 10 per cent, of course, experienced partial blockage of their earnings. In the 1960's special categories of investment, such as tourism, were established. Foreign companies could invest in those categories and repatriate additional sums under those circumstances.
19. One exception is the foreign oil companies which were guaranteed that they could repatriate part of their earnings at the TL 2.80 exchange rate, which continues in effect.

APPENDIX B

CALCULATION OF FACTORS RESPONSIBLE FOR TURKEY's DECLINING EXPORT EARNINGS, 1954 TO 1958

There are two alternative bases on which one can decompose the changes in a country's export earnings. First, one can form the identity:

$$\sum_i P_{it} X_{it} - \sum_i P_{io} X_{io} \equiv \sum_i (P_{it} - P_{io}) X_{io} + \sum_i P_{io}(X_{it} - X_{io})$$

$$+ \sum_i (P_{it} - P_{io})(X_{it} - X_{io}) \tag{B1}$$

where P_i is the price of the ith export commodity, X_i is the quantity of the ith good exported, and o,t subscripts refer to the initial and terminal periods. The first term on the right can be identified as the part of the change in export earnings attributable to price changes, the second term as the part attributable to quantity changes, and the last term as the result of interaction between price and quantity changes. A positive sign for the first two terms suggests that prices and quantities increased.

Second, one can use "shift and share" analysis. Then,

$$\sum_i (V_{it} - V_{io}) \equiv \sum_i s_{io} W_{it} + (s_{it} - s_{io}) W_{it} \tag{B2}$$

where V_i is the value of exports of the ith commodity, s_i is the Turkish share of world exports of the ith commodity, W_i is the value of world exports of the ith commodity, and o,t subscripts refer to the initial and terminal periods. In this formula, the left-hand side refers to the change in the total value of exports. The first term on the right indicates what exports would have been if the initial share of each commodity market had been maintained, while the second term reflects the change in share of exports.

Neither decomposition of the change in export earnings has a sound underlying theory. Both formulations reflect identities, and in that sense, neither can be given a "causal" interpretation.[1] Thus in eq. (B1), it might be that the quantity change was positive and the price change negative simply because a country was selling more at a lower price, and conversely. However, both formulations are useful in exploring the proximate factors accounting for changes in export earnings.

1. See J. David Richardson, "Constant-Market-Shares Analysis of Export Growth," *Journal of International Economics,* May 1971.

Tables B-1 to B-4 give the data and commodities which were used to compute the terms in equations (B1) and (B2). As can be seen, the commodities included in the computations cover over 80 per cent of Turkey's export earnings in 1953. Although the figures are given in TL, the exchange rate used to record exports was constant throughout the period. Dollar figures can be obtained by dividing by 2.8.

Table B-1
Actual commodity-specific export earnings, 1953–1958 (millions of TL)

	1953	1954	1955	1956	1957	1958
Wheat	164.3	188.3	35.0	49.7	0	7.7
Barley	34.9	6.7	15.4	25.1	0	15.8
Cereal n.e.s.	24.0	10.2	3.2	4.1	6.5	n.a.
Dried fruit	95.2	120.7	166.2	55.8	64.5	63.8
Oilseed cakes	23.4	25.0	29.8	30.9	20.4	15.9
Tobacco	238.7	240.5	249.2	261.9	388.8	235.9
Wool	31.4	24.4	30.8	27.0	40.8	n.a.
Cotton	220.3	146.8	128.2	73.5	116.0	62.7
Chrome	79.1	43.4	55.6	65.1	59.9	51.6
Copper	33.3	20.7	24.6	47.6	24.2	18.1
Value	944.6	826.7	738.0	640.7	721.1	518.8
All exports	1109.0	937.8	877.3	854.0	966.7	626.3

Source: See Table B-4.

Table B-2
Exports with actual prices, 1953 volume, 1953–1958 (millions of TL)

	1953	1954	1955	1956	1957	1958
Wheat	164.3	120.1	132.1	168.2	138.1	138.1
Barley	34.9	20.7	25.5	24.0	20.8	16.0
Cereal n.e.s.	24.0	20.0	49.5	20.0	55.8	55.8
Dried fruit	95.2	85.9	133.1	67.7	65.4	74.1
Oilseed cakes	23.4	109.7	95.3	27.7	25.3	16.9
Tobacco	238.7	267.4	297.6	309.0	314.8	301.1
Wool	31.4	32.3	29.8	37.1	66.7	66.9
Cotton	220.3	243.9	244.9	213.7	192.5	183.4
Chrome	79.1	81.4	67.9	67.9	67.9	67.7
Copper	33.3	31.3	35.9	43.9	29.4	25.1
Value	944.6	1012.7	1111.6	979.1	976.7	945.1
Ratio to actual	1.00	1.22	1.50	1.53	1.35	1.82

Source: See Table B-4.

Table B-3
Exports with actual volume, 1953 prices, 1953–1958 (millions of TL)

	1953	1954	1955	1956	1957	1958
Wheat	164.3	256.5	43.2	47.7	0	9.0
Barley	34.9	11.0	20.5	35.8	0	34.5
Cereal n.e.s.	24.0	12.5	1.6	5.0	2.8	–
Dried fruit	95.2	133.4	119.2	78.8	93.4	81.9
Oilseed cakes	23.4	5.2	7.2	25.3	18.7	21.6
Tobacco	238.7	214.4	199.8	202.1	294.7	186.8
Wool	31.4	23.7	32.5	23.7	19.3	–
Cotton	220.3	132.7	115.4	75.8	132.7	75.6
Chrome	79.1	42.8	67.1	74.9	68.5	61.1
Copper	33.3	22.0	22.7	36.1	27.4	23.9
Total	944.6	854.2	629.2	605.2	657.5	516.6
Ratio to actual	1.00	103.3	0.852	0.943	0.912	0.996

Source: See Table B-4.

Table B-4
Exports with constant shares, 1953–1958 (millions of TL)

	1953	1954	1955	1956	1957	1958
Wheat	164.3	124.3	125.2	183.7	168.8	152.9
Barley	34.9	24.1	29.4	40.9	37.5	39.2
Cereals n.e.s.	24.0	16.8	27.7	33.3	19.3	28.8
Dried fruit	95.2	112.0	108.6	103.3	105.3	116.8
Oilseed cakes	23.4	38.4	44.8	49.0	42.6	43.1
Tobacco	238.7	240.5	247.8	267.7	336.0	357.3
Wool	31.4	28.8	29.7	31.4	38.6	26.6
Cotton	220.3	248.6	178.6	213.9	271.9	219.5
Chrome	79.1	74.8	74.8	97.4	135.2	157.9
Copper	33.3	30.8	40.0	49.0	42.0	50.4
Total	944.6	939.1	906.6	1069.6	1197.2	1192.5
Ratio to actual	1.00	1.13	1.23	1.67	1.66	2.29

Notes: Exports of cereals n.e.s. and wool were not separately reported for 1958. 1957 figures for those commodities were used to compute totals for 1958.

Source: Values and quantities from *Yearbook of International Trade Statistics*, United Nations, various issues. Unit values derived by dividing value by quantity. Computed values as indicated in text.

Table B-2 gives the value exports would have had had the volume of each export remained constant at its 1953 level, while unit prices assumed their actual recorded values. In a sense, the sum over the commodities examined of export values gives an indication of the weighted change in export prices over the 1954-to-1958 period. If volume had retained its 1953 level for each export commodity, Turkey's export earnings would have increased through 1955, and would have remained above their 1953 level in each year under examination. Thus there is no way to attribute the decline in recorded export earnings to a deterioration in prices received by Turkey for her major exports.

The last row of Table B-2 gives the ratio of export earnings with volume constant to actual exports. With constant export volumes, export earnings would have been 50 per cent greater than they actually were in 1955 and 1956, and 35 per cent greater in 1957, even with no growth in the volume of exports and actual prices.

Table B-3 gives the values exports would have had with constant (1953) prices and the actual volume of exports. With constant prices, Turkey's exports would have declined even more than they in fact did. Actual export earnings in every year after 1954 were greater than they would have been had there been no changes in export prices. In an index-number sense, the weighted average price received by Turkey for her exports increased from 1953 to 1958.

Table B-4 indicates the value Turkey's exports would have assumed if the Turkish share of world exports of each commodity had remained constant. While it may be argued that Turkey might not have been able to expand her share of world exports without a reduction in price received, it is difficult to accept that argument for constancy of share, especially since the shares were computed on a value basis. Moreover, Turkey's share in international trade for the commodities listed ranged from 3.0 per cent for dried fruit to 1.8 per cent for copper. In none of these export groups was Turkey's share of the market very large. It seems reasonable in a growing market to assume that a country could maintain her share of the market without suffering terms-of-trade losses. Had Turkey maintained her share in each of her commodity markets, Turkish export earnings would have grown 23 per cent over the period 1953-to-1958, contrasted with an actual decline of 43 per cent.

The decline in export earnings can now be decomposed in accordance with (B1) and (B2). For the commodities in the sample,

$$-425.8 \quad = +0.5 \quad\quad -428.0 \quad\quad -1.7 \tag{B1}$$

total change   price change   quantity change   interaction

$$-425.8 \quad = 247.9 \quad\quad -673.7 \tag{B2}$$

total change   share constant   change in share.

Thus in a definitional sense the decline in export earnings resulted entirely from a reduction in export volumes, which was slightly offset by an increase in average price. Similarly, the Turkish loss in share of world markets exceeded the decline in export earnings.

APPENDIX C

THE 1970 DEVALUATION

In August 1970 the Turkish lira was devalued *de jure* and *de facto*. Although the writing of the main chapters of this book continued into 1972, the work was based on research completed early in 1971. At the time this Appendix was drafted (September 1972) enough facts were available to permit at least a broad description of the events leading up to and following the 1970 devaluation. No analysis undertaken only two years after the event can be definitive, especially in view of the fact that data are far from complete, even for 1971. The conclusions stated here then should be regarded as tentative.

An interesting aspect of the devaluation is its remarkable superficial resemblance to the 1958 experience. The outcome, however, has been surprisingly different, though it nevertheless appears to substantiate much of the analysis of earlier chapters.

The nominal devaluation was a two-thirds increase in the price of foreign exchange, from TL 9 to TL 15 to the dollar.[1] As in 1958, though, the stamp duties and certain other surcharges upon its imports were reduced while the exchange rate for most traditional exports was set at TL 12 per dollar. Thus the effective devaluation was considerably less than the nominal one. Simultaneously with the exchange rate-alteration some domestic taxes were significantly increased, the prices of a number of products sold by public enterprises were raised sharply, and foreign credits were extended to Turkey.

The effects of the devaluation upon Turkey's balance of payments and domestic economic activity were much more immediate than those of 1958, and contrast sharply with them. On the international payments side, export earnings rose rapidly, workers' remittances increased beyond the most optimistic expectations, and despite a massive liberalization of imports Turkey's foreign exchange reserves rose sharply, reaching $772 million at the end of 1971 contrasted with $477 million in July 1970.

Domestically the release of funds previously frozen in guarantee deposits plus the increase in the money supply resulting from increased foreign exchange receipts (especially workers' remittances) led to a rapid increase in the

---

1. When the dollar was devalued in December 1971 the Turkish lira retained its parity with continental European currencies and the dollar exchange rate became TL 14 per dollar.

price level, and despite some political uncertainties, to be discussed below, real GNP increased 9.2 per cent in 1971, according to provisional estimates by the SPO. That was the second highest real growth rate attained during the planning years. While the 1958 devaluation was followed by price stability and recession, with little immediate export response, the 1970 devaluation was followed by inflation, a rapid expansion of output, and a large increase in foreign exchange earnings from exports and other sources.

Before turning to more detailed consideration of the devaluation, the political events of 1969–1971 should be mentioned. There is again a strong superficial resemblance to 1958 and its aftermath. Elections had been held in October 1969, and the Justice Party under the leadership of Prime Minister Demirel was returned to power, receiving 46 per cent of the popular vote, compared to 52 per cent in the 1965 elections. Throughout 1969, 1970 and early 1971 there was increasing political violence in Turkey, with clashes between left and right wing extremists. Frequent encounters between students and police took place on several university campuses, and despite efforts of the government to handle the situation, violence continued. These events were so much at the center of political discussion that the devaluation went almost unnoticed.[2] By March 1971 the Turkish military intervened and informed the Prime Minister that he could either resign or face a military coup.[3] Demirel resigned, and a new government under Nihat Erim as Prime Minister was formed with the approval of the Turkish military leadership. Two Erim governments followed. The first lasted until December 1971 and the second until May 1972, when the Prime Minister resigned. The next government, under Ferit Melen as Prime Minister, again had military backing, although Parliament and political parties continued to function.

The Erim and Melen governments both imposed martial law and made strenuous, generally successful, efforts to stop the violence, with arrests and convictions of many suspected of encouraging the students or participating in the violence. Several changes in the administration of economic policy occurred under the first Erim government, the most important effect of these changes being that there was considerable uncertainty in the private sector as to the new government's intentions. Specifically relating to the trade regime, export price checks were resumed and rigorously enforced for a period of

---

2. The EIU has indicated that the devaluation strengthened Prime Minister Demirel politically, although many observers of Turkish politics disagree, believing that devaluation was a relatively unimportant issue at that time: EIU, *Op. Cit.* (Note 1, Chap. II), No. 3, September 1970, p. 2. The Prime Minister's proposed budget had been defeated in Parliament early in 1970, as several members of the Justice Party defected, but a new cabinet was formed at that time. The basis upon which the EIU formed its judgement is unclear.

3. *Middle Eastern Journal,* Summer 1971, p. 385.

several months, from May through the summer of 1971. In May and June there were widespread reports that goods were piled up at the docks awaiting price checks prior to export, since the government did not have the capacity to inspect all shipments promptly. But with the second Erim government most business uncertainty appeared to have ended. Although Ministers of both Erim governments made strong statements about intentions of major economic reforms, little of a substantive nature had been accomplished in that direction by the summer of 1972.

Thus the years 1969–1972 were a period of political change and unrest, and political questions occupied everyone's attention. But the causes of this preoccupation lay in factors essentially unassociated with the trade and payments regime or changes in it. Even the rapid price increases of 1971 and 1972, which were naturally very unpopular, did not become a major political issue, because the more important basic questions regarding the relationship of civilian politicians to the military occupied the center of the stage.

I. The situation pre-devaluation and the devaluation decision

As seen in earlier chapters, the premium on import licenses was rising almost continuously from 1964 to 1970. Liberalized List imports were the hardest hit, for approval of license applications was delayed. Moreover, even when licenses had been granted, currency transfers were delayed until foreign exchange became available. By late 1969, at the peak export season, it was estimated that the delay in transfer even under quota allocations was 30 weeks for industrialist, and 43 weeks for importers, reflecting about $300 million of import licenses which had been issued but for which no foreign exchange was available. That represented half of expected 1970 export earnings.[4] By June 1970 delays were even longer, and there were widespread reports of shortages of imported intermediate goods, especially steel products.[5] It was generally believed that these shortages would prevent the attainment of the goals set forth in the 1970 Annual Program.

Earlier recommendations for devaluation had been made by the IMF, OECD and other agencies, and there had been repeated discussions of devaluation within Turkey for several years. Some outside observers had expected the Prime Minister to announce a devaluation immediately after the 1969 elections, but when he did not do so expectations of a devaluation subsided somewhat.[6] In a sense, the fact that foreign exchange shortage had continued

4. EIU, *op. cit.* (Note 1, Chap. II), *No. 1*, March 1970, p. 3.
5. *Ibid., No. 2,* June 1970, p. 6.
6. When several deputies of the Justice Party left the party after the 1969 elections, they stated publicly that they had opposed an earlier devaluation proposal put forth by Prime Minister Demirel.

for so long meant that it could continue longer. The EIU reported in June 1970 that "there is now far less support for an early devaluation," and later termed the timing of the devaluation a "surprise."[7]

When the decision to devalue was made in August 1970, the situation was by no means as severe as that prior to August 1958, and external pressures were certainly less. The role of foreign donors in influencing the decision to devalue is unclear. The Consortium did not meet to make its 1970 pledges until July, and sizeable credits were extended to Turkey after the devaluation.[8] One of the arguments the Prime Minister made in defending the decision was that foreign loans were available as a result. It seems likely that the Consortium and its members had merely helped persuade the Prime Minister and others of the desirability of devaluation instead of making it a precondition of aid renewal, and that the timing was essentially a domestic political decision. Prime Minister Demirel appears to have been convinced for some time that the lira should be devalued but had been unable to do so due to opposition from within his own party. The industrialists in particular opposed the move, and they were among the key supporters of the Justice Party. The devaluation was announced shortly after Parliament had adjourned, which suggests that the timing may have been influenced by that fact. The factors influencing the Prime Minister in his decision are unclear. With heightened emphasis on growth during the 1960's the foreign exchange constraint was certainly viewed as a bottleneck to growth, and reported disruptions of production resulting from transfer delays and import shortages may have influenced the Prime Minister's attitude. After 1968, the SPO had emphasized the promotion of non-traditional exports, and export incentives had clearly met with some success. Devaluation was certainly consonant with the emphasis on new exports, and was probably an important factor influencing the Prime Minister's thinking.[9]

II. The devaluation package

When the exchange rate was altered in the summer of 1970, additional incentives for non-traditional exports were simultaneously established through changes in the rebate system, export credits and replenishment schemes. At the same time various changes in domestic policy took place. We

7. EIU, *op. cit.* (Note 1, Chap. II), *No. 2,* June 1970, p. 7; and *No. 3,* September 1970, p. 6.
8. *Ibid., No. 3,* September 1970, p. 13.
9. Betty S. Yaşer, "Economic Aspects of the Devaluation of the Turkish Lira of August 10, 1972," *Discussion Paper No. 5,* AID (Ankara), April 1972, p. 2.

Table C-1
Effective exchange rates, pre- and post-devaluation, 1970

	July 1970	September 1970	Per cent Increase
	(TL per dollar)		
Exports			
Traditional exports	9.38	12.00	27.9
Non-traditional exports	10.52	16.50	56.8
Imports			
Capital goods	13.16	19.68	49.6
Consumer goods	19.69	30.00	52.3
Intermediate goods	17.05	23.92	40.3
Imports with domestic substitutes	22.88	35.50	55.2
Tourism			
Buying TL	12.00	15.00	25.0
Selling TL	13.50	15.00	11.0
Other invisibles and capital	9.00	15.00	66.7

Notes: a) Import EERs were estimated by taking the pre-devaluation ratio of the
EER to the old exchange rate, subtracting 0.15 and the guarantee deposit *ad
valorem* equivalent, and multiplying by the new exchange rate.
b) For intermediate goods imports, it was estimated that the reduction in
duties on steel products reduced the weighted EER by 10 percent.
Source: Appendix A for pre-devaluation data. Estimates for post-devaluation imports
are the author's. Other post-devaluation data from text.

consider first the nominal and effective devaluation, and then the changes in
domestic policy. Although foreign credits were received as part of the package and imports were substantially increased, those components of the overall
policy change will be reviewed later, when considering the effect of devaluation.

Nominal and effective devaluation

Table C-1 summarizes the changes in nominal and effective exchange rates
that took place in August 1970. There were several exchange rates implicitly
in effect prior to 1970: the commodity exchange rate (TL 9 per dollar), the
workers' remittance and tourist buying rates (TL 12 per dollar), and the
tourist selling rate (TL 13.5 per dollar), applicable to Turkish residents wishing to purchase foreign exchange for foreign travel abroad. The latter rates
had been created by laws which provided subsidies and taxes outside of the
foreign trade regime. The three rates were equalized *de facto* at the TL 14.85

= $1 buying rate and TL 15 = $1 selling rate.[10]

On the import side, the stamp duty was reduced from 25 to 10 per cent, and guarantee deposit requirements were reduced by 50 per cent. The latter measure significantly reduced the cost of imports both directly and also because the delay in importing was reduced sharply. An import costing $1, subject to 100 per cent duty, had a landed cost of TL 22.8 pre-devaluation, and TL 35.6 post-devaluation, for a 56 per cent increase in the EER. An item subject to a 25 per cent duty had cost TL 14.87 pre-devaluation and cost TL 21.93 post-devaluation, for a 47 per cent increase in the EER. Thus the range of increase in individual import EERs was between 47 and 56 per cent, except for some intermediate steel products for which duty exemptions were granted with devaluation.[11] The net result, as indicated in Table C-1, was an increasing spread in import EERs, as capital goods and intermediate goods became slightly cheaper relative to consumer goods and to imports of goods also domestically produced.

The TL 15 = $1 exchange rate applied to all export commodities except cotton, figs, fig cakes, hazelnuts, molasses, oilcakes, olive oil, raisins and tobacco. Those commodities, of course, constitute the majority of Turkish exports. The ratio of the export EER to the import EER for non-traditional goods thus increased somewhat, and the degree of discrimination against export was slightly reduced. An exchange rate of TL 12 = $1 was set for the traditional commodities, but the government promised to gradually raise that rate to parity. The stated reasons for the lower exchange rate were that those exports were, in any event, competitive, even at the old exchange rates; and an increase in the exchange rates to TL 15 all at once would have resulted in unwarranted price increases. The rate for traditional exports was increased to TL 13 = $1 in July 1971.[12]

The Central Bank set up a "Foreign Exchange Equalization Fund" with the profits on the difference between its foreign exchange purchases and sales. The Fund was to be used to finance exports, although by 1972 the proceeds went directly to general government revenue. Yaşer estimates that

10. *De jure,* the workers' remittance rate became TL 11.25 = $1, with a $33\frac{1}{3}$ per cent subsidy still in force, and the Turkish travel rate became TL 10 = $1, with a 50 per cent tax upon it. The limit to the amount of foreign exchange that Turks could buy was $200, increasing to $400 in 1971.
11. The products were: cast iron products, ferro-alloys, scrap iron blooms, billets, steel bars, sheet iron in rolls, iron and steel rods and beams, high-carbon steel products and iron ore. Ministry of Industry permission was required. See Yaşer, *op. cit.* (Note 9), p. 22.
12. The tobacco rate had been increased in January 1971. The hazelnut rate was raised to TL 14 per dollar in March 1972. Since the TL was revalued to TL 14 per dollar in December 1971, the remaining disparity for other commodities was TL 1 per dollar.

for the five months when the fund was operative in 1970, revenues were TL 585 million.[13]

Rebate rates and the import replenishment scheme were altered for manufactured exports. A two-tier system was established for export rebates, with those firms exporting over $1 million entitled to rebate rates higher (ranging from 25 to 40 per cent) than those with smaller export values (up to 30 per cent). The intent of the two-tier system was of course to encourage larger export volumes and to foster consolidation of small exporting firms.[14] The new rebate rates were somewhat lower than the old, although the highest export EER (TL 21 = $1) was increased. The stated intention was "to lighten the burden on the budget."[15] The new import replenishment scheme allowed exporters 25 per cent of expected export earnings for importing goods needed in production.

The provisions for export credit and for interest rates payable by exporters were also altered. Not only was the Foreign Exchange Equalization Fund established, but 50 per cent of guarantee deposits and the interest earned on them were set aside for export credits. Interest rates for exporters were reduced, but there are a number of reasons for questioning the likely effectiveness of the scheme.[16]

Domestic policy changes

Several changes in domestic policies accompanied the changes in EERs. Some were passed by Parliament prior to devaluation and others were undertaken with devaluation. They included: changes in tax rates and imposition of new taxes, some changes in domestic price policies, and alteration in the general structure of interest rates. Some of the changes were very detailed and had little short-run impact. In other cases, subsequent economic policies eroded or offset the effects of the initial measures. Thus a brief description of the initial changes will suffice.

Taxes. In addition to changes in the stamp tax, higher production taxes were imposed on petroleum products and stocks, and taxes upon new construction were levied. A variety of miscellaneous new taxes were imposed: on the purchase of vehicles, on capital gains from real estate, and on sales of certain service and luxury goods (furs, TV, hotels, restaurants, etc.). Produc-

---

13. Yaşer, *op. cit.* (Note 9), p. 24.
14. No data are available to this author on the actual rebates given or rates applicable to individual export commodities since devaluation.
15. Quoted in Yaşer, *op. cit.* (Note 9), p. 22.
16. The system of export credits and subsidized interest rates is extremely complex, and need not be dealt with in detail. See *ibid.* for analysis of it.

tion tax rates were altered and, importantly, assembly industry production became subject to the production tax. A variety of other taxes (legal fees, documents, etc.) were likewise increased.

Data are not available to evaluate accurately the aggregate importance of the tax changes. Consolidated budget revenues from the 1971 budget are estimated to have increased from TL 14.4 to TL 18.5 billion. Of that increase, TL 2 billion, or half, came from import revenues and an additional TL 800 million came from the petroleum production tax.[17] In view of the Turkish inflation of 1971, it would appear that other tax changes were relatively small in their aggregate impact, although many Turks believe that the tax on new construction depressed building starts.

Price policy.   Government pronouncements following devaluation made it clear that the danger of inflation was recognized and that the government would adopt strong measures to combat it. The Prime Minister made strong statements that the prices of SEE products would not be increased, and that private sector firms unduly raising prices would be subject to various sanctions, including loss of incentives (exemption from duties on capital goods imports, investment priority status, and the like), "restrictions in their activities within the framework of the Foreign Trade Regime," and even imprisonment.[18]

Despite these statements of intent, actual government policy was less than determined both in August 1970 and afterwards. Several price increases were announced in August 1970. They included sugar, fertilizers, and agricultural support prices for wheat (6.3 per cent), hazelnuts (13.3 per cent), raisins (4.3 per cent), figs (17.5 per cent), cotton (18.5 per cent), and olive oil (23.8 per cent). In May 1971 the prices of a wide variety of SEE products were increased sharply. As will be seen below, all these increases combined with government fiscal policy and a favorable harvest in 1971 to produce sizeable inflationary pressure in the eighteen months following devaluation.

Interest rate and credit policy.   One of the steps taken with devaluation was a series of measures to increase the availability of credit to exporters and to reduce the interest rate paid by exporters. Those measures were part of a general overhaul of interest rates put into effect at that time. It resulted in a complex structure of twenty-eight different types of subsidies payable to banks for extending various categories of credit. At the time of writing, there are no data available with which the effectiveness of the scheme can be

17. Data from budget figures.
18. Speech of Prime Minister Demirel, quoted by Yaşer, *op. cit.* (Note 9), p. 19.

assessed, although there are grounds on which one can question whether the revisions will accomplish their desired goals.[19]

III. The effects of the devaluation

It is far too early to assess the overall impact of the devaluation package. Early results suggest that the devaluation was "successful" in improving the balance of payments, generating increased export earnings and liberalizing the import regime. It was less successful in terms of domestic price stability, although a large part of the resulting inflation originated from factors not necessarily associated with devaluation. We consider first the balance-of-payments performance, and thereafter evaluate the effects on the domestic economy.

Balance-of-payments performance

Table C-2 gives Turkey's balance of payments for the years 1969 to 1971. Exports by commodities are given in the top part of the Table. Exports rose from $537 million in 1969 to $677 million in 1971, for a 26 per cent increase in two years. That was well above expectations: the 1971 Annual Program projected 1971 exports at $640 million. The bulk of the increase was from 1970 to 1971, with cotton exports accounting for $51 million out of the $59 million increase between 1969 and 1970. The post-devaluation increases were in exports of industrial products ($36 million), cotton ($20 million), other crop exports ($18 million, of which $12 million was in fresh fuits and vegetables) and livestock products ($11 million). Hazelnuts, tobacco and mineral exports appear to have been relatively unaffected. As mentioned above, the first Erim government reinstituted export price checks for several months in the summer of 1971. The 1971 export performance is all the more remarkable in light of the uncertainties engendered by that episode.[20]

Consistent with the findings of Chapter VII, increases in the export EER appear to have had their greatest initial impact on non-traditional exports. The year 1971 saw an exceptionally good harvest, so that part of the increase must be attributed to good weather. But the response of industrial exports cannot be attributed to weather, and tends to substantiate earlier conclusions about the potential for new exports and their responsiveness to the exchange rate.[21]

19. For a full analysis of the changes, see *ibid.*, pp. 5 ff.
20. One of the motives for price checks was evidently the fear that there would be overinvoicing of exports eligible for high rebate rates.
21. In July 1972, SPO officials indicated that 1972 exports were running about $120 million ahead of 1971 exports.

Table C-2
Turkey's balance of payments, 1969 to 1971 (millions of U.S. dollars).

	1969	1970	1971
Exports f.o.b.			
Cotton	114	173	193
Tobacco	81	78	86
Hazelnuts	108	87	84
Other crops exports	59	62	80
Livestock	24	29	38
Industrial products	135	139	175
Minerals	17	20	21
Total exports	537	588	677
Imports c.i.f.			
Investment goods	−362	−439	−533
Intermediate goods	−403	−467	−590
Consumption goods	−36	−42	−48
Total imports	−801	−948	−1171
Invisibles			
Debt interest payments	−44	−47	−47
Tourism and travel	−5	4	21
Workers' remittances	141	273	471
Other (including offshore)	−48	−41	−60
Net current account	−220	−171	−109
Capital account			
Debt payment	−108	−158	−91
Private foreign capital	24	58	45
Projects credits	174	179	210
Consortium credits	106	217	89
Other (including SDRs)	61	135	95
Reserve movements	6	−236	−346
Errors and omissions	−37	−24	107

Notes: For imports by use categories, SIS gave monthly figures for 1971 and individual averages for pre-devaluation and post-devaluation periods for 1970. Simple averages of the figures were used to obtain the annual percentages.

Sources: Balance of payments components: Yaşer, *op. cit.* (Note 9), p. 69. Exports by commodities: *Ibid.*, p. 71. Imports by use: the percentage distribution given in *Monthly Bulletin of Statistics II*, 1972, SIS were multiplied by total imports.

Invisible earnings.   Although export earnings increased markedly, the big shift in Turkey's foreign exchange earnings originated in invisibles, especially workers' remittances. As Table C-2 shows, workers' remittances rose from $141 million in 1969 to $471 million in 1971. Part of the phenomenon was the result of workers switching their foreign exchange transactions from unofficial channels to official ones, as the black market all but disappeared after devaluation. The government implemented additional measures designed to induce workers to deposit their savings with Turkish banks (in long-term convertible accounts paying 9 per cent) rather than abroad, and also announced that Turks would not be questioned about the source of foreign exchange when it was deposited at local banks. Some of the increase in workers' remittances therefore reflected the counterspeculative flows, and thus undoubtedly represents a once-and-for-all phenomenon as workers moved past savings back to Turkey and others transferred funds to Turkey. Part, however, represents an increased flow, as funds move through official channels which formerly would have been deposited abroad.

Other invisible transactions showed much smaller changes. Tourism and travel changed from a small debit to a small credit item, which may again have reflected a move away from the black market. Debt-servicing items were not significantly affected.

Import liberalization. Imports rose from $801 million in 1969 to $1,171 million in 1971, for a 46 per cent increase over two years. Comparing the import data in Table C-2 with the program figures for 1970 (Table VI-2), imports of both intermediate goods and investment goods, particularly the latter, exceeded the Plan. In 1971 imports of intermediate goods rose to $590 million, and imports of investment goods also continued to increase rapidly.

Thus imports represented 10.2 per cent of estimated GNP in 1971, contrasted with 6.2 per cent in 1969,[22] and the absorption of purchasing power through the combined effects of higher import EERs and the increased real flow of imports was sizeable. As will be seen below, there is evidence of a slowdown in the level of economic activity in 1971, but in view of the rapid increase in imports, it was remarkably slight.

There is as yet insufficient evidence with which to evaluate the effects of import liberalization. There were frequent stories in 1971 of businessmen who had applied for import licenses well in excess of what they would in fact use, and of their discomfiture when granted the full amount applied for. The penalty of course was that either licenses had to be used or part of guarantee deposits forfeited. Most observers agreed that the influx of imports had virtually halted black market transactions and had increased competitive pressures for many Turkish producers. The long-run effects remain to be seen.

---

22. Exports represented 5.2 per cent of GNP in 1971 contrasted with 4.1 per cent in 1969. The TL values of imports were TL 17.7 billion in 1971 and TL 7.75 billion in 1969. *Monthly Bulletin,* Central Bank, March 1972.

Capital flows.   The combined effects of increased workers' remittances and export earnings reduced Turkey's current account deficit from $220 million in 1969 to $109 million in 1971, despite the increased flow of imports. On capital account, private foreign capital inflows increased somewhat and foreign aid (project and consortium credits) rose substantially, from $280 million in 1969 to $396 million in 1970, returning to $299 million in 1971. There was also a large positive errors-and-omissions item of $107 million in 1971, probably reflecting a reverse speculative flow.

The net result was a huge increase in Turkey's reserves, $236 million in 1970 and $346 million in 1971. Thus the swing in the balance of payments following devaluation was large by any standard, and Turkey's reserves were more than comfortable early in 1972.

In contrast to the 1958 devaluation, therefore, the 1970 devaluation resulted in a sharp and immediate improvement in the balance of payments. Part of the difference originated from the response of workers' remittances, and part can be attributed to the good harvest of 1971. But the export response was considerably greater than post-1958 and cannot be attributed entirely to these factors.

There are too many unknowns to evaluate whether foreign exchange earnings will continue to increase rapidly. One uncertainty is the rate of domestic inflation, to be discussed below. Another is the orientation of the Third Five Year Plan, which is being formulated at the time of this writing. Rapid increases in investment and orientation toward development of still more import-substitution industries (especially heavy industry) could offset much of the new incentive for exports created by the devaluation. On the other hand, if further moves in the direction of equalizing incentives are taken as imports are allowed to increase, the prospects for future growth in foreign exchange earnings would be much brighter.

The domestic economy

The aftermath of the 1958 devaluation was one of generally disappointing balance-of-payments performance but attainment of the domestic goal of price stability. The short-term results of the 1970 devaluation were a greatly improved balance of payments but frustration of the domestic goal of price stability.

Inflation.   Two exogenous factors contributed to the inflation. First, a new Personnel Law, passed in 1970, granted large salary increases to civil servants. The result was a 78 per cent increase in current government expenditures between the first half of 1970 and the first half of 1971, 85 per cent

Table C-3
Central bank assets, money supply, and price level 1968 to 1971

	1968	1969	1970	1971
Central Bank assets (millions of TL)				
Foreign exchange	278	1,153	4,301	8,772
Credits	15,961	18,835	20,483	22,191
Other assets	2,228	3,681	7,789	7,862
TOTAL	18,467	23,669	32,573	38,825
Money supply (millions of TL)				
Currency	8,237	9.081	11,850	13,917
Bank deposits	17,731	21,046	23,418	29,670
TOTAL	25,968	30,127	35,268	43,587
Price level				
Wholesale (1963 = 100)	129	137	146	169

Note: Gold is included with other Central Bank assets.
Sources: Central Bank assets from *Monthly Bulletin,* Central Bank, Jan.–March, 1972;
Monthly Bulletin of Statistics, SIS, II -1972; and Yaşer, *op. cit.* (Note 9), p.43.
Money supply from *Monthly Bulletin,* Central Bank, Jan.–March, 1972. Price
level: Ministry of Commerce.

of which are for salaries. To meet its increased salary obligations the government resorted to borrowing from the Central Bank. Second, the excellent harvest of 1971, combined with increased support prices for major agricultural commodities, resulted in a large increase in Central Bank credit to TMO.[23]

Partial offsets were the deflationary effects of increased imports and additional revenues resulting from higher customs duty receipts and profits from the purchase of foreign exchange at the rate of TL 12 = $1 and sales at TL 15 = $1, at least for the first year after the devaluation. However, Central Bank foreign exchange reserves increased sharply, as seen above, and much of the increase was directly monetized. This was especially true of workers' remittances. Table C-3 gives the relevant data.

As can be seen, Central Bank credits expanded rapidly between 1968 and the election year of 1969, but their increase after that date was about 8 per cent annually. However, foreign exchange reserves rose sharply, especially between 1970 and 1971, when TL 4,471 million of the increase in Central Bank assets of TL 6,252 million was the change in reserves. This was reflected in an increase in the money supply of 23.5 per cent during 1971.

The natural result was a rapid rise in the inflation rate. The increase for 1971 as a whole was 15.7 per cent according to the Ministry of Commerce

23. The manner in which large crops can lead to inflation was spelled out in Chapter II.

wholesale price index. Monthly figures show even sharper movements. The wholesale price index stood at 139 in July 1970, 150 in December 1970, 164 in June 1971, and 185 in December 1971. Thus from December to December prices rose 23 per cent.

There was some indication in the summer of 1972 that the rate of inflation was beginning to decelerate, but it had by no means subsided to pre-devaluation levels. Several factors should be noted. The sharp increase in Central Bank credits between 1968 an 1969 would have been reflected in quickened inflation in 1970–1971 in any event (see Fry's results reported in Chapter II). Also, the cumulative increase in the price level from July 1970 to December 1971 was 33 per cent, just over half the effective devaluation. Since Turkey would have experienced some inflation even without devaluation, it would appear that the increase in prices associated with devaluation in the subsequent eighteen months was less than one third the effective devaluation. Even then, stronger actions to offset the inflow of reserves might have reduced the initial impact on the price level.

The real danger to the success of the devaluation comes not from the inflation experienced in the first eighteen months but from the danger that continued inflation (at a more rapid rate than would otherwise have been the case) will erode the increase in the PLD-EERs that devaluation accomplished. The timing of the Personnel Law and of the raising of price supports were therefore unfortunate in that regard. Whether the government can slow down inflation is a critical question; and at the time of writing the outcome is still in doubt.

Effects on the level of economic activity. Despite the high rate of growth of GNP in 1971 there is some evidence suggesting that a mild, short-lived recession followed the devaluation. As with the price level, however, an important exogenous factor contributed. That was the uncertainty associated with the political violence and formation of the Erim government.

One indicator is the ratio of currency to bank deposits, which rose sharply from 43 per cent in 1969 to 51 per cent in 1970 and reached a peak of 77 per cent in March 1971 (see Table C-3), and thereafter declined to more normal levels. Part of the increase may have reflected the release of previously frozen guarantee deposits, although delays in depositing the unfrozen funds would still be explicable only by political uncertainties.

As with the aftermath of the 1958 devaluation, the construction sector appears to have been most adversely affected. According to the national income accounts, real construction grew at 8 per cent in 1969, 5.5 per cent in 1970, and 1.1 per cent in 1971.[24] The fact that taxes were imposed upon

24. SPO estimates at 1965 prices.

new construction at the time of devaluation undoubtedly contributed to the decline in the rate of expansion. The result was a shift in the composition of investment, away from construction and toward plant and equipment, as real investment rose an estimated 4.5 per cent in 1971.

Two other indicators also suggest recession in the private sector. Real private fixed capital investment is estimated to have declined 0.9 per cent in 1971, although investment in inventory rose 30 per cent over 1970 levels. The second was a reduced demand for bank credit from the private sector. Of an increase in deposits of commercial banks with the Central Bank of TL 3.3 billion in 1971, TL 0.5 billion were above legal reserve requirements, and there was a sharp shift away from private sector credits.[25]

Despite these factors, industrial output rose 8.7 per cent in 1971, although expansion had been only 2.5 per cent in 1970.[26] The fact of an excellent harvest in 1971 undoubtedly contributed purchasing power to the agricultural sector, which may have offset whatever decreases in demand originated from the construction sector. Thus to the extent that there was recession, it was extremely mild and took the form of a lower-than-average industrial growth rate rather than reductions in the level of economic activity.

An interesting question is what would have happened to the level of economic activity in the absence of the government's expansionist expenditure policies in 1970 and 1971. The existence of strong inflationary pressure suggests that government policies may have been too expansionist. On the other hand, the evidence indicates some slowing down in demand from the private sector. If that was so, government expenditure policies were necessary to prevent even greater recessionary forces from operating. Final judgment may well rest on whether the rapid price increases of 1970–1971 can be brought under control fairly quickly. If they can, the expansionist policies of the government may have buffered the economy from recession while enabling resource reallocation. If they cannot, the cost in terms of a more rapid rate of inflation in the long run way prove to be higher than Turkish policymakers are willing to accept.

IV. Conclusions

It is too soon to pass judgment on the 1970 devaluation. The contrasts with the 1958 devaluation however are of interest. And there are also some

25. Yaşer, *op. cit.* (Note 9), pp. 38 ff.
26. The slow rate of expansion in 1970 may have resulted from import shortages, although further data are needed before a definitive analysis can be made. Certainly the slow rate of growth for the year cannot be attributed to the effects of an August devaluation.

pertinent similarities. Similarities include the Personnel Law with its impact on current government expenditures; the change of governments and political uncertainty following each devaluation; resort to a lower EER for traditional exports; and a backlog of import licenses awaiting foreign exchange at the time of each devaluation.

The contrasts are more pronounced. First, the structure of the Turkish economy was markedly altered between 1958 and 1970, and government policies pre-devaluation were noncomparable. Second, the 1958 devaluation was aimed as much at altering domestic policy and eliminating inflation as it was at improving the balance of payments, if only because the former was a necessary condition for the latter. In 1970 the devaluation did not signal major changes in domestic policies and was aimed at improving the balance of payments. Third, the 1958 Stabilization Program virtually eliminated inflation, whereas the 1970 devaluation intensified it. Inflationary pressure resulted primarily from success in increasing foreign exchange reserves which increased the money supply. Finally, the 1970 devaluation resulted in an immediate improvement in the balance of payments, whereas the 1958 improvement was far smaller. Judged by its effect on the balance of payments in the first eighteen months, the 1970 devaluation was the more successful of the two.

Construction activity appears to have been retarded after both devaluations, and investment composition shifted toward plant and equipment. Private sector investment appears to have declined after each devaluation although manufacturing output has increased. These similar responses tend to confirm the analysis of earlier chapters that import shortages and currency overvaluation may lead to distortions of investment toward construction activity when insufficient imports are available. In addition, business activity becomes increasingly oriented toward short-term gains achievable through obtaining import licenses. When devaluation occurs these tendencies are reversed. Since construction investment has a higher fraction of domestic value-added than plant and machinery investment, the initial response is a slowdown in the rate of economic activity.

The Turkish economy remains heavily oriented towards import-substitution, despite the devaluation of 1970. Incentives for non-traditional exports were increased, but are still markedly less than incentives for import-substituting production. The prohibited list remains a highly protective instrument for encouraging new import-substituting industries, and to date there is no mechanism for gradual reduction of protection as industries become established.

Turkey's very ample foreign exchange reserves, combined with the opportunities for liberalization associated with her prospective membership in the Common Market, offer an opportunity to move gradually toward a more open economy. Whether that path will be chosen, however, remains to be seen.

APPENDIX D-1

DEFINITION OF CONCEPTS USED IN THE PROJECT

Exchange rates

1. *Nominal Exchange Rate*: The official parity for a transaction. For countries maintaining a single exchange rate registered with the International Monetary Fund, the nominal exchange rate is the registered rate.

2. *Effective Exchange Rate* (EER): The number of units of local currency actually paid or received for a one-dollar international transaction. Surcharges, tariffs, the implicit interest foregone on guarantee deposits, and any other charges against purchases of goods and services abroad are included, as are rebates, the value of import replenishment rights, and other incentives to earn foreign exchange for sales of goods and services abroad.

3. *Price-Level-Deflated (PLD) Nominal Exchange Rates*: The nominal exchange rate deflated in relation to some base period by the price level index of the country.

4. *Price-Level-Deflated EER (PLD–EER)*: The EER deflated by the price level index of the country in question.

5. *Purchasing-Power-Parity Adjusted Exchange Rates*: The relevant (nominal or effective) exchange rate multiplied by the ratio of the foreign price level to the domestic price level.

Devaluation

1. *Gross Devaluation*: The change in the parity registered with the IMF (or, synonymously in most cases, *de jure* devaluation).

2. *Net Devaluation*: The weighted average of changes in EERs by classes of transactions (or, synonymously in most cases, *de facto* devaluation).

3. *Real Gross Devaluation*: The gross devaluation adjusted for the increase in the domestic price level over the relevant period.

4. *Real Net Devaluation*: The net devaluation similarly adjusted.

Protection concepts

1. *Explicit Tariff*: The amount of tariff charged against the import of a good as a per cent of the import price (in local currency at the nominal exchange rate) of the good.

2. *Implicit Tariff* (or, synonymously, tariff equivalent): The ratio of the

domestic price (net of normal distribution costs) minus the c.i.f. import price to the c.i.f. import price in local currency.

3. *Premium*: The windfall profit accruing to the recipient of an import license per dollar of imports. It is the difference between the domestic selling price (net of normal distribution costs) and the landed cost of the item (including tariffs and other charges). The premium is thus the difference between the implicit and the explicit tariff (including other charges) multiplied by the nominal exchange rate.

4. *Nominal Tariff*: The tariff — either explicit or implicit as specified — on a commodity.

5. *Effective Tariff* or *Effective Rate of Protection* (ERP): The explicit or implicit tariff on value-added as distinct from the nominal tariff on a commodity.

6. *Domestic Resource Costs* (DCR): The value of domestic resources (evaluated) at "shadow" or opportunity cost prices) employed in earning or saving a dollar of foreign exchange (in the value-added sense) when producing domestic goods.

APPENDIX D-2

DELINEATION OF PHASES USED IN TRACING
THE EVOLUTION OF EXCHANGE CONTROL REGIMES

To achieve comparability of analysis among different countries, each author of a country-study was asked to identify the chronological development of his country's payments regime through the following Phases. There was no presumption that a country would necessarily pass through all the Phases in chronological sequence. Detailed description of the Phases will be found in Bhagwati and Krueger, *Foreign Trade Regimes and Economic Development: Experience and Analysis.*

Phase I: During this period, quantitative restrictions on international transactions are imposed and then intensified. They generally are initiated in response to an unsustainable payments deficit and then, for a period, are intensified. During the period when reliance upon quantitative restrictions as a means of controlling the balance of payments is increasing, the country is said to be in Phase I.

Phase II: During this Phase, quantitative restrictions are still intense, but various price measures are taken to offset some of the undesired results of the system. Heightened tariffs, surcharges on imports, rebates for exports, special tourist exchange rates, and other price interventions are used in this Phase, but primary reliance is placed on quantitative restrictions.

Phase III: This Phase is characterized by an attempt to systematize the changes which take place during Phase II. It generally starts with a formal exchange-rate change and may be accompanied by removal of some of the surcharges, etc., imposed during Phase II and by reduced reliance upon quantitative restrictions. Phase III may be little more than a tidying-up operation (in which case the likelihood is that the country will re-enter Phase II), or it may signal the beginning of the removal of reliance upon quantitative restrictions.

Phase IV: If the changes in Phase III result in adjustments within the country so that liberalization can continue, the country is said to enter Phase IV. The necessary adjustments generally include increased foreign exchange earnings and gradual relaxation of quantitative restrictions. The latter relaxation may take the form of changes in the nature of quantitative restrictions or of increased foreign exchange allocations, and thus reduced premia, under the same administrative system.

Phase V: This is a period during which an exchange regime is fully liberalized. There is full convertibility on current account, and quantitative restrictions are not employed as a means of regulating the *ex-ante* balance of payments.

APPENDIX D-3

LIST OF IMPORTANT TURKISH NAMES AND ABBREVIATIONS

Atatürk   The leader of Turkey's independence movement and of the country until his death in 1938.

Demirel   Prime Minister of Turkey from 1965 to 1971.

Democratic Party   The party led by Prime Minister Menderes, in power in the 1950's. It was dissolved after the May 1960 Revolution.

Ereğli Steel   A steel mill built in the 1960's at Ereğli with the help of U.S. aid.

EBK   Et ve Balık Kurumu. The state enterprise for meat and fish.

Étatism   The name given to the economic philosophy adopted during the 1930's, under which State Economic Enterprises and private sector firms would both participate in Turkey's economic development.

FFYP   The First Five Year Plan, 1963–1967.

Justice Party   A party formed in the 1960's which attained power in the elections of 1965. It is somewhat more free-enterprise oriented than the RPP, its largest competitor during the 1960's.

Kuruş   One one-hundredth of a Turkish Lira.

Menderes   Prime Minister of Turkey from 1950 to the May 1960 Revolution and leader of the Democratic Party.

NUC   National Unity Committee. The group which governed the country after the May 1960 Revolution until the elections in the fall of 1961.

RPP   Republican Peoples' Party. The major opposition party in Turkey from 1950 to 1961 and from 1965 to the present. Its most famous leader, and Prime Minister during the early 1960's, was İsmet İnönü. It is the party founded by Atatürk.

SEE   State Economic Enterprise, a government-owned firm engaged in economic activity.

SFYP   Second Five Year Plan, 1968–1972.

SIS	State Institute of Statistics (Devlet İstatistik Enstitüsü).
SPO	State Planning Organization (Devlet Planlama Teşkilatı).
TMO	Toprak Mahsulleri Ofisi (Soil Products Office).
Union of Chambers	Union of Chambers of Commerce and Industry, a semi-official body to which all private sector firms with ten or more employees belong. The Union bore a major responsibility for allocating imports among private sector firms, and has represented the interests of the private sector in government deliberations on many subjects.

Index